THE WESTERNS AND WAR
FILMS OF JOHN FORD

FILM AND HISTORY
Series Editor: Cynthia J. Miller

European Cinema after the Wall: Screening East–West Mobility, edited by Leen Engelen and Kris Van Heuckelom

Native Americans on Network TV: Stereotypes, Myths, and the "Good Indian," by Michael Ray FitzGerald

Bringing History to Life through Film: The Art of Cinematic Storytelling, edited by Kathryn Anne Morey

Hollywood and the End of the Cold War: Signs of Cinematic Change, by Bryn Upton

Smart Chicks on Screen: Representing Women's Intellect in Film and Television, edited by Laura Mattoon D'Amore

The JFK Image: Profiles in Docudrama, by Raluca Lucia Cimpean

Food on Film: Bringing Something New to the Table, edited by Tom Hertweck

Real War vs. Reel War: Veterans, Hollywood, and WWII, by Suzanne Broderick

Talking about Pauline Kael: Critics, Filmmakers, and Scholars Remember an Icon, edited by Wayne Stengel

The Westerns and War Films of John Ford, by Sue Matheson

THE WESTERNS AND WAR FILMS OF JOHN FORD

Sue Matheson

ROWMAN & LITTLEFIELD
Lanham • Boulder • New York • London

Published by Rowman & Littlefield
A wholly owned subsidiary of The Rowman & Littlefield Publishing Group,
Inc.
4501 Forbes Boulevard, Suite 200, Lanham, Maryland 20706
www.rowman.com

Unit A, Whitacre Mews, 26-34 Stannary Street, London SE11 4AB

British Library Cataloguing in Publication Information Available

Library of Congress Cataloging-in-Publication Data

Matheson, Sue.
The westerns and war films of John Ford / Sue Matheson.
pages cm. — (Film and history)
Includes bibliographical references and index.
ISBN 978-1-4422-6105-1 (hardback : alk. paper) — ISBN 978-1-4422-6106-8 (ebook) 1. Ford,
John, 1894-1973—Criticism and interpretation. 2. Western films—United States—History and
criticism. 3. War films—United States—History and criticism. I. Title.
PN1998.3.F65M35 2016
791.4302'33092—dc23
2015031674

Printed in the United States of America

To the memory of Mary Evelyn Matheson,
who understood survivor guilt

CONTENTS

ACKNOWLEDGMENTS

About four years ago, Philip Loy told me I should write a book about John Ford. Thank you for starting me on this project, Phil. I had grown up watching Hollywood movies and believed I was intimately acquainted with American culture. I couldn't have been more mistaken. Every time I watched a John Ford movie, the Old Master taught me more about filmmaking; more about my parents' generation before, during, and after the Second World War; and more about the America I thought I already knew.

While researching John Ford's life, I not only learned a great deal about him, I also met others who were equally fascinated by his work and the American West. I am immensely grateful to those people. Their interest and support kept me on track during the many days (and nights) I spent writing this book. Donna Coates directed me to Jonathan Shay's works on Vietnam veterans. Ray Merlock's unflagging belief in the viability of this project, sensible comments, and caring humor kept me writing. Debbie Cutshaw's keen interest in Westerns (of all kinds) validated my own fascination with Ford's work. Helen Lewis's steadfast encouragement and support of my ideas and Camille McCutcheon's infectious enthusiasm for Westerns and unending interest in Ford encouraged my fascination with this material. Andrew Patrick Nelson, who knows more about Westerns than I'll ever know, was always there to listen and offer excellent advice. John O'Donahue, who listened to me talk about John Ford—and whose work had the steadying effect of balancing mine—made sure I wasn't completely carried away by the power of Ford's artistry. It took him a while, but I have come to agree with him that Maureen O'Hara was indeed "a brassy broad."

To Gaylyn Studlar, who also likes mojitos and who understands John Ford much better than I, so many thanks—Gaylyn's interest in and superb work on Ford and his Westerns kept me watching his many movies. Many thanks are also due to my colleagues whose commitments to their work strengthened my own. Kathy Jackson-Merlock's balance and poise always erased the possibility of panic. Lynn Bartholome's sophisticated humor and energy buoyed my spirits. Mike Marsden's unfailing reasonableness and support of my work centered my thinking. Gary Edgerton's thoughtfulness and enthusiasm braced my beliefs about American culture. Gary Hoppenstand's enthusiasm for Westerns and guidance strengthened my judgment. Peter C. Rollins's kindness and knack for always saying what I needed most to hear motivated me to continue (I wish he was with us today).

I can't thank Jessica McCleary and the good folks at Rowman & Littlefield enough for their patience throughout the process of preparing this book, especially Cindy Miller, my editor, whose keenness for and love of the Western were infectious (and who has one of the best knives in the business). I couldn't have written succinctly about Ford without Cindy. I owe her an enormous debt of gratitude for her insightful readings and comments. Her guidance and common sense were invaluable. Cindy rocks!

To John Butler, who had an office next to mine when I needed to talk (about a John Ford who was not the seventeenth-century dramatist), a big thank you. I also owe many thanks to Sharon McLeod, who kept reminding me there would be life after Ford. I was so fortunate to be able to work closely with Shelly Doman at the University College of the North. A gifted researcher and librarian, Shelly loves tracking down data and minutiae. To Dan Smith, who gave me the all the time, encouragement, and support I needed to get my work done, thank you so much. To Virginia Goulet, who organized my research projects and kept me on track, and to Harvey Briggs, who cleared the way for this book in its final stage, I am so grateful. To Kathryn McNaughton, who provided me with funding in the early stages of this project, I am very grateful.

I met so many people interested in the life and work of John Ford who were exceptionally generous with their resources and time on my behalf. In particular, I cannot thank Dan Ford and Tag Gallagher enough for their kindnesses. Dan Ford gave me an open field in which to work at the Lilly Library. His patience was so encouraging. Thank you, Dan, for your help. I wrote Tag Gallagher a despairing note last summer, and he not only wrote back (at once), he also sent a cavalry unit to my rescue. Thank you, Tag.

I was incredibly lucky to be able to spend some time during the past two summers at the beautiful Lilly Library in Bloomington, Indiana. Listening to the voices of Ford, his family, friends, and Stock Company and reviewing their correspondence made an enormous difference to my understanding of the man and his movies. To Cherry Williams, the manuscripts curator, and the staff at the Lilly Library who made my work so enjoyable, thank you—especially, I owe thanks to Zach Downey, the public services assistant, for his time and interest in this project. To Tiffany Link, research librarian for the Maine Historical Society, who found Barbara Curran Feeney's obit, and to Janet Lorenz, researcher at the National Film Information Service, who located materials in *Moving Picture World*, *American Cinematographer*, and *Hollywood Reporter* for me, thank you.

To my children, Stuart and Rebecca, who patiently sat and faithfully watched John Ford's movies (all of them) with me, my thanks and love. Their insights and reactions to Ford's movies and to Ford himself were invaluable while I was writing. They not only listened to me talk (endlessly) about Ford, they also looked after our house, the dogs, the cats, and the goats when I had to be away at work. I couldn't have written this book without them.

Finally, of course, I must also thank John Ford—for the amazing movies that he made and the entertaining stories he told. His courage made this study worthwhile.

INTRODUCTION

He was a delightful rebel. [1]—John Wayne

As Carl Jung explains, every calling or profession has its own characteristic persona. "It is easy to study these things nowadays, when the photographs of public personalities so frequently appear in the press," Jung says,

> A certain kind of behaviour is forced on them by the world, and professional people endeavour [*sic*] to come up to these expectations. Only, the danger is that they become identical with their personas—the professor with his text-book, the tenor with his voice. Then the damage is done; henceforth he lives exclusively against the background of his own biography. [2]

In the case of the American filmmaker John Ford, Jung's statement is disturbingly accurate. A Hollywood celebrity, Ford lived his life against the background that Twentieth Century-Fox fashioned for him. As he did, the facts of his life merged with and became inseparable from his multifaceted legend fostered by Hollywood's self-contained studio culture and his own imagination. A command personality, he directed "fast, virile pictures"[3] and remained in character until the day he died: "a tough old retired director . . . well, half retired." In 1966, he told Bertrand Tavernier that he was only "waiting for someone to give [him] the go-ahead" to direct another movie.[4] In Hollywood, no one, it seems, really knew John Ford. He was "a mass of contradiction"[5]: kind and cruel, sentimental and cynical, optimistic and depressed, sincere and sardonic. His irascibility and indirection was "an elaborate performance,"[6] "a wall of protection,"[7] "a façade,"[8] "a personality that would hide his true nature,"[9] and a "smoke screen."[10] Actress Olive Carey, whose personal life and Hollywood career were closely connected to Ford,[11] pointed out, "Jack was one of the greatest hams of all time. He was a born actor. A complex, fantastic actor. He was never relaxed, never mellow, never allowed you to relax either. That's why he was such a good director, I guess. He was always playing a part for his own amusement. When he'd walk on the set, he'd have Danny Borzage play 'Bringing in the Sheaves' on his squeeze box. Oh, criminy, what a ham he was!"[12]

Many have attributed Ford's elusive (and often abrasive) personality to his Irish upbringing. Tag Gallagher, Joseph McBride, and Scott Eyman all begin their examinations of Ford by tracing the influence of his kith and kin and grounding their discussions of his works in his Irish heritage. Thomas Flanagan also has pointed out that Ford's personality, further complicated by his consciousness of and sensitivity to "a majority culture, from which the Irish, despite their bellicose loyalty to it stood somewhat apart,"[13] accounts in part for his multilayered (and, at times, conflicted) vision of America. Always sympathetic to the underdog, Ford adopted the stance of the outsider even in the industry in which he was so successful.

As Joseph McBride remarks, the evolution of John Ford's personality may be located in his family's marginalized position among New Englanders. Growing up in the Irish Catholic community of Mountjoy, encapsulated within the larger Protestant community of Portland, Maine, Ford did not remember Portland's Irish quarreling with members of the other minority groups in the multicultural area of Mountjoy, which included Jews, Italians, French-Canadians, and African Americans.[14] In Ford's reminiscences, Portland's Irish, Jewish, Italian, French-Canadian, and African American populations instead banded together against a common enemy—the Yankee establishment that dis_____ty Irish" and other immigrant laborers who _____ d during its economic boom in the second _____ury.[15] Speaking to his grandson, Ford re-_____ "a lot of Irish" in Portland: "We overpow-_____said. "We're a minority group, but we controlled the elections in high school and the athletic teams and even in the city elections we had places. The Ku Klux Klan tried to establish a footing in Portland but unfortunately the house they had out in Deering . . . one night it burned down, accidentally of course."[16]

Katharine Hepburn may have observed to John Ford, "You hacked your way through life in a most individual way,"[17] but it is no coincidence that his Stock Company was termed the Irish Mafia by Hollywood outsiders. Ford complicated his public's perception of himself (and by extension his Stock Company) by promoting himself as an Irish outlaw whose vision of the social good necessarily disregarded the rule of law. He observed that he was above all "a rebel": declaring himself anticlerical, he said, "I select my priests the way I cast my pictures. I hate sanctimoniousness."[18] Even when writing to his son, Pat, about the family's cash flow problems in 1963, Ford commented that he was grateful for being Irish because he "always felt better and fought harder" when the odds were against him.[19]

Still, Ford knew that however individual or eccentric or Irish he may have seemed to others, his personality was also the product of America, grounded in the broader, fundamental beliefs and principles of his time and place. A Victorian in his upbringing, his character was framed first by his parents and family, and then shaped by the trauma of the First World War (at home and abroad), the boom of the Roaring Twenties, and the despair of the Great Depression, before being reconfigured by the anxiety and sacrifice of the Second World War, the paranoia attending the Cold War, and the social reforms of the Sixties. As an American, Ford could not "stand people being persecuted or deprived of their freedom."[20] His vision of the American West, iconic of that ideal of freedom, became what Scott Eyman believes to be "the history of his time, mirroring it, transfiguring it, explaining America to itself."[21]

A first-generation American, Ford became a *seanchaí*, a traditional Irish storyteller. As Eyman notes, Ford loved telling stories and "would tell people the most outrageous falsehoods with a perfectly straight face. He would assert that his father had come to America to fight in the Civil War, when his father hadn't arrived in America until seven years after Appomattox."[22] The act of continually renewing his persona for public consumption enabled him to tell "stories for the sake of telling stories—to amuse his audience, of course, but mostly to amuse himself." Complex and complicated, rife with exaggerations, glorying in fantasy and enhanced by drama, Ford's stories transmitted important history and social norms while mirroring his listeners' expectations. He told Joel Sayre that he rode with Pancho Villa;[23] he told Jean Narboni and Andre S. LaBarthe that he was a cowboy in Arizona;[24] he even told Kay Gardella that all he watched on television was baseball.[25]

But Ford not only told stories, he also lived them. As Ford pointed out to Walter Wagner in 1973, his life had been the stuff of which storybooks are made. Reminiscing about his work with the Office of Strategic Services (OSS), he said, "This very supercilious and sarcastic man came up to me and said, 'Tell me, Commander Ford, when was the last time you were in Tibet?' I said, 'Exactly ten days ago, sir.' He looked so sort of flabbergasted. Then he said, 'I don't believe it.' And I replied, 'Screw you. It happens to be true.'"

It is tempting to think that at some point storytelling had taken over Ford's life. Unable to distinguish between fantasy and reality, the story-teller had become nothing more than an extension of his work, living in "a sort of play . . . [in which] actors come on wearing their different masks and all play their parts until the producer orders them off the stage." It often seemed that, as a Hollywood celebrity, John Ford epito-mized Erasmus's idea in "Praise of Folly" that living is only a perfor-mance, at best, "a sort of pretense . . . the only way to act out this farce."[26] However, Ford, who confessed to columnist Hedda Hopper in 1962 that he posed as "an illiterate,"[27] never lost sight of the fact that storytelling and filmmaking were art. It was he who taught Steven Spielberg to distinguish between art and life.

Coaching Spielberg, then a teenager, to be "a picture maker," Ford asked him, "Whadda you know about art?" "I wasn't expecting that question," Spielberg said in an interview with Brian Grazer and Ron Howard about meeting Ford.

> He said, "Tell me what you see in that painting." I said, "Well, I see two Indians on horses." He said, "No, no, no, no, no. Where's the horizon?" So I said, "Well, the horizon's way up above the head of the Indians." He said, "Fine. Walk on to the next one." He said, "What do you see in that painting?" And stupidly I said, "Well, there's some cavalry on horses." I hadn't learned anything, you know. He said, "No, no, no. Where's the horizon?" And I said, "The horizon is at the very, very bottom of the painting." He said, "O.K. Get over here." I stood in front of his desk: He said, "When you're able to

distinguish the art of the horizon—[at] the bottom of the frame or at the top of the frame but not going right through the center of the frame—when you're able to appreciate why it's at the top and why it's at the bottom, you might make a pretty good picture maker."[28]

Ford, the master storyteller and picture maker, never forgot that it is the camera, not the actor, who tells the tale.

Today, Spielberg still regards Ford as his mentor and watches Ford's films before making his own. "I have to look at *The Searchers*," he says. "I just have to almost every time, and there are some other films like *The Informer* that I have to look at and films like *Tobacco Road* which I love."[29] Likening the way that Ford "uses his camera to paint his pictures" to techniques used by "a classic painter," Spielberg finds Ford's static camera and his blocking and framing of scenes a celebration of "the frame, not just what happens inside of it."[30]

The origins of Ford's extraordinary talents as a filmmaker, critic Scott Eyman says, are elusive, but Ford's understanding of the devices intrinsic to the medium (pacing, framing, lighting, and characterization) is that of the inveterate reader who visualizes the story while scanning pages. Like Joseph Conrad, Ford acquired his love of reading and absorbed his storytelling skills from books during a life-threatening illness. While Ford was bed-ridden for months with diphtheria, his sister Maime read to him "until her voice cracked: Robert Louis Stevenson, Grimms' *Fairy Tales*, Mark Twain's *Tom Sawyer*, *Huckleberry Finn*, and *A Connecticut Yankee in King Arthur's Court*."[31] Dan Ford asserts that his grandfather, isolated from his peers, acquired "a sensitivity and an awareness" from being exposed to such texts during his illness.[32]

As an adult, Ford returned again and again to the vivid interior life of books after working on the set. At home and on his yacht, the *Araner*, he would relax and regenerate by reading what John Wayne described as "a cord" of books.[33] Ford's views of gender and community, self-sacrifice on the part of the individual, and death in his movies—derived from the nineteenth rather than the twentieth century—are found in the Victorian novels to which Ford listened while his sister read to him. As Gaylyn Studlar points out, Victorian sentiment informs what have come to be regarded as Fordian values regarding motherhood, womanhood, and death—men and women in his Westerns "submit themselves to the Christian sacrifice necessary to secure their communal (and national) identity."[34]

Ford's life and works reveal how deeply embedded the past still is in our present. His frontier narratives are not always faithful representations of history, but they are always culturally correct when one considers their historic and cinematic moments. Recognized as American classics by his contemporaries, their children, and their children's children, Ford's Westerns are transgenerational, communicating vital information about the American Character to their audiences. As Studlar observes, "Ford's Westerns present themselves as mythic discourse on the epic forging of national identity."[35]

World War, John Ford captured the optimistic ... America in his Westerns and military films. In ... ortrayed as a collective of courageous, self-reli... dividuals, embodying Thomas Jefferson's insis... and intrinsic value of the individual's rights to ..., and privacy. An important marker of the ... oughout Ford's Westerns, Jeffersonian individ... ...guards the nation's free institutions. As Cynthia J. Miller and A. Bowdoin Van Riper note, Frederick Jackson Turner's American frontier has always been a proving ground in the Western for "the dominant individualism" of the American Character and "the wellspring of the independent, indomitable American Spirit."[36] John Ford's prewar Westerns are no exception to this rule.

When Ford went to war, he underwent the sea change that complicated his worldview and deepened his understanding of personal self-sacrifice and America's "national character."[37] Like other World War II servicemen, he returned home transformed by the trauma of war. His films made after 1945, especially his Cold War Westerns, display increasingly critical examinations of military and combat culture and American involvement in the Cold War. These Westerns simultaneously "printed the legend" and critiqued it, expressing deep reservations about the military mind and American culture—complicating and darkening his viewers' understandings of America, born out of and regenerated through violence. Ford had become a veteran who returned to Hollywood to make movies for a nation of veterans, who likewise carried "the weight of friends' deaths *in* the war and were continuing to carry the weight of those deaths *after* the war."[38]

Veterans' issues, among them the topics of survivor guilt and posttraumatic shock syndrome, became central subjects in Ford's films. In

Ford's postwar Westerns and war pictures, one finds the veteran's deep and lasting commitment to the past, to tradition, to the dead, and to survivors encoded as a moral obligation, which Ford himself maintained until the end of his life. As stories about the lives of veterans and survivors of the Indian Wars, Westerns are themselves, at base, trauma narratives. Aptly, Ford's Cold War Westerns, particularly the Cavalry Trilogy and *The Searchers* (1956), resonated strongly with veterans and the families of veterans after the Second World War. In light of America's continuing conflicts in the Middle East, these Westerns still ring true for veterans and the families of veterans today.

The first four chapters of this book examine John Ford's career and development as a Hollywood director and chart the growing importance of the military and military culture to his prewar films. Chapter 1, "A Career Man," considers the development of John Ford as a persona, his beginnings as a director of Westerns for William Fox, his highly productive (and argumentative) relationship with Darryl F. Zanuck, and the effect that the Second World War had on his film career. Chapter 2, "Early Days in the Hollywood West," charts Ford's beginnings as a director of Westerns, his relationship with Harry Carey Sr. and the pair's approach to the Western, as well as the importance of the Sublime and the Hudson River School to his development as an artist. Ford's early Westerns, from *Hell Bent* (1917) to *The Iron Horse* (1924) are examined in this context. Chapter 3, "The Heroic West," examines Ford's subsequent work with the Western from *3 Bad Men* (1926) to *Stagecoach* (1939), which overturned and then established the Western's genre conventions for the next thirty years, as well as the further refinement of his "painterly eye" and the influences of F. W. Murnau, Frederic Remington, Charles Russell, Charles Schreyvogel, and Timothy O'Sullivan on his filmmaking. This chapter ends by locating Ford in Hollywood's response to the approach of the Second World War.

Chapter 4, "Not for Self but for Country," begins by examining Ford's lifelong love for the U.S. Navy and its codes of duty, tradition, and honor in his prewar naval films, *Salute* (1929), *Men without Women* (1930), *Seas Beneath* (1931), and *Submarine Patrol* (1938). This chapter also considers the importance of Ford's undercover work for the Navy before the Second World War to his career before discussing his very different treatments of the military in his Army pictures, *The Lost Patrol* (1938) and *Drums along the Mohawk* (1939), the creation of his

Field Photographic Unit, his decision to enlist in 1940, and America's preparation to enter the Second World War.

The next two chapters investigate Ford's movies regarding military life and culture. Chapter 5, "In the Navy," considers Ford's patriotic documentaries, *The Battle of Midway* (1942), *Torpedo Squadron 8* (1942), and *December 7th* (1943), made while serving in the Office of Strategic Services during the Second World War. Chapter 6, "War Stories," examines Ford's darkening vision of military culture and American manhood in *They Were Expendable* (1945), *When Willie Comes Marching Home* (1950), *What Price Glory* (1952), *Mr. Roberts* (1955), and *The Long Gray Line* (1955), as well as Ford's reaction to the Cold War during this period.

During the Cold War, Ford's Westerns offered audiences acerbic critiques of military culture that tempered many of his earlier ideas about the nature of war and the military. Ford's reactions to his wartime experiences, complex and protean, succeeding one another over time, are reflected in his trauma-centered subjects. The next three chapters, which consider the films comprising Ford's Cavalry Trilogy, begin a series of in-depth studies of his Cold War Westerns. Chapter 7, "Critiquing Combat Culture," reveals the veteran's critical eye on the military in *Fort Apache* (1948), in particular, military careerists and the accepted practice of whitewashing wartime blunders. Chapter 8, "Keeping the Faith," discusses the importance of survivor guilt, camaraderie, and brotherly love to the action of *She Wore a Yellow Ribbon* (1949). Chapter 9, "The War at Home," discusses Ford's analysis of the partisan nature of the American Character and the effect that war has on the veteran's family in *Rio Grande* (1952).

Ford's critique of American culture in his Westerns proved to be unrelenting as the 1950s continued. Chapter 10, "Veterans' Affairs," offers a reading of *The Searchers* (1956) as Ford's depiction of the veteran's experience, in particular, the blood pollution that veterans carry home from the war, the gulf that exists between the combatant and his community, and the resulting inability for veterans to re-enter society. Chapter 11, "A House Divided," examines how Ford continues to deconstruct popular notions of duty, honor, and patriotism while his cinematography actively involves the viewer in the experience of war throughout *The Horse Soldiers* (1959). Chapter 12, "The Nature of One's Service," explores Ford's use of film as an evidentiary medium throughout his investigation of military culture in *Sergeant Rutledge* (1960) against the background of the American civil rights movement. This chapter also views *Two Rode Together* (1961), generally considered to be an expression of its director's bitterness and disillusionment after the Second World War, as a social tragedy in which Ford transmits psychological truths about racism, mass hysteria, and individual hypocrisy as Hollywood blacklisting began to diminish. Chapter 13, "Deconstructing the Legend," examines Ford's commitment to honor the dead in *The Man Who Shot Liberty Valance* (1962) via its deconstruction of Western conventions. Chapter 14, "Questions of Just Conduct," reconsiders *Cheyenne Autumn* (1964), the John Ford film that almost everyone in 1964 seemed to love to hate, as another film concerned with the veteran experience, centering on issues of combat, combat trauma, and self-healing.

Actively engaged in shaping American culture throughout his career, John Ford recorded the growing pains of his country throughout the McCarthy period and the abatement of the Cold War, but never lost sight of the foundational ideas of America, especially the journey homeward that so deeply marks the American experience. However different Ford's postwar Westerns may seem to be, all communicate his concerns about his country's social and political problems. When speaking with Katherine Hepburn, Dan Ford commented that his grandfather's work has always recognizable for its "generosity of emotion." In it, one finds "honest sentiment and emotion, that's what makes it so strong."[39] "There's nothing small time about Jack Ford," Hepburn agreed.[40]

Like John Ford, there is nothing "small time" about his Westerns and war stories. They chart enormous changes in the heartbeat of American culture throughout the twentieth century. This book does not claim to be a comprehensive work on John Ford's interest in the military or the effect that the experience of the Second World War had on his films but hopes to generate more discussion about Ford's amazing life and work and break new ground for scholars, film historians, and general audiences everywhere.

1

A CAREER MAN

He was very cool. He was a cool appraiser within himself, I'm sure, of his own self. He would never let on what was going on in his mind. His motivations were secret.[1] —Katharine Hepburn

Because of John Ford's secretive nature, shaped in New England at the turn of the twentieth century, the complexities of his life and his work will probably never be completely resolved. Ford meant what he said when he stated that the truth about his life was "nobody's damn business" but his own. While dying, he told story after story about his life and times to his grandson, Dan, leaving behind a tantalizing record of family stories, tall tales, and memories of his wartime adventures. At various times a world-famous Hollywood film director, a world traveler, a spy for the Naval Reserve, an enthusiastic yachtsman, a dedicated OSS operator, a rear admiral, a hardened workaholic, and a periodic alcoholic, Ford worked hard (and played harder) with many of the people found in the twentieth-century's Who's Who.

Dan Ford's *Pappy: The Life of John Ford*, the most complete portrait written about Ford, offers insider glimpses into Ford's complicated and often conflicted private and professional lives. The book renders vivid cameos of Hollywood throughout Ford's career and provides valuable insights into Ford's relationships with actors, technicians, studio heads, politicians, influential Navy and Army officers, public personalities, and presidents of the United States.[2] Although Ford and his films have been examined extensively in terms of his Irish heritage, his strict Catholic upbringing, and his alcoholism, it seems that the more we know about the man, the less we know him. What Andrew Sarris refers to as "the John Ford Movie Mystery" continues, as Ford continues to elude definition.[3] James D'Arc points out that "there is the obligatory 'The End,' but there isn't an end to a John Ford film. The story continues. There is a sequel somewhere. Not from John Ford but from the person who's sitting in that theatre seat or in front of that television."[4] Screenwriter Lem Dobbs also remarks, "It's as if you want to pinpoint some kind of Rosebud that would explain everything and no one has found that with John Ford."[5]

Also born and raised in New England, Katharine Hepburn points out, when speaking with Ford at his home in Palm Springs shortly before his death, that she and he had been brought up to believe that there are some things "you wouldn't repeat. If you have any decency you just keep your trap shut."[6] Notably, while Hepburn talks with Ford about his life and work, he does just that, only interrupting her to comment when he feels that she is building him "into a hell of a heavy," to agree with her assessments of his sensitivities, to correct her when he feels she is wrong, and to ensure that her comments are being recorded.[7] Making sure that his grandson understands the importance of Hepburn's insights into his life, he tells Dan, "You have a chapter here."[8]

In his other conversations with his grandson, Ford continues to direct the research that went into the making of his biography, telling Dan to "kill" the tape when he couldn't think of anything else to say when responding to questions.[9] He would also double-check to confirm the tape recorder was turned off when he wished to discuss information that he wanted kept off the record. Often short, and sometimes cranky, when answering questions, he changes perceptibly during his interview with Hepburn. At first, the two simply seem to be old friends touching base with one another after many years apart. However, as their conversation continues, Ford's professional personality appears—revealing the personal, caring individual that his family, friends, and colleagues knew as Pappy. Pappy is most evident when Hepburn acknowledges her own difficulties with unwelcome publicity. At the time of their talk, she was in the process of consulting a lawyer about Metro-Goldwyn-Mayer, and Ford, concerned for her welfare, helpfully points out that "if you win, you lose the lawyer's fees."[10]

Ford's revealing conversation with Hepburn not only permits the listener a fascinating and spellbinding view of his continuing friendship with her, but also, and more importantly, illustrates how the Old Master of Hollywood related to people, in general, and actors, in particular. As Anna Lee, a veteran of the John Ford Stock Company, remembers in an interview with Dan Ford, Ford would "start talking—not about the scene—but about something entirely different—and instinctively you knew he was trying to tell you something. It was like magic; it was as if there was some kind of thought transference. That's the only way I can describe it."[11] What Lee describes as "thought transference" is evident in the following passages taken from his conversation with Hepburn. Tellingly, Ford shifts the focus of the conversation from himself to Hepburn before "directing" what appears to be her insight about his personality back to himself:

JF: You were talking about me having a split personality. So are you.

KH: Well, we are secretive New Englanders, but you're much worse than I am.

JF: You are a split personality. Half pagan, half Puritan.

KH: And so are you.

JF: True.[12]

Ford's extremely personal remark to Hepburn that she is "half pagan, half Puritan" remains unclarified. It is unclear whether he is alluding to their clandestine affair that took place in 1936 or to what they both saw as a New England penchant for strictly compartmentalizing one's life into public and private matters. By confirming Hepburn's return of the comment, Ford cannily awards this insight into his character to her, further protecting his privacy by retaining control of the information that would appear in his biography.

As Ford carefully constructs his persona for posterity, Hepburn even chides him about his propensity to reinvent himself for the public on tape, saying, "Now you're so sweet to everyone, and it is not your true self. And I don't want your grandson to misunderstand you."[13] Ford's responses to Hepburn permit a fascinating (and touching) glimpse of his continuing affection for her and, more important, an opportunity to witness him subtly directing her responses. A master manipulator of psychology, Ford introduces the importance of his own backstory to the project at hand before he and Hepburn construct the character of "John Ford" together. He then prompts her, as Anna Lee notes he did with his actors on set, guiding her impressions of the man she knew for his grandson:

> **KH:** [*to DF*] I think he has the most remarkable group of qualities that I've ever met in anyone. The most unusual assemblage of qualities that I've ever met.

> **JF:** I have?

> **KH:** Yes.

> **JF:** Name one. Never mind, don't.

> **KH:** No. I think he's enormously tough, terribly arrogant, enormously tender.

> **JF:** I am arrogant?

> **KH:** Yes, terribly arrogant.

> **JF:** I am . . . Caspar Milquetoast.

> **KH:** No. No. NO.

> **DF:** [*helping*] Very secure.

> **KH:** [*continuing*] "So, so sensi— [*pauses*]. No. Not all that. Very secure. Never smug. Never smug. Never phony and enormously, truly sensitive, which is a very rare quality and that you see in his hands more than anything. But true sensitivity and great nerve and speed which is why he did so much original stuff, I think. And never a follower—always a leader. Never was particularly concerned with, artistically never concerned at all with, what anyone thought because he took instead of [*pauses*] I don't think you ever really considered yourself as an artist did you? Because . . .

JF: No.

KH: [*continues*] You considered yourself as a sort of [*pauses*].

JF: [*inserts the correct term*] hard-working, hard-nosed, hard-boiled workman.

KH: Workman. Like a carpenter. Something like that.[14]

Having constructed the character of "John Ford" with Hepburn to his satisfaction, Ford does what a director will do when pleased with his actress—he compliments her on her work: "You're very perceptive. You're the best of all the interviews," he says. "Yeah, you're great."[15]

As Dan Ford points out, his grandfather's personal and professional lives cannot be "cleanly and evenly divided" because "the demands of the movie factory always came first."[16] The "endless parade of writers, actors, and producers who were always passing through John's life . . . had first call on his attention."[17] Even when Ford escaped from his public life to the privacy of his yacht, the *Araner*,[18] the people who accompanied him on fishing trips down the coast to Mexico were often the people with whom he worked, like Wingate Smith, Dudley Nichols, Preston Foster, John Wayne, and Ward Bond. Later, Mary Ford's naval friends also became her husband's friends and business associates, as Ford divided his career between Hollywood and the Navy. Ford may have been away from the pressures of the Studio and the OSS while on vacation or leave, but he was never entirely divorced from his work. Thus, very few people felt they ever really knew the man who appeared to the public as John Ford. Actor George O'Brien, for example, lived in close quarters with Ford while vacationing with him in the Far East in 1931. Many years later, O'Brien, who regularly starred in Ford's films during the 1920s, shared hotel rooms and bunked in cramped quarters with the director on a tramp steamer, and saw him at his best and his worst, confided to his son that he felt that he still did not really know the man who, without explanation on their return from the Philippines, cut him out of his inner circle of friends and did not cast him in another role until making *Fort Apache* (1948). O'Brien's observation identifies Ford as a social persona, designed, as Carl Jung would say, to make an impression upon others and to conceal the true nature of the individual engaged in the role being played.[19] Paradoxically, John Wayne, who took O'Brien's place among Ford's friends, attributed his close friendship with Ford to their lack of personal intimacy: "We had a nice relationship," he tells Dan Ford. "We never had to explain to each other. We never complained."[20] In Hollywood, personas are a common phenomenon, but Ford's use of one is highly unusual. As Lem Dodds points out, "You know, it's amazing. Everyone knows that actors change their names when they come to Hollywood. That John Wayne's name isn't John Wayne and Woody Allen's name isn't Woody Allen. Or Rock Hudson or Tony Curtis or Kirk Douglas—they're all phony. And writers use pseudonyms. You know, in the history of famous directors in Hollywood, do you know how many change their names? Who have completely made up names? John Ford."[21]

It wasn't until the shooting of *Two Rode Together* (1961) that Harry Carey Jr. recognized the overlapping of professional and social networks had created a catch-22 situation for John Ford: "He wanted very much to be 'one of the boys,' but to do that, he would have to give up that mystique and authority he possessed." Remembering one night when Ford visited him after supper, Carey observes, "John Ford, the great motivator, the film genius, the man who enabled you to do things you never thought yourself capable of doing, who never gave you a good scene to do and then cut it from the final print, was there in our room, trying his best to be a 'regular guy.'" Ford was, according to Carey, "really a very lonely man."[22] In Los Angeles, Ford was also unable to find a social network that offered him an escape from the pressures of filmmaking and family. John Wayne understood how badly John Ford needed periods of rest and relaxation to recover from the stress of making films. He remembered that "Jack kinda liked me because we could go out on his boat and stay for maybe two or three weeks. And he'd bring a cord of books; while I was reading one, he'd read three. It didn't depend on continuous or continual conversation. . . . He was certainly not a drunkard. . . . On occasion to let off steam this man hit the bottle."[23]

Like many of his contemporaries, Ford measured his self-worth and social importance by his industry. He was happiest when he was directing. To Peter Bogdanovich, Ford says, "To me, [making a film] was always a job of work—which I enjoyed immensely—and that's it."[24] John Ford began his career in Hollywood employed as "a ditchdigger" by getting a job on "the labor gang at Universal when Carl Laemmle Sr.

was running the studio."[25] He worked his way through the system as an assistant propman, an extra, a stuntman, a cameraman, and an assistant director for his brother, Francis Ford. In three short years, at the age of twenty-two, he became an action director, specializing in Westerns. Tellingly, Ford attributes his success to his productiveness and his belief in the American Dream: In a 1973 interview with Walter Wagner, he confided, "I think if you work hard enough, you will succeed."[26] Accordingly, Ford judged his actors and the members of his family by their dedication to the task at hand, encouraging them to put the collective nature of filmmaking ahead of their personal needs. "A director can either make a film or break it," he says to Wagner.

> He must hypnotize himself to be sympathetic toward the material. Sometimes we are not. Being under contract you make pictures that you don't want to make, but you try to steel yourself, to get enthused over them. You get on the set, and you forget everything else. You say these actors are doing the best they can. They also have to make a living. As a director I must help them as much as I can. I think a director can help an actor or an actress, and he can also help the cameraman, the electricians and everybody else. I think he brings a great deal to a film.[27]

Always pragmatic, Ford points out to Wagner that he directed films for "money, to pay the rent," but also acknowledged that "there is an art to the making of a motion picture."[28] Citing Frank Capra, George Cukor, George Stevens, and George Sidney as examples, he stated, "There are some great artists in the business," but modestly added, "I am not one of them." This, of course, could not be further from the truth, but Ford, who lived and spoke in terms of indirection to protect his private life from public scrutiny, expected his listener to know that he was a master filmmaker.

At the end of his life, John Ford had become all things to all people. Few remembered that this Hollywood celebrity began his life in Portland, Maine, as John Martin Feeney, and fewer still knew that he died still bearing that name. Even film historian Joseph McBride was startled to discover that Ford was really a social persona. John Feeney had retained his birth name throughout his life. "I went to Ford's funeral," he said, "and I first discovered this when I looked at his coffin. . . . The family had engraved John M. Feeney on there. And I thought that's a surprise."[29]

JOHN FORD AT WORK

Attempting to reconstruct the personal life of John Ford is like trying to square a circle, capture a unicorn, or chase a rainbow, but reconstructing the career of John Ford is quite another matter. Born on February 1, 1894, John Martin Feeney reinvented himself not once but twice in his first seven years of working in Hollywood. After arriving in Hollywood as the son of the wealthiest saloonkeeper in Portland, Maine, and the younger brother of Francis Ford, John Feeney became Jack Ford, adopting his famous brother's name when Fox erred in making out his first paycheck. Then Jack Ford, the young director of silent Westerns and close friend of Harry Carey Sr., became John Ford. When *The Iron Horse* was released, "they made him change Jack Ford to John Ford," as Mary Ford says, because Jack "didn't sound dignified enough."[30]

Ford became the Old Man of Hollywood that he is today because he and Fox's publicists skillfully constructed, encouraged, and promoted a personality designed for public consumption. A master of image management, Ford understood how to construct personas on screen and off. As Bill Clothier points out, "This is true—the Old Man made John Wayne and Wayne has never failed to admit this."[31] Throughout his life, Ford's forte was understatement. As Wayne points out, Ford disliked obvious displays of sophistication, hypocrisy, and even social amenities if they were false: "You know what kind of wit he had," he says, commenting that Ford could usually make people enjoy being the targets of his humor. "He could zing 'em, and they'd go away loving it."[32] Undoubtedly the most famous incident in which Ford displayed this occurred when at the Director's Guild meeting of October 15, 1950. As Joseph Mankiewicz remembers, Ford stood up and began his attack on a faction of the guild headed by Cecil B. DeMille by saying, "My name's John Ford. I make Westerns"[33]—deftly allying himself with the fundamental American values associated with that genre.

Fifteen years before, however, it is doubtful that John Ford would have thought of introducing himself as a director of Westerns. As Charles J. Maland noted, Ford, the only major director to identify himself so closely with the Western, downplayed his Westerns at times in his career because many held the genre in low esteem. Before the Second World War, Ford was first known as a "money" director in Hollywood whose box office hits were brought in on time and under budget, and later as an aesthete whose movies (also brought in on time and under budget) garnered Academy Awards. It was only after *The Informer* (1935) won four Academy Awards (for Best Actor, Best Director, Best Screenplay, and Best Score), the National Board of Review (USA) award for Best Film, the New York Film Critics Circle Award for Best Film, and the Venice Film Festival's award for Best Screenplay that Ford became known as a director interested in exploring Irish culture using expressionist film style, even though he had begun his successful career as a director of "dusters" and broke into making A-list movies with *The Iron Horse* in 1924. Ford's connection with the Western, an association that occurred late in his career, is one that became common with *cinéastes* during the early 1960s and is the one best known today.

Ford's involvement with the Western later in his career may seem puzzling at first, but, as Maland notes, directors were much more likely to gain the attention of filmgoers and critics before 1960 if their films were associated with a particular genre: Chaplin's tramp-centered comedies, for example, Frank Capra's screwball comedy and social-problem films, and Hitchcock's thrillers all elicited a great deal of attention compared to the attention received by directors (like Howard Hawks and John Ford) who worked in a wide variety of genres.[34] Ford, who began his career making Westerns, returned to directing the genre films after the Second World War to save Argosy Productions from his costly "art" film, *The Fugitive*. At this point in his career, the Western became the source of Ford's "money-makers." Six of his eight films between 1946 and 1950 were Westerns, and he also directed five consecutive Westerns between 1959 and 1962, starting with *The Horse Soldiers* and ending with his work *How the West Was Won*. Most of these movies were successful at the box office. *Fort Apache*, for example, in 1948 was a commercial success that returned $2.8 million in its first six months and put Argosy back in the black—proof to "the intrepid" Ford, who on his return to Los Angeles was celebrated by the press as a war hero, that "the public shared his visions of military glory and was ready for more pictures based on the stories of James Warner Bellah."[35]

Ford's image as a director of Westerns rests on his work done with the genre in the late 1940s through the 1950s. One article that appeared in the *Saturday Evening Post* on July 23, 1949, was particularly important to the making of this reputation: in "Hollywood's Favorite Rebel," Frank Nugent, who had praised *Stagecoach* highly in his 1939 review, described Ford as "one of the greatest directors who ever lived"; a "big shambling man with a corrugated face . . . and a gift for making pictures which reminded Hollywood that the movies are not just an industry but an art."[36] Nugent finished his article by offering the paradox to his readers with which we are still familiar: John Ford is a man who is proud of the awards displayed on the mantel in his living room, but who never shows up at the star-studded dinners to claim them. Above all, Ford, according to Nugent, who socialized with the director, is a modest, private man—a public persona who shuns publicity.[37]

Many critical commentators have found Nugent's characterization of Ford as a paradox attractive. Joseph McBride, Tag Gallagher, Ron L. Davis, Peter Bogdanovich, and Andrew Sinclair have all remarked on what appears to be Ford's puzzling nature,[38] but the image of Ford as a complicated, card-playing man's man existed long before "Hollywood's Favorite Rebel" was published. The review's similarities to Fox's portrayal of Ford as a modest family man *and* a virile individualist before the Second World War suggest that Nugent's portrayal of Ford's public image was not news to his fans and followers.

Picture Show ran a full-page spread on John Ford at home and at work, sent by the Associated Press Feature Service to 114 newspapers across the country on January 21, 1939, to promote the opening of *Submarine Patrol*, released on November 25, 1938.[39] Presented as a family man, Ford walks in his garden, escapes the "bright lights" of Hollywood on his 110-foot ketch, smokes his pipe after dinner, and spends his evenings playing "hearts" with his wife and friends and reading books on Irish subjects.[40] According to *Picture Show*, John Ford was a star who refused to live like one. His lifestyle was certainly not that of the rich and famous. He lived in a modest nine-room house with a garden and no swimming pool. His wife also said they've always been happy there so "why move to a palace?"[41]

As a call-out for the feature helpfully announces, "John Ford at 43 is a $100,000-per-film Hollywood Director and Motion Picture Academy award winner. But you'd never suspect it, the way he lives. His idea of a swell time isn't a nightclub party, but a quiet evening at home with baked beans for dinner, a good book, and a pipe. Nor, to see him at work—in old clothes, talking softly, encouraging [sic] always cool—would you guess that he directs fast, virile films."[42] Fox's account of Ford as an average American husband devoted to hearth and home, of course, was nonsense. In his early forties, Ford was experiencing a midlife crisis after the death of his mother, and his marriage with Mary could not be considered ideal or satisfying. On the set however, *Picture Show* finds Ford to be as modest and disarming as he is at home. The captions beneath their thrillers, *Seas Beneath* (1931), *The Hurricane* (1937), and *Submarine Patrol* (1938), inform readers that Ford, being "no judge" of his own work, "never attends galas or premieres."[43] Ford, in fact, avoided attending premieres after *The Informer*'s preview because his temperament was not well suited to the stress that previews created—he was so upset by the tepid reception of *The Informer* that he "sneaked past a cluster of grim-faced RKO executives," sat down on the running board of his car, and vomited in the parking lot.[44] Suffering from nervous exhaustion after he made his films at Twentieth Century-Fox, Ford typically handed his footage over to Darryl Zanuck to be edited and left for several weeks of rest and relaxation aboard the *Araner*, sailing to Mexico or Honolulu to get away from pressures of his workplace.

Picture Show's account of Ford, which suggested that he preferred to direct "he-man" stories, is also highly inaccurate. The films he helmed were chosen for him by his studios. A "full-blown disaster epic" and romantic action money-maker,[45] *Hurricane*, praised for its special effects, was assigned to Ford by Sam Goldwyn, who exercised dictatorial control over his pictures.[46] Another big moneymaker, *Submarine Patrol*, was a straight adventure film, a studio potboiler made on the assembly line.[47]

The most glaring instance of image management in *Picture Show*'s account of Ford as a director, however, lies in its depiction of Ford tricking Victor McLaglen into producing an Oscar-winning performance in *The Informer* by withholding lines from the actor until he was on the set. As Dan Ford notes, his grandfather's direction involved turning "the actor to a trembling wreck": the night before the movie's key scene was to be shot, Ford took his leading man aside and told him he was not needed the next day and to take the night off and to "relax." He had friends take McLaglen to a party where, by midnight, as Ford intended, McLaglen had drunk himself unconscious and passed out on a piano. Early next morning, the actor was summoned to the studio and put right to work on the court-of-inquiry scene. McLaglen's badly hungover performance "won him an Oscar." Not surprisingly, throughout the shooting of *The Informer*, "he shook, lost weight, and couldn't sleep at night. He also swore he was going to quit acting—after he killed John Ford."[48]

Given the phenomenal success of his movies in the late 1930s, it is not surprising that Ford continued throughout the rest of his career to promote himself to the public as the unflappable director and respectable family man fashioned by Twentieth Century-Fox in 1939. As Hollywood's industry standards changed, Ford steadfastly refused to make movies that would alter his professional image, so much so that, in *Searching for John Ford*, Joseph McBride notes that the director's complaints about Hollywood being "a market for sex and horror" became a familiar and tiresome refrain of his later years.[49] Even on his deathbed, Ford remained true to the public persona found in the *Picture Show*'s spread: in 1973, terminally ill with cancer and unable to eat, he claimed to be living his life at home just as he did in 1939: "I still practically live on baked beans," he says while Dan Ford interviews him. "Of course, they aren't as good as the ones [my mother] cooked—I don't know what her secret was, but she could make baked beans that would make your mouth water."[50]

Ford's (and Fox's) emphasis on his modesty has supported the general assumption that he was only interested in promoting his reputation as a Navy man after the Second World War. However, as John Wayne points out to Dan Ford, John Ford was keenly aware of and very sensitive about his public image in Tinsel Town. Like his wife, he too enjoyed the prestige awarded to a major director: "Your granddad liked that a lot more than he pretended, you know," he tells Dan Ford. Revealing yet another aspect of Ford's personality, Wayne says,

> It used to kill him when down at the isthmus, I was aboard the boat for Christ's sake as much as he was, and when the sightseeing boat would come down. It would be "oh that's the *Araner*; that's John Wayne's boat and that's John Wayne up there." Now Jack'd get up and say, "It's *not John Wayne's* boat! It's *John Ford's* boat!" And I'm

sittin' there laughin'. God, it was fun. He'd say, "You son of a bitch. I'll stop you coming on here." I said, "Well, you do and I'll sink my ship." Those were great days. You can't look back. You're not supposed to, but it's pretty hard not to when there were guys like Ward and Jack.[51]

Katharine Hepburn also concurs with Wayne's assessment of Ford's concern about his public image; she notes, "Although he never will admit it, Jack is an enormously ambitious man—and he had a tremendous amount of energy so he wasn't about to sit back and accomplish nothing."[52]

Ford's sense of humor also contributed to the making of his reputation. He and the members of his Stock Company were always playing practical jokes on one another. While *Wagon Master* (1950) was being filmed, Ford encouraged a dogfight to take place. The dogs, however, did not cooperate. One ran away, and the other attacked Ward Bond, a Stock Company veteran who worked in twenty-five of Ford's films and was one of the director's closest colleagues. The dog "ripped the whole length of [Ward's] pant leg wide open"; Harry Carey Jr. had never seen Ford "laugh so hard"—after yelling "cut and print." After Ford learned that Bond was all right, he asked for a vet to "give the poor dog a shot, just in case he bit Ward."[53] During the shooting of *Rio Grande* (1950), Ford and his entire location crew decamped quietly one afternoon from the Colorado River, leaving Ben Johnson and Harry Carey Jr. walking home in 1872 cavalry uniforms with about twenty catfish because they had been "fishing on company time" (with Ford's permission).[54] According to John Wayne, Victor McLaglen vowed he'd never play another joke on John Ford after a prank resulted in him being arrested and thrown in jail: "Jack got even with him," Wayne says. According to Wayne, McLaglen was "thrown in the jug" for something he did not do—sponsoring someone who was illegally in the United States into Mexico. "They wouldn't let McLaglen call the studio, and they kept him in that jail for two days."[55]

Not surprisingly, Ford's fearsome reputation became part of the horseplay in which members of his Stock Company indulged themselves. Harry Carey Jr., for example, remembers McLaglen taking the opportunity to warn him about Ford's bullying while they were en route to the shooting location of *She Wore a Yellow Ribbon* (1949). Carey took McLaglen's every word about the director seriously, but McLaglen, who, Wayne says, admired and respected Ford, was having some fun and pulling the young actor's leg by asking the younger man whether Ford was "mean" to him and warning him that the director was "a sadist" and "a bad one." McLaglen frayed the eager young actor's nerves further, saying, "A fucking sadist, he [Ford] is. But ya can't let it bother ya, lad. You mustn't let it bother ya."[56]

Carey's insider memories of Ford after the Second World War, however, need to be considered carefully, because he did precisely what McLaglen warned him not to do: he let John Ford bother him. As a result, his memories of Uncle Jack are, at times, far from being objective and, because of his own problems with alcohol, at times, far from credible. Carey himself admits that "over the years [he] had dwelt too much on stories of Ford harassing [him]" and points out that his Uncle "Jack was a man for all seasons, but not for all actors."[57] Carey remembers that during the filming of *Two Rode Together*, he was so nervous that his mother encouraged him to wash "Greenies" down with rum.[58] Unlike Widmark, who found Ford "tremendously funny,"[59] Carey was "jealous of others [to whom Ford was] paying attention."[60] When he did have the director's attention, Carey found John Ford to be "scary."[61] "I didn't like him," Carey says, "and wished he'd get back to the boat he kept bragging about."[62] Habitually on edge around Ford, he was "so scared" that he was shaking even when the director was being pleasant.[63] On and off the set, the sort of father-son relationship that Carey desired to have with Ford was simply impossible. As Carey points out, on location in Death Valley while shooting *3 Godfathers* (1948), the Old Man was "bearable or unbearable—never nice."[64] While learning to act, Carey "mistakenly" kept thinking that he, not John Ford, was "right."[65] Carey even claims to have been furious after reading that the director "bullied" a performance out of him before conceding the point and saying "the author was right."[66]

Ford's view of the relationship between a director and his actors, shaped during his own apprenticeship in silent film, differed radically from Carey's. "It isn't a question of freedom," he remarks to Dan Ford. "At least in my day the actor had no freedom; the director was the man on the spot and he was in charge. And the actors did as the director said. It wasn't a question of freedom at all."[67]

Carey's complicated love-hate relationship with John Ford provides readers with a great deal of insight into how closely Ford managed the young man's career and how Carey himself affected Ford's reputation. Carey attributes Ford's decision to make him a star in *3 Godfathers* to Ford and his father's professional parting of ways in 1921, but it is more probable that Ford, who, Harry Carey Jr. states, "never apologized for anything in his life,"[68] was instead fulfilling a deathbed promise to his old friend. Ford, who had Carey Jr. transferred out of the Pacific theater to Washington during the Second World War to ensure his safety, rescued the Careys from bankruptcy during this period, and then cast Olive Carey in his Westerns after her husband's death to ensure her financial stability, considered the young man to be a member of his own family. In 1954, he finally spelled out what he considered this relationship to be to Carey, instructing the young actor to call him "Uncle Jack."[69]

Another of the many stars that Ford created was Ben Johnson. The World Rodeo Roping Champion arrived in Hollywood with a load of horses that Howard Hughes ordered for *The Outlaw* in 1943 and was working as a double and a stuntman in Westerns when Ford cast him in larger roles. Often paired with Harry Carey Jr. in Ford's films, Johnson's star enjoyed a meteoric rise in the Western, playing major characters first in *She Wore a Yellow Ribbon* and then in *Rio Grande* and *Wagon Master*. On October 25, 1948, *Variety*'s "Twinkle Twinkle Little Star" listed Johnson as a "top talent."[70] The article notes that "Johnson, an Oklahoma cowboy, is so favorably considered by John Ford and Merian C. Cooper that he was handed the star role of latter's 'Mr. Joseph Young of Africa' for his first screen appearance, and now is in 'Yellow Ribbon.'"[71] Johnson commented after visiting Ford for the last time in Palm Springs, "That John Ford, I worked for him for six years. I mean, he was a mean old bastard, but if you listened to him, you could learn something. He was a real educator. The last words Ford ever said to me was, 'Ben, don't forget to stay real.' I think that's pretty good advice anywhere."[72]

As Johnson's anecdote demonstrates, John Feeney played his part out to the end. He never stopped being John Ford, the "money" director and Old Master of Hollywood—even while dying. Lying in bed and calling for more games of poker and bottles of Guinness, he reminded his grandson that his public persona is simply another legend:

> I've started a lot of good actors, from good actors to stardom but the
> supplementary crews. . . . I like to use my own actors. . . . My God,
> the names of the actors I've started in this business. I mean it is
> amazing. Amazing. I know there was a myth about the John Ford
> Stock Company which isn't true. What is the John Ford Stock Com-
> pany? I don't know. . . . These legends keep coming up and most of
> them are untrue but what the hell. I mean, I love actors and actress-
> es. There is a compulsion about them to express something. I go
> along with it.[73]

Ford was keenly aware of his contribution to the making of Hollywood's
stars, and he also knew how the stars that he discovered and developed
contributed to the making of his own reputation. In 1975, Andrew
Sarris's *The John Ford Mystery Movie* begins its treatments of Ford and
his movies by saying, "We seek out the man only because of the movies,
and not, as with Stroheim, Welles, and even Renoir, the movies because
of the man."[74] Since then, it has become a general wisdom to regard
John Ford as a rebel, a stubborn (and driven) auteur director whose
personal vision transcended the obstructions of the Hollywood studio
system despite his protests that he was, at base, a studio man—a hard-
nosed, hard-working journeyman director, merely a traffic cop in front
of the camera.

JOHN FORD AND DARRYL F. ZANUCK

To a large degree, Ford's success as a filmmaker, and later as an independent producer/director, can be attributed to the years he spent
working for Twentieth Century-Fox. Throughout the 1930s and 1940s,
being employed at Twentieth Century-Fox meant being directed by the
man whom Ford named "Darryl F. Panic." As Lem Dobbs observes,
Zanuck, as Twentieth Century-Fox's executive producer and production head, was a "director of the director." George F. Custen argues
convincingly Zanuck was as dominant a creative force at Twentieth
Century-Fox as John Ford and points out that the effect that Zanuck
had on Ford's work and career should not be overlooked or underestimated. Custen points out that "people who have written appreciatively
of *The Grapes of Wrath* and another classic, *How Green Was My Valley*, have seen them as sterling entries in the canon of John Ford"—

casting the producer as the "fellow with whom, in the Faustian pact between art and commerce struck in Hollywood, creative people like Ford were forced to deal."[75] He reminds his readers that "with all the forces at work in the culture of Hollywood, militating against accomplishing anything of value, it was Zanuck who . . . acquired the rights to the books . . . fought to get them made into movies . . . cast the roles . . . staffed the film's production team . . . supervised the music, the sets, and the scripts."[76] As he notes, it was also Zanuck who edited all the movies he assigned to Ford that were produced by Twentieth Century-Fox. "Taking nothing away from the other creative people upon whom these films depend for their collective lives," Custen says, "on the whole it was Zanuck who afforded the world of each film its definitive contours."[77] It was Zanuck's marketing of Americana at Twentieth Century-Fox that made it possible for Ford to direct *Young Mr. Lincoln* (1939), *Drums along the Mohawk* (1939), and *The Grapes of Wrath* (1940), not Ford's creative vision. It was under Zanuck's supervision, then, that John Ford developed into a master filmmaker.

With this in mind, it is not surprising that Ford, notoriously impatient with interviewers (and especially with academics) who desired to promote their views of him as a cinematic poet, acknowledged the perception of himself as an auteur, but also attempted to correct it. Returning to Fox's Americana and that studio's underpinnings of his public image, Ford, when talking with interviewers, cast himself as a studio man: "a hard-nosed, hard-working director with a sense of humor and no temper, temperament, or inhibitions."[78] Promoting himself as a rugged individualist engaged in an American Dream remarkably like that found in Zanuck's films, he remarked to Eric Leguèbe, "Sex, obscenity, violence, ugliness, decadence, degeneration don't interest me. Excesses disgust me. What I like is effort, the will to go beyond oneself. For me life is to be in the face of friends who you punch in the nose, and then you drink and sing together. It is the attraction to real women, and not the Miss Bovarys. It's the fresh air, the great outdoors, the great hopes."[79]

At Twentieth Century-Fox, Ford's relationship with Zanuck was compartmentalized and complicated. When Zanuck arrived at Fox in 1935 and recut the Ford-Rogers comedy *Steamboat around the Bend* (1935), Ford was "appalled."[80] Later, he would agree with Philip Dunne's assessment that Zanuck was "the most talented producer in the history of movies"[81] and cited Zanuck as a genius in the editing room. At first, however, Ford advanced the more antagonistic side of his relationship with the producer, calling Zanuck a "hyperactive manipulator" with a "Napoleon complex."[82] In *Don't Say Yes Until I Finish Talking*, Mel Gussow points out that *Prisoner of Shark Island* (1936) was one of "the rare instances of an argument between Zanuck and Ford." Zanuck, who had decided Warner Baxter's Southern accent was unbelievable, visited Ford's set and told him the accent had to be dropped. Ford "snapped": "If you don't like it, get someone else." Zanuck's reply left no doubt in anyone's mind who was in charge of the film: "God damn it to hell," he shouted. "Don't threaten me! People don't threaten *me*. I threaten them!"[83] Warren Baxter changed his accent.

For his part, Zanuck was reported to have been furious that in *Prisoner of Shark Island*, many of the touches lauded by one critic as evidence of Ford's genius were in fact the result of Zanuck's own direct editorial intervention—Nunnally Johnson, hired as a full-time writer by Twentieth Century-Fox in 1935, recalls that "this woman [film critic] chose four points which I happened to know all about. One was a big cut which to her was an example of Ford's elliptical directing, which I knew was a cut that Zanuck had made with Ford screaming like a banshee against it."[84]

As the two men learned to work together harmoniously, open disagreements disappeared, although Ford continued to foster the impression on his sets that he and the production head were at loggerheads and commented on the interference of producers in his interviews during the latter half of the 1930s. In 1936, for example, he complained to Emanuel Eisenberg that producers have "got to turn over picture-making into the hands that know it. Combination of author and director running the works: that's the ideal. Like Dudley Nichols and me. Or Riskin and Capra."[85] In 1939, he even took a not-so-oblique jab at Zanuck while promoting the release of *Stagecoach* to Michel Mok. Proud of the fact that no animals were injured during the shooting of his movie, Ford says, "The S.P.C.A. watched us every minute, and a good thing too. They raised all kinds of hell with Darryl Zanuck for what was supposed to have happened to the horses in *Jesse James*. The only creature hurt in making our picture was a press agent who got in the way of a posse. Fortunately there's no society for the prevention of cruelty to press agents."[86]

Studio correspondence at Twentieth Century-Fox, however, reveals that the Ford-Zanuck collaboration had become mutually respectful. Outlining his concerns about inconsistencies and characterization in *My Darling Clementine* (1946), Zanuck, for example, recommends to Ford in a memo dated June 25, 1946, that he talk to Sam Engel and recommends that the editing of the movie be turned over to Zanuck: "You trusted me implicitly on *The Grapes of Wrath* and *How Green Was My Valley*," he reminds Ford.

> You did not see either picture until they were playing in the theatres and innumerable times you went out of your way to tell me how much you appreciated the Editorial work. We won Academy Awards with both pictures and I recall your telling me that in your opinion the cutting job on Valley, which was a difficult subject, was the best job you had ever seen. You will recall on both jobs I made a number of radical changes. You provided me with ample film to work with as you have done in the case of *Clementine*.[87]

Zanuck's hand as a screenwriter is also evident in Ford's films. When we consider the sequence in *The Grapes of Wrath* portraying the Joads' arrival in town in tandem with Zanuck's report, "'The Grapes of Wrath' Conference on Screenplay of July 13, 1939," it is evident that Ford had adopted Zanuck's suggestions. Custen points out that "the sequence as shot is a virtual transcription of the memo, down to the lines of dialogue."[88]

Tellingly, when no longer employed by Twentieth Century-Fox, Ford continued to use what he considered to be one of Zanuck's greatest contributions to their films during their collaboration: "proper music—and sound effects."[89] In *The Battle of Midway* (1942), for example, Ford borrows not only "The Red River Valley" from *Grapes of Wrath* to score the uneasy peace on the atoll the night before the Japanese attack, but he also does so via a single, lightly played accordion—validating, by imitation, Zanuck's decision to use only an accordion to render the folk song and re-creating the mood that he himself recognized in *Grapes of Wrath* as "very American and very right"[90] in *The Battle of Midway*.

Lightly played folk songs from the Ford-Zanuck collaboration also reappear in Ford's postwar Westerns produced by Merian C. Cooper

for Argosy Pictures, in particular those sung by the Sons of the Pio-
neers, as well the haunting strains of "Lara's Theme" associated with
Anne Rutledge (Pauline Moore) in *Young Mr. Lincoln*, which is reused
in conjunction with Kathleen Yorke (Maureen O'Hara) in *Rio Grande*
and Martha Edwards (Dorothy Jordan) in *The Searchers* (1956). When
one compares Ford's heavy-handed and ultimately maddening repetition of "Anchors Aweigh" in *Salute* (1929) and its unimaginative replication in *Men without Women* (1930), *Seas Beneath*, and *Submarine
Patrol* with its subtle and much more appropriate use in *The Battle of
Midway*, it is evident that Ford benefited from Zanuck's direction of
the director.

Although the public was never aware of it, the major architect of the
destiny of every single Twentieth Century-Fox release, Ford's films
included, was Darryl Zanuck.[91] Ford may have denied all but the small-
est creative power to producers, but at Twentieth Century-Fox, the
very concept of major films can be traced directly to Darryl Zanuck. In
story conferences *and* in the editing room, Zanuck was the creative
equal of John Ford on the set. Not only are the collective lives of Ford's
films attributable to Zanuck, but the collective life of its director's reputation must also, in part, be attributed to Ford's production head. With
this in mind, it is not surprising that Ford, assigned to assist Zanuck in
producing films in North Africa during the Second World War, greeted
his boss with "Can't I ever get away from you? I'll bet a dollar to a
doughnut that if I ever go to Heaven you'll be waiting at the door for
me under a sign reading 'Produced by Darryl F. Zanuck.'"[92]

Because Hollywood studios until the late 1950s were not just corporations but extensions of their founders, and of the production heads
who oversaw their programs,[93] the similarities that existed between
Ford's and Zanuck's professional lives are highly instructive. Both men
were anomalies in an industry defined by immigrants or first-genera-
tions Jews (Ford was a first-generation Irish American Catholic from
Portland, Maine; Zanuck a first-generation Swiss American Protestant
from Wahoo, Nebraska), yet both mastered its dynamics—Ford became the greatest director and Zanuck the most influential producer in
the history of Hollywood.

In 1973, Ford confided to Walter Wagner, "I have no idea why I
have survived in this business. Luck, I guess."[94] Clearly, however, the
reason for Ford's success was Darryl Zanuck. After 1935, the quality of

Ford's output skyrocketed. Dan Ford remarks that however negative his grandfather's feelings about working with Zanuck may have been, Zanuck's efforts to improve the studio had resulted in "an exceptionally creative atmosphere": "Zanuck was, in fact, steering him toward his best work."[95] The Ford-Zanuck collaboration struck an ideal balance on screen because both men agreed that the story was the essential ingredient of a successful film. Ford's interest in character was balanced by Zanuck's in plot. From 1939 to 1946, Ford's films swept the Oscars, and he collected three coveted New York Critics Awards back to back in 1939, 1940, and 1941. As Dan Ford quips, during the Ford-Zanuck collaboration, John Ford became "hotter than boiler plate."[96] When Lindsay Anderson, a British film director who had been a longtime admirer, visited Ford for the last time, he asked him if there had been any producer with whom he had enjoyed working. Ford replied, "Zanuck. He knew the business. When I was finished a picture I could go off to Catalina on my boat and fish. Didn't have to hang around. I could leave the editing to him. None of the others knew anything."[97]

With Zanuck at the helm, Twentieth Century-Fox was a hard-nosed corporate culture that rewarded creativity, efficiency, and craftsmanship. Known as a "money" director who brought his films in on time and under budget, John Ford excelled in this environment because, in many ways, his working habits and preferences mirrored those of the studio's production head. Like Zanuck, Ford was known for his ability to draw the best out of the people with whom he worked. Also like Zanuck, Ford had a penchant for remakes. 3 Bad Men (1926) was a remake of Marked Men (1919), and 3 Godfathers was a remake of 3 Bad Men. Ford even proposed remakes of Jean Renoir's The Grand Illusion (1937) and Four Sons (1928) to Zanuck, although neither picture was made because of the likelihood they would not draw crowds at the box office. Ford was known for his courage, his industry, and the fast pace he set while directing. Zanuck was respected for the same qualities: William Wellman admired Zanuck for "his guts" and the speed at which he worked "to make a good picture quickly." According to Wellman, Zanuck was "the hardest-working little guy you have ever seen in all your life."[98] Like Zanuck, Ford was a member of the Los Angeles Athletic Club—where he aligned himself with an old boys' network of film industry workers. Ford, during the 1930s, was a regular at the club after work. Writers discovered that the best place to pitch a story idea to him was in the club steam room, where he was invariably in "a relaxed and open frame of mind."[99] As well, both men volunteered for military duty well before Pearl Harbor. Ford joined the Naval Reserve in 1934; Zanuck was commissioned a Reserve lieutenant colonel in the Army Signal Corps in January 1941.

Because of these professional and personal overlaps, it is not surprising that both John Ford and Darryl Zanuck were also masters of what Custen terms "the subtle art of lying in Hollywood,"[100] displaying "split" personalities as they and their families attempted to maintain private lives while being celebrities. People in the industry were often surprised by Ford's and Zanuck's respect for their wives' opinions. They should not have been, for both of these men who sought complete control over their product at work (Ford over his actors and technicians, Zanuck over his directors) had married up in the world, thereby creating intense personal pressures at home. Like Mary Ford, Virginia Zanuck was better educated and more refined than her husband. A gracious hostess, like Mary, Virginia was also an efficient manager, at ease in almost any social setting. Ford and Zanuck also valued being thought of as good family men, but both had affairs during their marriages. In 1939, Ford was still atoning for his affair with Katharine Hepburn, which began during the production of *Mary of Scotland* (1936) and lasted well into the summer of 1936. His infatuation with Hepburn had, as Dan Ford puts it, "blown the lid off any pretense of monogamy, and after it was over, Mary, playing the part of the ideal Hollywood wife, seemed to have given John a free rein to indulge in extramarital affairs—her only stipulations being, first, that she wasn't to know about them, and second, that they were not to become public knowledge."[101] Like Virginia Zanuck's unspoken accord with her husband, Mary ignored Ford's infidelities as long as he was discreet. Unlike Virginia Zanuck, however, Mary did not divorce her partner—she "intended to be Mrs. John Ford until the day she died"[102]—preparing and delivering his meals on request while she maintained a separate bedroom. As Dan Ford points out, "with her Rolls Royce and her charge accounts in every Beverly Hills store,"[103] Mary Ford was very much the Hollywood Matron.[104]

Zanuck's and Ford's professional and personal overlaps are also apparent on screen. Ford has often been noted for his ability to craft a distinctive American world in his movies, particularly his Westerns, whose epic scale and intensely personal stories offer American iconography and ideology. In part, what has come to be known as the "Gordian" style draws its inspiration from Darryl Zanuck's vision of Americana, in which the American past is presented "in a visually perfect but highly modified form."[105] Ford's apprenticeship in the art of sentiment, undertaken when directing Harry Carey Sr.'s character studies at Universal, suited him admirably for Zanuck's knack of foregrounding the human element while rewriting, simplifying, and sanitizing history. Working at Twentieth Century-Fox in the 1930s, Ford participated in producing popular culture that influenced the way Americans thought about themselves. Whether or not they were historically accurate, the images found in Ford's films that were produced and edited by Darryl Zanuck furthered the viability of the American Dream to their audiences. Indeed it may be said that Zanuck's visual look rekeyed America's iconography rather than merely recording history.[106] In the same way that Zanuck's musicals "reconciled Victorianism with its successor culture,"[107] Ford's Westerns also united America's past with its present. The Second World War and its aftermath may have refocused much of American cinema's agenda,[108] but in Ford's Westerns, especially his Cavalry Trilogy, Zanuck's nostalgia for Americana and the ideal American family lingers.

The origin of what has come to be regarded as the "Gordian" family occurred in 1939 in *The Grapes of Wrath* and *How Green Was My Valley* (1941). Under Carl Laemmle and William Fox, in Ford's earlier movies this family does not appear. Rather, these post–World War I pictures often showcase highly dysfunctional single- or no-parent families. In *Hell Bent* (1918), both parents are dead and the brother pimps out his sister; single-parent fathers are responsible for the unhappy state of affairs in *Straight Shooting* (1917), *Bucking Broadway* (1917), *The Iron Horse* (1924), and *3 Bad Men* (1926). The gender of the single parent is reversed in *Four Sons* (1928) and *Pilgrimage* (1933); in these films, single-parent mothers are unable to halt the disintegration of their families.

Ford's experiences with Zanuck's methods of producing stood the director in good stead after he left Twentieth Century-Fox to work with Merian C. Cooper at Argosy. As an independent producer, Ford borrowed pages from Zanuck's book, alternating between big ideas and prestige pictures like *The Fugitive* (1947) and *The Quiet Man* (1952) and popular money-makers like *Fort Apache* and *Rio Grande*. Like Zanuck, Ford's preproduction was painstaking. He prepared his postwar films so thoroughly from script to casting that the movie was completely formed in his head before it was shot. When Ford left Zanuck, he also remained, in many ways, a Twentieth Century-Fox product, carefully maintaining his public image created by the studio and producing and directing movies that appealed to the public's appetite for Americana to finance his art films.

Ford's pictures, however, did change in other ways. Many commentators remark on the differences in Ford's work after he returned from the Second World War. Ford returned unhappily to Twentieth Century-Fox after the war to complete his contract with the studio. His last film while working for Fox was a Western, a remake of Allan Dwan's *Frontier Marshal* (1939). During production, Ford indulged himself, focusing on grace notes and character in what was to become *My Darling Clementine* (1946), and after viewing the rough cut, Zanuck reshaped the film as he had formerly done with *The Grapes of Wrath* and *How Green Was My Valley*. As Dan Ford points out, "In recutting *My Darling Clementine*, Darryl Zanuck, the editor supreme, markedly improved it" by eliminating thirty minutes of "unrestrained sentimentality, boozy, rowdy humor [and] low comedy," and when released in November 1946, *My Darling Clementine* grossed $4.5 million.[109] Lindsay Anderson points out that Ford "didn't like what Zanuck did to *Clementine* . . . all through the war, he'd been his own boss."[110] Eyman concurs that artistic control, always very important to Ford, divided the two men over *Clementine*'s editing. As Anderson notes, *Stagecoach* (1939) may be very good prose but *Clementine* is poetry.[111]

Many commentators, Dan Ford among them, have noted that Ford's vision of America darkened because of his experiences during the Second World War. The military, which had been an avocation before 1941, became the centerpiece of his life. As Dan Ford observes, "he now ruled his Stock Company in an almost military manner."[112] Other insiders also noticed the change in Ford. John Wayne remarked to Dan Ford that his grandfather had become "a lot kinder and a lot more sympathetic."[113] As Wayne points out, John Ford had "stopped playing soldier." Simply put, he had become one. Ford returned home a veteran. His decision to leave Twentieth Century-Fox was undoubtedly influenced by the insider scandal created by the Senate War Investigating

Committee's investigation of Darryl Zanuck, who had produced a high number of Army-Hollywood films while collecting a salary from his studio. The inquiry determined that Zanuck had violated Section 41 of the U.S. Criminal Code because he had not "placed his Fox stock in trust for the duration of his time in the Army."[114] Although no charges were filed, the collateral damage created by Missouri Senator Harry Truman's accusations of conflict of interest confirmed for Ford, wishing to continue in the Naval Reserve, what his wife had been telling him for years: that Hollywood had become "seedy, shoddy and full of hucksters."[115] Turning down Zanuck's generous offer to renegotiate his contract for $600,000 a year—including a nonexclusive clause that allowed him to work elsewhere—and telling the production head that he would no longer work as a "piece goods worker in the Hollywood sweatshops,"[116] Ford not only gained artistic control when he left Twentieth Century-Fox, he also protected his identity as a war hero and turned his back on Hollywood's corporate culture.

In hindsight, Ford's rejection of Zanuck's offer seems at first to be irrational. How could he have given up the financial stability, artistic freedom, and automatic recognition that working for Twentieth Century-Fox would have given him? As Custen reveals, "Since the hearings were secret, when Zanuck resigned from the Army it was assumed to be because at age forty-one, he had done his duty," and "only a few army personnel, Zanuck, and his family knew how close he had come to being involved in a scandal that would have wrecked his life and career."[117] But somehow or other, Hollywood's scuttlebutt ensured that gossip about the inquiry did get out. Industry insiders were well aware of the scandal in which Darryl Zanuck had been involved even though the inquiry had "ended quietly."[118] Talking to Dan Ford, Wingate Smith expressed his disgust, without naming names, about profiteers working in Hollywood who made it their business to profit from the war. Having returned to civilian society, Ford, as a veteran with ambitions to further his career in the Naval Reserve, could not continue working for the scandal-ridden Twentieth Century-Fox. It simply would not have been "right" to do so.

There is no question that John Ford returned home from the Second World War deeply scarred by his combat experiences. As Dan Ford points out to John Wayne, "The war really affected him . . . he lost a lot of his people."[119] In 1949, Ford revealed the overlap in his professional and personal lives to Thomas A. Dawson, commenting that making Western pictures had become a crusade with him since the war.[120] In part, this crusade was his mission to rescue Argosy Pictures from bankruptcy; in part, making Westerns also expressed his personal affiliations with military life and culture after the Second World War.

At work, Ford had begun wearing fatigues and his Navy baseball cap to work on the set. He joined veterans' organizations and became what his daughter Barbara called "a ribbon freak,"[121] seeking more medals and awards for his service in the OSS. He went out of his way to help other veterans and created the Field Photo Home for veterans who had served with him in the OSS.[122] After the war, Ford also integrated his interest in the military into his filmmaking, in particular, into his Westerns.

McBride points out that Ford's postwar Westerns deal with war and military issues, and, in general, Ford's postwar body of work is "more nakedly individualistic, more deeply emotional, in many ways more pessimistic, fascinatingly and sometimes maddeningly self-contradictory, often defiantly quirky and self-indulgent to the point of perversity."[123] Accusing Ford of living in an "imagined nineteenth-century Eden, extrapolated from the world just before he was born," McBride, however, does not look past Ford's postwar inclusion of popular Americana acquired during his stint at Twentieth Century-Fox to the critique of Americana that is embedded in his work. When Ford said, in 1949, "I am sure that means there are millions of people left still proud of their country, their flag, and their traditions,"[124] he was not just referring to Americans in general, he was also referencing the population of veterans who had just returned home from battle, as he pointed to the success of *Fort Apache* and *She Wore a Yellow Ribbon*. Free from Zanuck's control, and finally at liberty to include his own interests in his films as he saw fit, Ford's Westerns came to constitute a body of work, the profile of which articulates a distinctive "presentation of self" that became its most valued asset. As a John Ford Production, Ford's Westerns announced their identity in the same way that pictures produced by Zanuck at Twentieth Century-Fox constituted that organization's corporate "presentation of self."[125] What McBride considers Ford's "own recognizably 'Fordian' value system, a reflection of his own inner desires and conflicts," is the director's branding of his work.[126] Ford's postwar Westerns, therefore, may appear at first to be patriotic flag-wavers, but they are, at base, films made for veterans—sophisticated compositions that question the world that they supposedly mirror. A master craftsman, Ford combined the lessons he learned while making Westerns and military movies before the Second World War with his own wartime experiences to create a subtle but powerful dialectic in his postwar Westerns that addresses the veteran's homecoming experience in all its beliefs, hopes, and disillusionment.[127]

Ford's valorization and critique of military and combat culture in his postwar Westerns leaves an extremely complex film legacy for his viewers to consider, not only in the context of his life, but more importantly in the context of his life's work. As creative collaborations, films always reflect the talents and interests of the producers, cameramen, cinematographers, writers, and actors with whom any director works. Ford himself notes that what remained constant throughout this process was his eye for composition and a talent for visual nuance that was developed and refined as he became proficient in rendering realistic and expressionistic styles of presentation during his early days at Universal and Fox, his ideal representations of landscape and documentary presentation at Twentieth Century-Fox, and the influence of his realistic training and propaganda films produced for the OSS during the Second World War. Toward the very end of his life, Ford still considered himself to be "a very good cameraman" who influenced others.[128] In her final conversations with Ford, Hepburn compares him to "a real old sort of Renaissance craftsman" who could "just do it without a hell of a lot of conversation."[129] The fact that he didn't argue with her assessment speaks volumes. A director, a patriot, and a critic, John Ford wanted not only to be remembered for his work but also to be defined by the films he made without Darryl Zanuck's assistance. In his own final analysis, he was "an author of westerns, war stories where men count more than events, and comedies where the strength of feelings counts"—"the rest," he says dismissively, "are the rest."[130]

2

EARLY DAYS IN THE HOLLYWOOD WEST

From *Straight Shooting* to *The Iron Horse*

None of us thought we were making anything but entertainment for the moment. Only Ernst Lubitsch knew we were making art.[1]—John Ford

Before directing, Ford worked for his brother Francis, mastering the art of acting and the mechanics of the movie camera. He became a carpenter and cared for properties, and when Francis's actors refused to jump over cliffs or be blown up by dynamite or grenades, he worked as a stuntman. He rode as a Klansman in *Birth of a Nation* (1915) for D. W. Griffith, whose movies he watched when they were shown at the old Philharmonic Auditorium in Los Angeles. In 1916, he also worked as an assistant director in charge of crowds of extras and groups of cowboys. As Allan Dwan—a pioneering Canadian-born American silent film director, producer, and screenwriter—remembers, when Ford began helming pictures in Hollywood, he was "a natural": "There wasn't any doubt about who the boss was. . . . He'd give them all specific pieces of business. He'd say, 'You there, when you ride over the hill, throw our hat up in the air; you over there, get shot and fall, and you, I want you to get shot at the top of the hill but make it all the way down before you keel over.' He'd pick those things out for himself. He directed the crowd scenes and he was starting to make a name for himself. He wasn't directing principals, but he was directing."[2]

Then, in early June of 1917, Ford was offered the opportunity of a lifetime: the chance to begin his apprenticeship by directing Harry Carey Sr., who had gone to Carl Laemmle and asked to work with Ford. Laemmle, who had watched Ford direct a group of cowboys, had no objections. Over the next four years, Ford and Carey would make more than twenty films. At Universal, scripts were little more than rough drafts that outlined the action and the shots. Olive Carey remembers that her husband and Ford would "sit around this tiny kitchen with a wood fire going in the stove and drink Mellow Wood. They would talk, talk, talk, late into the night and Jack would take notes. They molded the whole thing between them and the next day they'd go out and shoot it."[3] Characterization and plot line were foregrounded in the young director's early two-reeler Westerns. After the Ford-Carey collaborations were shot, George Hively would summarize the story on the screen and turn what was considered to be the script for the film in to the front office. "Every once in a while, Universal would decide they needed a story department so they'd hire some writers and send us these terrible scripts," Olive says. "Harry and Jack would take one look at them and say, 'Christ, that's horrible,' then throw them away and go back to their own stuff."[4]

DEVELOPING HIS PAINTERLY EYE

As film critic Andrew Sarris observes, Ford "was spotted as a stylist surprisingly early in his career," and the persistence of his stylistic control over a half century of directing (from *Straight Shooting* in 1917 to *Seven Women* in 1966) is "a remarkable feat of directorial fidelity."[5] What many critics refer to as his distinctive "Fordian" style can be attributed, in part, to his apprenticeship under his brother Francis Ford and to his "fantastic eye for the camera."[6] Olive Carey remembered, "He lined up all the shots. He was fascinated with everything, went into great detail about everything. He delved into all sorts of different things."[7] A student of both his brother Francis and D. W. Griffith, Ford learned the nuances of camerawork: the iris-in, the close-up, and the fade-in. Ford's compositions also display the influence of D. W. Griffith's use of foreground framing with the action staged deeper in the picture. As Ford's "painterly eye" developed throughout his career, his growing familiarity (and comfort) with the work of the Hudson River School of landscape painting, the principles of classical composition, and the Claude landscape, which draws the viewer's eye toward the horizon of the picture, becomes apparent.[8] More than forty years later, during the filming of *Cheyenne Autumn*, Ford smiled when Bernard Smith commented, "I have a feeling you have studied medieval and Renaissance painting,"[9] after learning his plans for action in the foreground, background, and far distance of a scene. Imitating D. W. Griffith, Ford had begun composing his shots by using elements of Renaissance landscape painting early in his career.

As Dan Ford notes, the influence of D. W. Griffith's *Birth of a Nation* on Ford's filmmaking is apparent even in his grandfather's earliest surviving film, *Straight Shooting* (1917): "There is one sequence where the cattlemen assemble their forces, salute their leader, and ride into ranks that exactly copies a parallel scene, the assembly of the Klansmen."[10] Because of its well-drawn characters, powerful plot, and sophisticated camerawork, audience reactions to *Straight Shooting* were enthusiastic, with *Universal Weekly* applauding it as "the most wonderful Western picture ever made."[11] Starring Harry Carey Sr. as Cheyenne Harry, *Straight Shooting* is the story of a one-sided range war over water rights during which a ruthless and powerful rancher, Thunder Flint (Duke R. Lee), harasses an honest and penniless farming family, the Sims. After witnessing Sweet Water Sim's grief over the death of his son, Ted (Ted Brooks), Harry gives up working for Flint, enlists the help of his outlaw friends, defends the farmers, and helps drive off Flint and his gang of thugs. The grateful Sim (George Berrell) tries to adopt Harry as his son, but the cowboy declares that he cannot "be a farmer." He "belongs on the range." Sim then wants Harry and his daughter Joan (Molly Malone) to marry, but after much thought, Harry, in spite of his feelings for Joan, nobly decides against becoming the old man's son-in-law. "Sam, I'm leaving Joan to you," he declares to the girl's long-suffering boyfriend, Danny Morgan (Hoot Gibson). "Bless you and goodbye." Danny (aka Sam Turner) is delighted by Harry's decision to continue on as a drifter, until he realizes that Joan no longer loves him. *Straight Shooting*'s conclusion remains tantalizingly open-ended. As promised, Harry gives Joan his final answer as to whether he will remain with her or leave the farm at sunset, but we do not learn if their embrace indicates that he has changed his mind and will stay.

In *Straight Shooting*, Ford's "painterly eye" immediately establishes the orderliness and unity of the natural world. As Scott Eyman points out, Ford's "compositions, usually in deep focus, have balance, depth, and spaciousness." Ford uses trees and foreground bushes to construct natural frames for the action, and "interior sets were built in real locations so authentic exteriors can be seen through windows and doorways."[12] The film opens in deep focus, as a group of Herefords crests a hill and begins to descend toward the camera and the valley below them. Ford then cuts to an iris-in shot that establishes the villain, Flint, wearing what at first appears to be a black Trail Boss Stetson and sporting a black moustache, which he later twirls nefariously as he plots to destroy the farmers infesting his land. At the height of his power, Flint is literally placed above his hired hands, who appear on the slope beneath him with his cattle clustered far below, each appearing to be no bigger than their master's hand. Once the viewer's eye has dropped to the valley floor, the milling cattle, undifferentiated by size, direct the eye back to the figure of Flint, whose presence dominates and unbalances the screen.

Ford's unusual use of depth illustrates the preceding intertitle's comment that the "the ranchers' empire, vast grazing land . . . [a] once endless territory" appears to be no more. This, however, appears not to be the case. After Flint and his cowhands ride out of the frame, it becomes evident that there are no farmer's fences cutting and dividing his pasture into tiny, compacted spaces because the camera cuts to another shot of the valley, which displays the liberating three-dimensional quality of the terrain that audiences have come to associate with Ford's expansive West—that balanced spaciousness of the land created by a graduated sequencing that leads the eye from the foreground to a background of hills or buttes and then upward into the liberating far distance of the sky.

In this shot, Ford emphasizes the movement of the eye as it travels through the empty foreground, dips into the valley's midground, and then moves through the cattle to the trees behind before climbing the hills in the background. Throughout this shot, the eye's movement is encouraged by the three riders cresting the steep rise. When they near the right-hand side of the screen, they turn their horses and approach the camera. Ford maintains his camera placement and cuts to a closer shot of the trio. As a group, these riders then gallop from the upper right-hand corner of the foreground to exit the frame at the lower left corner of the screen. Their movement mirrors the bold, broad diagonal lines created by the group of cattle. Behind the cattle, this diagonal is repeated by a parallel line of the large shade trees. Behind these trees, a similar diagonal is found in the low, rolling slope on which trees and bushes grow. Behind this, another hill, without trees and brush (and therefore devoid of movement), stabilizes and balances the entire composition. Its ridge invites the eye to move upward to the top along the right-hand side of the frame.

The three-dimensional nature of Ford's compositions is also evident in his interior shots. Visitors to the farmhouse and the ranch house are seen through screen doors, while the interiors occupy the foreground of these shots. Here, Ford uses iris-in shots, as he would later use the close-up, to reveal characters' emotions and reactions. Ted's death, for example, elicits strong expressions of grief from his father and sister. When Sim and Jane discover Ted's dead body, Ford's camera isolates Jane, signaling the enormity of her grief and helplessness. Undergoing a life-changing experience while he witnesses the family's despair, Harry's face is also isolated, and the viewer's gaze is directed toward the highlights carefully placed in his eyes, revealing his regret and grief. As Ford later says to Mark Haggard in 1970, "the main thing about motion pictures is: photograph the people's eyes. Photograph their eyes."[13]

KIDDING THE WESTERN HERO

Filling a niche of their own, Ford and Carey's Westerns were not designed to compete with the other Westerns being made at the time, especially the movies starring the sensational Tom Mix at Universal. The biggest Western star in Hollywood at that time, the athletic Mix, in his white hat, was a children's matinee idol, the "good" cowboy who saved women (and children) from black-hatted villains. Like Mix, Carey's on-camera persona of the "good" bad man also rescued the weak and the innocent from the wicked but, in doing so, parodied the fantastic excesses of the Mix Western. Many years later, Ford reminded Peter Bogdanovich that Carey's character, Cheyenne Harry, was "sort of a bum . . . instead of a great bold gun-fighting hero."[14] In *Straight Shoot-*

ing, for example, Carey plays a saddle tramp, a highly questionable character who has a drinking problem and cheats at cards.

Well aware of the discrepancy that existed between the reality of settling the American frontier and the distortion of the American West in Hollywood, Ford and Carey made Westerns for an adult audience. According to Ford, these movies "weren't shoot-em ups"—they were character stories set in a historical presentation of frontier life. "We tried to do it the real way it had been in the West," Ford said. "None of this so-called quick-draw stuff, nobody wore flashy clothes and we didn't have dance hall scenes with girls in short dresses."[15] With this in mind, it is not surprising that at the beginning of the two-reeler *Hell Bent*, Fred Worth, a novelist, receives a request from his publisher that reads: "Dear Mr. Worth, We would like it if the hero in your next story were a more ordinary man, as bad as he is good. The public is already tired of perfect men in novels who embody every virtue. Everyone knows such people do not exist. Sincerely yours, H.T. Barber, Assistant to the Publisher." Worth considers Barber's request. Lost in thought, he wanders with his hands in his pockets out of his living room. The film cuts to him standing beside a framed copy of Frederick Remington's *The Misdeal* hanging on a wall. In profile, Worth considers the painting, removes the pipe from his mouth, and taps his chin reflectively. As he thinks, the camera slowly tracks toward the picture until it fills the screen. Having entered the world of Worth's imagination, the camera pauses for a moment to allow the viewer to consider Remington's romantic re-creation of the Old West. Then, the hanging smoke in the saloon, created by the gunfight caused by the misdeal, begins to swirl in the shot, and the figures of the cowboys come to life.

As Barber requests, Ford's hero is "an ordinary man who is as bad as he is good." Harry Carey, paradoxically wearing a black hat and riding a white horse, is responsible for the disaster in the saloon; a card cheat, he escapes his pursuers, stopping only long enough to discard three hands containing four aces each from his pockets. Ironically, as the movie's romantic lead, this social pariah becomes more committed to protecting Mary Thurston (Neva Gerber), forced by her shiftless brother to work as a saloon girl, than he is to filling his pockets with other people's money. Having fallen in love with her, however, he must first be "domesticated" so that he can become part of polite society. At the beginning of his courtship, Harry gets drunk and forgets his manners at the bar, kissing Mary without her permission. Slapped for his rudeness, he restores his image as a gentleman by carrying her over a muddy street and then walking her home. Inviting him in, Mary educates her admirer by teaching him how to drink tea. Harry stays on in Rawhide, as an intertitle suggests, because of "the novelty of the pleasures of tea drinking or maybe . . . ," but their budding romance is interrupted when she is kidnapped by the outlaw leader, Beau Ross (Joe Harris). In the manner of a virtuous Dime Store hero, Harry recovers her and the stolen gold after capturing Ross. Redeemed, he proposes to Mary, but the movie ends before she answers his question. Throughout, the predictability of *Hell Bent*'s romantic subplot comments on the Western's dime novel underpinnings. Harry may cheat at cards and be an inept lover, but in matters of revenge and survival, he embodies every virtue.

Among the narrative clichés that *Hell Bent* renders the most humorous is that of the stereotypical relationship of the horse and his rider. Harry not only rides into the Best Bet Saloon like free-spirited cowboys of classic Westerns; he also rides up a flight of stairs and into a room, looking for a place to sleep. In the room, he finds Cimarron Bill (Duke R. Lee), the man destined to be his best friend, who will save his life after the two sing "Sweet Genevieve." While they argue over whether they will double up and share the room, Harry's faithful four-legged friend, who also spends the night in the room, takes advantage of the situation (and the distraction offered by the music) to eat the men's mattress that is stuffed with hay.

Hell Bent's tongue-in-cheek narrative is fueled by the triptych of large Western desert landscapes that is displayed over the bar at the Best Bet Saloon. Reminding the viewer of the carefully crafted nature of the film, a huge Remington-esque painting of two running horses is flanked by a framed desert scene featuring dunes and buttes on its left side, and, on its right, there is a desert scene featuring a canyon pass, its sandy floor improbably dotted with large saguaro cacti. Signaling *Hell Bent*'s visuals as Western clichés, these pictures introduce scenes that follow in the same way that *The Misdeal* introduces and frames the story of Harry Carey, cowboy and card cheat. Much like a painting coming to life, Ford cuts from *The Misdeal* sequence to a shot of Harry, riding toward the camera, seeming to have emerged from a backdrop designed to look like a picture. Featuring a highly artificial walled city, sand dunes, and huge saguaro cacti, this backdrop prefigures the fantastic desert landscapes of the triptych at the Best Bet Saloon.

Later, when Harry and Ross, reduced to crawling on their bellies across the sand, experience a mirage in the desert, another obvious backdrop appears, filled with buttes and cacti, before being replaced by another featuring a palm-lined oasis. Then the first backdrop returns, further announcing the presence of the soundstage. Oddly, these scenes could have been shot on location. Clearly man-made, like the landscapes hanging on the wall of the Best Bet Saloon, they remind the viewer that the Western is, at its base, a product of Hollywood. When Harry and Ross are seen walking through the desert on location, large saguaro cacti improbably planted in sandy dunes serve to emphasize the unnatural (and undoubtedly fictional) nature of their setting.

In spite of their irreverent treatments of genre conventions and character, the action of Ford and Carey's Westerns remains that of the morality play—wrongs were righted as good triumphed over evil in the end. In *Bucking Broadway*, Cheyenne Harry's girlfriend and his boss's daughter, the irresistible Helen Clayton (Molly Malone), is swept off her feet by Eugene Thornton (Vester Pegg), a wealthy, smooth-talking city slicker who convinces her to break her promise to marry Harry, who could only afford to give her a small wooden heart that he had whittled himself. Helen runs away with Thornton to New York, where he proves himself to be a cad and a bounder. She is saved from disgrace by Harry, who, publicly humiliated by her rejection, receives her cry for help, finds her in the big city, and rescues her during a rip-roaring fistfight between Thornton's friends and the ranch hands in a showdown on the terrace of the Columbia Hotel. After Harry has knocked Thornton out, Helen mends the broken heart he had given her, and the lovers are reunited.

Establishing the independent spirit of the West at the beginning of *Bucking Broadway*, Ford's sophisticated compositions and camerawork demonstrate his great sensitivity to proportion and balance, using deep focus to emphasize the spaciousness and depth of the Western landscape in his long exterior wide shots. Ford allows his camera to pan only once while following a bucking horse. Backlit, Buck Hoover (William Steele), the leader of the cowboys, and his horse are foregrounded on a bank, beneath and behind which three cowhands ride toward the camera. One horseman leaves the group and gallops along the riverbank beneath Buck's horse while his comrades splash down the shallow stream in the small valley. Framed by the trees and hill in the background, this shot was captured on the first take.

Ford's three-dimensional use of depth is emphasized several scenes later when a herd of cattle is revealed in another valley. Here, the classical composition is again carefully composed: foreground, midground, and background are perfectly balanced, each occupying one third of the screen. The effect created is one of great depth and spaciousness, emphasized by the men on horseback who appear in the foreground over the lip of the ridge while a small group of cattle are driven down the hills in the background toward the large herd grazing in midshot. Ford's framing here creates the painterly effect that became his trademark—that of presenting action on screen as a picture that moves within the limits dictated by its frame. Even when the cowboys are riding to Helen's rescue down Broadway, Ford's camera, positioned on the back of a moving vehicle, does not change perspective; the men and horses charging toward the camera remain foregrounded within the frame while the buildings and sidewalks that frame them slide away into the background.

Ford's treatment of space in the big city is as sophisticated and balanced as his depictions of the West. For example, the very long take that establishes the fistfight at the Columbia Hotel is conducted on a classically proportioned three-tiered terrace. As the cowboys and Harry rush to Helen's aid, they swarm up a marble staircase that leads the eye upward to a latticed dining area stretching across the background. Enclosed by a marble railing, a fishpond, flanked by marble balconies providing natural frames, encompasses much of the foreground. After city slickers are thrown off the balconies and into the pond by the cowboys, they attempt to clamber over the railing but fall backward into the water. Behind them, groups of struggling men fill the stairs and the dining terrace that is pushed over early in the fight. Two men in the foreground manage to climb out of the pond and begin wrestling in front of the railing on the floor of the dining area. A third man balances this action by popping over the railing located at the rear of the pond and joining the fight on the stairs. Throughout, Ford's camera does not move.

In *Bucking Broadway*, Ford's close-ups, like the iris-in shots found in *Straight Shooting* and *Hell Bent*, isolate details of a scene and provide viewers with insights into the plot and characters' thoughts and feelings. Close-ups of Helen's goodbye letter to her father and shots of Cheyenne Harry's purse being surreptitiously returned to his jacket pocket by the thief who stole it establish character and motivation. Ford's dynamic editing of close-ups linking a steam radiator with a hissing rattlesnake at the Columbia Hotel reveals how out of his depth Harry is in the big city. Similarly, a close-up of Harry's roughened hands and the tiny, wooden heart, just larger than the size of his thumbnail, establishes the depth and sincerity of the cowboy's feelings for Helen. Significantly, close-ups of faces in *Bucking Broadway* are reserved for interior shots and used to convey private moments of heightened emotions, such as when Helen is shown the house that Harry has built for her, when Harry proposes to her, and again during Harry's reaction to the news that Helen has jilted him.

The ending of the Ford-Carey collaboration has generally been attributed to Ford's unhappiness about the glass ceiling at Universal under which he worked while directing Harry Carey Sr. *Marked Men*, filmed in 1919, was the last Ford-Carey collaboration. Dan Ford attributes Ford's parting of ways with Carey to his grandfather's "difficulty in dealing with success," citing "jealousy, competition for money and recognition" as factors that combined to undermine the success of the Ford-Carey relationship.[16] In particular, Ford notes that his grandfather's salary as a director, which doubled from $75 a week in 1917 to $150 a week in 1918 and then to $300 a week in 1919, was a point of real tension between the two men. Unlike Ford, Carey was making $150 a week in 1917, $1,250 a week in 1918, and then $2,250 a week in 1919.[17] For Ford, the relationship with Carey presented an artistic barrier as well as a financial one. Working with Carey, Ford established himself as a first-rate action director but was also pigeonholed as a director of Westerns, having made more than twenty-five in only three years. Leaving the partnership with Carey proved to be a sound business decision and a smart career move. In 1919, William Fox, general manager Winfield Sheehan, and studio manager Sol Wurtzel were building a stable of leading directors to elevate the prestige of Fox's movies. Ford, still very much a journeyman director, took advantage of Fox's patronage and the studio's commercial framework to develop his own career and increase his income. Making films in genres other than the Western, his salary and his professional standing increased dramatically—in 1921, his income of over $27,000 more than tripled what he earned in 1919; in 1922, he earned over $37,000; and in 1923, he made almost $45,000.[18]

Ford's first film for Fox Studio was *Just Pals* (1920), the story of a small-time conman who becomes a small-town hero, starring Buck Jones. After viewing *Just Pals*, William Fox was convinced that John Ford was not only a talented director, he was also an artist. On January 29, 1921, Fox wrote to Sol Wurtzel, stating that *Just Pals* was "one of the most artistically done pictures that I have reviewed in years . . . [and] if Jones is properly directed, he can play any part."[19] *Just Pals* was an important movie for Ford because it proved he could work effectively outside the parameters of the Western, it favorably impressed his patron, and it was an opportunity for the young director to work with Fox's veteran cameraman, George Schneiderman. Ford's association with Schneiderman began their ongoing collaboration at Fox, furthering Ford's visual style. When talking with George J. Mitchell, Ford revealed that he considered himself "very lucky in getting a good crew and a good cameraman."[20] In *Straight Shooting*, *Hell Bent*, and *Bucking Broadway*, Ford's cameramen—George Scott, Ben F. Reynolds, and John W. Brown—faithfully recorded their director's set-ups and sight-lines, producing the classically balanced compositions and effective close-ups that Ford desired. Schneiderman, in particular, garnered the director's favor, his work enhancing Ford's fluid compositions by creating high art images in his Westerns. "Schneiderman was one of the early cameramen and a great one," Ford remembered in 1964. "He could do anything."[21]

THE IRON HORSE—HIGH ART IN THE WILD WEST

After *Just Pals*, Ford directed ten romantic action dramas: *The Big Punch* (1921), *Jackie* (1921), *Little Miss Smiles* (1922), *Silver Wings* (1922), *The Village Blacksmith* (1922), *The Face on the Barroom Floor* (1923), *Three Jumps Ahead* (1923), *Cameo Kirby* (1923), *North of Hudson Bay* (1923), and *Hoodman Blind* (1923). Schneiderman worked as Ford's cameraman on *Jackie*, *The Village Blacksmith*, *The Face on the Barroom Floor*, *Cameo Kirby*, and *Hoodman Blind*. By the time Schneiderman was assigned as cameraman to Ford's next picture, the veteran cameraman and the young director had developed a close working relationship. Ford's eleventh project for Fox was a Western originally entitled *The Transcontinental Railroad*. Shooting began in Nevada after a blizzard, and Ford remembers asking Schneiderman, "What'll we do? We only have four weeks to make it." According to Ford, Schneiderman replied, "There must have been snow when they built the railroad so why don't we shoot anyway?"[22]

When one considers Ford's work history, it is not surprising that Fox, wanting to imitate Paramount's success with James Cruze's *The Covered Wagon* (1923), assigned this film to their talented young director. The Western, after all, was Ford's forte. Ironically, the very genre that held Ford back in the teens propelled him into the forefront of Hollywood directors in the 1920s. Bearing the name *The Iron Horse* on its release, this film won Ford international recognition. Almost ninety years later, *The Iron Horse*, named to the National Film Registry, was recognized nationally as being culturally significant.

A director who prided himself on his reputation to bring movies in under budget and before their production deadlines, Ford's performance during the shooting of this picture was atypical: not only did the film run over budget, but Ford was also unable to meet his shooting schedules. The movie cost Fox $450,000 and the actors and crews extra time on location because the weather did not cooperate during production. Ford chose Wadsworth, Nevada, as *The Iron Horse*'s location because *The Covered Wagon* had been shot nearby. Beale's Cut mountain pass in Newhall, California, also appears in the film.

As Dan Ford points out, the small filmmaking army of *The Iron Horse* troupe that came to be known as Camp Ford was plagued by deplorable living conditions in the movable tent town and the A. G. Barnes Circus train cars that served as their accommodations on site, as well as "bitter cold winter weather, blizzards and deep snow drifts."[23] In a working atmosphere that began to resemble the Wild West, with bootlegged liquor and a brothel, Ford took what Richard Ashton terms "an almost reckless approach to the filming of action sequences."[24] The director also took liberties with the actual events that occurred during the making of the transcontinental railway, in spite of the opening intertitle, which claims *The Iron Horse* to be "accurate and faithful in every particular of fact and atmosphere." He did, however, remain faithful to the spirit of the building of the railroad, making the look of *The Iron*

Horse as authentic as possible by using "two genuine Central Pacific and Union Pacific locomotives, 'Juniper' and '116' to re-enact the wedding of the rails" at Promontory Point, and the film has come to be considered "a historical picture that conveyed a strong sense of national pride . . . a celebration of heroic enterprise, of hope, of the country stretching gloriously to its full length."[25]

Supported by Fox's massive promotion campaign, *The Iron Horse* premiered at the Lyric Theatre in New York on August 28, 1924, and proved to be a huge hit, earning $2 million at the box office. As Dan Ford points out, the film, advertised as "a romantic picture of the East and the West," is the "work of a mature John Ford."[26] *The Iron Horse*'s action contains original shots, "including the technique of placing the camera in a pit and stampeding a herd of cattle overhead" and recording Pawnee on horseback, galloping to rescue the embattled railworkers. The film's camerawork also includes "more angles, cutaways, and close-ups" and "[its] editing [is] far more complex."[27] These changes, however, do not demonstrate a radical departure from the classical underpinnings found in the earlier examples of Ford's visual style discussed above. In *Straight Shooting*, *Hell Bent*, and *Bucking Broadway*, Ford also regularly changed camera angles, used cutaways, and employed close-ups. Even Ford's acclaimed use of menacing shadows cast along the sides of boxcars by mounted Cheyenne just before Walsh's train is attacked in *The Iron Horse* may be traced back to his use of blacks in *Hell Bent* as the shadows of riders cast on a rock wall in the desert multiply the forces of the search taking place while Cheyenne Harry rescues Mary from Thunder Flint.

The Iron Horse charts the building of Abraham Lincoln's dream of a railroad joining the eastern and western coasts of the United States. Dave Brandon (George O'Brien) and his father set out to help find a route for the rails. They find the route, but they are ambushed, and Dave's father is killed. Twenty years later, as the railroad is finally being built, Dave convinces the construction superintendent, Thomas Marsh (Will Walling)—who providentially happens to be the father of his sweetheart, Miriam (Madge Bellamy)—to use the route that his father discovered. In spite of interference from a corrupt landowner and an Indian attack on the railway workers, the railroad is built through Brandon's Pass and connected at Promontory Point, Utah. When the "golden spike" is finally driven in, Dave and Miriam are united, and Dave's and his father's dreams are fulfilled.

Throughout the story, Ford's classical compositions of Western landscapes evoke the visual groundwork found in the Ford-Carey collaborations. In the Cheyenne Hills and again during a cattle drive from Texas, Ford's three-dimensional landscape shots typically contain elevated foregrounds that allow the eye to dip into an expansive midground before traveling up to a background of hills and then ascending to the far distance of the Western sky. Schneiderman's exacting attention transmits Ford's delicate and fluid balancing of foregrounds, midgrounds, and backgrounds. Movement is often an important component of Ford's three-dimensional presentations of the West. For example, when the hostile Cheyenne ride to war, their single line of horsemen, moving from right to left, gallops beside a pond in the shot's foreground. Behind them, another line of warriors, simultaneously moving from left to right, creates a counterpoint to the movement in the foreground. The internal balance within the frame created by these crosscurrents is supported by the tall bank that towers in the background, providing a horizontal line that encourages the viewer's eye to ascend up to the mountains behind and then to the sky located in the shot's far distance.

Ford's treatment of the cattle drive from Texas begins by establishing visual balance very much like the balanced proportions he uses in *Straight Shooting*, *Hell Bent*, and *Bucking Broadway*. As the drive begins, a horse and rider halt in the foreground at midscreen. His figure on horseback should dominate the shot as Thunder Flint does while he surveys his "empire" at the opening of *Straight Shooting*, but here, Ford's lack of frames allows for an easy flow of movement from left to right: the cattle enter the left-hand side of the screen and pour through the midground behind the cowboy to exit the shot on the right. Behind the line of moving cattle are the distant plains of the background. The viewer's eye is drawn farther back to the even more distant mountains, and the far distance of the sky is plainly visible, inviting the eye to ascend before exiting the picture.

Ford's most spectacular beauty shot in *The Iron Horse* is a classical exercise in the presentation of perfect proportions. Riding to war, the hostile Cheyenne are mirrored, galloping in single file on a cut bank located above the still waters of a lake. In *Hell Bent*, Cheyenne Harry's reflected image before he dismounted to drink on his way to Rawhide does not perfectly mirror the horse and rider, but in *The Iron Horse*, the composition of the image and its double is precise and harmonious. Cutting the screen exactly in half, the reflected image in the water is itself divided equally into a foreground, midground, and background. Exquisitely proportioned, the foreground contains the reflected sky and hill, and the mounted warriors are perfectly balanced by the reflected image of the cut bank, which in turn is balanced by the equal proportions occupied by the actual riders, the backdrop of the hills behind them, and the far distant sky.

Later, a scene featuring the cattle crossing a wide, shallow river also offers Ford several opportunities to experiment further with the viewer's perceptions of space. In these shots, the foreground is extended to include half of the screen containing the water through which the cattle swim, diminishing the sweep of the barren midground to the mountains in the background and then to the far distant sky. The foreground's enormous spaciousness creates an epic sweep that expands as the figures of men and animals diminish in the distance. Because of the great distances recorded in these shots, it takes time for the cattle and the men who trail them to traverse such a space.

As George Sydney points out, Ford never includes striking pictorial scenes just for effect. Everything is done to enhance the scene, to tell the story.[28] Easy passage through the West is a concern that drives the tale of *The Iron Horse*: Dave's father dies looking for the shortest route for the railroad; Dave works as a Pony Express rider facilitating the passage of information through the frontier; Miriam's father must build the tracks on the most efficient route to connect East and West before Congress's deadline runs out. Because film, for Ford, is always "a silent medium,"[29] shots in *The Iron Horse* are carefully composed to develop the narrative and advance the passage of both the characters and the viewer's eye across the screen. In the Cheyenne Hills, a cavalry unit moves from right to left along the top of a ridge that intersects the foreground and midground. Railway tracks in other shots afford easy passage to travelers and denote the importance of passage to Dave and Miriam, who linger on them, as well as emphasize the significance of vanishing points as trains move between towns that appear and disappear for the railway workers moving farther along the line. When one considers the history of Western settlement, it is entirely appropriate that the Cheyenne who oppose it ride away toward the vanishing point in the distant hills and disappear, and that the friendly Pawnee emerge from a vanishing point located in those hills and fill the screen with their presence.

Ford's picturesque presentations of Brandon's Pass point to a crucial development in his understanding and use of aesthetics. Seen from a low angle, the pass, a narrow rift framed by towering crags of sparsely tree-topped rock, is represented by a shot of a nineteenth-century landscape painting—not a photographic image of the actual, natural phenomenon. Observed by Dave's father and then surveyed by Dave, the pass is the means by which a small army of engineers will unite both the continent and the country. To the viewer, however, the pass communicates what Barbara Novak identifies as a religious, moral, and frequently nationalist concept of nature in American painting that contributed to the aggressive conquest and settling of the United States.[30]

As Novak explains, landscape attitudes in mid-nineteenth-century America were influenced by the late eighteenth century's understanding of the Sublime, expressed in terms of majestic scale and size and particularly exemplified in terms of mountain scenery.[31] In works of art, the Sublime indicated the presence of the divine, and the observer's reaction of awe at once created the desire to transcend the human condition and the awareness of one's insignificance in the context of the eternal. Throughout the nineteenth century in America, the more ambitious works of the Hudson River School Christianized and connected the Sublime with the picturesque.[32] In *The Iron Horse*, Brandon dreams of making the Sublime experience of the West available to all by reclaiming the "wilderness" of the natural world "clean to California." Aptly, he tells Tom Marsh that he will do so "with the help of God."

In American art, light is the means by which artists express Sublime experiences; landscape artists, in particular, use light to turn matter into spirit.[33] Similarly, in photography and film, light is a common convention used to express the transcendent experience of love. In 1936, when talking with Howard Sharpe, Ford considered lighting to be his "strong point"[34]—a strength that was already apparent in 1924, during the production of *The Iron Horse*. A sophisticated means for conveying the film's portrayals of love, light reveals the characters' emotional states. Romantic leads, particularly women, often appear to be radiant when backlit, having luminous halos (or even spiritual auras when brightness outlines the contours of their entire bodies). Framed in light, these characters seem to emit brightness and look as if they have become sources of light themselves. In *The Iron Horse*, Miriam is carefully and heavily backlit throughout most of her scenes. Whenever Dave appears, she seems to glow from within. The addition of carefully placed highlights that appear in her eyes whenever she talks with him further the impression that she is generating the brightness that surrounds her. When Dave breaks his promise to her not to fight with Jesson (Cyril Chadwick), however, this effect disappears. Disappointed by the man she loves, Miriam's happy spirit is diminished, and, accordingly, the glow that she seems to have been emitting disappears.

The evening before the golden spike is driven into the rails uniting East and West, Dave is seen standing alone on the railroad tracks with his hands clasped behind his back, looking at the "consummation of his father's dream." Backlit in the strong light, Ford's wide shot foregrounds Dave's figure on the tracks before the huge emptiness of the desert framed by the Western sky. Linking his past with his present, Dave has accomplished what he set out to do because his love for his father fuelled the courage of his convictions, but having "driven the last spike" into "the buckle of the girdle of America," he finds himself alone. As the tracks on which he stands signify the inevitability of time and progress (each tie representing a step toward the completion of his dream), he sits down to consider his work (and his situation) more closely. Ford cuts from the wide shot that establishes the context for Dave's contemplation to a closer look, to emphasize Dave's emotions as he touches the rails. Bathed in light spilling over his head, shoulders, and forearms, his shadowed face registers the enormity of his emotions at his accomplishment and the loss of his father, who made that accomplishment possible.

Ford's intertitle preceding this sequence not only announces the arrival of the Central Pacific and Union Pacific locomotives, "Juniper" and "116," the next day, it also presages Miriam's appearance as Dave sits musing. Ford cuts back to a wide shot, and Miriam immediately enters the frame, walking down the tracks toward Dave. Moving toward him and the source of the sunlight, her face and form present a brighter, more optimistic figure than his. Her glowing backlit hair shines so brightly that it appears to be surrounded by a halo. When Dave stands up and turns his back to her, his shoulders remain outlined in light, but the brightness that one would expect to see outlining the shape of his head is gone. Miriam's shining presence, however, remains—it is evident that she loves him still.

The next day, at the joining of both the rails and the lovers, Dave, allied with the Central Pacific, and Miriam, with the Union Pacific, begin the scene separated. Their emotional states, however, are reversed. It is now Dave who is backlit and glowing. He refuses to join his sweetheart, however, until the ceremony unites the West with the East, noting that then "we'll belong to both sides—and to each other." A highly emotional experience for every character involved, the wedding of the rails not only joins Dave and Miriam at last, it also enables them (and all those who celebrate the union of West and East) to transcend their individual differences in their collective identity.

Ford uses light to articulate the "joyous exultation" evoked by the fusing of West and East. As Leland Stanford (uncredited), president of the Central Pacific, and Thomas C. Durant (Jack Ganzhorn), vice president of the Union Pacific, pound in the golden spike, their backlighting and that of the engines and the crowd of workers attending the ceremony brightens appreciably. After the tracks have been symbolically joined, the camera reveals that Miriam too is glowing, now also outlined in light. And when Dave joins her, their shining figures are united by an uninterrupted line of light that outlines their bodies and interlocked arms. They run hand in hand from the ceremony like newlyweds from the altar. The picture taken of the event is, in effect, their (and the country's) wedding photo. Ultimately, it is love that motivates both work and relationships with others, that orders human existence, and that makes life meaningful.

Not every character in *The Iron Horse* experiences or is capable of feeling the transcendent experience of love. Intelligent but immoral, Ruby (Gladys Hulette) is "the bright—but not too particular—star of the 'Arabian Nights' dance tent," a character lacking in the translucent quality of light associated with Miriam's idealized, loving nature. A beautiful but debased woman, Ruby is a dangerous predator—she is a seductress, a prostitute, and a murderess. A saloon girl, she is never backlit, whether she is employed by the happy-go-lucky Judge Haller, who dispenses "likker" and justice indiscriminately, or the ruthless Deroux, a cutthroat capitalist cut from the same cloth as Thunder Flint in *Straight Shooting* and Eugene Thornton in *Hell Bent*. The absence of light associated with Ruby is a significant element in Ford's character-ization of amoral characters in *The Iron Horse*, the con artists and sociopaths who take advantage of others during the expansion of the West. Unable to transcend their selfish natures, none of the characters frequenting Judge Haller's court and saloon, aptly named "Hell on Wheels," is backlit. Even Miriam and Dave lose their "halos" when they enter "Hell on Wheels." Shot against the saloon's tent wall, both charac-ters throw shadows that darken on the white canvas as they become angry with one another.

The film's greatest contrast with the shady side of human nature found in the saloon is located in the natural world of the American West. Illustrating the defiant nature of Native Americans resisting Eu-ropean settlement of their world, Ford's presentation of a backlit Chey-enne war chief, dressed in leathers and feathers, is not so much an acknowledgment of the director's appreciation for Charles Russell's de-pictions of vanishing Americans as it is an elaborate statement of the Sublime. Foregrounded and filling the screen, the warrior's spectacu-larly backlit headdress acts as a halo, framing the man's face and shoul-ders. Each eagle feather on the side of the headdress emits light, shin-ing like a spoke in a saint's aureole while white tufts of fur attached to their tips float in the air, suspended like the thin clouds seen in the sky behind the figure. Sanctified in this manner, the warrior is turned into spirit and, as such, becomes an American archetype embodying the land stretching out behind him. Ford uses the natural backlighting of the sunlight in this shot to signify the divine, indicating that the Native American figure on screen is the point where human nature meets God—a glowing bridge between earth and heaven, the secular and the sacred.

In spite of its outstanding camera work, Ford's first masterpiece, *The Iron Horse*, seemed to have little effect on his career. After critical and commercial success, he went back to Fox and continued to learn his craft while "grinding out studio potboilers and program fillers."[35] "After *The Iron Horse*, he was still the same guy," stuntman John Weld recalls. "I was [with him] for three years, and all during that time, he was progressing, getting better and better, getting to know more and more about what he was doing."[36] Ford would not return to the Western until 1928, when he directed what was billed to be his next super-film, *3 Bad Men*.

3

THE HEROIC WEST

From *3 Bad Men* to *Drums along the Mohawk*

I think first as a cameraman, I consider myself a cameraman rather than a director.[1]—John Ford

Like *The Iron Horse*, *3 Bad Men* was proclaimed to be "in a class by itself" by Fox's in-house magazine,[2] but when the picture was released in October of 1926, it failed at the box office, in spite of its strong plotline, well-drawn characters, and attention to historical detail. It took the studio years to recover the films' costs—among them, the construction of a full-size reproduction of the town of Custer as it was in 1877 and the location shooting at Jackson Hole, Wyoming, the Mojave Desert, and Victorville, California, required for Ford's authentic treatment of the Dakota land rush.[3]

3 Bad Men tells the story of three thieves, Bull Stanley (Tom Santchi), Mike Costigan (J. Farrell MacDonald), and Spade Allen (Frank Campeau), who abandon their habit of "finding horses that nobody had lost" and help Lee Carlton (Olive Borden) and Dan O'Malley (George O'Brien) find happiness creating a home and family with each other. One of the most violent movies of its time, *3 Bad Men* showcases Layne Hunter (Lou Tellegen), an outrageously presented villain who embodies the worst qualities of Thunder Flint in *Straight Shooting*, Eugene Thornton in *Bucking Broadway*, and Beau Ross in *Hell Bent*. A ruthless, womanizing, power-hungry capitalist, Hunter is one of Ford's most violent silent antagonists. Prefiguring Doc Holliday (Victor Mature) and

Old Man Clanton (Walter Brennan) from *My Darling Clementine* and Liberty Valance (Lee Marvin) from *The Man Who Shot Liberty Valance* (1962), Hunter is the embodiment of authority and humanity gone wrong. As historian Joseph McBride notes, Hunter—made up to look like a vampire and dressed like a dandy—appears to be a "satirical exaggeration of iconic Western villainy."[4]

But McBride steps to Ford's defense regarding this poorly drawn character, revealing that "the picture John Ford made wasn't the one that reached the screen."[5] In part, studio interference is to blame. Scenes featuring Bull's sister, Millie (Priscilla Bonner), which culminate in her brutal beating by Hunter, were left on the cutting room floor. If they had been retained in the film, Hunter's inhumanity, denoted by his strange, bloodless face and demonstrated in his wholesale performances of terror—including savagely thrashing an elderly parson as he attempts to steal a map to an old man's gold mine, burning down the church in Custer, and ordering the murder of an old prospector—would have had to have been regarded as monstrous rather than tongue-in-cheek.

Bull, a good bad man, avenges his sister, whom Hunter, a genuinely bad man, disgraces, casts off, and kills. Bull and his comrades are then killed in a shoot-out with Hunter's thugs. Ford's presentation of the "good bad man," a paradoxical figure first popularized by the moral dilemmas of William S. Hart's serious Westerns, reveals the hypocrisy of the society that the outlaw saves.[6] In *3 Bad Men*, Ford's noble outlaws not only establish the strong moral tone of his Westerns, they are also their director's expression of the quintessential American. All are socially marginalized but fundamentally "good" working-class heroes who are spiritually redeemed by their actions. In *3 Bad Men*, Lee, a blue-blooded Virginian, immediately knows (as does the audience) that "her men" are natural aristocrats. Aptly, in the movie's final scene, the spirits of the three "bad" men live on, appearing as ghostly riders on a darkened horizon and overseeing Lee and Dan's cozy life together in their rustic cabin in the Black Hills. Ensuring the outlaws will not be forgotten, the happy couple has named their son "Bull" Stanley Costigan Allen O'Malley, in their memory.

Aesthetically, *3 Bad Men* is a fascinating intersection in Ford's career, bridging the compositions and influences found in his early films with the distinctive look that is evident in his later Westerns. As Dan Ford notes, *3 Bad Men* "has the same feel, the same 'aura,' and many of the same shots" as his grandfather's sound Westerns and "stands as one of John Ford's better films, and quite possibly his best silent film."[7] Borrowing from William S. Hart's movies, Ford also adopts moments from D. W. Griffith. As Tom Paulus suggests, Griffith's influence on Ford's early films goes "beyond mere homage and extends to narrative structure, editing and mise-en-scène."[8] As in *Straight Shooting*, Ford turns to Griffith's assembly of the Klansmen to serve as a model for the sequence in *3 Bad Men* in which Layne Hunter's henchmen assemble, salute their leader, and ride in ranks with flaming torches to terrorize the settlers and burn the church. Far from oblique, Ford's reference to the Klansmen even showcases the burning of a cross on the church lawn.

Ford's landscape treatments in *3 Bad Men* continue to demonstrate the classical proportions and the balanced presentation of the natural world found in *Straight Shooting*, *Hell Bent*, and *Bucking Broadway* and that his audiences associated with the American West. Human figures are often engulfed in the vast expanse of the scenery,[9] as in one scene, set in the spring of 1876, that begins with a shot of a large poplar tree blocking the viewer's line of sight being chopped down by the diminished figure of a Native American. When the tree falls, the immense upward sweep of the Rocky Mountains, behind a settler's cabin on the bank of a rushing river, is revealed while the Indian and his wives, foregrounded on the opposite shore, appear small in comparison. Establishing "the trackless immensity of the west" in the Black Hills of Dakota as a place where immigrants "seek the reality of their dreams," Ford's next shot, of the trading post at Custer, repeats this composition. Here, the viewer's eye first encounters "the outriders of progress" and their horses balanced against tepees, trees, and an ample log building. Filling the upper half of the screen, the sheer face of the Rockies stretches to the sky far above them.

By the early twentieth century, the North American public had been educated to believe the West to be a vast, open place in which the American Dream was actualized. *3 Bad Men*'s understated introduction of the Western plains, with "the eager thud of hoofs and the creak of wagon wheels," corresponds perfectly with this popular perception. Ford directs the viewer's eye through the parallel lines of covered wagons and horses moving from left to right through the frame, revealing an immense foreground of open prairie. A thin slope of trees leads on, to a background formed from the towering rocky face of the distant mountains shrouded in cloud. The vast scope of the shot is immediately recognizable, identifying the place as the West in which *Straight Shooting*, *Hell Bent*, *Bucking Broadway*, and *The Iron Horse* are also set.

CAPTURING THE OLD WEST

As Graham Clarke points out, American photography, while being dependent on English models, also established its own terms of reference related to the settlement of the continent and the vast spaces that the eye had to measure and contain.[10] Timothy O'Sullivan, a Civil War photographer who was involved in a number of government expeditions to the Western territories and photographed the scenes of Colorado, Nevada, and New Mexico during the 1870s, is an exemplary figure in this development. Working in the West, O'Sullivan photographed extreme landscapes like the Grand Canyon and the Nevada desert that were also painted by Albert Bierstadt, a member of the Hudson River School, after the Civil War. Available to the public and popularized in stereoscope, O'Sullivan's black-and-white images, like Bierstadt's paintings, depict the grandeur of the land.

Adopting the balanced compositions of photographic images already representing the Old West, Ford borrows their historical authenticity. His Westerns take on the "feel" of the Old West of the nineteenth century and further popularize images familiar in the late 1800s and throughout the twentieth century. A prime example of Ford's aesthetic indebtedness to Timothy O'Sullivan can be seen in *3 Godfathers*. Borrowing O'Sullivan's composition in *Desert Sand Hills Near Sink of Carson, Nevada* (1867), a quintessential nineteenth-century American landscape image, Ford's shot of the settlers' covered wagon awaiting the birth of the baby mirrors O'Sullivan's depiction of his own wagon. As in O'Sullivan's image, the settlers' covered wagon is dwarfed by the immensity of the sand dune on which it rests and the vastness of the desert stretching toward the horizon. Echoing O'Sullivan's perception of the incompatibility of the human condition and the West that defines the settlers' relation to the land, Ford's desert is unmarked by signs of human habitation and, like O'Sullivan's, resists definition.

Like O'Sullivan, Ford had embarked on what Clarke terms "a mythic enterprise,"[11] mapping and ordering images of the American West as a physical reality and a national symbol. Ford's replication of the work done by other American photographers in the West places his films within America's photographic landscape tradition and complicates his contribution to our images of the American West.

Building on his camerawork in *The Iron Horse*, Ford noticeably adds elements of the Sublime to his landscape treatments in *3 Bad Men*. A. J. Russell's *Driving of the Golden Spike at Promontory Point, Utah* (1869) makes art out of the wilderness by using the men and machines to frame the event's ledges as if the scene were a pastoral landscape. Carefully reconstructing Russell's historic documentation of the meeting in *The Iron Horse*, Ford also makes the American West picturesque while promoting its mythology. Including the figure of Russell making art, ordering the unordered the wilderness, in this sequence, Ford reminds the viewer that they are, in fact, witnessing a "rendition" of history—a fictional film.

When filming the Old West, Ford, conscious of the camera's ability to transform the Real into the Ideal, consistently uses the landscape conventions of the Old Masters to create an artistic authenticity in his Westerns that his audiences recognized, responded to, and in some cases mistook for historical faithfulness. Ford introduces elements of the picturesque early on in *3 Bad Men*, carefully directing the audience's eye through his large-scale compositions. As the three bad men dismount on a bank above a winding river to watch the wagon train move to Custer, the movement created by the figures of the men and horses directs the viewer's eye from left to right, into the river. Rather than exiting the scene, the viewer's eye moves up the riverbank into the midground of the screen, only to be directed back to the left side of the frame by the slow countermovement of the wagon train rolling on to Custer, and then once more upward to the far distant mountains and rolling cumulus that are building into storm clouds.

Here Ford's use of light has matured and complicated since *The Iron Horse*, connecting the action of the three bad men's story with Dan and Lee's tender romantic subplot. When Ford's three bad men first appear on screen, they are dramatically shot in silhouette from a low angle against a sunset. Naturally backlit, Bull, Mike, and Spade signal the transcendental nature of the landscape in which they are set and foreshadow the sacrifices they themselves will make as they journey westward with Dan and Lee. Aptly, Ford's backlighting of the outlaws accords with Emerson's observation that "from within or from behind, a light shines through us upon things and makes us aware that we are nothing, but the light is all."[12] Like the romantic leads in *The Iron Horse*, the romantic leads in *3 Bad Men* are also backlit, but Ford's use of light to convey sentiment in *3 Bad Men* is more controlled and sophisticated here. As Dan and Lee's love for one another grows, so do the lines of light radiating from their figures. After they have married, Dan and Lee continue to emit light in their brightly lit cabin at the story's end.

Ford's Dakota land rush sequence in *3 Bad Men* is an exercise in landscape photography's ability to connect with the viewer's sense of limitless space found in the West. As those who are participating in the land rush are at the start, waiting for the cannon to be fired, Ford's camera pans the line-up and the ground over which the settlers will travel. Encompassing hundreds of wagons and riders on horseback, the shot stretches out to demonstrate the epic nature of the race: "We used over two hundred vehicles—stages, Conestoga wagons buggies, broughams, every blasted vehicle there was—and hundreds of men riding horses, all waiting for the signal to cross over riding like hell."[13] Accentuating the suspense of the start, Ford changes camera angles, cutting in shots of the cavalry holding the line in check until high noon. As Dan Ford points out, this land rush contains what is perhaps the most famous single shot in Ford's silent films: an actual baby is accidently abandoned on the dry lake bed during the race and rescued just before being flattened by the onrushing wagons and riders. With the camera shooting out of a pit to provide the lowest possible camera angle (and the child's point of view) to accentuate the drama, stuntman Lefty Hough's arm reaches into the frame and picks up the little girl just before she is trampled.[14]

3 Bad Men's land rush not only prepares Ford's viewer for the exciting chase scene that occurs in *Stagecoach* (1939) thirteen years later, it also demonstrates Ford's proficiency with the moving camera, even before he encountered German director F. W. Murnau, who is credited with changing the ways that shots were framed, actors blocked, and sets designed and built. His innovative use of moving and subjective cameras freed filmmakers from the limitations of the tripod, enabling the camera to manipulate the viewer's perspective in much the same way that the first-person narrator directs the reader's perception of a narrative.

William Fox invited Murnau to work at Fox in 1926 to strengthen his connections with the lucrative European market and increase the prestige of his studio. In *Becoming John Ford*, writer/director Janet Bergstrom points out that Murnau's arrival "was preceded by a whole year of publicity, so everybody on the Fox lot knew that he was coming. Everybody was told he was the world's most important director." Ford, interested in painting and gifted when it came to lighting, benefited from the experience of watching Murnau work, from "being able to talk to him," and from "seeing what he could do with *Sunrise*." Murnau admired Ford's work, as well, wiring him that *Mother Machree* (1928) was "a beautiful picture" and advising William Fox that *Four Sons* was "one of the greatest box office values that has ever been shown on the screen."[15]

Once at the studio, Murnau lived up to Fox's expectations, directing his own cinematic masterpiece, *Sunrise* (1927). After seeing the rushes, Ford declared *Sunrise* the best movie that he had ever seen. It is not surprising that Ford would understand and appreciate Murnau's filmmaking and find the possibilities offered by German expressionism exciting. The aesthetic sympathies of his Westerns, especially those displayed in *The Iron Horse* and *3 Bad Men*, are similar to those found in Murnau's expressionist works, borrowing the symbolism embodied in American landscape painting and photography. Ford's stereotypical characters and use of backlighting convey not only the dramatic emotions of his films, they also embody and express the American Character.

Murnau's presence at Fox helped facilitate John Ford's development as an artist by expanding his visual vocabulary to include the film aesthetics of the early twentieth century's avant-garde. A prime example of German expressionist filmmaking, *Sunrise* offered Ford more avenues through which human feelings and emotions could be explored. *Sunrise*'s extreme stylization, deliberately artificial lighting accentuating deep shadows and sharp contrasts, and camera angles that emphasized the fantastic and the grotesque would later influence Ford's early antiwar films: *Four Sons*, a psychological study of maternal love, and *Pilgrimage*, a disturbing examination of suffocating and destructive motherliness. Both films borrow techniques that Murnau pioneered—using fog, a moving camera, elevated and canted sets, heavy shadows, and symbolic mise-en-scène. Ford's appreciation for Murnau's complete control and creative manipulation of *Sunrise*'s mise-en-scène, lighting, and camera work translated into the Academy Award–winning expressionism of *The Informer*.

While experimenting with the new visual means of telling stories, Ford did not simply exchange one technique for another. Like the painters and photographers with whom he identified, Ford adopted European techniques and then made them his own. His rich, highly individual vision expresses his personal understanding of the American experience as a working-class phenomenon. "I am of the proletariat," he affirmed to George J. Mitchell. "My people were peasants. They came here, were educated. They served this country well. I love America."[16]

STAGECOACH

Looking back on his career, Ford often noted that the movies he made at Fox were assigned to him rather than chosen—"They were thrown at you, and you did the best you could with them."[17] In 1935, Twentieth Century Pictures bought the bankrupt Fox studio and continued that practice; as Philip Dunne points out, "Darryl Zanuck's Twentieth Century-Fox was no place for an Auteur. Movies were made on what amounted to an assembly line: writers wrote, directors directed, actors acted, cutters cut, and Zanuck himself supervised every detail of each stage of production."[18]

The history of Ford's first sound Western demonstrates the control that the box office and studio executives exerted on directors and producers during this period. While spending a year and a half shopping "Stage to Lordsburg" around Hollywood (1937–1938), Ford and Merian C. Cooper approached David Selznick's International with the project. At first, Selznick reluctantly agreed to make *Stagecoach*, but after some thought recanted his decision and attempted to modify his agreement, causing Cooper and Ford to walk out of his office and go to Walter Wanger for their production funding.

Selznick's lack of enthusiasm stemmed from his conclusion that the picture, being "just another Western,"[19] would not recover its print costs unless stars were cast and, after some thought, had decided to continue with the project only if Gary Cooper and Marlene Dietrich were cast as the Ringo Kid and Dallas. On June 29, 1937, he wrote to John Hay Whitney, board chairman of Selznick International, and John Wharton, the company's treasurer, that "we must select the story and sell it to John Ford instead of having Ford select some uncommercial pet of his that we would be making only because of Ford's enthusiasm. . . . I see no justification for making any story just because it is liked by a man who, I am willing to concede, is one of the greatest directors in the world, but whose record commercially is far from good."[20] As McBride notes, Selznick then cited *The Informer* as Ford's "one really great picture" but listed *Mary of Scotland* and *The Plough and the Stars* (1936) as examples of his "outstanding failures."[21]

André Bazin considers *Stagecoach* to be "the ideal example of the maturity of a style brought to classic perfection." For Bazin, the film strikes "the ideal balance among social myth, historical reconstruction, psychological truth and the traditional theme of the Western mise-en-scène."[22] *Stagecoach* established Ford "once and for all as the Western filmmaker par excellence"—"despite the deepening and enrichment of his subsequent work in the genre," McBride says, "no other Ford Western, not even *The Searchers*, has achieved anything like the same stature in the popular consciousness"[23] Grossing over $1 million in the first year of its release, *Stagecoach* received seven Oscar nominations, including one for Best Picture.

Stagecoach begins by creating sympathy for the socially marginalized: Doc Boone (Thomas Mitchell), an inveterate alcoholic, and Dallas (Claire Trevor), a common whore, are run out of Tonto by representatives of the town's Law and Order League. Members of the respectable middle class, the League is stereotypically presented as a group of sexually repressed and socially repressive old women. In their ugly bonnets and high necklines, Mrs. Gatewood (Brenda Fowler), the banker's wife, and her friends are, as Dallas comments, "things worse than Apaches."

As Richard Slotkin points out, violence is a key element of "frontier psychology." Indian war, Slotkin notes, dramatically symbolizes American settlers' cultural anxieties and becomes the means by which their economic and spiritual regeneration is accomplished.[24] In *Stagecoach*, such violence is a way of life. Beginning with the terrifying news that a new Indian war is about to begin in the American West, the anxiety expressed at the outset of this film resonated strongly with American audiences, who were bracing for the Second World War to begin. Ironically, even worse than the enemy outside of the frontier town is the enemy within, busy bestowing "the blessings of civilization" on Tonto's hapless inhabitants. Mrs. Gatewood is a far more violent and fearsome figure than Geronimo could ever hope to be.

An Irish American, Ford himself was keenly aware of the social violence that was (and arguably still is) part and parcel of the working-class experience of America. Mary Ford pointed out to her grandson that "Jack was a well-known Irish Catholic, and my family was Scotch Presbyterians. . . . [My father] wanted to know if he [Jack] could speak English."[25] As Slotkin observes in *Gunfighter Nation*, Ford uses Western types to present the film as "a folktale or fable" rather than historical realism.[26] Like the folktale and fable, *Stagecoach* is a teaching tale about social violence in a country founded on an egalitarian ideal; Ford's character studies provide psychological insights into the nature of the American Character.

Throughout *Stagecoach*, it is impossible to escape this violence. Inside the coach, the social and psychological skirmishes experienced in Tonto continue. Uncomfortably confined within the Concord coach, Lucy Mallory (Louise Platt), an officer's respectable wife, is wedged against a window to avoid being tainted by her forced association with a whore, a corrupt banker, a drunken doctor, a notorious gambler, and, finally, a convicted killer. By the time the Ringo Kid (John Wayne) joins the ensemble, there is so little room in the vehicle that its most antisocial pariah must be seated on the floor. When Lucy is offered a drink of water, Dallas gets one as well—albeit not in a silver cup.

When the travelers are no longer in the stagecoach, their freedom of movement is only physical; social restrictions continue to imprison them. Lucy refuses to eat with a whore, and she and the other more "respectable" characters put as much distance as possible between themselves and Dallas. Ironically, Ringo remarks to Dallas during their first meal together that it is not possible "to break out of jail and into society" in the space of a week, for society itself is imprisoning.

Ford's restricted interiors at these rest stops express the constricted social and psychological spaces that their characters inhabit. Whether the travelers are seated in a dining room, standing around a bar, working in a kitchen, or delivering a baby in a bedroom, the rooms that contain them all have unusually low ceilings that block any possibility of upward mobility and confine the viewer's eye to the characters. Doc Boone and Dallas, for example, take over Lucy's bedroom during and after the birth of her baby, filling the camera's frame and emphasizing the smallness of the room and Lucy's mind.

Ford synthesizes two styles while shooting *Stagecoach*—the montage and the long take. At the first way station, his intercutting between characters seated at the dining table exemplifies what André Bazin terms "expressionist montage," heightening Lucy's "brutality" and Dallas's shame.[27] Ford's use of shadows also heightens the viewer's awareness of the travelers' social and psychological states. At the second way station, when Ringo considers escaping to Lordsburg, for instance, Ford presents the narrow passageway in which he stands as an unnaturally long, darkened hallway leading to a brightly lit doorway that serves as an opening to the outside world and freedom. Ford's expression of the outlaw's dangerous state of mind as he stops in the middle of the passage to discuss escaping to Lordsburg with Chris (Chris-Pin Martin) is highly telling, using heavy shadows created by Chris's lamp as Ringo stoops to light a cigarette to reveal the harshness of Ringo's resolve. Throughout this scene, Ford's presentation of the shadowy corridor and its brightened ending reminds the viewer that marriage to Dallas (who is to be found waiting for Ringo outside the doorway) is the light at the end of his tunnel.

Ford's naturalistic use of backlighting provided by hotel windows and nighttime shadows, as Ringo walks Dallas through the seedy side of Lordsburg, demonstrates both his exceptional command of the camera and his versatility as a director. The long tracking shots along the boardwalk hotels that appear behind the couple as they walk through the redlight distinct realistically document the increasingly sordid nature of the reality awaiting Dallas. When Ringo and Dallas finally approach her destination, Ford's sudden introduction of heavy shadows and harsh lighting trades social realism for psychological insight, dramatically transforming what has been a realistic presentation of the neighborhood into an expressionist shadow world signaling the debasement of those who inhabit it. Whatever Dallas may say about herself, Ringo is correct when he observes that is no place for her. Heavily backlit and emitting a strong, steady light, she does not belong in the shadows.

Throughout *Stagecoach*, shadows often express destructive tendencies or foreshadow death. Preceded by his gigantic shadow, the Ringo Kid, for example, enters Lordsburg intent on revenge. When Luke Plummer (Tom Tyler) learns that the Kid is in town again, he stands up, placing his face in deep shadow before throwing down the death hand of two black aces and eights that he has been dealt. Even sympathetic characters, like Doc Boone, have their attendant darknesses. Boone's exaggerated shadow, signaling his alcoholism, precedes him when the doctor enters the bar in Tonto to have a drink before stepping into the stagecoach.

The deep shadows that Ford uses to characterize Ringo's showdown with the Plummers in Lordsburg seem natural. As the combatants walk down the main street, their shadows loom on the wall of a building at its corner, announcing the men and their ominous intentions. These shadows disappear as the men come into view and round the corner, stepping beyond the scope of the street light that created their shadows. The equally murderous Ringo Kid, silhouetted and walking toward the Plummers, appears at first to be a shadow himself. He too immediately loses his shadowy form when he walks forward into the brightness cast by another street light. Only then does his white hat appear, placing him on the side of the angels.

Ford's decision to use expressionist techniques in the streets of towns and the interiors of buildings, but place them within a natural setting, complements his treatments of the landscapes shot in Monument Valley. In his presentations of the stagecoach traveling through Monument Valley, Ford creates opposites in his images of nature and civilization, as well as open and constricted spaces, illustrating that the relationship between the land and the individual defines the American Character. As Tag Gallagher points out, "Scenery is not simply a given, but a participant in drama."[28] Emphasizing the importance of the presentation of the frontier, Ford himself stated to Bill Libby that "the real star of my Westerns has always been the land. I have always taken pride in the photography of my films, and the photography of Westerns in general has often been outstanding, yet rarely draws credit. It is as if the visual effect itself was not important, which would make no sense."[29]

Author and naturalist Michel Guillaume Jean de Crèvecoeur would agree that *Stagecoach* is geographically situated to shape the American Character. In *Letters from an American Farmer*, he writes, "Men are like plants: the goodness and flavour of the fruit proceeds from the peculiar soil and exposition in which they grow."[30] Monument Valley, emptied of human habitation, is a quintessential image of the frontier world and thus a natural setting for heroism. Throughout *Stagecoach*, social outcasts who have been corrupted by "the blessings of civilization" are transplanted from town to nature and return to the heroic condition. As Ford's ship of fools travels through Monument Valley, Doc Boone redeems his debased nature by caring for Lucy and healing Samuel Peacock (Donald Meek); the gambler Hatfield (John Carradine), a corrupt Southern aristocrat, re-establishes his chivalric identity by escorting Lucy through the wilderness; Dallas is socially and spiritually redeemed by love. In Lordsburg, located west of Tonto, the heroic age of society prevails: Gatewood is caught and punished for his crime and the Plummer boys pay the ultimate price for murdering Ringo's father and brother.

ENCOUNTERING THE SUBLIME IN MONUMENT VALLEY

However, as McBride points out, Ford's "intercutting between the petty squabbles inside the coach and the magnificence of the landscape outside comments on the existence of a greater system of moral and spiritual values, recognized more by the audience than by the characters themselves."[31] Expressing the heroic age in its epic scope, the sweep of the Western landscape of Monument Valley at first appears to offer the viewer's eye unbounded possibilities—Ford's first image of the Valley creates a sense of wonder as the viewer experiences the limitlessness of the space recorded on the screen. As the mass of the butte gives way to the sense of space created by the light in the sky, a world of form and energy is apparent—the cloud formations subtly mirror the landforms beneath them—the American Ideal expressed in the Real.

Ford's large prospects of Monument Valley, emptied of human presence and revealing an ideal image in an ideal land, do not express the condition of paradise. Very different from the English ideal, Ford's Arcadian West is expressed as an ideal wilderness, a terra incognita, an extreme borderland in which the environment, emptied of human presence, serves for the dramatic conflict of man and nature.

Generally, Ford's camera is placed on the Valley's floor, his low horizons emphasizing the height and mass of its buttes and the towering grandeur of the sky above them. On occasion, the camera seems to be suspended above the Valley, allowing the viewer's eye (like the waiting Apaches') to survey the larger landscape that composes Monument Valley and its massive cutaway forms. The downward plunge of the eye toward Monument Valley's floor and the tiny stagecoach that traverses it emphasizes the three-dimensional nature of the pristine space through which it travels. Directed toward the background, the viewer's eye again ascends to the far distant sky before the camera pans sharply to the left, revealing the Apaches waiting on the Valley's rim for the travelers to pass by.

As Barbara Novak points out, sky in American art has a clearly identifiable geography[32]—and Ford's skies in *Stagecoach* reflect the influence of painters whose work emphasizes transcendental feeling. As the source of light, spiritual as well as secular, Ford's skies operate as "the chief organ of sentiment," much like those of the English painter John Constable.[33] Backlit, clouds in *Stagecoach* are emotional and intellectual hieroglyphs, ever-changing manifestations of the Ideal informed by the Real. In the nineteenth century, landscape painters considered the cirrus cloud to represent man's noble impulse to rise higher in the natural and the divine orders. Aptly, Ford introduces Ringo against a backdrop of cirrus clouds that radiate like a halo spreading outward and upward from his form.

Like Albert Bierstadt, John Ford is also a master of the use of cumulus clouds. These clouds not only mirror the shapes of the land beneath them, as when the stagecoach and cavalry go their separate ways, they also comment on the action of the movie. At times, Ford's horizon is so low that it the cumuli hang well into the midground of the screen. Shot from a low angle, the stagecoach appears to be able to drive among them, reconfiguring the mundane into the Sublime. Monument Valley thus becomes a natural form alive with potential meaning—part of a larger mythology of the American West. With this in mind, it is not surprising that in 1968, Darryl Zanuck declared, "Ford could get more drama into an ordinary interior or exterior long shot than any director and . . . his placement of the camera almost had the effect of making even good dialogue unnecessary or secondary. . . . He was an artist. He painted a picture—in movement, in action, in still shots. He would never move a camera setup—move in or zoom in. You would look at the set and think maybe you need a close-up, but you didn't. He was a great, great pictorial artist."[34]

Courtney Fellion argues that in *Stagecoach*, Monument Valley is a "fictional, fantastic landscape" supporting America's Manifest Destiny.[35] She observes that "like the gates of heaven, the space of the West is where men are measured."[36] Ford's treatment of the larger mythology of the American West, however, calls for closer examination of what first appears simply to be Monument Valley's picturesque presentation. *Stagecoach* was not written and directed to the film industry's standards and cannot be considered to support popular national values of morality and religion. As McBride points out, *Stagecoach* "snub[s] its nose against 'respectable' American bourgeoisie values while exalting raffish egalitarianism."[37] The film violates all the censorial canons of its time and, as Ford pointed out, "there's not a single respectable character in the cast."[38] Indeed, if one judges the Ringo Kid by his actions, the gates of heaven would surely be closed to the stone-cold killer. As John Ford himself points out, "The leading man has killed three guys."[39]

Michel Mok makes it clear in 1939 that Ford and Dudley Nichols were optimistic that *Stagecoach* would "mark the end of elaborate, insipid screen slush, [and] start a vogue for simple, direct, intelligent film drama."[40] At the conclusion of *Stagecoach*, Ringo and Dallas transcend the sordid reality of the West in Lordsburg and ride off to a better, happier life, but this is clearly a fairy-tale ending. Can any viewer be expected to take their escape to a perfect world seriously? Ringo has no bullets left in his gun, and in the Valley, the Apache are still there, waiting for unlucky travelers.

As Gallagher points out, Ford's modus operandi throughout *Stagecoach* rests on the creation of contrast to highlight the film's contradictions.[41] Monument Valley may appear peacefully pastoral, but its majestic landforms are also expressions of tremendous force. A frontier wilderness, the Valley's natural majesty embodies both Thomas Hobbes's violent and John Locke's peaceful states of nature.

For Locke, the state of nature is "directly antithetical to the state of war. The former belongs to order, and the latter is a deviation that violates it."[42] Monument Valley expresses the order, unity, and harmony of that classical ideal. But as the setting of an Indian War, Monument Valley as depicted in *Stagecoach* is also a place that Crèvecoeur—who echoes Hobbes's insight that the natural state of man is that of war—would immediately recognize as part of the American frontier with which he was familiar. In *Letters from an American Farmer,* he writes that living in a natural state on the frontier men are "often in a perfect state of war, that of man against man . . . [and] that of man against every venerable inhabitant of these wild woods of which they are come to dispossess them."[43]

In *Stagecoach*, the bellicose nature of the people living on the frontier of the popular imagination is never in doubt. Only Peacock, the whiskey drummer from the East (Kansas City, Kansas), displays "a little Christian charity" to his fellow travelers. The rest spend their time arguing and insulting one another. Even when the West's inhabitants are not sparring with one another in the stagecoach, war defines their characters. Much of the settlement of the Southwestern plains and Texas was the result of the Southern diaspora that took place after the Civil War, and as the stagecoach travels to Lordsburg, it becomes evident that the antagonism of North and South is continuing long after the Civil War has ended. Doc Boone declares himself to have been "honorably discharged from the Union Army after the War of the Rebellion," only to be corrected immediately by Hatfield, who served the South under Lucy Mallory's father during "the War for the Southern Confederacy."

Ford did not make another Western after *Stagecoach* until he returned from the Second World War. Incredibly, *Stagecoach* at once popularized and legitimized the idea of the West in the twentieth century, reviving the genre's place in the Hollywood A-list. *Stagecoach* can be seen to be "the most optimistic of Ford's Westerns," as its ending suggests that there is "a simple place outside the confines of the dehumanizing landscapes of our industrial reality, a magic place where our sentimental pastoralism is not only a dream, but a fact."[44]

GATHERING TOGETHER WESTERN ICONOGRAPHY

In his postwar Westerns, Ford continues to investigate the nature of the West and the figures contained within it—in particular, the cavalrymen who took a different trail in *Stagecoach* and vanished off screen into Monument Valley. In his postwar Westerns, especially those of the

Cavalry Trilogy, Ford's treatments of military life and culture on the frontier, enhanced by elements borrowed from the works of Charles A. Russell, Frederic Remington, and Charles Schreyvogel, strengthened images of his West into an iconography that movie viewers now associate with the American frontier. Ford's cavalry became—in *Fort Apache*, *She Wore a Yellow Ribbon*, *Rio Grande*, and *Sergeant Rutledge* (1960)—what the public imagination was told it was by Teddy Roosevelt: "a rough and ready army whose competence [was] based not upon the drill book but upon a whole way of life."[45]

Ford points out to Bill Libby that "some time ago we reached the point where they would let our characters get out of the elaborate dress that once passed in movies for cowboy clothes, and let us put John Wayne, for example, into a part without a coat and with suspenders showing,"[46] but he also notes that he consciously incorporated elements of Western art into his Westerns. Speaking to Peter Bogdanovich, Ford remarks, "I like *She Wore a Yellow Ribbon*. I tried to copy the Remington style there—you can't copy him one hundred percent—but at least I tried to get in his color and movement, and I think I succeeded partly."[47] In 1964, Ford also recalls, "When I did *She Wore a Yellow Ribbon*, I tried to have the cameras photograph it as Remington would have sketched and painted it. It came out very beautifully and was very successful in this respect, I think."[48] This, of course, would come as no surprise to a viewer familiar with Ford's canon. Remington's compositions, founded on tension and suspense, focus on action frozen at the point of its maximum impact. *Hell Bent* obligingly supplies the corresponding story. Disseminated in mass publications (and reinforced by Western dime store novels and penny dreadfuls), the exciting action in Remington's work that captured the popular imagination was often the first glimpse that readers had of the West. America's reading public was well acquainted with Remington's work. Catering to their tastes for violent action, he turned out more than three thousand pictures, almost all Western subjects.[49]

On screen, Ford ensured that Remington's still images were translated into thrilling and recognizable action. In *Stagecoach*, shots of the exciting chase and cavalry charge on Dry Salt Lake echo Remington's *Downing the Nigh Leader* (originally published in *Collier's* April 20, 1903). The result was box office gold. Ford, who knew what popular audiences responded to, returned to Remington and the Western when making *Fort Apache* to recoup the losses of his art movie *The Fugitive* and continued to make Westerns to finance Argosy's later projects.

Of course, Remington is not the only artist from whom Ford borrowed material to authenticate the depictions of figures in his West. As Pat Ford recalls, his father kept "a collection of Schreyvogel close by his beside." Appreciating the way in which the artist's figures "frequently rush fill tilt at the spectator threatening to jump right out of the screen,"[50] Ford "pored over the book to dream up action sequences for his films."[51] In *Stagecoach* (as well as in earlier movies like *The Iron Horse* and *3 Bad Men*), Ford's figures do jump right out of the screen, thundering toward the camera, positioned in a pit, and leaping over it, into the audience. Ford also used elements of Charles Russell's depictions of ranchers and Native Americans to give his Westerns a sense of artistic authenticity. "Most Westerners really dressed in simple, rugged clothing, and were often very dirty," Ford commented to Bill Libby. "When I did *The Searchers*, I used a Charles Russell motif."[52] Incorporating elements drawn from Remington to express the frontier's military life and culture, elements from Schreyvogel to depict violent conflict and exciting action, and elements from Russell to portray cowboys and Native Americans, Ford conveyed Western images that were already deeply embedded in the American imagination—stock types and narrative situations predefined a century earlier.[53]

Central to the success of these figures is Ford's idiosyncratic borrowing from the work of Timothy O'Sullivan. As Ford noted to Libby, "The thing most accurately portrayed in the Western is the land. I think you can say that the real star of my Westerns has always been the land."[54] Tailoring his appeal to an audience educated about the West by nineteenth-century stereoscopic panoramas of the frontier and theatrical paintings and prints, Ford echoes many nineteenth-century philosophers' fascinations with the opportunities that the natural world offered urban dwellers, commenting, "We all have an escape complex. We all want to leave the troubles of our civilized world behind us. We envy those who can live the most natural way of life with nature, bravely and simply. . . . We all picture ourselves doing heroic things."[55]

HOLLYWOOD BEFORE THE SECOND WORLD WAR

A long and anxious year during which Hitler marched into Sudetenland and invaded Poland, 1939 was, as Dan Ford notes, "the year of John Ford" in Hollywood.[56] Facing the inexorable approach of war in Europe, American audiences turned to stories of the Western frontier to escape the oncoming catastrophe, if only for a few hours. John Ford collected his New York Critics Award for *Stagecoach* on December 26, 1939. *Stagecoach* has been credited with reviving American audiences' interest in the Western, but it was not the only Western to be released during what was to be Hollywood's Western renaissance. Other major Westerns made during the period from 1939 to 1940 included *Union Pacific* (1939), *Jesse James* (1939), *Dodge City* (1939), *The Oklahoma Kid* (1939), *Frontier Marshal* (1939), *Destry Rides Again* (1939), *Northwest Passage* (1940), *The Return of Frank James* (1940), *The Westerner* (1940), *Arizona* (1940), *Dark Command* (1940), *Santa Fe Trail* (1940), and *Virginia City* (1940) as well as Ford's frontier epic *Drums along the Mohawk*. These films allowed American audiences to forget about the war in Europe by immersing them in American legend and history.[57]

Well before the Japanese attacked Pearl Harbor, Ford had planned his departure from Hollywood. As the Nazi presence increased in Germany and Europe, directors, writers, composers, and actors who were not sympathetic to the Third Reich fled Germany. Many eventually arrived in America. Billy Wilder, Fredrich Hollander, Peter Lorre, Erich Maria Remarque, Max Kolpe, John Wengraf, Carl Esmond, Otto Preminger, Sig Arno, Victor Borge, Werner Klemperer, John Banner, Lilli Palmer, Felix Bressart, Ludwig Donath, Otto Reichow, Peter Van Eyck, Sig Ruman, Jean Gabin, Kurt Katch, and Hedy Lamarr all made their way to Hollywood. Arriving in New York, Gabin summed up the dilemma that he and his fellow Frenchmen were facing: "Those who are pro-British say every night in their prayers, 'Dear God, let the gallant British win quickly,'" he related "And those who are anti-British pray, 'Dear God, let the filthy British win very soon.'"[58]

By 1941 there were so many European émigrés working in the American film industry that Gerald P. Nye, a noninterventionist Republican senator from North Dakota, attacked Hollywood as "a raging volcano of war fever."[59] But, as Mark Harris points out in *Five Came Back: The Story of Hollywood and The Second World War*, Hollywood's creative class, its directors, writers, actors, and independent producers, were more forthright in making their political sympathies known than were studio heads.[60] In 1938, Ford petitioned Darryl Zanuck to finance a remake of Jean Renoir's 1937 antiwar classic, *Grand Illusion*, but Zanuck turned the project down, noting that "I have investigated and found that this picture has been released all over Europe, which would make a remake a very dangerous proposition."[61]

In spite of reluctance to support anti-Nazi projects on the part of many of the studio heads, by the late 1930s and the early part of the 1940s, some war-related films began to be released. Warner Bros. had ceased working with Germany (in 1934) and shut its offices in Austria in 1938. The Warners, Jewish immigrants from Poland who were "ardently pro-Roosevelt . . . didn't tiptoe around their hatred of Fascism and of Hitler, and were increasingly unafraid to go public and to use their position to influence others."[62]

Anatole Litvak's *Confessions of a Nazi Spy* (1939) was the first anti-Nazi movie made in Hollywood before the start of World War II. Based on the espionage activities of German American Bund in New York in 1938, *Confessions of a Nazi Spy*, starring Edward G. Robinson and Paul Lukas, was released on May 6, 1939. Litvak, a Ukrainian-born Jew who left Germany for France as the Nazis rose to power in the early 1930s, was offered a four-year contract by Warner Bros. and became one of Hollywood's leading directors by the late 1930s. Despite being banned in Germany, Japan, and eighteen Latin American countries, *Confessions of a Nazi Spy* was selected as one of the best films in 1939 by the National Board of Review and broke records at the box office. The film was also rereleased the next year with a new ending that showed the effects of the Nazi occupation of Norway, Holland, and Belgium. According to the *Los Angeles Examiner* on June 6, 1939, German Propaganda Minister Joseph Goebbels responded to the release of *Confessions of a Nazi Spy* by ordering the production of a series of documentaries on American unemployment, organized crime, and judicial corruption. In Europe, theater owners who ran the movie reported instances of vandalism and threats, and seven theater operators who screened the film in Warsaw were reportedly hanged following the German occupation. In August 1939, *Hollywood Reporter* noted that five Danzig citizens were arrested by Nazi authorities for having traveled to Gdynia, Poland, to see the film. In his autobiography, Jack

Warner noted that the film probably put him on Adolf Hitler's personal death list. [63]

Released on October 8, 1939, by Ben Judell's Producers Distributing Company, Sam Newfield's *Hitler—Beast of Berlin*, unlike *Confessions of a Nazi Spy*, did not fare well at the box office. This sensational, low-budget picture, which charted the activities of the German Underground resisting Hitler, gave American audiences their first glimpse of life inside concentration camps but was considered to be too inflammatory by the censorship boards of some states to play in theatres. *Hitler—Beast of Berlin* was shown again on April 1, 1940, in Britain and on September 25, 1941, in Mexico, but still failed to interest the public.

Ignoring the Nazi juggernaut may have allowed studios to protect their European markets for a short period of time and provided an escape in the United States for isolationists and interventionists, but, as Harris points out, theaters were not only places of "shelter from the troubles of the world," they were also the venues in which most Americans experienced vivid images of the Second World War for the first time in newsreel documentaries. In June 1940, theatergoing Americans saw Winston Churchill take over from Neville Chamberlain as prime minister and witnessed the occupation of Paris by the *Wehrmacht*. [64] As the war began, antiwar activism in Hollywood increased accordingly, and with it, the release of anti-Nazi and pro-British movies. Alfred Hitchcock's *Foreign Correspondent*, a pro-British thriller in which a young American reporter tries to expose Nazi agents in London, was released in 1940. In the movie's final broadcast, Johnny Jones (Joel McCrea) involves his American audience in the London Blitz: "I can't read the rest of the speech I had, because the lights have gone out, so I'll just have to talk off the cuff. All that noise you hear isn't static—it's death, coming to London. Yes, they're coming here now. You can hear the bombs falling on the streets and the homes." Jones says, "Don't tune me out, hang on a while—this is a big story, and you're part of it. It's too late to do anything here now except stand in the dark and let them come . . . as if the lights were all out everywhere, except in America."

Begging his listeners to safeguard the American way of life, Jones continues, "Keep those lights burning, cover them with steel, ring them with guns, build a canopy of battleships and bombing planes around them. Hello, America, hang on to your lights: they're the only lights left in the world!" Other pro-British movies included stirring historical dramas like Michael Curtiz's *The Sea Hawk*, starring Errol Flynn and Brenda Marshall, and Alexander Korda's *That Hamilton Woman*, starring Vivien Leigh and Laurence Olivier, released in 1940.

An Argosy Pictures and Walter Wanger coproduction, Ford's antiwar statement was released in 1940. Like *Stagecoach*, *The Long Voyage Home* was a ship-of-fools story set during the early days of the Second World War, but unlike *Stagecoach*, it did not appeal to its audiences. Nonetheless, Ford and cinematographer Gregg Toland's expressionistic treatments of material drawn from four short Eugene O'Neill dramas earned him his third New York Film Critics Award. On October 9, 1940, Bosley Crowther of the *New York Times* declared *The Long Voyage Home* "inspired" and to be "one of the most honest pictures ever placed upon the screen." Crowther appreciated the film's "loose and unresolved" plot about a group of the merchant marines en route to London in a "rusty old tub loaded deep with highly explosive ammunition" and lauded Ford's insights into human nature: "Out of human weakness there proceeds some nobility." Crowther deemed it "far more gratifying than the fanciest hero-worshiping fare." Brilliantly expressing the uncertainty of a world poised on the brink of war, *The Long Voyage Home*, filmed during the summer of 1940, was deemed the "deliberate fumbling onward toward a goal which is never reached, toward a peace which is never attained."[65]

In 1940, Charlie Chaplin lampooned Adolf Hitler in *The Great Dictator*. Considered by Crowther, in his October 16, 1940, *New York Times* review, as "from one point of view, perhaps the most significant film ever made," *The Great Dictator* is a withering revelation "through genuinely inspired mimicry, of the tragic weaknesses, the overblown conceit and even the blank insanity of a dictator. Hitler, of course." A powerful piece of anti-Nazi propaganda, Frank Borzage's *The Mortal Storm* (1940) was also released by Metro-Goldwyn-Mayer. As Crowther summarizes, *The Mortal Storm* is "a grim and agonizing look . . . finally taken into Nazi Germany—into the new Nazi Germany of 1933, when Hitler took over the reins and a terrible wave of suppression and persecution followed." United Artists distributed Roy Boulting's *Pastor Hall* (1940) in the United States, providing audiences with a filmed introduction by Eleanor Roosevelt. Based on the true story of Pastor Martin Neimuller, who was sent to Dachau concentration camp for criticizing the Nazi Party, *Pastor Hall* depicts Nazi stormtroopers terrorizing a German village before sending its heroic minister to a concentration camp. And, on the day the United States began peacetime conscription for men between the ages of twenty-one and thirty-one, Paramount released *Arise, My Love* (1940), a romantic drama that made use of extensive and explicit anti-Hitler dialogue.[66]

A few more pro-British American intervention films were released in 1941. Twentieth Century-Fox premiered Fritz Lang's *Man Hunt*, the first of that director's anti-Nazi movies, on June 13, 1941. Based on Geoffrey Household's novel *Rogue Male*, Dudley Nichols and Lamar Trotti's screenplay tells the story of Captain Allan Thorndike, a British big game hunter who sets out on a "sporting stalk." While on vacation in Bavaria, Thorndike gets Hitler in his sights only to be caught, beaten, and left for dead. Thorndike escapes back to London where he is harassed by German agents and aided by a young woman. After eluding and killing the German agents, Thorndike joins the RAF as a Bomber Command crewman and unexpectedly parachutes into Germany with his hunting rifle to finish what he started. Another pro-intervention film, Twentieth Century-Fox's *A Yank in the R.A.F.*, premiered on September 26, 1941, at Grauman's Chinese Theatre in Los Angeles. Based on the real-life activities of American volunteers in the Royal Air Force, *A Yank in the R.A.F.*, a romantic drama, was initiated by Darryl F. Zanuck, who wrote its story under the pseudonym Melville Crossman, and utilized airborne combat footage. Crowther gave the "thoroughly enjoyable show . . . a thumb's up," noting that "never have Darryl F. Zanuck and Twentieth Century-Fox owed so much to so few as they do for the pulsing excitement contained in their new film."[67]

Premiering on July 2, 1941, Howard Hawks's Oscar-winning *Sergeant York* received a rave review in *Variety*, which deemed it "a clarion film that reaches the public at a moment when its stirring and patriotic message is probably most needed."[68] Crowther, however, remarked in the *New York Times* that "the suggestion of deliberate propaganda is readily detected here."[69] As Harris points out, *Sergeant York*'s phenomenal success at the box office proved to be "the last straw for a cadre of isolationist politicians," prompting Nye to accuse the "foreigners" who ran Hollywood of promoting war.[70]

Undoubtedly, the oddest of Hollywood's prewar movies was produced and edited by Darryl Zanuck in January of 1941. Graphic and frank, John Ford's social guidance film *Sex Hygiene* (1941) was made "for the Army," not for general release to the American public. As Ford told Peter Bogdanovich, Zanuck, an officer in the Army Reserve, had pitched the project to Ford, saying, "These kids have got to be taught about these things. It's horrible—do you mind doing it?" Ford remembers that "it really was horrible; not being for general release, we could do anything—we had guys out there with VD and everything else. I think it made its point and helped a lot of young kids. I looked at it and threw up."[71]

The film was a prime example of how straightforward the Ford-Zanuck collaboration had become. In a memo to Ford dated January 25, 1941, Zanuck requests five or six more close-ups and two more scenes—one in which the unlucky Pete (Charles Tannen) leaves the recreation hall and the other in which Tannen leaves a woman's apartment. Stating that U.S. Army Project #40 is "an excellent job," Zanuck carefully specifies what the scene requires:

> After he walks out of the recreation hall, I want to go to a closeup insert of an eight-ball on the pool table, with the white ball behind it. I want to lap dissolve from this to a stock shot of a gramophone playing, and then I want to lap dissolve from that to a closeup of a half-smoked cigar parked on a ledge in a dingy dark hallway. The camera pulls back, revealing the hallway—it is empty. A door opens and Pete (Tannen) comes out of the doorway. He starts down the hallway; he remembers his cigar where he parked it; gets it; lights it, and strolls past the camera. We fade out on this and fade in on the film already shot, where the commanding officer tells about the new cases.[72]

Zanuck concludes, "I would like to knock this stuff off as quickly as we can. I imagine you can do it easily in one day. I am convinced that the officers in the War Department and the Chief Signal Officer will be delighted with this film."[73] Zanuck was correct. Two days later, in a letter bearing the letterhead of the War Department, Office of the Chief Signal Officer, Washington, Zanuck writes to Ford that

> Major General J.O. Mauborgne, Chief Signal Officer of the United States Army, has asked me to express his personal appreciation to you for your cooperation in helping us to film the first Signal Corps Training Film to be made in Hollywood by the motion picture indus-

try. . . . The Film has turned out to be an excellent example of the possibilities for making Training Films here with industry facilities, and we are very grateful to you for the interest which led you to contribute your services to this national Defense activity without remuneration.[74]

As with the sequence of the Joads' arrival in *The Grapes of Wrath*, Ford's sequence transcribes Zanuck's memo shot for shot.

On September 11, 1941, Ford, who had been an important part of the Naval Reserve's undercover prewar reconnaissance along the California and Mexican coastline, received orders to report to Washington, D.C. Abandoning his brilliant career in Hollywood for the Navy three months before the Japanese invasion of Pearl Harbor, Ford himself did not understand why he was "giving up money, career, security, family and freedom for the iron regimen of the military,"[75] but as Mary Ford pointed out to her grandson, Ford valued self-sacrifice in himself (and others) above all else. Her memory of Ford secretly rushing off to war without saying good-bye seems somewhat fanciful and romantic: Ford "said he had to make a quick business trip to Washington and he'd be gone a [few] days," she says, then notes that he sent for her "when he got right to Washington," saying "he was going to be a little delayed."[76] Taking Barbara with her, Mary joined Ford "in Washington a couple of weeks before the thing really broke,"[77] renewing their acquaintance with people with whom Ford had become friendly while shooting pictures with the Navy twenty years earlier.

4

NOT FOR SELF BUT FOR COUNTRY

From *Salute* to *Submarine Patrol*

It was just a lot of hard work. . . . Then later they cut the hell out of it.[1]—John Ford on *Seas Beneath*

Growing up in Portland, Maine, John Ford understood the sea. "If you go to Portland, Maine, you understand him," Dan Ford says. "It reeks of John Ford. What you hear all the time, constantly are seagulls . . . it's definitely a waterfront town. It smells of the sea."[2] Scott Eyman concurs, noting that the sea was part of the necessary chemical components of Ford's very being: Ford, Eyman remarks, "needed the sea. I think it was just something that just called his soul."[3] Robert Elswit, ASC, also comments on the natural affinity between Ford and the sea: "He was in love with the sea." Elswit notes, "He had a boat from the time he was twelve."[4] As a result, Ford made four films about life in the Navy that played to enthusiastic audiences before the Second World War: *Salute* (1929), *Men without Women* (1930), *Seas Beneath* (1931), and *Submarine Patrol* (1938).

Filmed partly on location at the Naval Academy in Annapolis, Maryland, *Salute* resonated strongly with audiences at the box office, ending the year as Fox's top-grossing movie. A formulaic coming-of-age story, the film in many ways prefigured Ford's postwar treatment of military culture in *The Long Gray Line* (1955). Paul Randall (William Janney), heir to wealth and privilege, enters the U.S. Naval Academy and develops into an adult. Between episodes of interservice football games and romantic rivalry, he matures, demonstrating determination and becoming a team player. An accountable, independent thinker, he becomes the officer his ancestors and his grandfather—"all Navy men"—expect him to be, as well as a suitable companion for the attractive Nancy Wayne (Helen Chandler), a naval officer's daughter. He is, at the movie's end, a Navy man.

Joseph McBride remarks that filming and living at Annapolis for several weeks enabled Ford to cultivate more friendships with Navy brass. Having a taste of what it would be like to be one of them, Ford portrayed on screen what he wanted for himself: a vocation that combined male camaraderie with patriotic fervor and the acceptance he craved from the American establishment—and from his wife.[5] Tag Gallagher, however, reads *Salute* very differently. This movie is a comedy of manners, he points out, arguing that *Salute* critiques instead of applauds life in the Navy. Pointing out the excessive emphasis put on duty and tradition throughout the film in the U.S. Naval Academy's ceremonies, uniforms, exercises, hazing, and music ("Anchors Aweigh" is played at every possible occasion), Gallagher finds in Ford's presentation of the Navy and its traditions "a formidable myopia."[6] When Paul's love interest, Nancy Wayne, teaches him how to sing "Anchors Aweigh," it becomes apparent, Gallagher argues, that "wars are not caused, says Ford, by 'bad' people, but by 'innocent' ones, for whom war becomes an extension of every fine impulse."[7] Accordingly, he believes that Ford critiques Nancy and Paul's indoctrinated, ingenuous dutifulness as the cause of most social evils.

In *Salute*, Gallagher continues, "evil" is latent, at worst, and even attractive, noting that Paul, Nancy, and the Navy still need "a mammy" to look after them. This need is answered by the character of Smoke Screen, played by Stepin Fetchit, whose performance is in keeping with the theatrical traditions of the "original Negro," whose duty is to act "as a mirror satirically reflecting establishment values—like many Ford 'fool characters.'"[8] Gallagher observes that "Tradition and Duty, growing out of ethnic origins, result in generally gloomy consequences," since duty precipitates noble tragedy in Ford's movies,[9] but *Salute* proves to be an exception to this rule—ending on an upbeat note before any such tragedy occurs. The Navy football squad fights a much stronger Army squad to a standstill on the field, because Paul, cooperating with the senior who mercilessly hazed him, is able to tackle his brother, a star quarterback who has been his competition on and off the field throughout the movie, and prevent him from scoring another touchdown. Working together, the Navy men disrupt the Army's ability to advance and even the score despite the odds being against them. The game ends in a tie that both sides celebrate.

Salute's football game allows the viewer to consider a very different approach to the subject of competition in this movie. Ford's recurring wide shots of the spectacle, whether they be of marching bands performing during pregame activities or of the teams playing on the field, emphasize teamwork and illustrate that the players' cooperative spirit is the true foundation of the game. On the field, the powerful Army team's strength is its weakness. As the Army team's star athlete, John Randall (George O'Brien) is solely responsible for his team's success. When the Navy team bands together and succeeds in stopping the football hero, they succeed in stopping their entire opposition. When the game is over, John thanks Paul for humbling him: "I had a spill coming to me," he tells his brother. "I've been a big shot here too long. In fact, it was good to learn I could be spilled, 'cause Paul, when I get that ole commission and go out to the Army, I'll only be a punch shavetail. . . . I'm thankful to you. I'm proud of you."[10] Demonstrating good fellowship and respect, John and his teammates stop by the Navy's dressing room to congratulate them on their success, demonstrating the cooperative spirit expected of members in the branches of the U.S. military.

THE IMPORTANCE OF TEAMWORK

During the thirties, Ford made three more movies concerned with the subject of teamwork in the Navy: *Men without Women*, a peacetime drama about an unlucky submarine crewmen; *Seas Beneath*, a First World War naval combat film; and *Submarine Patrol*, another combat film set during the First World War that contains elements of romance and comedy.

Men without Women is the story of a dishonored naval officer, Quartermaine, who masquerades as Chief Torpedoman Burke (Kenneth MacKenna) and redeems himself by staying behind in a sunken submarine so that his crewmates can live. Painstakingly structured, its action begins by establishing the lack of moral fiber in the crew and officers of the unlucky submarine (the S-13) as they participate in a pub crawl in the fleshpots of Shanghai before shipping out to sea. Visiting what is reputed to be "the longest bar in the world," the men are not interested in looking at photographs of women; what they want is available "in the flesh." Prostitutes, liquor, and opium are all accessible to anyone willing to pay for them. As a seaman belts out a decadent, jazzy version of "Frankie and Johnnie," submariner Joe Cobb (Walter McGrail) nego- tiates for not one but two prostitutes, keeping both women for himself when his shipmate Curly Pollock (George LeGuere) backs out of the deal. The crewmen, who are interested only in drinking, manage to quickly overindulge in the two hours allotted to them. By the time they stumble out of the bar, they are roaring drunk, accosting more prosti- tutes, who are displayed behind barred windows along the men's way back to the dock. In spite of one woman's tempting promises, the sailors do not stop for long: "Not me, baby, not in a cage," another submariner, Radioman Jenkins (Stuart Erwin), tells one woman. "I've got *some* mod- esty left."

Arriving at the submarine, the men are immediately relieved of the liquor they attempt to smuggle on board. Without wine, women, and song, they immediately regain their self-control and act like Navy men. Shortly after the submarine puts to sea, she is rammed by a freighter and sunk. The new ensign, Albert Edward Price (Frank Albertson), is forced to take over command when the captain is lost during the sinking of the submarine. Price is clearly a Navy man—a highly rational and self-disciplined individual who embodies the best traditions of the U.S. Naval Academy—competence, character, and compassion.

As an officer *and* a gentleman, Price knows that his crew's survival depends upon their ability to function as a team, which, in turn, rests on their willingness to follow orders. As long as the crew cooperates with their commanding officer and does the "right thing," they may be res- cued. Some of the enlisted men, however, prove to be unable to re- strain their impulsive natures. Lacking self-discipline, they begin to argue and then fight over the oxygen cylinder on board. Driven insane by the possibility of slow suffocation after learning that the gun trunk access and torpedo tubes are jammed inoperable, a melee erupts on board. During the mutiny, Pollock becomes psychotic. Holding a deto- nator above his head and believing himself to be "the avenging angel," he shrieks, "The vengeance of the Lord is here! . . . Blasphemers, you are all going to eternal damnation!" Forced to protect his crew, Price shoots him. The shock of Pollock's death reminds the seamen that they must work together to survive. There are no more outbreaks of violence or disruptive behavior, even when, one by one, the men begin to die. Ford effectively uses screenwriter Dudley Nichols's visual symbolism in this sequence to evoke sentiment from his viewer: a small wooden boat, carved to keep a young seaman's mind off the catastrophe, refuses to float. As its maker slowly succumbs to the chlorine gas that is leaking through the submarine from the switchboard in the control room, the clumsy child's toy is placed in the water of the torpedo room—there it capsizes and slowly sinks while Navy divers hurry to the submarine's resting place.

Trained for self-sacrifice, Price and Quartermaine both offer to stay aboard the submarine after the salvage team arrives and slowly repairs one of the torpedo tubes. Both understand that one man must sacrifice himself to ensure the survival of the other, as it is impossible to activate the torpedo tube once one is inside it. As Price points out, being responsible for the safety and well-being of his men, the commanding officer must stay with the ship. Quartermaine, however, seizes the opportunity to redeem himself and his reputation by being the last man aboard. He knocks Price unconscious, stuffs the young officer headfirst into the torpedo tube, and then ejects him into the ocean. Left behind, Quartermaine becomes the submarine's thirteenth man. Rather than being unlucky, he dies a noble and tragic figure, *and* his self-sacrifice ensures that he is no longer one of the socially damned.

Men without Women is striking because of Ford's experimental use of underwater photography to document naval rescue crews welding the hull of the doomed submarine resting on the ocean's floor. This very early sound movie also broke new ground by employing technicians with microphones hung from fishing poles during dolly shots in bars and down streets to capture sound deemed at the time to be impossible.[11] As McBride is points out, *Men without Women* also marks the beginning of Ford's creative partnership with Dudley Nichols, a long-lasting relationship between the director and a writer-producer that helped Ford reach his full artistic maturity.[12] Nichols's polished craftsmanship, as well as his effective control of dramatic structure, is evident.

Released in 1931, *Seas Beneath* is another action film that also depicts the brotherly bond of Navy men, but this time through the relationship existing between the dutiful American and German sailors of the First World War. Ford's underwater photography in this picture is remarkable—largely due to naval support of the project, which was shot off the Isthmus and Santa Catalina. The Navy contributed the USS *Argonaut*, SS-166, Ex V-4—which was, at the time, the largest submarine in the world—as well as destroyers, cruisers, other submarines, and naval personnel to its making. As in *Men without Women*, duty drives the narrative action in *Seas Beneath*—its characters must make sacrifices of love, liberty, or life for their principles.

A Twentieth Century-Fox production, *Seas Beneath* is another early example of Ford's creative partnership with Dudley Nichols. It is the story of a U.S. Mystery Ship that is on a mission to find and sink a U-boat—the U-172—that has been disrupting Allied shipping. Posing as a harmless three-masted schooner, the Mystery Ship, fitted with a gun capable of sinking the U-172, acts in concert with an American submarine to scuttle the enemy's plans. En route, her captain and crew stop at the Canary Islands, become friendly with the sister of the U-172's commanding officer, meet the U172's crew, and run afoul of locals, who prove to be German spies.

Interwoven among scenes of high-seas action, the romantic subplot between American Commander Robert Kingsley (George O'Brien) and German Anna Marie von Steuben (Marion Lessing) is patently unbelievable but serves to illustrate the theme, which runs throughout the movie, of duty being a universal value for military men. Kingsley and Anna fall in love but are separated by their differing loyalties. Unlike the crew of *Men without Women*, every naval man (and woman) in *Seas Beneath* can be counted on to do "the right thing." In this film, the conflict lies not between individuals, but countries. Loyal to a man, Kingsley's and von Steuben's crews execute their orders without question or complaint. Under fire, Kingsley and his men, in particular, exhibit the Navy man's traits of self-reliance and self-control. Professional sailors, the German submariners, like their American counterparts, exhibit socially correct behavior: as their submarine sinks underneath them, they exhibit no loss of self-control or tendencies toward violence, only refinement—shaking hands politely with one another as the water rises above their knees. Rescued by Kingsley and his men, they are, of course, model prisoners.

Only the spy, Fraulein Lolita (Mona Maris), whose machinations first trap and then destroy the naive, young American Ensign Richard Cabot (Steve Pendleton), is depicted as despicable and self-serving. A mercenary, Lolita's self-interest contrasts sharply with Cabot's professionalism. After being drugged, Cabot falls asleep. Like his fellows, Cabot has come ashore pretending to be an ordinary sailor, but the markings inside his naval cap divulge the identity of the Mystery Ship to Lolita and her henchmen, who sell this information to the Germans. When Cabot regains consciousness the next day, he discovers that the Mystery Ship has already left on its mission. Unwilling to remain ashore, Cabot redeems himself by stowing away on the German's supply boat. After knocking a hole in the bottom of the supply ketch's hold, he disrupts the submarine's refueling. Like *Men without Women*, *Seas Beneath* demonstrates that doing one's duty enables the individual to transcend his or her limitations, be they personal, social, or political. Shot in the act of sabotage, Cabot dies a martyr's death but is forgiven by Kingsley and the crew when they find his body floating in a German life jacket.

Shot in the studio at Twentieth Century-Fox, *Submarine Patrol* bears many similarities to *Salute*, *Men without Women*, and *Seas Beneath*. A studio potboiler based on William Faulkner's 1936 script, *Submarine Patrol* is the story of a rundown, plywood submarine chaser, the S.C. 599, and her motley crew during World War I. Prefiguring the PT crews in *They Were Expendable* (1945), *Submarine Patrol* contains two closely linked plots in its ship-of-fools story, that of Lt. John C. Drake (Preston Foster), a naval officer demoted for negligence who is put in command of the S.C. 599, and that of Perry Townsend III (Richard Greene), heir to wealth and privilege who manages simultaneously to fall in love *and* become a naval man.

Assigned to the S.C. 599 for letting a destroyer run onto the rocks, Drake is told that his crew is made up of "green, unseasoned men" and only "four old-timers." He is expected to do "his best." The disgraced officer begins redeeming himself by whipping his disorderly crew into shape and making Townsend into a Navy man, before ultimately regaining his honor by finding and destroying the notorious U-26. Townsend, like Paul Randall in *Salute*, is born into a wealthy family. Unlike Randall, Townsend is not the product of a Navy family. He is overbearing, enthusiastic, and arrogant. Offering his services to Rear Admiral Joseph Maitland (Charles Trowbridge), the Commandant of the Yard, at the beginning of the picture, Townsend says, "I hear you need some good men for your Navy so here I am." Discovering that he will not be serving on a "tough, sawed-off, little battlewagon" but a boat belonging to the "Splinter Fleet," the millionaire playboy complains, expecting to be transferred, but is told that the Navy, a meritocracy, "has very little patience with pull or influence. We don't play favorites. Being a Townsend was important before you enlisted, but it doesn't count anymore." He is told to go back to his vessel and be "a good sailor."

Townsend and Drake are not happy with their assignments, but both develop into "good" Navy men as they serve on the S.C. 599. Learning to work with and respect others, Townsend, a competent mechanic, develops into a highly prized engineer. The transformation of the civilian volunteer, who, at first, can only think of himself, into a crewman who is responsible for the well-being of his mates is completed when he is unable to attend his own wedding. As Townsend's note to Susan Leeds (Nancy Kelly) indicates, his responsibilities to the S.C. 599 come first; she and the wedding will just have to wait. His "liberty cancelled," he is sailing at once for Malta and then "for duty in the Baltic." Teaching the haphazard crew of the sub chaser the art of self-control and self-sacrifice, Drake leads by example, and by doing so acquires those values himself.

The crewmen of the S.C. 599, who began their adventure by mistaking a garbage can for a periscope, also become Navy men. Every one of them volunteers for the dangerous mission of hunting down the U-26. Before leaving to pilot the rowboat that will guide the S.C. 599 through the minefield, the old-timer Mike Quincannon (J. Farrell MacDonald) shakes Drake's hand and pays him the ultimate compliment: "Sir, it is a fine thing to have served with the son of your father."

Throughout *Submarine Patrol*, Ford obeys the Hollywood dictum if something is successful, imitate it. The action scenes, in which the S.C. 599's crew demonstrates their coolness under fire, draw heavily on those found in *Men without Women* and *Seas Beneath*. When the sub chaser's hull is breached during the sequence that showcases the destruction of the U-26, the panic that occurs is accentuated by Ford's introduction of harshly lit clouds of steam, brilliant sparks, and gushing water, elements borrowed from the sinking submarine in *Men without Women*. As in *Seas Beneath*, the element of surprise is critical when attacking the U-boat. What appears to be a 40-mm cannon is unveiled on the deck of the S.C. 599 at the last minute before the fighting begins. Also, as in *Seas Beneath*, the S.C. 599's hold catches on fire during the fighting and has to be extinguished.

THE NAVY MAN ON THE *ARANER*

Considering Ford's love of the sea, and his interest in the Navy, it is fitting that three years after shooting *Seas Beneath*, he purchased a boat of his own. 1933 and 1934 were excellent earning years for John Ford,[13] so in June of 1934, he bought himself a 110-foot gaff-headed ketch with a wide transom, which he renamed the *Araner*. In the following September, he was commissioned as a lieutenant commander in the U.S. Naval Reserve. Between 1935 and 1939, Ford performed reconnaissance missions in the *Araner* for the Navy, turning in regular reports on the Japanese fishing trawlers that were active in Mexican waters. In one account he reports the findings of a trip on the *Araner* along the Baja and through the Gulf of California. After finding little that was unusual, Ford encountered the Japanese shrimp fleet lying at anchor in Guaymas harbor. Fourteen steam trawlers and two mother ships at anchor were not an unusual sight at Guaymas, but Ford's impression of the fleet's personnel was not favorable. The crews that came ashore for liberty wearing "well tailored flannels, worsteds and tweed suits . . . black service shoes smartly polished . . . [the men] were about average height . . . young . . . good looking and very alert," carried themselves "with military carriage . . . hair well cut." On board each trawler, "three or four young officers were stationed, who never went ashore unless in uniform. The uniform, with the exception of the cap badge and strike was the regulation braid-bound Imperial Navy uniform, smartly out and well pressed. The Cap badge while not regulation had the Rising Sun motif." Ford wrote, "These men were tall, straight as ramrods, high cheek boned, with aquiline features, definitely aristocratic. For want of a better word I would call them the Samurai type of the military caste. (During three trips to Japan I have studied this type very closely. I am positive they are Naval men.)"[14] Summing up his impressions of the trawlers and their crews, Ford concluded,

> It is my opinion that the crews and officers of this shrimp fleet belong to the Imperial Navy or Reserve. . . . It is my opinion that these young men are brought here from time to time to make themselves absolutely familiar with Mexican waters and particularly the Gulf of California. The two mother ships are supposed to have sounding devices on them. . . . It is plausible to assume that these men know every Bay, Cove and Inlet in the Gulf of California, a Bay which is so full of islands, and so close to our Arizona borderline.[15]

As Dan Ford points out, his grandfather was determined to make his career in the Naval Reserve as successful as his career in motion pictures, actively seeking out the patronage of his commanding officer, Captain Claude Mayo.[16] Ford's interest in and willingness to volunteer his time and expertise to the Navy did not go unnoticed. By 1940, he was well established, and well connected, in the Naval Reserve.

FORD ON THE ARMY

Throughout the 1930s, Ford also directed movies about life in the Army. In these films, ideas about duty, tradition, and honor figure prominently. Set during the First World War, *The Lost Patrol*—a 1934 combat film and box office success starring Victor McLaglen and Boris Karloff—is the story of a British Army patrol lost in the Mesopotamian desert. The unit's commanding officer has been killed, and the Sergeant, uninformed of their orders, decides to try to rejoin the brigade. Eventually the eleven men reach an oasis, where Arabs steal their horses and the men are picked off by snipers one by one. A British pilot finds the patrol and lands to help the survivors, but he too is killed. In the end, only the Sergeant (Victor McLaglen) is left alive. Ironically, he manages to kill all the Arabs, only to have another British patrol, attracted by the smoke of the burning plane, arrive moments after he has done so.

Functioning in circumstances similar to those found in *Men without Women*, *Seas Beneath*, and *Submarine Patrol*, the Sergeant's patrol is cut off from the outside world. It functions as a microcosm of society and becomes an allegory about human nature. In the opening shot of the movie, the patrol, lost in a sea of sand, appears to be walking on water. The huge sand dunes over which the soldiers ride resemble the ocean swells in *Seas Beneath*. A land-locked ship-of-fools story, this Ford-Nichols collaboration showcases enlisted men, under stress, who become deranged. Lost in the desert without its officer, the patrol is like a ship without a pilot. The individuals of the patrol are also lost, being at the mercy of their own self-destructive tendencies.

Inaction, not action, creates the dramatic tension on which the film's narrative rests. As Gallagher points out, in *The Lost Patrol*, "the plot leads its characters, as opposed to characters leading the plot." Nothing much happens "beyond the encroachment of aloneness and insanity."[17] While the patrol attempts to fight off an unseen enemy, the absurdity of their situation heightens each soldier's isolated, alienated existence. Aptly, the soldiers, whose lives are predicated by action, find themselves at a loss or, if you will pardon the pun, at sea.

Entrusted to the care of the Sergeant, the men of the patrol form a ragtag band in which old-timers and raw recruits display a number of antisocial tendencies. Sanders (Boris Karloff), who becomes increasingly obsessed with religious dogma and the "wickedness" of his companions, ends his life by compulsively dragging a gigantic homemade cross up a gigantic sand dune to the waiting Arabs, who quickly finish him off with one shot. Abelson (Sammy Stein), a callous individual who displays a sociopath's resistance to authority, foolishly disobeys his Sergeant's orders, suffers from heat stroke, and runs into the empty desert to attack an unseen enemy. He too is shot in short order. Unable to control his thirst for revenge, Quincannon (J. M. Kerrigan) marches into the desert to die. A narcissistic sadist who speaks of "the joy of killing Arabs," Brown (Reginald Denny) disappears into the desert on a "hunting expedition" and does not return. Pearson (Douglas Walton), young, pathetic, and unable to concentrate, is shot in the back while on guard duty. A sniper kills Hale (Billy Bevan), the patrol's exhibitionist who shows off on the top of a palm tree while he is surveying the enemy's terrain. Even the group's stock Englishman, Bell (Brandon Hurst), an old-timer, is severely flawed. Critically injured at the time Pearson was killed, he staggers from his bed when hearing shots and collapses, dying of his head injury.

Unlike their companions, the remaining three members of the patrol appear to be reasonably well-adjusted, mentally balanced individuals, capable of following orders and cooperating with their companions, but they too prove themselves inadequate to the tasks before them. MacKay (Paul Hanson) and Cook (Alan Hale) are tasked with finding their brigade and rescuing their companions. They leave the patrol in good spirits, but their mutilated bodies are returned later that evening, strapped to the horses that the Arabs had taken earlier. Morelli (Wallace Ford) loyally follows the Sergeant's orders but becomes increasingly hysterical when left alone. Finally, his exasperation with Sanders— whose constant proselytizing to "save" him will not allow him to sleep— drives him over the edge. Ironically, he becomes as irrational as Sanders. He meets his end by behaving like the man he despises. After rushing into the desert to save Sanders, who, suffering a psychotic lapse, is re-enacting Christ's journey to Cavalry, he is shot while attempting to bring the wounded man's body back to safety.

The Lost Patrol, thought to be an unusually serious adventure film at the time of its release,[18] can be considered "a study in the lack of leadership."[19] In part, the patrol's difficulties are due to command failure. Because their young officer "kept his orders in his head" and failed to communicate them to the Sergeant before dying, the Sergeant, like his men, has no idea where they are, where they are going, or what they are supposed to do. With "the orders locked up in that dead kid back there," the patrol is not only lost; it also lacks direction. The men's activities are meaningless: they are "a patrol, patrolling and not knowing where they're at." In part, the patrol's failure is also due to the soldiers' inability to work with one another. The success of the patrol unit, much like the success of the Army's football team in *Salute*, rests on one individual. When that individual is removed, the ability of the unit to function crumbles.

Lack of character, however, is the major reason for the Sergeant's failure. His decisions to post a guard over the horses and then stay at the oasis are well reasoned. A competent and compassionate noncommissioned officer, he does his duty to his men by ensuring that their mounts are able to carry them and allowing his men time to regain their strength before ordering them to their patrol. But after the horses are lost, the Sergeant abrogates his responsibilities and loses the respect of his men. Attributing their situation to "bad luck," he shifts his accountability for the patrol's losses elsewhere. Thereafter, his actions become meaningless. His men cease to follow his orders. As he himself notes when Brown disappears, they have become "insubordinate swine."

The Sergeant seems to have more to live for than his men, but at the last, he too goes "bughouse." When Morelli is shot, the Sergeant digs himself a grave and then goes berserk, laughing maniacally as he uses the submachine gun he has salvaged from the plane to cut down the Arabs as they rush him. Before shooting the last Arab, throwing his fist in the air, he shouts, "Quincannon! I got 'em! Quincannon! Brown! There they are!! I got 'em! Morelli, Pearson! Pearson, Morelli!! McKay, look! Look at them!!"

By the time another patrol arrives to rescue him, the Sergeant has gone completely mad. Unable to speak when the officer asks him, "Where's your men? Where's your section?" he can only look at his companions' sabres glinting horribly as they protrude from their owners' graves. As the cavalry leaves to rejoin the brigade, they return the way they came, retracing the path that the Sergeant's patrol took when it arrived at the oasis. Here, Ford invites his viewer to consider the meaninglessness of the men's sacrifices: no ground has been captured; there has been no advance at all.

Ford uses sand to highlight the lack of spirituality among the alienated, suffering men. Bleak and uncompromising, the desert itself becomes the patrol's enemy. The entirety of its terrifyingly pristine wilderness contains no human activity. The desert's two primary elements, sand and light, are both subject to continuous change, but the surface of the dunes is consistent and continuous. Ford's desert lacks the enormous scale of his Westerns, but each grain of sand, each dune, speaks to the emotional and spiritual emptiness of the men trapped in the arid landscape. Retracing their steps in the constantly shifting sand, the line of horsemen appears to be retreating, leaving only the marks of the horses' hooves in the sand as the picture fades to black. Those too will vanish quickly. There will be no trace of the men having been there. Only the desert will remain.

In 1938, this ending must have been particularly disturbing. Without direction, the futile efforts of the Sergeant's patrol question the possibility of success as the world braced for another war. Not surprisingly, *The Lost Patrol* resonated strongly at the box office with American audiences who had witnessed the collapse of social order due to lack of direction in Europe; Hitler's violation of the Treaty of Versailles; Germany's invasion of the Rhineland, Austria, and Czechoslovakia; Italy's taking of Ethiopia; and the civil war in Spain.

When one considers Ford's earlier and much more optimistic military movies, *The Lost Patrol* provides a sharp contrast to the successful undertakings of Robert Kingsley's Mystery Ship and John Drake's S.C 599. The dearth of effective leadership and lack of team players in *The Last Patrol* is startling in comparison, and the soldiers' sporadic moments of self-sacrifice are meaningless. Ford had not abandoned his interest in the military and military culture. Rather, *The Lost Patrol's* emphasis on the psychological dimension of combat indicates a broadening of his observations that includes a modern sensibility not generally attributed to him.

MARTIAL UNDERPINNINGS

Released the same year as *Young Mr. Lincoln*, Ford's first color film for Twentieth Century-Fox, *Drums along the Mohawk*, showcases the director's understanding of a different side of the American Character before the Second World War. As Robin Wood observes, *Drums along the Mohawk* is "perfectly conceived for, or a perfectly logical product of, its contemporary historical moment—America just emerging from the Depression; the world on the brink of a war to defend Democracy against Fascism." The film dramatically illustrates the perseverance and durability of the American Character—"the American people in microcosm struggling against hardship and disaster, overcoming them and preparing for new effort."[20] Nominated for two Academy Awards and grossing over $1 million at the box office in 1939, this Technicolor flag-waver, based on a 1936 novel of the same name by Walter D. Edmonds, charts the lives of settlers suffering British, Tory, and Indian attacks on the New York frontier during the American Revolution. While examining the foundations of the American Character, *Drums along the Mohawk* offers a compensatory vision of mankind to its viewer, making sense of the pervasive awareness of social collapse that was occurring as the world was once again on the brink of war.

Whereas *The Lost Patrol* may be seen to be a modern expression of the frontier experience, *Drums along the Mohawk*—the story of Gilbert and Lana Martin, a young married couple who leave the safety of colonial New York to build a new life on the upstate frontier, only to find themselves at war with the British and their allies—is a much more traditional treatment of that subject in terms of its approach to the story of the American Revolution.

As the Revolution develops, the Martins, who are civilian volunteers, are burned out of their home. Reinventing themselves, they find work with a wealthy widow, support the war effort, and raise a family. McBride complains that Ford takes a cartoonish approach to character and grossly oversimplifies the history of the Revolutionary War period,[21] but *Drums along the Mohawk* makes no pretense of being a historical documentary of the American Revolution. Its treatment of American history is a prime example of Darryl Zanuck's transformation of the American past at Twentieth Century-Fox into the visually perfect and highly modified form associated with that studio before the Second World War. Rustic, hand-stitched samplers as intertitles announce the presence of Americana throughout the movie.

First among the American types involved in the unfolding drama is a Zanuck natural, the Yeoman. An ideal representative of republicanism, Gil Martin (Henry Fonda), "a natural born farmer," is the embodiment of the honest, hard-working American Yeoman whose compassion, cooperation, and neighborliness reveal his self-sacrificing nature. The American yeomanry, unlike the peasantry of Europe, were independent freeholders, a society of sturdy individuals "ideally suited for republicanism."[22] At the time of the Revolution, most Americans were farmers, who assumed that they were living in the age of agriculture, only glimpsing the beginnings of the age of commerce. As Thomas Jefferson noted, they considered themselves God's chosen people, in whom "he had made his peculiar deposit for substantial and genuine virtue."[23] Citing Jefferson, Gordon S. Wood points out that it was the presence of America's yeomanry that made virtuous republican government possible—after all, "corruption of morals in the mass of cultivators is a phenomenon of which no age nor nation has furnished an example."[24]

The duty of the American Yeoman to help his neighbors established a tradition of neighborliness on the frontier. This is readily apparent in *Drums along the Mohawk*: as an intertitle announces, "It was the custom for neighbors to come from miles around to help a newcomer clear his land." Compassionate and cooperative, Gil's neighbors help one another burn brush, fell trees, and dislodge tree stumps. However, the yeoman is also fiercely independent; as Noah Webster observed, they are "substantial independent freeholders, masters of their own persons and lords of their own soil."[25] The American Yeoman is willing to work with others but unwilling to work *for* others. Even after being burned out of his farm, Gil is reluctant to lose his independence by going to work for another person. Standing in front of the ruined hearth and chimney, the remains of his cabin, he categorically refuses to give up his freedom when Lana (Claudette Colbert) suggests that they work for Mrs. McKlennar (Edna May Oliver). "Lana," he says, "you can't hire out, a girl like you." When Lana suggests there would be no harm in talking over the matter with the woman whose hired help has left her, he refuses. "No! Hired help," he spits out disdainfully. "No!"

Unfortunately, it is winter, and there is no other solution to the Martins' dilemma. They must hire themselves out to survive and soon are employed by Sarah McKlennar. A freeholder herself, Sarah also demonstrates the virtues of the American yeomanry. Ford locates this character in what appears to be a beneficent natural world. The pastoral beauty of her frontier farmland, evident in its stunning blue skies, healthy crops of corn, and spotlessly white flocks of sheep, is stunning in Technicolor. Sarah, like her neighbors, is a product of her times and remarkable for the simplicity of her needs and the generosity of her spirit. In the eighteenth century, enlightened thinkers presumed everyone to possess a common moral and social sense that united people in natural affection.[26] Inviting the Martins to work for her, she provides them with a house and furniture as well as a livelihood. Because of their natural affection for one another, Sarah, Gil, Lana, and their son, over time, become an extended family unit, and when Sarah dies, she bequeaths her farm, all of her belongings, and even her hoard of "gold pieces" to the young couple because they have been "like her own flesh and blood."

Published in 1893, Frederick Jackson Turner's highly popular address "The Significance of the Frontier in American History" asserts that America's frontier experience produced a social and psychological phenomenon characterized by the qualities of strength and inventiveness that settlers acquired after jettisoning colonial institutions and ideas in order to survive in the wilderness. The hardships involved in settling a new land also produced in the American Yeoman the distinctive qualities of individualism, materialism, and egalitarianism and ensured his resistance to centralized political power. Before their farm is burned, Gil and Lana begin their lives together by casting off the colonial institutions of her genteel family in Albany. Gil takes her to live in a cabin, not a frame house. There she learns to be self-sufficient, working in the fields and doing her own housework. Thus, when Sarah interviews Gil, she also inspects Lana's hands. Pleased with the calluses she finds, she hires them.

Like Gil and Lana, Sarah, too, embodies the regenerative impulse that underpins the American Character. Refusing to give up her home after her husband's death, she has had to reinvent herself, staying on her farm, tending her meadow, and caring for her livestock. Her natural social and moral sense of the world, however, is tempered by her classical martial virtue. Brought up on Army life, she tells Gil and Lana, "When I give out an order I expect it to be obeyed." The contributions made by Sarah to the Martins' Americanization are particularly important. Sarah, a feisty, forthright individual, provides a useful contrast while Lana develops into an American. Ford's comic touches perfectly illustrate the fundamental differences between the colonial mindset and the American psyche. When Lana arrives at Gil's cabin, she is at first appalled by its primitive condition and then terrified by Blue Black (Chief John Big Tree), an Indian neighbor who comes to visit. Hearing her panicked screaming, Gil has to rush from the barn and "rescue" his helpless wife from his good friend. Throughout the movie, Lana undergoes the difficult process of shedding her colonial mores for American principles. Having shed her colonial standards long ago, Sarah, unlike Lana, is able to take care of herself in the wilderness. The older woman is also startled in her home by Native Americans, but her response to the intruders could not have been more different. Disturbed from an afternoon nap by two tall, muscle-bound men, painted for war and intent on burning down her house, the elderly woman, instead of screaming and cowering, sits up in bed and snaps, "What do you want? What are you doing in here? Answer me! What do you mean coming in my house?"

Lacking Lana's passivity, Sarah reacts aggressively when threatened. When the Indians reply, "Burn house," she leaps out of bed at the men, shouting, "Don't you dare! You filthy, drunken, dirty rascals!" Chasing them around her bedroom, Sarah is too small to dissuade them from burning the house, but she does oblige them to carry her out of the room on her beloved bed: "I won't move a step without my bed. My husband bought me this bed when I was married," she tells them. In the meadow, Gil, seeing the smoke, rushes home and finds Sarah, abandoned by the Indians who could not make the bed fit through a door, sitting on it in the living room, watching the other pieces of her furniture burn. Luckily, Adam Hartman (Ward Bond) arrives to warn his neighbors that they will have to take refuge in the fort—another attack is on its way. He slings Sarah, in spite of her protests, over his shoulder and accomplishes what Gil, Lana, Daisy (Beulah Hall Jones), and the Indians were unable to do—he prevents the virtuous woman from allowing herself to be burned to death.

In *Drums along the Mohawk*, every American citizen, man and woman, serves in some capacity during the Revolution. When Gil and the other men march off to battle, Sarah, Lana, and the other women in the neighborhood work on the home front, caring for their farms until their husbands come home. When the soldiers return, Sarah's farm serves as a medical station and refuge for the wounded. As the Revolution continues, Lana becomes like Sarah. She needs only the basics of life and her family to be happy. When she and Gil again take refuge in the fort at German Flats, both display the virtue of self-sacrifice: Gil volunteers to leave the fort and bring back reinforcements, and when the war demands that Lana sacrifice her husband for the good of those awaiting rescue, she does so. Telling Lana that he must go for help, Gil asks, "Say that you're not afraid . . . that you want me to go." Lana's reply demonstrates how greatly she has changed during her marriage. She says, "I am not afraid. I want you to go." Transformed, Lana, taking Gil's musket, becomes a soldier herself. Wearing a militiaman's jacket, she becomes the front line of defense for the women and children huddling in the church—courageously shooting and killing a Mohawk warrior who breaks into the sanctuary.

When Gil returns to the fort to help rescue his wife, he finds that she and his son have survived. The final sequence of the movie reveals the Yeomen, having defeated the enemy, proceeding to reinvent themselves once again. As the fort and the community within it are repaired, Ford celebrates the birth of America. Bearing their new country's flag, which displays "thirteen stripes for the colonies and thirteen stars in a circle for the Union," a group of militiamen arrive with the news that

"Cornwallis surrendered to Washington at Yorktown last week." Uniting Church and State, the community fixes the flag to the church steeple. As "My Country 'Tis of Thee" accompanies the raising of the flag, Ford celebrates America's diversity. His egalitarian low-angle shots, which emphasize the presence and importance of a smiling Daisy, Sarah's black house servant, and Blue Black raising his hand to acknowledge and bless the Union, may seem incongruously modern, but, as Wood points out, thinking of others as their equals was a crucially important development of the enlightened eighteenth century. "Even those as aristocratic as William Byrd . . . and Francis Fauquier, a colonial governor of Virginia conceded that all men were born equal," he says, offering Byrd's observation that "the principal difference between one people and another proceeds only from differing opportunities of improvement" and Fauquier's 1760 declaration that "White, Red, or Black; polished or unpolished, Men are Men."[27]

Dressed in red, white, and blue, Lana, like the "pretty flag," not only symbolizes the country that the Yeomen have been fighting for but also stands for what Gordon S. Wood notes as the "domestication" of classical virtue in America[28]—expressing friendship and sympathy, the women's relationships with one another while their husbands were at war displayed the moral and social sense of the new republic. Illustrating the work ethic for which the American Character is famous, Gil takes his wife home, commenting, "I reckon we'd better be getting back to work. There'll be a heap to do from now on." In Ford's final analysis, the needlework on the final intertitle reminds his viewer that America, represented as a community of cabins, belongs to the Yeoman.

Unlike the British soldiers in *The Lost Patrol*, the American Yeomen in *Drums along the Mohawk* are all civilian volunteers whose virtues ensure the success of the American Revolution. As Ford demonstrates in these movies, republics demand far more morally from their citizens than do monarchies from their subjects.[29] In *The Lost Patrol*, each man's desire to do what was right in his own eyes was restrained by the institution that he served—by the professional standing Army to which he belonged. As a result, the "dubious" situation in which they found themselves at the beginning of their story did not change at its end. In contrast, Gil and Lana's willingness to take up arms to defend their country, and to sacrifice their personal desires for the sake of the public good, helped construct a society of equal and virtuous citizens. Built from the bottom up, a republic must consist of patriots. In *Drums along the Mohawk*, the martial nature of the frontier experience is an integral component of the American experience, underpinning what Robin Wood terms Ford's "dedication to the development of a civilization"[30] —in short, the United States.

In 1934, John Ford joined the U.S. Navy. "I don't think it was because he envisioned a war as much as he wanted to be in the Navy," Dan Ford mused. "It was almost natural that he would become a reserve naval officer. Ford had a certain expertise. He had the ability to make motion pictures and he also had access to studios, he had access to ins and outs, and he had access to the newsreel departments."[31] As the Second World War approached, Ford's overlapping professional and personal lives provided an outlet for his patriotism off screen.

In 1940, Ford's feelings about the war and his desire to participate in it went from strong to passionate when he learned that Merian Cooper had walked out on a $100,000-a-year vice presidency at RKO to help his old friend Claire Chennault organize the Flying Tigers, a quasi-mercenary band of pilots who flew for Chiang Kai-shek. Ford, who by this time was well connected in the Naval Reserve, began to develop his Naval Field Photographic Reserve. Operating without authorization, he recruited some of the most skilled professionals in Hollywood (among them cinematographers Gregg Toland and Joe August; soundman Sol Halprin; special effects man Ray Kellogg; editor Robert Parrish; and writers Garson Kanin and Budd Schulberg). He also recruited actor Jack Pennick, an ex-Marine, to teach them military discipline.[32] That summer, Ford's Field Photographic Unit, known as Field Photographic, developed the Cunningham Combat Camera, a lightweight 35-mm camera on a rifle stock. When Ford boarded the Union Pacific Streamliner and reported to Washington, D.C., in 1941, Field Photographic had been gathered up, not by the Navy, but by William J. "Wild Bill" Donovan, who had recently been appointed Coordinator of Information by President Roosevelt and given orders to create the Office of Strategic Services—the OSS. Accountable only to Donovan, and beyond that, to the president of the United States, Ford was well suited for the work required of him. As Robert Parrish notes, "For Ford, the O.S.S. was no different from Twentieth Century-Fox. You manipulated when you had to, and if you didn't get what you wanted through channels you simply went around them. He had no more respect for bureaucrats and professional military types than he had for producers or production managers back home."[33]

Ford's first assignments for the OSS after the Pearl Harbor attack involved filming a report on Iceland's viability as a hub for Allied landings and transports and preparing a study on the security of the Panama Canal. Field Photographic was then ordered to document the reconstruction of American forces that was taking place at Pearl Harbor. Ford gave Gregg Toland (his cinematographer on *The Grapes of Wrath*) and Samuel Engel, a Hollywood writer-producer, this task. Six weeks later, he visited Honolulu, where he received orders to film the Doolittle raid, one of the first secret missions of the war, aboard the aircraft carrier USS *Hornet*.[34] After Admiral Chester Nimitz called Ford in late May to tell him that several Field Photo cameramen would be needed to cover a dangerous assignment in the Pacific, Ford volunteered himself, packed a bag, and returned to Pearl Harbor, where a destroyer took him to the Midway atoll, a refueling stop for fliers that was located in the North Pacific about halfway between California and Tokyo.

5

IN THE NAVY

The Battle of Midway

I, John Ford, do hereby agree to offer the auxiliary yacht "Araner", of which I am the sole owner to the United States Government for the duration of the present National Emergency. [1]—John Ford

On May 25, 1942, Fleet Admiral Chester W. Nimitz asked Ford for photographic documentation of "a dangerous mission." [2] Ford, who had sent Gregg Toland and Sam Engel to Honolulu to work on *December 7th*, [3] answered the call himself and requested that a young Navy photographer, Jack MacKenzie Jr., accompany him. The two arrived "at Midway on May 28." [4] Once there, Ford was informed by his friend "Massie" Hughes, in command of the Midway Sand Island Seaplane Base, that the Japanese code had been broken and the attack was imminent.

On June 3, Ford flew reconnaissance with Hughes in an amphibious patrol bomber (known as PBYs). They met enemy planes 320 miles north of Midway and reported the position of the enemy ships that housed them. On their return, Cyril T. Simard, the commandant of the U.S. Naval Air Station, asked Ford to provide a detailed account of the bombing while he was photographing the attack. [5] The next day, Ford, situated on the roof of the Eastern Island powerhouse and acting as an observer, delivered a description of the battle by telephone while he and MacKenzie filmed the beginning of the attack. The first bomb was dropped by the Japanese at 06:30. Eight minutes into the battle, when the powerhouse was hit by a Japanese dive-bomber and badly damaged, Ford and MacKenzie "prudently" climbed down from their perch and continued to film the battle. Even under fire, Ford reminded his cameraman to "concentrate on filming *faces*."[6] MacKenzie ran to the airfield's control tower and then began filming images as he moved around the base, recording the island's aircraft hangars and hospital on fire while Ford continued to record the bombardment by the power plant. Working in the midst of the bombardment, Ford was knocked unconscious by flying concrete. Regaining consciousness, he continued filming even when hit by shrapnel.[7] By 06:55, all the Japanese planes had left the area. In all, the battle over Midway's islands lasted only twenty-five minutes.

On June 14, John Ford left Midway and stopped in Hawaii with eight cans of 16-mm Midway footage for Robert Parrish to edit in the United States. After speaking to Parrish, Ford returned to Los Angeles on June 16 with an arm "slightly bruised from elbow to wrist"[8] and three days later was proclaimed an "intrepid" war hero by Louella Parsons on the front page of the *L.A. Examiner*.[9] When the film was completed, Ford avoided the Navy censors by taking it directly to the White House and screening it for President Roosevelt, Eleanor Roosevelt, members of the Joint Chiefs of Staff, presidential press aide Stephen Early, and FDR's chief of staff, Admiral William Leahy.[10] The five hundred 35-mm prints of *The Battle of Midway*, screened in theaters two months after the Navy buried its dead, prompted strong audience reactions: "Parrish was astonished when people screamed and wept and had to be helped out of the theatre by ushers."[11]

Critical responses to *The Battle of Midway* have also been highly emotional. Tag Gallagher states that "the most significant fact of *The Battle of Midway* is that it is authentic, and Ford at every moment wishes to remind us of this." For Gallagher, "There is a unique sort of 'reality' here; there is a closer proximity to life than exists in Ford's fiction films. The confrontation is starker, more vivid, more deeply encountered. And it is personal."[12] Joseph McBride, also deeply affected, deems the film to be "an extraordinarily vivid and eloquent meditation on war, one of the rare pieces of propaganda that is also a timeless work of art."[13] Dismissing documentary film historian William T. Murphy's description of *The Battle of Midway* as "crude propaganda" that "substitutes moral and emotional feelings for information," offering "no broad perspective of the battle,"[14] McBride argues that Ford's purpose in making the eighteen-minute film was not to reveal military strategy or provide a comprehensive historical record but to remind the American public of the sacrifices necessary to preserve their way of life.[15] Agreeing with McBride, Andrew Sarris notes *The Battle of Midway* is only "ostensibly a documentary . . . [because Ford] focuses here on the ordinary scale by which the most gallant heroes are measured. It is not the battle itself that intrigues Ford, but the weary faces of rescued fliers plucked out of the Pacific after days of privation."[16]

MORE FICTION THAN FACT

Part propaganda, part poetry, *The Battle of Midway* is much more fiction than it is fact, convincing its viewers that it portrays real events when it does not. Ford invites this misconception when he opens the film with a title card that reads, "This is the actual photographic report of The Battle of Midway." The fact that the Battle of Midway did happen gives the film much of its emotional impact, yet a great deal of the action shown in *The Battle of Midway* happened before and after the battle itself took place.

Ford's skilled use of synthesis is apparent throughout the film. When one compares the "authentic scenes" of Ford's version of the Battle of Midway with the incidents that actually took place on and around the island of Midway in early June 1942, it is impossible not to notice the many carefully scripted, fictional elements and instances of sophisticated montage used to tell the film's story. Ford, however, begins by diverting attention from these elements via his introduction of a map of the world at the outset of the film to establish both its educational value and the authority of its narration. After viewing the map, the authenticity of the film's opening footage in the air and on the water of the island from Massie Hughes's patrol bomber is unquestionable—as is Irving Pichel's voice-over characterization of the atoll as viewers' "front yard." The perception of Midway as a piece of American real estate is furthered by the presence of a group of Marines, who, dressed as if on parade, march on the dock in formation behind their battalion flag. Adding to viewers' perception that they are watching a documentary, Ford introduces Midway's gooney birds as the natives of Midway.

If one believes the narrator, there seems to be little to do in this sleepy, tropical place except bird-watch. En route, Ford discovered that his destination was Midway and that "everything and everybody was on KV [a form of alert]." Regardless, however, he "proceeded to make a pictorial [film] history" of the island. "I photographed the Gooney Birds," he said. "I photographed the PT's and all that sort of thing. I didn't believe much in the impending action, if it did come I didn't think it was going to touch us. So I worked, spent about 12 hours a day in work, had a good time."[17]

In actuality, Midway was a hive of military activity at the time that Ford was shooting his footage. Since mid-May, the Marine Sixth Defense Battalion had been digging slit trenches and fortifying the beaches with miles of barbed wire. Informed well in advance of the arrival of the Japanese fleet, ground forces at Midway had been raised to maximum, according to the Combat Narratives of the Office of Naval Intelligence.[18] When Ford arrived in late May, the troops on the Midway atoll were finishing their preparations to repel a full-scale invasion:

> The islands were almost entirely surrounded by underwater obstacles with extra precautions at the more likely beaches. Gun crews were generously provided with Molotov cocktails (anti-tank grenades). A large number of water mines had been planted, as well as numerous antipersonnel and antitank mines of both the controlled and contact variety. . . . One PY boat was stationed at Pearl—Hermes and 4 YPs (converted tuna fishing boats) were stationed at Lisianski, Gardiner's Pinnacles, Laysan and Necker Islands to make rescues. Motor Torpedo Boat Squadron ONE consisting of 11 PT boats . . . was dispatched from the Hawaiian Sea Frontier Forces and placed under the direction of the Commanding Officer, Midway. . . . Finally 19 submarines were assigned to cover the approaches to Midway . . . six patrolled sectors of the 150-mile circle, three patrolled sectors of the 200-mile circle, and the remainder were assigned station patrol. All submarines were on station by June 3rd.[19]

Midway's airstrip and airspace were also stretched to their maximum capacities. Because of the threat of a dawn attack, "searching plans were sent out as early as possible each day—usually about 0415."[20] B-17s flew in from Hawaii and PBYs searched to distances of seven hundred miles looking for the Japanese fleet.[21] "On the third of June, the first day of actual contact with the enemy, there were at Midway, in addition to the planes of the Marine air group, the following: 14 PBY-5's, 16 PBY-5A's, 4 B-26's, 17 B-17's, 6 TBF's (with 2 PBY-5's and 1 B-17 out of commission)."[22]

At the beginning of Ford's *The Battle of Midway*, there is no evidence of the enormous military preparation that was taking place. There is nothing to suggest that an invasion is expected or that plans are being made to repel it. Instead, the pilot of a patrol bomber returning from a routine patrol is greeted by the plane's ground crew in their bathing suits. Then, shifting away from this lightheartedness, the film foreshadows the violence of the battle to come. Even the gooney birds "seem nervous[;] there is something in the air." Cutting to staged shots of backlit and silhouetted figures of men watching the sun set while an American flag moves in the gentle wind, Ford evokes the American Character by inserting an accordion player picking out the tune of "The Red River Valley" to underpin a sequence of staged shots featuring soldiers scanning the skies. Drawing on his experience depicting Americana at Fox, Ford's treatment is at once subtle and sophisticated. The viewer is assured that America, even in the South Pacific, remains God's country. This message is transmitted in the unmistakeable vocabulary of the storm clouds and florid sunset that grace the sky and is reflected in the calm ocean. The scene conveys an inspiring and convincing message akin to that encoded in the landscapes of the Hudson River School. The sublime cloud formations at the end of the sequence transform the South Pacific into an idiom of glory and power that expresses the greatness of America. Ford's final dramatic shot of huge bands of light shining through clouds that are so red, they appear to be shot through with blood, makes it apparent that war is coming.

Ford's depiction of the activity on the Midway atoll the following morning, on the other hand, is grounded in purely practical matters. The sequence appears to be documenting preparations for war, but close examination of the footage reveals that there is an enormous amount of slippage between the voice-over narration and images on the screen. The viewer is told there is "excitement . . . the dawn patrol has sighted an enemy fleet," but the aerial shots of the island reveal no fleet and are taken with the sun high—not at dawn. A council of war is held, and as Jane Darwell's voice comments on how similar the crewmen look to people she knows at home, it becomes apparent that Ford is inserting shots of B-17s about to take off on patrols to look for the Japanese fleet before June 3. In the background, B-17s are parked and being serviced along the runway. While planes lumber into their take-offs, Ford cheats on the actual number departing: No. 12437 takes off four times.

After the last B-17 leaves, the narrator's voice shouts, "Suddenly, from behind the clouds, the Japs attack!" as Ford cuts to a shot of five planes flying into view. The only clouds visible are found miles away on the horizon, but the fast pace of the editing that follows leaves the viewer little time to recognize the unsuitability of the narrator's comment. The Americans' experience of Japanese "perfidy" at Pearl Harbor amplifies the believability of the event: for American audiences in theatres in 1942, history is attempting to repeat itself at Midway. This time, however, the American forces are ready for them. Slippage between the narrator and the footage is once again evident as an anti-aircraft gun responds immediately to the enemy threat, tracking a single plane that evades the exploding flak. This footage, however, could not have been shot at the actual moment of the first attack. Ford and MacKenzie were located on top of the powerhouse, and the anti-aircraft battery in question was nowhere near them. Instead, the gun was located on a white sand beach a stone's throw from the water. More slippage occurs as Ford cuts to footage of SB2U-3s taking off that was shot on June 1.

Ford himself was well aware that his account of the Japanese attack was much more a matter of fiction than fact. As he recollects, the American planes "had all pulled off early in the morning. . . . [The Japanese] planes were picked up coming in the radar . . . and so we had about, I think, nearly a half-hour's warning. Of course, the Marines took off about 20 minutes before [Japanese] planes arrived and as a matter of fact, as we know, they attacked the first five planes coming in and did a hell of a good job. So there was nothing on the ground for them [the Japanese attackers] to hit."[23]

According to the *Combat Narratives of the Office of Naval Intelligence*, on June 3, by 04:30, all planes that were "fit for service were in the air."[24] The *Executive Officer's Report of the Battle of Midway*, marked confidential, notes that Midway's air raid siren did not sound until 05:55 and that the first bombs were dropped on Eastern Island where Ford was located at 06:35.[25] Although there were no American bombers on the ground, Ford shows fliers responding immediately to the incoming Japanese planes. "There go the Marines!" the voice-over announces, as several Devastators, considered obsolete in 1942, lift off from a runway—on which one sees B-17s parked. Ford's handheld camera, located beneath the propellers of a B-17, pans to follow the Devastators as they leave the ground, and for a split second, MacKenzie and his camera can also be seen. Ford cuts in MacKenzie's shot of the same planes leaving, thereby doubling American "response" to the Japanese.

The powerhouse on which Ford and MacKenzie were stationed was hit by a bomb and lost electricity at 06:38, and by 6:41, all the telephone lines except Aviation Radar and Aviation Radio were out. Between 06:35 and 07:10, fourteen bombs were dropped on Eastern Island by enemy bombers. During this time, two pilots, White and Armistead, landed with damaged aircraft, and Japanese fighters strafed gun positions and attempted to shoot down crippled fighters circling the field. At 07:20, the radar screen showed no near targets and the enemy retiring, so all fighters were directed to "land and reservice."[26]

Ford's exciting version of the battle is not a chronological narrative. Instead, spectacular shots of debris from the roof of the powerhouse as it is blown to bits, fighter planes screaming overhead, and Japanese Navy dive-bombers dropping their bombs are introduced amid short clips of burning hangars, men running through piles of smoking debris, and billowing, smoky clouds from fires rolling across the beaches. As the Marines run the Stars and Stripes up the flagpole, the tattered ends of the flag unfolded by the men signal that the viewer is witnessing the re-creation of the event, not the event itself.

After the flag has been raised, the intent faces of anti-aircraft gunners and medics, supported by the droning of planes passing overhead, convey that the battle continues to rage, despite the fact that there are no formations of Japanese bombers visible in the sky. Instead, the viewer is presented with images of the aftermath of the action, in which the skies are empty. A short shot of a plane crashing, and an even shorter (and highly improbable) aerial shot of a Zero cutting across the top left-hand corner of the screen, are cut in to suggest that the battle continues. The images of what appears to be a burning fuel dump, buildings and hangars smashed and in flames, and the huge clouds of smoke billowing upward behind them seem to have been shot during the inspection of Midway's facilities after the battle. At this time, it was revealed that the powerhouse had been "decimated"—that "gas lines from the main gasoline stowage were broken," that "there were bomb hits in the vicinity of Sick Bay and VMSB Engineering Tents," and that the Eastern Island C.P., mess-hall, and PX had been destroyed."[27] "Six (6) enlisted [men] had been killed, with approximately twenty (20) enlisted [men suffering] minor cuts and bruises."[28]

PARALLELS AND PROPAGANDA

As the symbol of the rising sun burns on the mutilated wing of the wreckage of a Japanese Zero, the film's narrator announces: "Meantime, our warships stalked the Jap fleet." Ford's treatment of the naval battle that took place 150 miles northeast of the Midway atoll carefully parallels his presentation of the attack on Midway Island. Again, the element of surprise is emphasized at the beginning of the attack. This time, however, the American fleet has turned the tables on the Japanese. "Suddenly the trap is sprung," the narrator exclaims. "Navy planes roared from the decks of our carriers . . . Navy bombers . . . Marines . . . tons of destruction over a 300-mile battle area." Shots of fighters and torpedo bombers leaving the deck of what is generally assumed to be the morning of June 3 on the USS *Hornet* are used to represent these aircraft carriers launching their planes into the air. As McBride notes, "Most of the footage of air and sea combat in Ford's documentary was shot by US Navy Lieutenant Kenneth M. Pier, who flew on planes off the *Hornet*, 'with a little 16mm camera you could carry in your coat pocket—and did he do a swell job!' said MacKenzie. 'His film had a lot to do with the success of the picture that was released to the public.'"[29]

The departures of the planes, however, strike a false note. Edited out of sequence, first a Wildcat, then a Devastator, a dive-bomber, and then a final Wildcat fly off to battle. In reality, the Navy airmen would have had to leave squadron by squadron, not plane by plane—the Wildcats left the *Hornet* first, they were then joined by the dive-bombers, and then finally by the Devastators. On the morning of June 3, the *Hornet* was not under attack by enemy aircraft. As it launched its planes, the aircraft carrier was stationed 150 miles northeast of the Midway atoll, within striking distance of the Japanese fleet by air but not by sea. Nevertheless, in *The Battle of Midway*, the carrier's gun crews begin to load and shoot their weapons. Shortly after, enemy aircraft are shot out of the sky. Here, the pace of Ford's editing increases dramatically, matching the speed of the cuts during the battle that took place on Midway.

The startling contrasts between the color and nature of the clouds and seas in these shots suggest that some of the footage used in this sequence was recorded during gunnery practice, not during combat. One man is found lying down, relaxing on the flight deck, as the guns blast away. In another shot, officers mug for the camera while the aircraft carrier's guns are engaged—no enemy planes are evident in the sky. A sailor, watching the guns work, stands with his back to the camera. Leaning nonchalantly against a railing with his relaxed hand behind him holding a rag, this sailor is disinterested in what should be a matter of life and death. A shot of a Zero flying overhead and framed by the wires of the carrier's rigging is recognizably the same shot that was used in the earlier attack sequence on Midway Island. Ford's skillful presentation of the naval battle captures the tempo and disjointed nature of combat, but the film narrative made from these snapshots does not document the military action that actually took place.

An even more fantastic presentation concludes the film. On June 3, the *Hornet*'s airmen did not launch a single successful torpedo attack against the Japanese Fleet and the *Hornet* had no visual contact with the enemy. Nonetheless, *The Battle of Midway*'s narrative voice-over insists that "the invasion forces were hit and hit and hit again," and Ford offers his viewers shots of burning ships as evidence of the superiority of the American Navy. "Men and women of America—here come your neighbors' sons home from the day's work," the narrator announces. Pilots are seen emerging from their planes as the soundtrack plays "Onward, Christian Soldiers."[30] However, the Wildcats from which the men emerge could have not been in combat. They are not riddled with bullets or flak. Indeed, after their day's "work" at war, not a single plane was missing. In reality, most of the Wildcats launched from the *Hornet* did not return to the carrier. Their pilots, finding themselves without enough fuel to return home, either ditched in the Pacific and waited days for rescue or limped to a runway on the atoll to be reserviced and refueled.

Shots of E. Scott McCuskey and Jimmy Thach, both flying aces, posing in a plane with "seven meatballs" on its side are particularly instructive. Never assigned to the USS *Hornet*, McCuskey flew from the USS *Yorktown* (CV-5), while Thach and Fighting Squadron Three flew from the USS *Lexington* (CV-2) during the early stages of the war, before being assigned to the *Yorktown* during the Battle of Midway. Ford's next shot showcases another pilot, who coincidentally also has "seven meatballs" on a plane that is parked (remarkably) in the same spot as McCuskey's and Thach's. In this shot, the flier is already standing and about to step out of the cockpit when Henry Fonda's voice asks, "How many more today, Skipper?" In response to Fonda's question, he modestly holds up four fingers. After several more shots of pilots leaving their planes, the same man climbs out of a different Wildcat, one sporting only "six meatballs" and leans against its wing.

Once again Ford changes the tone of the narrative. Leaving behind the flight deck with its staged presentations of the ebullient, returning heroes, the film returns to the cleanup work being done on Midway Island in the aftermath of the attack there. Over shots of burning hangars, the debris of crashed fighters, a horribly twisted propeller, and the gentle, curious gooney birds, the camera ironically juxtaposes peaceful natural images with the violence of war. "Tojo swore that he would liberate the natives," narrator Henry Fonda comments on the presence of gooney birds amid the wreckage. "They're just as free as they ever were."

The film's burial scenes provide a resolution typical of Ford's narrative films. Also used in many of his Westerns, the burial scene demonstrates group solidarity and the continuity of past and future. It emphasizes renewed commitment to the cause, as well as solemn tribute to those whose new "home" will be their grave on the frontier—be that frontier in a fictional West or on a real Midway Island. Vincent Casaregola notes that the burial also represents ties to a home left behind and to the social rituals that shape people's lives.[31] In *The Battle of Midway*, Ford's presentation of the burial at sea of "our heroic dead" serves not only to remind the viewer of the soldiers' ties to home but also to connect viewers with the rituals of the war effort, including them in the military's rituals of mourning and the renewal of identity that such rituals evoke.

The Island of Midway was not just a battlefront located in the Pacific Ocean; it was also the home front of every American who was watching this movie in 1942. Because the Battle of Midway was fought on American soil, the film suggests, every person in America had a stake in its outcome. Having won the battle, however, did not mean that the war was over. Now that "our Front Yard is safe," the narrator's voice-over reminds the viewer, "there is still the big job to be done."

In part, this job involved locating and rescuing the airmen who had gone missing in action. Ford's careful chronicling of the Navy's search for survivors—"for men who flew to the last round of ammunition and to the last drop of gas and then crashed into the sea"—serves to further create a common community for the viewer, by uniting the men who care for their lost companions at the front with the anxious families waiting for confirmation that their loved ones had been found alive. The narrative voice-over proclaims that eleven days later, men are still being found and, with the help of Henry Fonda's voice-over, applauds the efforts of the men rescuing the downed fliers: "Well done, Massie Hughes . . . Logan Ramsey . . . Frank Vesser," the narrative voice-over intones while Fonda joins in with the comment, "That's thirteen for Frank!"

As Dan Ford points out, Ford and MacKenzie spent days on Midway after the battle, photographing the aftermath.[32] Documenting the "memorial service beside a bomb crater; a line of PT boats going out through iridescent blue water carrying the flag-draped coffins of the navy's dead . . . the President's son, Marine Corps Major Jimmy Roosevelt, who had served at Midway, [and the survivors] paying homage to the Marine dead."[33] Ford collected the materials he needed to complete *The Battle of Midway*, then he quietly returned back to Pearl Harbor with his film.

Back at Pearl Harbor, the fortunes of war smiled on John Ford, in the form of Marc Mitscher, the captain of the USS *Hornet*. Interested in the possibilities that photographs and film could offer the Navy, Mitscher had ordered all of his pilots and virtually every flight operation on board the aircraft carrier to be photographed or filmed. Mitscher talked with Ford and, as a result of their conversation, supplied him with the footage taken on board the *Hornet* for use in *The Battle of Midway*.

When Ford delivered eight cans of the Midway footage to Robert Parrish in Honolulu, he ordered Parrish to cut the film in Hollywood and not in Hawaii. In light of new information about the Battle of Midway that has recently been released, the materials in Parrish's possession were red hot. Ford advised Parrish that "as soon as it's discovered in Honolulu that I've smuggled the film past the Navy censors they'll come snooping around with enough brass to take it away from us."[34]

The "top-secret" nature of the materials that Ford had spirited away from Navy censors was even hotter than his instructions to Parrish first indicated. America's first victory over the Japanese had been incredible. Outgunned and outmanned, American forces at Midway had beaten the odds and turned the tide of the Second World War in the Pacific. The aftermath of the battle was deemed by the Navy to be a time for celebration, not for the revelation of a number of ugly truths that were circulating among the men who had flown and fought at Midway. Prior to speaking with Ford, Marc Mitscher had just filed a sanitized and highly irregular account of his aircraft carrier's performance during the Battle of Midway with Admiral Raymond Spruance of the *Enterprise* (CV-6) to endorse and forward to Fleet Admiral Nimitz. This report was so unreliable that Spruance took the extraordinary step of noting on the endorsement page that there were "a number of inaccuracies."[35] In his own after-action report, Spruance noted that the data presented by the *Enterprise* (CV-6) was the more "reliable" of the two carriers. "Where discrepancies exist between *Enterprise* and *Hornet* reports," Spruance wrote, "the *Enterprise* should be taken as more accurate."[36]

Mitscher's document, which is the *Hornet*'s only written account of the actions taken by the crew, lessened the responsibility that he held for the dismal performance of the *Hornet* Air Group on June 4. That day, almost everything that could have gone wrong, did, for the *Hornet*'s Air Group—escorting fighters were ordered to give no protection to Waldron's Devastators, which were decimated to a man by the enemy's fighters; they were directed away from the Japanese fleet; the Wildcats and dive-bombers got lost and ran out of fuel without ever firing their guns; and the *Hornet*'s commander, Stanhope C. Ring, had lost all control over his Air Group, as his men finally broke formation and attempted to return to the carrier. Grossly incompetent, Mitscher's performance at the Battle of Midway was so dismal that it should have ruined his career.

We will never know the subjects of Mitscher and Ford's conversations when the two men spoke, or what their agreement in Honolulu amounted to, but it is safe to assume that Navy scuttlebutt would have been circulating in Honolulu about the events that occurred on board the *Hornet* on June 4. Ford's instructions to Parrish to work in Hollywood and stay at his mother's home effectively removed his editor from contact with stories such as these that would have been circulating at the time. Even so, Parrish objected to the corniness of the commentary read by Fox actors Henry Fonda, Donald Crisp, and Irving Pichel, and especially "the emotional voice of the typical American mother represented by Jane Darwell."[37]

In the meantime, feelings in the Services continued to run high about the Battle of Midway. Arguments between Army and Navy pilots as to which had contributed more to the victory erupted, and fights broke out all over the Royal Hawaiian Hotel. The sole survivor of Torpedo Squadron Eight, Tex Gay, whose story was featured in *Life Magazine*, was sent to the United States to boost the Navy's version of the Battle of Midway. With this in mind, it is not surprising that Ford had Parrish actually measure the footage allotted to each service in *The Battle of Midway*, to ensure that each was given equal on screen—or that at the last minute he ordered a five-foot close-up of James Roosevelt saluting to be included in the film.

A celebration of the American Character that revises the events of June 4, 1942, *The Battle of Midway* was never screened by the military censors. Ford and William Donovan instead screened the film to President Roosevelt, who, deeply affected by the appearance of his son in the funeral sequence, wanted "every mother in America to see this picture."[38] When *The Battle of Midway* was released, the legend became fact.

It was only after *The Battle of Midway* was completed that Ford had Parrish show the film to Gregg Toland and Sam Engel, who were still working on their original version of *December 7th* (1943). McBride reports that, when viewing Ford's elegiac sequence of the burial at sea to the accompaniment of "My Country 'Tis of Thee," Engel actually jumped out of his chair, shouting, "The sonofabitch stole our scenes! That's exactly what we have in our picture, the stuff we told him about in Pearl Harbor!" As Parrish, Toland, and Engel walked out of the projection room, Engel was beside himself. "Don't you see what's happened?" he exclaimed. "The bastard sabotaged our picture! Everything we've been working on for six months!" Toland and Engel did not insert a burial at sea sequence into either the long or shortened versions of *December 7th*. The unedited footage that they had shot for such a sequence, however, is available at the National Archives. When Parrish informed Ford about Engel's outburst, Ford admitted, "Maybe he's right."[39]

Ford's elegiac sequence during the burial at sea in *The Battle of Midway* also borrows heavily from the visual rhetoric of the Hudson River School. Like his earlier treatment of the bloody sunset foreshadowing the action that will erupt on Midway's Sand Island, this sequence draws the viewer's attention to the presence of the divine. As the PT boats and their solemn crews carry the flag-draped bodies of the dead to their final resting place, verse four of "My Country 'Tis of Thee" is sung: "Our father's God to Thee, / Author of liberty, / To Thee we sing." As the choir sings, "Long may our land be bright, / With Freedom's holy light, / Protect us by Thy might, / Great God our King," Ford's camera pans upward to heaven and rests on the large, puffy cumulus clouds riding in the brilliant blue of the tropical sky—an inspiring visual message that affirms the rightness of the dead men's sacrifice. The camera leads the viewer's eye upward into the heavens before panning back down to a wide shot of Midway Island and then cutting to a stunning shot of white birds and B-17-s circling above the ruined runway as a Marine, using binoculars, scans the sky above while black smoke from a burning oil dump billows past his knee. Ford's compelling use of visuals forms an effective argument: that the human sacrifice that took place during the Battle of Midway has resulted in liberty and the maintenance of American values.

The Battle of Midway's emotive ending is very different than its beginning, in which the opening intertitles declare the film to be "the actual photographic report of the Battle of Midway." The viewer is reassured that "the following authentic scenes were made by Navy photographers." Even though Ford's final shot replaces reason with emotion, *The Battle of Midway* continues to be regarded as a documentary, its footage is deemed to be actual footage of the battle, and the film itself has been advertised on amazon.com as "an historic event not to be missed."

TORPEDO SQUADRON 8

Torpedo Squadron 8 (1942), another moving elegy about the action at Midway made by Ford, has rarely been screened in public. McBride points out that "the decisions to keep the film private and not incorporate the footage into *The Battle of Midway* probably stemmed from fear of a negative effect on the morale of the American public."[40] Keeping the news private about the ill-fated squadron of torpedo bombers from the USS *Hornet* was another story. The Navy public relations office sought out and recruited Tex Gay, the only survivor of the debacle, to take part in an extensive public relations campaign regarding the action in the Pacific theater. Informing the American public of the resounding victory at Midway, Gay traveled to the United States. His face and story appeared in almost every newspaper in the country. One headline read, "Ensign Gay Sole Survivor of Torpedo Squadron Eight at Midway."[41] A celebrity, Gay was "called upon to make speeches at business conventions . . . invited to appear on Nelson Eddy's radio program . . . [and] received a musical tribute from big band orchestra leader Kay Kyser."[42] "Placed on the invitation lists of celebrities," he began to meet "movie stars. He began to receive fan mail and even marriage proposals. Twentieth Century-Fox wanted to make a movie of his life."[43]

If the story of Torpedo Squadron Eight elicited such an overwhelmingly positive response from the American public, why did Donovan assign John Ford the project of making a short film created out of 16-mm color footage taken of the members of the squadron before they took off on their suicide mission? Why was this movie made only for private distribution to the families of the airmen? And why did Ford have Joe August and other messengers personally deliver 8-mm copies of the elegiac eight-minute film to the families? Unlike *The Battle of Midway*, *Torpedo Squadron 8* does not attempt to write an "official" history of the airmen's engagement with the Japanese fleet. Instead, the film awards the young men the status of secular saints.

Torpedo Squadron 8 has great poignancy, and in part, that poignancy rests on dramatic tension produced by the knowledge that the young men posing for the camera did not return from what McBride accurately terms "their suicidal mission."[44] Breaking radio silence shortly after their take-off, Squadron Leader John Waldron led his men without air cover to the Japanese fleet while Squadron Commander Ring continued to fly west, away from the enemy, with the Air Group's Wildcats and dive-bombers. Every plane of Torpedo Squadron Eight came within sight of its target but was shot down in short order during the squadron's bombing run. Not one of the squadron's torpedoes hit an enemy ship. Ensign Tex Gay survived his plane crashing into the ocean by clinging to a floating seat cushion from his submerged aircraft.

Like *The Battle of Midway*, *Torpedo Squadron 8* begins with an edifying intertitle eulogizing the fallen airmen:

> On June 4, 1942, near Midway Island in the pacific, many naval aviators and flight crews gave their lives to unflinchingly pursue and destroy a powerful Japanese invasion force of superior aircraft carrier strength.
>
> These men of Torpedo Squadron Eight are gone.
>
> The memory of their courage and determination will forever be an ideal for Navy flying men to follow. These men, pilots, and flight crews, of the squadrons who participated in this action, have written the most brilliant pages in the glowing history of our naval air forces.

As this intertitle announces, the value of the sacrifices made by the men of Torpedo Squadron Eight lies in their ability to inspire others to acts of heroism. Unlike *The Battle of Midway*, which depends heavily upon fast-paced editing and the visual rhetoric of its combat sequences for effect, *Torpedo Squadron 8* proceeds at a leisurely pace, encouraging the viewer to meditate on the nature of the airmen's self-sacrifice. After beginning the film with a wide shot of a squadron of planes warming up on the flight deck, Ford introduces two group photos of the men of Torpedo Squadron Eight, suggesting that the aircrews are waiting to leave on their mission. Each shot lasts approximately ten seconds and gives the viewer ample to recognize the individuals. Strains of "Anchors Aweigh," the fight song of the U.S. Naval Academy, increase the impression that the men of the squadron, lined up like a sports team, with the pilots standing behind their kneeling crewmen, are eager and spoiling for action.

At this point, however, the music fades, and the viewer is left with only the roar of the engines, as Ford cuts to two men working together to hand-crank a plane to get it started. The game now being played is that of war. Having established the nature of the squadron and its cheerful camaraderie, Ford's montage turns to the implementation of the men's training, aligning the tactical with the practical, via a sequence during which Devastators roll down the flight deck toward the camera to take off. The final shot of the planes accelerating to leave the carrier is pure movie magic, since Waldron's Devastators were the last planes to leave the *Hornet* on the morning of June 4. To complete the image of the squadron leaving the aircraft carrier behind forever, Ford inserts a reverse-angle shot of a Dauntless dive-bomber leaving the flight deck away from the camera. The plane dips below the edge of the deck as it quits the carrier and hangs uncertainly in the air for a moment before beginning to gain altitude and joining its fellows.

Begun as a eulogy in praise of the dead, *Torpedo Squadron 8* becomes an elegy in which Ford laments their loss. Throughout this sequence, there is no voice-over narrating the action. Instead, the viewer's sense of loss and anxiety is increased by the sound of aircraft engines announcing the planes' take-offs. After the Dauntless lumbers off the flight deck, the engines continue to drone, and an intertitle bearing the Navy Cross, which was awarded to every man in the squadron, appears. Beneath the medal the words "In Memoriam" signal the finality of the airmen's absence. After this intertitle fades to black, Ford begins introducing the airmen, crew by crew.

The sequencing of these introductions is established by the first seven-second intertitle, which fades up from black and simply bears the names Lt. Commander John Charles Waldron and his Chief Radioman Horace Franklin Dobbs, on a memorial topped with air-force wings. Ford then cuts to footage of Waldron and Dobbs standing comfortably together by the starboard wing of a Devastator. During this nine-second shot, as the men smile and chat with one another, requiem bells, joining the sound of the engines, begin to toll. Ford does not allow the viewers to hear the men's voices. This distancing of the viewer from the airmen has the effect of emphasizing the distance between the living and the dead.

Creating an honor roll of the fallen, Ford repeats the sequence of a memorial intertitle and footage for each aircrew. As the second sequence begins, the music of "Anchors Aweigh" returns to score the sequences, replacing the sound of aircraft engines. During the presentation of the memorials, the structure of the scenes remains the same. The footage, however, recalling happier times, changes: the airmen are shown alternately kneeling under the wing or in front of the plane, sitting on the starboard wing, holding the plane's propeller, and in some cases even drawing a face on the torpedo itself. As the honor roll continues, the face on the torpedo changes until it is rendered complete.

Acting as a counterpoint to the visual conventions of the documentary, Ford's scoring of *Torpedo Squadron 8* offers its viewers commentary that takes the place of a narrative voice-over. When the fourth aircrew, Lt. Raymond A. Moore and Tom Hartsel Pettrey, Airman 1st Class, is introduced, the upbeat treatment of the tune of "Anchors Aweigh" changes. The music slows noticeably and at times changes from a major to a minor key, introducing a somber, darker, and disturbing mood as the young men continue to smile and mug for the camera. Expressing grief, the score mourns the passing of the men. At times, the rhythm hesitates and the tone deepens, as a heavy brass component introduces minor notes into the melody. The conflicts that these fluctuations in tone and meter create in the harmony and rhythm of the film suggest to its viewer the terrible conflict that is about to be experienced by the young men showcased before the aircraft. Periodically, phrases of "Anchors Aweigh" are heard, acting as a wordless, nostalgic refrain.

Five minutes into the film, the score turns from its expression of grief to elegiac consolation. "Onward, Christian Soldiers" takes the place of what has remained of "Anchors Aweigh," transcending the discord, gently swelling, and finally supporting Ford's cutting of intertitles and footage. Fifty-nine seconds later, a women's choir begins to sing "Onward, Christian Soldiers," slowing the tempo. The hymn finishes before the final two intertitles are shown without footage of the men being named. Instead, each of these intertitles is introduced by the peal of the church bell. In the silence that follows, Ford offers his viewers a requiem for the repose of the airmen, reassuring the viewer that the dead have been properly cared for—a black-robed minister conducts a funeral service that ends honoring the dead with the volleys of a seven-gun salute on board the aircraft carrier. Following the squadron's graveside military honors, the final intertitle of the film awards the men the Distinguished Flying Cross, framed against a background of white cumulus clouds on a brilliant blue sky. Beneath this award of valor lies a line from the Gettysburg Address presented in the same shade of white as the clouds above it: "That we here highly resolve that these dead shall not have died in vain."

Ford returns to the visual style of the Hudson River School to intensify the meaningfulness of the airmen's sacrifice and heighten his viewer's response. He introduces the presence of the divine by cutting to an inspiring seascape in which a convoy of ships is located on the horizon, with one silhouetted ship overshadowed by a gigantic cloud formation. Cutting to a shot of a similar ship at sea, later in the evening, *Torpedo Squadron 8* acknowledges the gathering darkness created by the loss of the squadron, but as the women's choir continues to sing, the silhouette of a seabird floats across the gloom off the screen, suggesting the flight of a soul. The viewer's eye, following the bird, is attracted to a break in the clouds that allows a small amount of light through and affords a glimpse of the heaven lying behind them.

As the choir continues its chorus, the final shots of the film complete the argument begun in the first intertitle. Ford cuts directly to a startlingly bright shot, as white clouds act as a backdrop for a plane that is attempting to flying upward at a ninety-degree angle. Before the plane reaches the top of the screen, Ford cuts back to the same shot. Starting from the same place, this time the pilot transcends his own earthly limitations. The tiny aircraft streaks upward and exits the screen.

Torpedo Squadron 8 not only mourns the loss of the individuals on screen, it also consoles the viewer and celebrates the squadron's sacrifice. In doing so, this film expresses many of the puzzling dynamics about the military that are evident in Ford's movies after the Second World War, and which Ford seems to have been unable to resolve in his films. Of these, the need for Americans to remember and honor their dead becomes an insistent theme.

DECEMBER 7TH

December 7th (1943) also lays the groundwork for Ford's later preoccupation with the dead. Bearing the working title *The Story of Pearl Harbor: An Epic in American History*, work began on *December 7th* almost as soon as the attack on Pearl Harbor had ended. Donovan biographer Anthony Cave Brown asserts that "the root cause of the intelligence failure that produced the Pearl Harbor disaster" was that "the Army and the Navy had ignored the presidential order that Donovan was to see all intelligence having a bearing on national security."

December 7th can be seen, in part, as Donovan's vehicle to strike back at Army and Navy intelligence for failing to keep him in the loop.[45] Ford's cinematographer Gregg Toland, who proved to have little respect for military protocol, was assigned to direct the film with Samuel G. Engel serving as writer-producer.

Instead of being a short newsreel-like documentary, *December 7th* morphed into a sprawling, feature-length docudrama. Ford flew to Honolulu on January 24, 1942, and discovered them planning to combine actual footage of the attack that had been filmed by C .P. Daugherty of the Fleet Camera Party stationed aboard the USS *Argonne* and Lt. Commander Edward Young of the USS *Mugford* with a range of re-creations, miniatures of American ships and Japanese bombers, scenes that depicted prewar life in Hawaii, and dramatized scenes illustrating America's reluctance to go to war. The project bore little resemblance to what Donovan wanted—a brief documentary about "what had happened at Pearl Harbor and who was to blame."[46]

Before leaving Pearl Harbor to document Doolittle's B-25 bombers leaving to bomb Japan, Ford shot footage of the salvage operation to save damaged ships, one of which was still burning, and directed some of the reenactments of the attacks. Returning from the *Hornet*, he continued to help Toland and Engel before being ordered to Midway late in May. Toland and Engel continued to annoy military brass and work on the project in Honolulu after Ford's departure. Subsequently, more scenes for *December 7th* were also shot at Fox and filmed at the Los Angeles National Cemetery. Becoming the most controversial of the films shot by Field Photographic, Toland and Engel's *December 7th* xenophobically attributes much of Japan's success to spying on the part of Hawaii's Japanese Americans and argues for eighty-three minutes that the United States had been unprepared and caught sleeping during the surprise attack at Pearl Harbor.

In general, the Navy was not impressed. In particular, Admiral Harold R. Stark, who had been the chief of naval operations at the time of the Pearl Harbor attack, complained that *December 7th* would damage the war effort by giving "the distinct impression that the Navy was not on the job, and this is not true. . . . I am not concerned with minor inaccuracies, but great harm will be done and sleeping dogs awakened if the picture is released as it now stands, leaving the impression that the Navy was asleep."[47]

Ordered shelved, the long version of *December 7th* was radically revised by Robert Parrish, Budd Shulberg, and James McGuinness into two much shorter versions, one of which was shown to servicemen and went on to win an Academy Award, while the other was shown to factory workers as part of the Navy's Industrial Incentive Program to boost the war effort on the home front in 1943. Introduced by statements from the War Department and the Secretary of the Navy, the thirty-four-minute version of *December 7th* immediately establishes that the film is presenting "factually the conditions existing in Hawaii prior to December 7th, the story of the Japanese attack there on December 7th, and the present conditions in Hawaii as they pertain to preparations for future action." In short, *December 7th* is "a complete motion picture factual presentation." Very little of *December 7th*, however, can be considered a documentary. From its staged reenactments of sailors and airmen rushing to the defense of the harbor, to a shot that transforms a dragon's head found on a Shinto temple in Honolulu into an image of Tojo crowing over the American defeat, much of the film is what McBride terms "fakery."[48]

Ford's appeals to his viewer's sentiments reveal observations about the fallen similar to those that appear in *The Battle of Midway* and *Torpedo Squadron 8*. The film's narrative voice-over directs the viewer's reaction to shots of the wounded being bandaged and carried to hospitals as "sorrow, yes, bitter, grievous, mortifying sorrow, for on this Sabbath day 2,343 officers, and enlisted men of our Army, Navy, and Marine Corps gave their young lives in the service of our country." Introducing the viewer to representatives of the fallen, *December 7th*, like *Torpedo Squadron 8*, edifies and eulogizes the dead, but in this sequence, the dead speak simply about themselves, while the images of their bereaved parents and a child born after his father's death create gut-wrenching emotional impact.

December 7th's understated, factual treatment of the voice-overs is particularly effective. Robert L. Kelly speaks first, over a close-up of his portrait. He announces himself to be a member of the "United States Army," establishes his hometown, and then introduces his parents sitting in their living room. The viewer is then introduced to five other service members whose short speeches parallel Kelly's. As Gallagher notes, the "*same* voice continues throughout the presentations of six more dead soldiers in this sequence, each representing different services, different regions, and different origins."[49] When the narrative voice-over notes this incongruity and asks, "How does it happen that you all sound and talk alike?" the reply is "We are all alike. We are all Americans." Like the dead, the viewer too is an "American" and so participates in an identity that transcends his or her individuality.

After the Battle of Midway, Marc Mitscher was relieved of command of the *Hornet* and served on shore until being given command of Carrier Division Three in 1944. Stanhope Ring, awarded the Navy Cross for his actions on June 5, 1942, during attacks on the Japanese cruiser *Mikuma*, served as Mitscher's operation officer during this period. Eventually, both men moved up the Navy's chain of command. In the end, Mitscher became commander-in-chief of the U.S. Atlantic Fleet with the rank of admiral, and Ring was promoted to vice admiral on his retirement. While Mitscher and Ring served on shore, Ford continued to be active in the field. After screening *The Battle of Midway* at the White House, he was flown to London to organize Field Photo crews to cover the invasion of North Africa under the auspices of his old production head, Darryl Zanuck. Operation Torch began on November 8, 1942, and Ford's camera crews covered all three of the operation's landings. Ford himself landed on the Tunisian coast later in November and spent several days filming with Zanuck before the two men separated. Zanuck left the front, but Ford continued on, spending six weeks in the field. He returned to his office in Washington, D.C., on December 31, 1942, and between January and August 1943, he worked there, fighting what he called "the paper war."[50]

6

WAR STORIES

They Were Expendable

Send the Commie bastard to me; I'll hire him. [1]—John Ford

In April of 1943, Spig Wead and Jim McGuinness flew to Washington to convince John Ford to direct a movie based on W. L. White's *They Were Expendable*, an account of the adventures of Lt. John Bulkeley and his squadron of PT boats during the American withdrawal from the Philippines. Although he was interested in the project, Ford was not eager to return to Hollywood. He was reluctant to leave his unit—his men were scattered, working on various fronts—and, as Dan Ford points out, Darryl Zanuck at this time was being criticized for making films at Fox while serving in North Africa. Ford believed that he too would come under fire for making a commercial picture for profit while still in uniform. As he bluntly confided in McGuinness, "Every congressman would be after my ass." [2]

Jim McGuinness, however, continued to be enthusiastic about the project and pressed the matter, even visiting when Ford was at home in California to plead his case. Interested but unwilling, Ford continued to put the project off, informing McGuinness that his commitment to the war came first. Heavily involved in providing photographic coverage for the upcoming Normandy invasion, he told McGuinness that picture making in Hollywood would simply have to wait. Then, when *December 7th* won its Academy Award as the best documentary subject of 1944,

Ford informed McGuinness that he would definitely not return to Hollywood until after the war. McGuinness would have to get himself "another boy or forget the whole goddamn thing."[3]

Ford spoke too soon. On June 6, 1944, the fortunes of war smiled on Wead and McGuinness. Itching to get closer to the action taking place on Omaha Beach, Ford left the *Augusta*, which was floating at some distance away from the fighting, and joined John Bulkeley, who was in charge of a squadron of PT boats operating off the Normandy coast. For five days, he worked with Bulkeley on the PT boat, experienced a running machine-gun duel with a group of German E-boats off Cherbourg, and developed an easy rapport with the Congressional Medal of Honor recipient. "If Jim McGuinness or Eddie Mannix knew where I was, they'd die," he told Mark Armistead.[4]

They Were Expendable was a movie destined to be made. Delighted with Bulkeley's candor and modesty, Ford "realized that Spig Wead and Jim McGuinness had been right."[5] He decided to return to Hollywood and make the film. On September 14, 1944, Rear Admiral Aaron S. Merrill wrote Charles Cheston, the acting director of the OSS, requesting Ford be made available for the project: "I am very desirous of having that interesting book, *They Were Expendable* put on the screen in order that it may reach a larger percentage of our public," Merrill states. "The Metro-Goldwyn-Mayer Company is undertaking the production and they have requested from the Navy the services of Commander John Ford, USNR, as Director of the film. This request was based on the belief that Commander Ford is better qualified through his dual experience as a director and as a Naval officer than anyone else."[6]

Ford offset any possibility of public criticism of his directing and producing a commercial picture while in uniform by having the $300,000 that he received from MGM deposited directly into an account belonging to the Field Photo Homes, Inc., a nonprofit, charitable corporation that he created to serve as a "living memorial" to preserve the memory of the men of Field Photographic who died during the war and to continue the community that the Field Photographic Unit had become after the war.[7] After script changes and delays, shooting began on February 1, 1945, in Key Biscayne, Florida, with the Navy's blessing. A big-budget action picture, *They Were Expendable* offered the Navy's public relations office an enormous return because of its propaganda value. Accordingly, the Navy lent MGM the PT boats used in the film.

"The culmination of four years of the most intense personal experience" in John Ford's life,[8] *They Were Expendable*, hailed by Lindsay Anderson as "a heroic poem,"[9] is arguably Ford's most definitive statement after three and a half years of warfare. According to John Wayne, while working on *They Were Expendable*, "Jack was awfully intense . . . and working with more concentration than I had ever seen. I think he was really out to achieve something."[10] In part, *They Were Expendable* is about the tragedy of the American withdrawal in the Philippines and "the cost of war."[11] But in part, this film is also about how war teaches those who experience it that their commitment to a cause is greater than their commitment to themselves, and that this justifies their actions.

When Ford congratulated Al Wedemeyer on his appointment as Chiang Kai-shek's chief of staff, he also noted in his letter that he would be returning to Hollywood to make *They Were Expendable*. "My militaristic ego has been somewhat deflated," he writes. "I have been ordered to make a commercial picture called *They Were Expendable*. While I will at least get a chance to spend Christmas with the folks and play with my grandson's electric train, still I'm a bit ashamed that a great warrior like me should be in 'movie land' while the good people are fighting." Distancing himself from the possibility of personal gain from the project, he ensures that Wedemeyer knows that "the picture won't last forever, while the war seems a bit indefinite yet. I am getting a big chunk of dough for the picture, which I am turning into a trust fund for Pennick and the boys."[12]

DARKENING THE AMERICAN CHARACTER

Here Ford's emphasis on self-sacrifice may be read as an unconsidered patriotic reaction, but, as Dan Ford observes, *They Were Expendable* cannot be considered a simple propaganda film. Its dark, realistic interiors and clean, strong visual style, which flawlessly combine documentary effects, announce it to be an art film.[13] *They Were Expendable* considers not only the effect of war on the human condition but, more importantly, the darkening effect that war has had on the resilient nature of the American Character.

Based on William L. White's story of the adventures of Motor Torpedo Boat Squadron 3, a PT unit stationed in the Pacific, *They Were Expendable* depicts the resistance of American forces during the Japanese invasion of the Philippines. The character of Lt. John Brickley (Robert Montgomery) is based on Bulkeley, who evacuated General Douglas MacArthur from Corrigedor, and the character of Lt. Rusty Ryan (John Wayne) is based on Robert Kelly, Bulkeley's executive officer. Sent to Manila to defend the Philippines from Japanese invasion in December 1941, Motor Torpedo Boat Squadron 3 is considered expendable but not effective—until the men demonstrate the PTs' ability to intercept and sink Japanese cruisers. Outgunned and outnumbered, the PTs and the American forces in the Philippines delay the Japanese invaders as long as they can in hope that they may be relieved, but the garrisons at Bataan and Corrigedor are slowly overwhelmed. Brickley and his men evacuate MacArthur (Robert Barrat), his family, and a group of VIPs, and then return to continue the fight. They are doomed—the Japanese forces gradually decimate the squadron, sinking the boats and killing their crews. When the last PT boat has been hauled away, the enlisted men who have managed to survive join what remains of the U.S. Army and the Filipino guerrillas. Brickley, Ryan, and two ensigns are airlifted out of the Philippines on the last plane because they are needed to train PT boat officers and crews in the United States.

Ford's examination of the effect of the war on the American Character during the film is best illustrated in Ryan's touching elegy for Squarehead Larsen (Harry Tenbrook) and Slug Mahan (Murray Alper). Having taken the bodies of their comrades to a Catholic Church, the crewmen of Boat 34 are shocked and dismayed to discover that Larsen and Mahan cannot be properly buried. The priest is not present to officiate the ceremony because he is at the hospital and has been there for two days giving last rites to dying men. Ryan takes the priest's place, but he cannot perform the appropriate funeral rites. He is only able to affirm that "[a] serviceman is supposed to have a funeral" and explains to his men that the religious and social ritual of the funeral is of paramount importance because the "escort . . . firing squad . . . [being] wrapped in the flag he served under and died for" is "a tribute to the way he spent his life." In war, Ryan concedes, "you've got to forget those things and get buried the best way you can," and this is precisely what he proceeds to do for his men. Paying tribute to their lives, his simple elegy discovers the meaningfulness of Larsen's and Mahan's lives in their relationship with their comrades. Larsen and Mahan lived like Americans: "They were just a couple of blue jackets who did their job," he says. "Did it well." Both, Ryan notes, were indispensable to the men with whom they served—"34 boat couldn'ta got along without 'em."

Ryan finds Larsen's and Mahan's lives meaningful, not because they killed the Japanese fliers and soldiers who were their enemies, but because they were part of community that loved and supported its members. As Ryan points out, in war the heroic masculine ideal, celebrated for its physical strength and aggressive instincts, is not what is remembered. What matters to the men who survive were Larsen's and Mahan's abilities to nurture the bodies and the souls of their crewmates. Ryan remembers that Squarehead Larsen was "the best cook in the Navy" and that he "loved the old *Arizona*"; Mahan, he says, "was always quotin' verse. Bits of poetry." The crucible of war may make men out of boys, but their masculinity is made meaningful by their abilities to care for others.

As historian Anthony E. Rotundo points out, American manliness is a role that is learned and reinforced over the course of a lifetime.[14] Ford, who boyishly rushed off to the great adventure that war promised in 1941, without saying goodbye to his wife and children, returned to the United States in 1945 to make a film about the deeply embedded values of pre-twentieth-century manliness taught to him by his parents. Among these values, the importance of a man's altruism cannot be overstated. Dan Ford notes that, when making *They Were Expendable*, his grandfather "had trouble adjusting to what he thought of as the commercial and self-serving attitudes of everyone else on the picture. . . . 'Working for free,' . . . he expected the same sort of dedication from his actors and technicians. He was upset to learn that not everyone was as altruistic as he was."[15]

NEW ENGLAND MANHOOD

It is not surprising that every American male character in *They Were Expendable* exhibits altruism under the pressure of war and represents a type of manhood that blurs the characteristics of two much earlier masculine ideals: on one hand, the Christian Gentleman, a nineteenth-century phenomenon, and on the other, *communal manhood*, the roots of which were embedded in New England before 1800. A product of the middle-class family in nineteenth-century America, the ideal of the Christian Gentleman was, in essence, an ethic of compassion that directed a man's attention to the needs and concerns of others. This ideal stressed love, kindness, and compassion—"these were not only worthy attitudes for a man—they also formed the basis for right actions on his part."[16] Because the Christian Gentleman privileges the needs of society over those of the individual, expressions for this gender ideal include philanthropic activities and acts of self-sacrifice.[17]

Ford's own life abounds in altruistic instances of "right actions" prescribed by these foundational ethics. Throughout the early part of his marriage, for instance, Ford would deprive himself and his family in order to send monthly checks to his parents. In the Ford family, this was the "right thing" to do when a son left home and began working. As Mary Ford pointed out to her grandson, "He loved me and he loved the children but his mother and father always came first. If there was going to be a shortage anywhere, he shorted us and the house because they got their thousand dollars a month right on the first regardless."[18] It was Ford who had Harry Carey Jr. transferred out of the Pacific theater to Washington, at his parents' request, for the duration of the war, and when the Careys were about to lose their home at Corona Del Mar, Ford ensured that Olive Carey received $25,000. She did not discover this until talking with Dan Ford after his grandfather's death. Ford's altruism in North Africa is more well known. While investigating a downed German Ju-88, he prevented a captured German airman from being shot by the Free French. When a Free French lieutenant began "slapping [the prisoner whom Ford had turned over to him] around," it was Ford who stepped in, saying, "Ok, that's enough. The prisoner stays with us."[19]

The American soldiers and sailors in *They Were Expendable*, even the quick-tempered and formidable Rusty Ryan, are, at the core, Christian Gentlemen. The men of Boats 34 and 41 are not simply patriots who fight the Japanese because they happen to be "the enemy." Ford ensures that the viewer understands that Brickley and Ryan attack and destroy a Mogambi-class cruiser to ensure that the food ships carrying Red Cross supplies are able to deliver their precious cargo. This sort of altruistic behavior in the men involved in the fighting is emphasized many times throughout the film.

Kindness and compassion are the foundations of the squadron's behavior, whether the PT men are entertaining and serenading Lt. Sandy Davyss (Donna Reed) over a dinner of soup and jam or enabling a crewmate to die with his dignity intact. Here, Ford is being neither fanciful nor sentimental, for the Christian Gentleman draws much of his manliness from an earlier concept of *communal manhood* that was developed in the social world of colonial New England, where a man's identity (and by extension, his wife's and children's) was inseparable from the duties he owed to his community.

In colonial New England, men fulfilled themselves through public usefulness more than by their economic success, and the social status of the family into which a man was born determined his place in the community more than did his individual achievements.[20] The crewmen in *They Were Expendable*, like men in colonial New England, value their public usefulness. Contributing to the war effort in a meaningful way is so important that Rusty attempts to embark on a dangerous mission when he should be in a hospital for blood poisoning. Being governed by a set of duties owed to others, these men need to do more than simply run mail and messages back and forth across the lagoon. Thus when a sailor arrives to announce that "the General has awarded the Silver Star for gallantry" to every man in the squadron, the crews ignore him. The practical activity in which they are engaged, diving to ascertain the seaworthiness of the hulls of their ships, is far more meaningful to them than the news that they have each received a medal.

Brickley's squadron is a tightly knit community. Before departing, the crew visits hospitalized ensign "Andy" Andrews (Paul Langton) for the last time. The arrival of the Japanese is imminent, and they all know that they will be unable to take their wounded crewmate with them. Immediately apparent, the affection of the men for one another is an exercise in altruism on the part of every man present. After some horse play and being reassured that the gang and the 34 Boat are fine, Andrews offers his crewmates cigarettes, but the men, knowing what is about to happen, politely refuse the gift. Andrews will need the comfort more than they. Brickley lets him know that "we've got a patrol we've got to get ready for. Job's yours any time you can make it." Although the men part saying, "See you next week," they know that there is no likelihood of doing so. The Japanese Army will have overwhelmed the island hospital by then. Andrews, who has heard the scuttlebutt, is aware of this as well. "That was a nice act you boys put on," he tells Brickley. Knowing he will die, Andrews has written out his will and gives it to Brickley with letters to send home. His last words to Brickley express his concern for the men with whom he served, "*Brick*, I'm sorry I couldn't do more for the squadron."

In *They Were Expendable*, Ford creates an ad hoc "family" of military men and women that gradually breaks up in the service of a higher cause, national survival in the face of enemy aggression. This theme of the military as an extended family resonates in Brickley's farewell to the members of his squadron left behind with the Army on Bataan: "You older men, with longer service records—take care of the kids. Maybe . . . that's all. God bless you."[21] The responsibility of the older men to their younger crewmates is also a prime example of the American male's "public usefulness"—after all, "men who carried out their duties to family and community were men to admire."[22]

When Brickley and Ryan are ordered to return to the States without their men, it is evident that Brickley, as a father figure, has failed in his duty to support, maintain, and care for his men. Unable to convince General Martin (Jack Holt) to allow his men to accompany him, Brickley comments to Ryan that leaving the men behind for the Japanese will "make a fine pair of heels out of us." The men's reaction to this news, however, is one of caring and compassion. Instead of feeling betrayed by the man expected to care for them, they congratulate their officers. Jonesy (Arthur Walsh), who is to be left behind, will definitely need more good fortune than his commanding officer, yet he makes a point of wishing Brickley "good luck." Mulcahey (Ward Bond), also deemed to be expendable, approaches Brickley to wish him well: "Sir," he says, "I'd like to shake your hand." When Brickley replies, "That'll be a pleasure," the two clasp hands. Abandoning military protocol, Mulcahey exclaims, "The book doesn't mean much here so I'm going to say so long, Brick; you've been a swell guy." Ironically, Brickley's value has never rested on his authority as an officer or a father figure. He leaves his unit being "one of the guys."

At the beginning of the film, it is evident that the relationship between John Brickley and Rusty Ryan is a friendly one but has ceased to be that of father and son. Ryan, Brickley's executive officer, decides to apply for transfer to a destroyer. Quitting the squadron, he comments that he "can't build a Navy reputation riding a plywood dream." When Brickley asks Ryan, "What are you aiming at? Building a reputation or playing for the team?" Ryan replies, "Look, Brick, for years I've been taking your fatherly advice and it's never been very good. From here on in I'm a one man band."

The invasion of Pearl Harbor, however, forestalls Ryan from leaving the squadron. During the ensuing action, he becomes a team player or, if you will, "one of the guys." His relationship to Brickley is rarely that of a junior to a senior officer. Indeed, the only time Brickley gives Ryan a direct order occurs when Ryan, who has contracted blood poisoning, attempts to go on a mission. Because Ryan would have jeopardized the lives of his crewmates and possibly the success of the mission, Brickley orders him to go to the hospital. While he is being treated, Ryan begins to acquire moral knowledge and undergo the self-transformation that enables him to become a team player. He learns self-sacrifice, when, in the end, he must choose between his love for Sandy and his orders. It is a difficult decision. When he decides to leave on the last plane out of the Philippines, it is because he still has "business here."

In the military, professional relationships are paramount, for they not only impart social knowledge but also create and sustain trust. Valuing the strength of character that is necessary to follow orders, it is one's manliness, ultimately an ethics of compassion and self-worth, that enables men to be morally effective, socially useful citizens, *and* powerful individuals. Dutiful behavior is an essential expression of one's manhood, one's integrity, and one's virtue.

War, in *They Were Expendable*, is an exercise in moral philosophy. The final sequence of the film is not only about the American withdrawal from the Philippines, it is also about discovering the work of being moral, of learning self-direction, and of cultivating integrity. As they straggle along through the long afternoon shadows on a beach while the transport plane bearing their officers flies overhead, the men Brickley has left behind become emblems of the sturdiness and indestructibility of the American Character. Ford's unusual use of close-ups that linger on the men's faces as they look up and watch the plane fly away function very differently than earlier close-ups used in the film, creating an inspiring sequence, as uplifting strains of the "Battle Hymn of the Republic" begin to swell.

After the group returns to their duty and continues down the beach, Ford cuts back to a final close-up of Mulcahey, leaning on his crutch, still watching the plane leave, as strong male voices begin to sing, "My eyes have seen the glory of the coming of the Lord." Only then does Ford permit the viewer to see what the men have experienced. As in *The Battle of Midway*, the viewer is assured of the presence of the divine in the South Pacific. The images of the lighthouse, sea, clouds, and another florid sunset gracing the sky encourage the viewer to meditate on the inspiring light into which the aircraft flies. A cloud formation framing the left-hand side of the screen transforms this light into a symbol of glory and power. There can be no doubt before the shot fades to black that Brickley, Ryan, Cross (Cameron Mitchell), and Aiken (Jeff York), like MacArthur, will be back to even the score. As the refrain of the "Battle Hymn of the Republic" triumphantly increases in volume, and the transport plane soars away into the light, this knowledge is made apparent: MacArthur's epitaph for the Philippines, "We will return," speeds toward the viewer from the center of the screen.

They Were Expendable is a transitional film between Ford's wartime service and his return to Hollywood mythmaking.[23] In this film, elements of Ford's postwar narrative film style are indeed evident. Expressing his "feelings with a blend of emotional simplicity and the seemingly effortless artistry of a master craftsman,"[24] Ford effectively incorporates the clean, realistic treatments of the documentary style, painterly effects borrowed from the Hudson River School, and the power of effectively sparse musical scores of his war documentaries into the film and then transfers these filmic techniques to his later projects. Working in the field during the Second World War had broadened and strengthened his already exceptional skills as a photographer, director, and editor, deepening and expanding the expertise that had won him his back-to-back Oscars for *The Grapes of Wrath* and *How Green Was My Valley*.

RETURNING HOME TO THE COLD WAR

It is not surprising that Ford rejected the limitations imposed by the studios, their producers, and their soundstages when he returned to work in Hollywood after the Second World War. His war experiences, which ended when Field Photographic disbanded on September 28, 1945, had been to him "the most eventful, rewarding, and satisfying period in his life."[25] Before the Second World War, the military had been "an avocation for Ford who used it as a way of gaining social status,"[26] but when Ford returned to Hollywood, John Wayne and Henry Fonda both noticed changes in their old friend and director's personality. Wayne explained this change to Dan Ford by saying, "He stopped playing soldier." "It took me a while to realize it, but a big change had come over Jack," Wayne said. "Before the war there had always been an edge to him. But after the war, after he had been out there he was a lot kinder and a lot more sympathetic."[27] According to Fonda, Ford had become "a lot easier man to be around."[28]

After the Second World War, Ford continued to make films that were concerned with military matters. During the first half of the Cold War, he directed *When Willie Comes Marching Home*, *This is Korea!*, *What Price Glory*, *The Long Gray Line*, and *Mister Roberts*. In part, these films continued to develop the themes and craftsmanship of Ford's earlier movies; in part, they also commented on Ford's concerns during the period in which they were made. No longer just "a hardworking journeyman director," Ford began to use the medium at which he excelled to continue the work he had begun during the Second World War. A master storyteller and filmmaker, he applied his knowledge and talents to define the American Character and establish the importance of its continuance in the minds of his viewers. In doing so, these films illustrate the effect that the Cold War had on his thinking and filmmaking.

Ford's critiques of the American Character in these films are necessarily oblique. Ford made them during the Red Scare in Hollywood, a time when his name, according to his daughter Barbara, was at the top of "Joe McCarthy's list . . . along with Edward G. Robinson and a lot of others."[29] Barbara, who knew her father to be "a Roosevelt man," considered him to be a "bleeding heart" liberal.[30] Although Ford's name is not listed among those found in the now infamous publication *Red*

Channels, he nevertheless did find himself, like others, placed under suspicion during this period. Nonetheless, his conflicted behavior in regard to the volatile, shifting political terrain that was the American film industry in the 1950s has worried many commentators. McBride, for example, is puzzled that Ford, whose father had been a Democratic Party ward boss, had always identified himself as being left leaning until 1947, but called himself "a state of Maine Republican" at the Screen Directors Guild board meeting on October 21, 1947—the second day of the HUAC hearings. This was "the first recorded instance of Ford referring to himself as a Republican," McBride notes. "By 1950, Ford's public comments on the issue of communism [had become] simply boilerplate cold war rhetoric, devoid of subtlety or nuance."[31] What had happened to the man who had been a defender of civil liberties during the Depression and the Second World War? Given the situation in which Ford found himself, the answer is a straightforward matter. Ford, who had left the financial security of Twentieth Century-Fox and was attempting to establish an independent film production company, Argosy Pictures, with Merian C. Cooper, began to straddle the ideological and political divide in Hollywood in order to be able to work.

To appreciate the difficulties presented by the Red Scare for Ford throughout the 1950s, it is necessary to consider the effect that Cold War blacklisting had on the members of the Hollywood film industry, in general, and on Ford, in particular. The systematic blacklisting of artists on the basis of alleged membership in the American Communist Party, sympathies with progressive political causes, or the refusal to assist in investigations into Communist Party activities began on November 25, 1947. The day after ten writers and directors were cited for contempt of Congress for refusing to testify to the House Committee on Un-American Activities, the Motion Picture Association of America (MPAA)—represented by a group of extremely high-powered studio executives that included Louis B. Mayer (MGM), Harry Cohn (Columbia Pictures), Spyros Skouras (20th Century Fox), Samuel Goldwyn (Samuel Goldwyn Company), Albert Warner (Warner Bros.), William Goetz (Universal-International), and Dore Schary (RKO Pictures)—fired the group, which came to be known as the Hollywood Ten.

The reasons for and notice of their dismissal were printed in the *Motion Picture Herald* and *Daily Variety*: the MPAA deplored "the action of the 10 Hollywood men who have been cited for contempt by the House of Representatives" and deemed those actions to have been "a disservice to their employers." The MPAA then invited Hollywood talent guilds to "work with us to eliminate any subversives: to protect the innocent; and to safeguard free speech and a free screen wherever threatened." The MPAA stated that it would no longer knowingly employ "a Communist or a member of any party or group which advocates the overthrow of the government of the United States by force or by any illegal or unconstitutional methods," and if a member of the Ten wished to resume working in Hollywood, he would have "to be acquitted or [have] purged himself of contempt and declares under oath that he is not a Communist."[32]

Given the hostility of the climate in which Ford was working, it is not surprising that Ford's Western Union telegraph to John Wayne, dated June 1, 1950, informed him that Jim McGuinness "would like you back on the seventh for motion picture alliance conference with motion picture council," but counsels Wayne, who was staying at the Grand Hotel in Queretaro Mexico, that "if you're having a good time and the work is progressing with your help I'd advise you stay until we actually need you." Ford's heads-up to his friend ends with "I'm a nervous wreck."[33]

Exactly three weeks after Ford sent this message to Wayne, *Red Channels: The Report of Communist Influence in Radio and Television* was published at the apex of the Red Scare. Issued by the right-wing journal *Counterattack*, *Red Channels* listed 151 actors, writers, musicians, broadcast journalists, and others, claiming that they had been involved in Communist manipulation of the entertainment industry. Some of the listed had already been denied employment because of their political beliefs, history, or association with suspected "subversives." The MPAA blacklisted the rest. Among those were Eddie Albert, Harry Belafonte, Leonard and Walter Bernstein, Dolores del Rio, John Ireland, Frances Farmer, Burl Ives, Gypsy Rose Lee, Zero Mostel, Dorothy Parker, Irving Pichel, Edward G. Robinson, Pete Seeger, Artie Shaw, and Orson Welles.[34]

Only two months after *Red Channels* had been released, Ford, who had been hailed as Hollywood's "No.1 Hero" by Louella Parsons, learned that he was being considered by Steve Early as "a bad risk" to the United States.[35] As Wingate Smith wrote in his letter to Major General Kirke B. Lawton, deputy chief signal officer, dated August 2, 1950, "a bomb exploded . . . [and] the whole of Hollywood and half the

Navy wanted to take it up."[36] Lawton immediately followed up on Smith's letter, and any questions about Ford's loyalty were immediately laid to rest. By October, Ford had received his security clearance and the Navy was making arrangements for him to travel to Korea to make the combat documentary *This is Korea!* released on August 10, 1951, by Republic Pictures.

Considering the circumstances of its preproduction, it is not surprising that *This Is Korea!* lacks the subtle Fordian comments about military culture that are found in *The Battle of Midway*, *Torpedo Squadron 8*, and *December 7th*. As Tag Gallagher remarks, the film's soldier's-eye view of the bleak, desolate nature of this war conflicts with "preppy cold-war jargon of the narration, which makes us wince . . . [and which] Ford was so right to use."[37]

Only four months later, Frank Capra wrote to Ford for help. In spite of his distinguished service during the war making patriotic films for the Army, Capra too had fallen under suspicion:

> Today I got the enclosed letter which is pretty shocking to me. The investigating boys evidently think I'm a friend of the Commies. . . . Could I count on you as a friend and brother director, to write me a letter addressed to the Army-Navy-Air Force Personnel Security Board, that I can forward to them, stating just what you know about me as a person, and what I have stood for in the Guild? I hate like Hell to put you to this trouble, John, and I apologize all over the place. But there are times when a man just has to call on his friends.[38]

Earlier in December, the Army-Navy-Air Force Personnel Security Board had "after careful consideration of the information available to it . . . tentatively concluded that it [could not] grant consent for [Capra's] access to certain classified matter at [the] California Institute of Technology, VISTA Project." This information indicated that Capra had been "a member of the communist inspired picket line in a Hollywood Citizens Newstrike" in 1938; had been "sponsor and national Vice-chairman of the Russian War Relief . . . [and] active in the National Federation for Constitutional Liberties" in 1941; and had "contributed to the Joint Anti-Fascist Refugee Committee" in 1943.[39] Ford, who had been photographed with Capra when they had visited the picket line together during the Hollywood Citizens Newstrike in 1938, wrote back at once: "Dear Frank[,] Am shocked at letter. What were we fighting for? Have already talked to same people regarding you earlier this week. Will send letter immediatly [*sic*]. Merry Christmas and love to you and yours. Siempre JACK."[40] After Ford and others had contacted the Army-Navy-Air Force Personnel Security Board, Capra's concerns were resolved very quickly. On January 14, 1952, he thanked Ford for the clearance for Project VISTA that was awarded him. "Dear Juanito," Capra writes, "The Army-Navy-Air Force Personnel Security has granted me full clearance thanks to friends like you. The whole thing was worth it just to know how much your pals think of you. I'm deeply grateful to you, John. In fact I could get awfully corny and tell you that I love you very much."[41]

SOCIAL FARCE

Released in 1950, *When Willie Comes Marching Home* offers its viewers a coherent critique of American patriotism—a subject frequently referred to by witnesses called upon to testify and demonstrate their loyalty to the State during the hearings of the House Committee on Un-American Activities. Jack L. Warner, for example, claimed to be "very proud to be an American" because he had spent "three-odd months in Europe and . . . saw the consequence of people who killed laws, who destroyed freedom of enterprise, individual enterprise, private enterprise" and was "naturally in favor of anything that is good for all Americans."[42] The subject of patriotism was as popular in Hollywood as it was at the HUAC hearings. Given Ford's shifting ideological and political stances throughout this time, his treatments of the American Character in his narrative films concerned with war are particularly instructive. As John Wayne points out to Dan Ford,

> Although [Ford] was a private man, he was certainly articulate with that camera and he told his feelings through people. I don't think that anyone in the business realized as much as he that pictures are about people. They're not about how to build a bridge or how sail a battleship into battle. They are about people. He made his mark and showed his feelings about the world and the community and his friends through his handling of people in pictures. I think this is a side of Jack that very few people realize.[43]

A film that Ford considered "one of the funniest ever made," *When Willie Comes Marching Home* is the story of William Kluggs (Dan Dailey), the first citizen of Punxatawney, Western Virginia, to enlist in the war effort. Because his life is directed by the fortunes of war, Kluggs, by chance and very much against his wishes, is posted at home for the duration of the war. Irony after irony makes his life both miserable and hilarious. After first being lionized by his fellow citizens for enlisting, he becomes a social pariah for having done so. Being the best gunner on the airfield, he is considered to be too valuable to send to war and is retained as an instructor at the Punxatawney airbase. The social criticism he receives by serving at home is worse than the hardships of serving in the field. At the dinner table, his father, embarrassed by his presence at home, finally explodes, "So you can't talk them into sending you overseas, but do you have to hang around here where people can see you?"

Wanting to do the "right thing," Kluggs, an officer and a Christian Gentleman, is a team player who desperately wants to play. Obeying the orders of his commanding officers, he stops "bellyaching" and does "his job." Incongruously, Kluggs really is not as interested in "all that hero stuff" as his superiors think. His requests to serve overseas are simply the means by which he attempts to escape the condemnation of his parents and neighbors. When a chance opportunity to serve overseas does arrive, his tour of duty lasts only four days. After parachuting into France, being captured by partisans, and witnessing the launch of a V-2 rocket, Kluggs evades the Gestapo and is sent as a courier bearing top-secret photos of the launch to London before being rushed back to Washington to advise General Marshall. Made horribly ill by being constantly forced to drink liquor and exhausted from questioning, he barely avoids being incarcerated in a psychiatric ward. He hops a freight train home after breaking out of the hospital, only to be clubbed by his father when climbing in the kitchen window of his home. The movie ends with Kluggs, escorted by MPs, flying to Washington to be decorated by the president. His family, fiancée, the Legion band, and the entire town couldn't be prouder of him.

The product of middle-class parents living in a middle-class neighborhood in a small town, Kluggs is the embodiment of the average American male. Indeed, it is his "American-ness" that enables him to survive being captured by the suspicious French partisans. Being

American, Kluggs is privy to information that only an American would have. He knows that Dick Tracy is a "gendarme" and that the Lone Ranger says, "Hi-yo, Silver," but what finally convinces the French resistance fighters not to kill him is his knowledge of and passion for baseball. "Who are you trying to kid?" he sneers to the partisan questioning him. "The Yanks are on the American League. Right now they're neck and neck with the St. Louis Browns." Everyone in the room relaxes when Kluggs demonstrates that he knows and follows professional baseball.

His recommendation for the Good Conduct award occurs so often that it becomes a running joke in the story. He comments, "It got so I had the Good Conduct Medal with oak leaf clusters." A loving and dutiful son, he also remains faithful to his fiancée and is kind not only to the neighborhood children but also to animals. When his neighbors begin to complain that he has not been shipped overseas to serve, Kluggs, despite his hurt feelings, remains pleasant and mild-mannered. Devoted to the good of his community, he repeatedly appeals to his commanding officers to assign him to combat duties. And even when his fellow instructors and students will have nothing to do with him, he continues to perform his duties at the airfield faithfully, governs his passions rationally, and altruistically submits to his fate and to his place in society.

Kluggs's strength of character ultimately proves to be an ethics of self-worth. His mother defends his reluctance to divulge top-secret information to her, saying, "I know my son, and I know whatever he's done is right!" Even his father proclaims Kluggs's innocence before the military police break down his front door, shouting, "Look, son, maybe I've been picking on you and all that, but I know my boy, and I know no matter what happens you did your duty!" In the end, his morally effective actions are rewarded, and when Kluggs leaves Loring Field, the town of Punxatawney turns out to honor him as a socially and publicly useful citizen *and* a powerful individual.

MILITARY FARCE

Ford's other Cold War comedy, *Mr. Roberts*, was shot at locations on Midway Island and at the Kanoehoe Marine Corps Air Station in Hawaii. Hospitalized with a ruptured gallbladder, Ford was unable to finish directing the film and shares the credit for directing with Mervyn LeRoy. Released in July, *Mister Roberts* was the second top-grossing film of 1955, drawing in $8.5 million. Jack Lemmon won an Academic Award for best supporting actor for his portrayal of Ensign Frank Pulver, who spends more time planning how to date nurses than he does working. But because of an argument with Henry Fonda over his direction of the project, Ford "was soured on the entire project [and] . . . disassociated himself from it altogether."[44] Nonetheless, it is possible to understand what attracted Ford to the project in the first place and recognize his hand at work in the film.

Like *When Willie Comes Marching Home*, *Mister Roberts* is also an apolitical social farce that charts the adventures of an average American officer who is unable to convince his superiors to transfer him to combat duty. Like Kluggs, Doug Roberts (Henry Fonda) has proved to be indispensable because he is good at his job. Because he is "a good cargo officer," Roberts is the reason that his captain will be "going places." Captain Morton (James Cagney) has decided that Roberts is going to help him wear "the cap of a full commander" and informs him that he is "never getting off this ship." Thus, like Kluggs, Roberts, who has been applying to be transferred to a destroyer since he joined the crew of *The Reluctant*, has had every one of his requests turned down.

Roberts also resembles Kluggs in his good nature and devotion to the good of his community. He is a team player who desperately wants to play in another position. Everyone on board, with the exception of Captain Morton, likes the college graduate. A dutiful officer to his men, unlike Ensign Frank Pulver (Jack Lemmon), who is "the most hapless, lazy, disorganized and, in general, the most lecherous person" he has ever known, Roberts cares for others. When a crewman who has been working in the hold collapses from heat stroke, Roberts countermands his captain's orders. Responding to Mannion (Philip Carey), who pleads, "It's murder down there. Can't we take our shirts off?" Roberts replies, "Sure, take them off," and allows his men to strip. This kindness earns him ten days in his quarters for insubordinate behavior. After serving his sentence, Roberts remains devoted to his men, whom he thinks "are the greatest guys on this earth." Rational and self-controlled, he remains pleasant and mild-mannered even when Morton bullies him, and continues to perform his duties as *The Reluctant*'s cargo officer faithfully. Because his men have not been allowed off the ship for a year, he altruistically gives up his chances of transfer to attain their shore leave by promising Morton not to write any more letters. He is only transferred because his men risk prison by forging Morton's signature on paperwork that they themselves have created.

Tag Gallagher sees Roberts as a typical Fordian hero, mediating "community tensions, searching for a middle way between chaos and repression—a way of tolerance."[45] In part, Roberts does provide a middle path between Morton and his crew. Yet, in the end, Roberts's strength of character tips the scales in the men's favor. Recognized for his sterling virtues, he is decorated by his men, who award him the Order of the Palm for "action against the enemy, above and beyond the call of duty." Ironically, that enemy is his superior officer, Captain Morton. Challenging Morton, Roberts is willing to sacrifice his career for the welfare of his men. He cares *and* supports those who depend on him. *The Reluctant* may be a tightly knit community and the social-climbing Morton its nominal head, but time and again *The Reluctant*'s men turn to Roberts, counting on him to preserve political order, ensure productive activity, and take care of their needs. For Roberts, the moral responsibility to his crew overshadows his social responsibilities in the military community.

When Roberts leaves *The Reluctant*, at first there is no one to take his place and protect the men from Morton's irascible temper. The hapless Pulver, *The Reluctant*'s new cargo officer, whom Morton has deemed "gutless," refuses to intercede on their behalf. News of Roberts's death, however, changes Pulver. Inspired by Roberts's sacrifice, he honors his friend's wish that he not "let those guys down." Acquiring the courage of his convictions, he becomes like Roberts, a useful citizen *and* a powerful individual whom his men and the viewer can respect. After leaping to his feet and dumping Morton's palm tree overboard, he strides into the captain's cabin and demands, "What's all this crud about no movie tonight?"

As in Ford's treatment of the American withdrawal from the Philippines in *They Were Expendable*, the sacrifice of one individual of *The Reluctant*'s community in *Mister Roberts* ensures the survival and growth of the American Character in the others. Roberts's resistance to Morton's unbridled authority becomes the reaction of every crew member, even Pulver. As John Wayne points out to Dan Ford, the inspiring

effect that virtuous behavior has on others is a recurring subject in
Ford's films: it is the "recognition of the human virtues when there's
trouble," Wayne notes. "They kind of fade into the background when
there is no cause or no hardship or no community effort."[46]

ROMANTIC FARCE

What Price Glory, a remake of Raoul Walsh's pioneering antiwar statement, is a much more pessimistic consideration of the American Character for Ford. It is the story of a veteran Marine company, one of the
first American units to fight in France during the First World War.
When not at the front, its commanding officer, Captain Flagg (Jimmy
Cagney), divides his attention between training new recruits and competing with his longtime rival, Top Sergeant Quirt (Dan Dailey), for the
affections of an innkeeper's daughter, Charmaine (Corinne Calvet).
After the company has suffered losses at the front while attempting to
capture a German Officer (Frederic Brunn), Flagg and Quirt, who has
been wounded, first fight and then cut cards to determine who will
marry Charmaine. Flagg wins, but decides to return to the front when
the company is recalled to the fighting. Corporal Kiper (William De-
marest), who receives his discharge papers, also refuses to leave his
comrades and follows Flagg. Quirt too joins the troops as they march
back to war.

In 1926, dispelling the notion that "it is sweet and right to die for
your country,"[47] Walsh's original film conveyed the message that war is
"a dirty, bungled mess." Like Walsh, Ford created a cynical, modern
depiction of the First World War soldier in Europe, causing Gallagher
to deem the film "the *volte face* of *When Willie Comes Marching
Home.*"[48] Ford's pessimistic treatment of the persistence of the
American Character in this movie is meant to puzzle the viewer. There
is no reason why the men persist in responding to the call to arms. In
fact, the men themselves do not even understand their compulsion to
return to the battlefield when they are ordered back in as "the big push"
is going on. Flagg, having just decided to marry Charmaine and settle
permanently in France, can only say, "There's something. Something
about this profession of arms, some kind of religion with it that you
can't shake."

It is an absurd situation. The men do not know where they are going as they march off down the street; "nobody knows." Kiper, whose discharge papers have been held back for a year, follows his platoon, even though he is free to leave the unit. Wounded, Quirt aptly comments to Charmaine, "What a lot of blasted fools it takes to make an army," before he too limps off to join Flagg. As the "Marine's Hymn" swells enthusiastically, Ford's final shot reveals the men retracing their steps, returning through the blasted, lifeless landscape of a First World War battlefield to the front that lies out of sight behind a small rise. The film ends on a note of futility, as the soldiers and the audience alike know that in the trenches to which Flagg is marching there is no escape from the harsh realities of war.

The sequences in which Flagg and his men are hidden by tall grasses and heavy meadow also evoke the battlefield on which Mother Bernle's loved ones die in *Four Sons*. Lit by lurid dawns and surrealistically orange sunsets, these are places of death, not resurrection. The skies above the men are lit only by flares and rockets. Nothing lives in the bare earth and bomb craters, and blasted, lifeless trees litter the landscape. As Flagg and his men discover, it is impossible to find meaning in the grotesque, unnatural condition of the land. In the trenches, men who die simply disappear. There can be no requiem for the fallen, for the heroic dead are never found. One of the raw recruits, wounded by a potato masher, sarcastically challenges Flagg to make the game that they are playing a meaningful activity: "Let the 30-day wonder speak his piece," he spits at his captain. "Why don't you get off the bench and play Captain Flagg? Why don't you get in the game? There are two minutes left and we can use a hero. We can use a hero." Because of their unethical behavior, the men's relationships with one another have also become debased. In the field, teamwork is what one would expect of veterans. They succeed in capturing a German officer, but even that activity proves to be meaningless. Ordered back to the front, they do not receive the leave promised to themselves and their men. War becomes meaningless activity that the men are doomed to repeat again. *What Price Glory* also functions as a strong critique of a negative aspect of the American Character that Ford personally experienced at the height of the Red Scare: the disorganized, drunken, and piggish behavior of Flagg, Quirt, and their fellows allows Ford to make a scathing comment on the viability of individuals who persistently and simply respond to the call to war when that activity has no meaning.

MAKING MEN OF BOYS

As Harry Carey Jr. points out, *The Long Gray Line* "is never talked about much, in spite of the fact that it starred Maureen O'Hara and Tyrone Power at the height of their careers."[49] Adapted from Marty Maher's *Bringing Up the Brass: My 55 Years At West Point*, published in 1951, *The Long Gray Line* is the story of an Irish immigrant whose disorderly life is transformed as he becomes involves in West Point's athletic program as a trainer, equipment manager, and surrogate father to every cadet he teaches. Unlike *What Price Glory*, *The Long Gray Line* has all "the right ingredients for a Ford movie"—all of "Ford's favorite flavors" are present: "the West Point military pomp and circumstance, the brass and the shining silver of the sabers . . . the accent on the physical—the virility of the place, the mental toughness and the dedication of the cadets; along with the lightheartedness and laughter of blooming healthy youths."[50] There is also, Carey notes, "a hallowed, ethereal quality" to the walls and buildings.[51] McBride agrees, pointing out that *The Long Gray Line*, shot at West Point, "has all the trappings of an Eisenhower-era patriotic spectacle designed to glorify the American military system."[52] A box office success for Harry Cohn's Columbia Pictures, *The Long Gray Line* grossed over $5.6 million.

For McBride, *The Long Gray Line* suffers from "the overly broad comedy of its first half, which offers too stark a contrast with the nightmarish darkness that follows."[53] Yet when considered alongside *What Price Glory*, *The Long Gray Line* presents a successful recovery and rehabilitation of the American Character. Every cadet works to exhibit the qualities of kindness, compassion, and care that Marty (Tyrone Power) instills in them by his example. Making boys into Christian Gentlemen is the business of West Point, an elderly Marty informs a visiting congressman who sneers at the school's institutions, wanting "more realism, less tradition." Leaders in the United States "don't just happen," Marty points out. "They're made."

Ford's careful detail throughout the film emphasizes the order and teamwork of the West Point cadets as they drill, exercise, and eat. As Marty himself grows into being a part of the military community on the Hudson, his behavior also becomes rational and self-controlled. Demanding strength of character from his cadets, he, too, develops into a morally effective and socially useful citizen. When his son dies soon after birth, Marty begins to father his student "charges." At first, Marty is unable to understand the important implications of maintaining high moral standards for oneself. Sitting in the cooler, he is unable to believe that friend Jim O'Carberry (Martin Milner) put himself on report because "at the hop we're on our honor not to go off limits. I went. I had to report it." "You mean you do something wrong, and get away with it, nobody the wiser," Marty asks, "and then you have to tell them that you broke the rules?"

Unlike Marty, O'Carberry is a quintessential Christian Gentleman. He understands that virtuous behavior is the agent that "upholds communities, maintains union, friendship and correspondence amongst men."[54] Later, Marty also realizes that manliness is an exercise in moral philosophy that teaches that the individual must be responsible for his own behavior. Thus when his surrogate son, "Red" Sundstrom Jr. (William Leslie), does the "right thing" by leaving West Point and joining the Army rather than graduating and dishonoring himself and his class, Marty is very proud of him. When Red, wounded, returns "home" with his mother to wish his surrogate father a Merry Christmas, he asks Marty to pin his captain's bars on him. Overcome with emotion, Marty sits down while his "family" celebrates Christmas with him.

Ford's use of sentiment, evident in Marty's relationships with his father, wife, colleagues, and cadets, resolves the earlier conflict between moral and social values. Concluding his life story, Marty says, "So, you see, sir, it's been my whole life. Everything I treasure in my heart living or dead is at West Point. I wouldn't know where else to go." Returned to West Point by the president of the United States, who is a former student of his, Marty is treated to a review put on by his cadets. As the orderly rows of young men march by to Irish airs like the "Garryowen,"[55] Marty's past and present, the Old World and the New, are reconciled. When "Red" comments, "If only Old Martin [Marty's father] and Mary [his wife] were here," his mother replies, "They are here, and the others." Mary O'Donnell (Maureen O'Hara), Old Martin

(Donald Crisp), Captain Kohler (Ward Bond), Corporal Heinz (Peter Graves), and Jim O'Carberry all appear to Marty to watch the review as well. Transcending time, the rituals of the review have the power to bring the past to life. Emblems of sturdiness and indestructibility, Marty's cadets, past and present, recover and rehabilitate the American Character that proved to be so problematic in *What Price Glory*. In *The Long Gray Line*, West Point's enduring traditions create an eternal present, in which the actions of the living resurrect the dead, thereby ensuring their immortality. Appropriately, as the final shot of the film fades to black, church bells toll victoriously.

John Ford may have shrouded himself in mystery, as Tag Gallagher asserts, and presented "a complex, perhaps multiple, individuality to the world that was direct and devious, charismatic and sardonic, amusing and caustic," at times self-consciously Irish and Catholic,[56] but when we look at the emphasis on moral excellence over social transcendence in his films, the man and his behavior become instantly understandable. Apolitical when directing and voting, Ford supported the man, not the party to which that man belonged. Answering Hepburn's question about his political philosophy, he simply says, "I don't have any. I'm a registered Democrat—family influence. I've never voted until the last election. I voted for Barry Goldwater. Well, he's a close personal friend. Barry Senior. I voted for Dick Nixon. He's a close personal friend."[57] To Ford, ideological, political, and social divides were not measures of worth. Moral excellence and self-sacrifice were the measures of a man, and the subject of the first Western that he made for Argosy Pictures after the war—*Fort Apache*.

Sergeant Tyree (Ben Johnson) brings Nathan Brittles (John Wayne) news that he has been recalled to duty as the chief of scouts at the rank of a lieutenant colonel in *She Wore a Yellow Ribbon. Courtesy the Lilly Library, Indiana University, Bloomington, Indiana*

In cavalry uniforms designed by John Ford, Second Lieutenant Ross Pennell (Harry Carey Jr.) and Lieutenant Flint Cohill (John Agar) disagree over who will court Olivia Dandridge (Joanne Dru) in *She Wore a Yellow Ribbon* (1949). *Courtesy the Lilly Library, Indiana University, Bloomington, Indiana*

Captain Nathan Brittles (John Wayne) and his troopers prepare for an attack under the spectacular cloudscape of Monument Valley in *She Wore a Yellow Ribbon* (1949). *Courtesy the Lilly Library, Indiana University, Bloomington, Indiana*

John Ford in a candid moment on the *Araner*. Courtesy the Lilly Library, Indiana University, Bloomington, Indiana

Maureen O'Hara talks with John Wayne during lunch with Harry Carey Jr. and Ben Johnson while working on *Rio Grande* (1950). *Courtesy the Lilly Library, Indiana University, Bloomington, Indiana*

Standing before an authentic Sibley tent, Lt. General Phil Sheridan (J. Carrol Naish) gives orders while Lt. Colonel Kirby Yorke (John Wayne) observes in *Rio Grande* (1950). *Courtesy the Lilly Library, Indiana University, Bloomington, Indiana*

Captain Flagg (James Cagney) orders his men to the front in *What Price Glory* (1952). *Courtesy the Lilly Library, Indiana University, Bloomington, Indiana*

A relaxed John Ford, who considered himself a cameraman first and foremost, leans on a Mitchell camera and chats with George O'Brien, USNR, in Korea. *Courtesy the Lilly Library, Indiana University, Bloomington, Indiana*

Cadets on review at West Point during the shooting of *The Long Gray Line* (1955).
Courtesy the Lilly Library, Indiana University, Bloomington, Indiana

John Wayne visits John Ford on the set of *The Long Gray Line* (1955). *Courtesy the Lilly Library, Indiana University, Bloomington, Indiana*

A striking bird's-eye view of the cadets at the chapel in *The Long Gray Line* (1955). Courtesy the Lilly Library, Indiana University, Bloomington, Indiana

John Ford cuts the cake and celebrates his birthday with friends and veterans of the Field Photographic Unit at the farm. Wingate Smith stands beside him to the left, Harry Carey Jr. talks to John Wayne behind Ford, and Jack Pennick, third from the right, is visible in the back row. *Courtesy the Lilly Library, Indiana University, Bloomington, Indiana*

Ford employs landscape conventions common to Civil War photography as Colonel John Marlowe (John Wayne) watches Blaney and his 2nd Iowa return north in *The Horse Soldiers* (1959). *Courtesy the Lilly Library, Indiana University, Bloomington, Indiana*

Marshal Guthrie McCabe (James Stewart) and First Lieutenant Jim Gary (Richard Widmark) search for lost children in *Two Rode Together* **(1961).** *Courtesy the Lilly Library, Indiana University, Bloomington, Indiana*

A paint-splattered Jimmy Stewart punches John Wayne for John Ford on the set of *The Man Who Shot Liberty Valance* (1962). *Courtesy the Lilly Library, Indiana University, Bloomington, Indiana*

Rear Admiral John Ford, USNR (Ret.). *Courtesy the Lilly Library, Indiana University, Bloomington, Indiana*

7

CRITIQUING COMBAT CULTURE

Fort Apache

Emanuel Eisenberg: Then you do believe, as a director, in including your point of view in a picture about things that bother you?

John Ford: What the hell else does a man live for?[1]

Between 1947 and 1950, Argosy Pictures released five Westerns. Three of the five, *Fort Apache*, *She Wore a Yellow Ribbon*, and *Rio Grande*, now known as Ford's Cavalry Trilogy, are considered to be celebrations of military life and culture in the United States. Based on short stories published in *The Saturday Evening Post*, *Fort Apache*, *She Wore a Yellow Ribbon*, and *Rio Grande* echo the Victorian military ideals of James Warner Bellah, who had grown up on cavalry posts while the American frontier was closing—as Dan Ford points out, Bellah's stories speak of "an honor, spirit, tradition, that is largely gone in America" and "are rife with the aristocratic watchwords of duty, honor, and country."[2] John Ford was drawn to Bellah's "Massacre," and Argosy Productions purchased the rights to the story in 1947. Because Bellah was "a blatant racist,"[3] Ford hired liberal thinker and former *New York Times* critic Frank Nugent to research the period thoroughly before writing the screenplay. When Nugent, having read dozens of books on the subject, returned from exploring the Indian country of the Southwest, Ford told him to "forget everything you've read and we'll start writing a movie."[4] McBride remarks that this comment has been interpreted as a sign of Ford's indifference to historical truth in the cavalry films, but believes instead that Ford's attention to American history during *Fort Apache*'s preproduction signals its director's intention to avoid the failure of *My Darling Clementine*.[5] Nugent's and Katherine Cliffton's extensive research into the customs, manners, and physical details of Army life in the West during the 1880s enabled Ford and his art director, James Basevi, to successfully create a modified version of military culture on the frontier, what critic Bosley Crowther deems in the *New York Times* to be "a salty and sizzling visualization of regimental life at a desert fort."[6]

As Dan Ford observes, Ford's Cavalry Trilogy are among his most famous films, in part, because they "reflect his wartime experience and his fascination with the heightened sense of community among fighting men."[7] Crowther remarks, however, that *Fort Apache* is more than a demonstration of "the screen as a most potential medium for capturing the 'look' of history and of life"—in Ford's "rich blend of personality, of the gorgeously picturesque outdoor western scenery, of folk music and intrinsic sounds," there is also a "new comprehension of frontier history."[8] In *Fort Apache*, Crowther recognizes "a new and maturing viewpoint upon one aspect of the American Indian wars," remarking that this movie's plot is not what one would expect of Western grounded in George Custer's story. "Here it is not the 'heathen Indian' who is the 'heavy' of the piece, but a hard-bitten Army colonel, blind through ignorance and a passion for revenge," he points out.

> And ranged alongside this wilful white man is a venal government agent who exploits the innocence of the Indians while supposedly acting as their friend. . . . From the moment that sullen Colonel Thursday, a demoted general of the Civil War, lays down the law to his regiment upon taking over the post, there is tension and dismay at Fort Apache, a critical garrison on the Arizona frontier. And from the moment he crosses notions of Apache psychology with Captain York, his experienced and indulgent "second," a showdown is obviously ahead.[9]

This "new comprehension of history" may be attributed to Ford finally being in control of preproduction, production, and postproduction. Clearly, *Fort Apache* is not cut from the same cloth as *Drums along the Mohawk* and then carefully recut under Zanuck's watchful eye at Twentieth Century-Fox. Even Ford's innovative use of infrared film, used in the outside shots, transmits a modified version of reality that is diametrically opposed to the Technicolor vision of a pastoral frontier found in *Drums along the Mohawk*. Popular in the 1930s among enthusiasts, the first infrared photographs to be published appeared in 1910 in the February edition of *The Century Magazine* and the October edition of the *Royal Photographic Society Journal*. Ford would have been well acquainted with infrared film, which accentuates texture, contrast, and depth for aerial photography, as his Field Photo units used it during the Second World War. Infrared enables photographers the opportunity to create highly dramatic images because of its tendency to darken skies and is often the film stock of choice for fine art images. Working beyond the boundaries of conventional filmmaking, Ford and cameraman Archie Stout employed infrared in *Fort Apache* to transmit the experience of hyperreality in Monument Valley. Contrasted against the white clouds, the skies in this movie are particularly dramatic, suggesting the presence of the Sublime in Monument Valley and creating a visual dynamic between interiors and exteriors. Transformed, the skies above Monument Valley reaffirm the Western hieroglyph, but unlike the firmaments in *Stagecoach*, these darkened heavens emit a terrible beauty.

Critical reactions to *Fort Apache*, like its reviews, have been mixed. According to Max Westbrook, Ford's cinematic comments on the West are, like John Wayne's brief dance with Shirley Temple in *Fort Apache* (1948), "decorative rather than substantive."[10] Like all Westerns, *Fort Apache* invokes history for the purposes of propaganda, to convince by association, Westbrook says, and habituates its audiences not only to accept the basic premises of the social order but also to ignore their irrationality and injustice.[11] He concludes, "That's America. And if the propaganda is hard to swallow, accept the cover-up and plunge on. That's the higher loyalty."[12] However, as Richard Slotkin points out in *Gunfighter Nation*, Ford's invocation of history and propaganda in *Fort Apache* is not designed to justify anyone's "higher loyalty." A "seminal work" of American mythography, *Fort Apache* "visualizes and verbalizes the process by which truth becomes myth and by which myth provides the essential and socially necessary meaning in our images of history."[13]

As Slotkin remarks, of all the major Hollywood directors, John Ford was the most reluctant to make fictional films about combat. Noting that *They Were Expendable* was made under some official duress, Slot-kin argues that Ford's unwillingness to fictionalize the war was a reaction to wartime censorship, which forbade his telling the truth about combat or his criticizing American tactics and policies.[14] It is also possible that Ford's reluctance to fictionalize the war may be attributed in part to the furor that *December 7th*'s potentially damaging criticism of America's unpreparedness at Pearl Harbor created in Washington. By the summer of 1943, Darryl Zanuck had weathered the Senate War Investigating Committee's inquiry into Hollywood's role in the war, but Ford and *December 7th* had become so controversial that Donovan posted him to the China-Burma-India Theater of Operations (CBI) as technical observer and named Ray Kellogg deputy chief of Field Photo. During the rest of the war, Ford remained nominally in charge, but Kellogg remained the unit's acting chief for most of that time while Ford was either in the field or on inactive status while directing *They Were Expendable*. Ford could have been flown to Asia, but Donovan sent him there on a very slow freighter, protecting his friend by rendering him incommunicado. On September 19, Ford left New York for Calcutta, a journey that lasted "fifty-five days and took [him] through stops at Cuba, Australia, and Ceylon."[15]

CRITIQUING COMBAT CULTURE

Unlike his combat films, Ford's Westerns after the Second World War offered him ample scope and the distance needed to critique combat culture and command errors. As Tag Gallagher points out, "it is puzzling that so flagrant an irony as *Fort Apache's* is commonly mistaken for chauvinism by so many of Ford's critics. . . . [Ford's] portrait of the cavalry is a scathing indictment of arrogance, idiocy, racism, and caste-ridden inefficiency."[16] *Fort Apache* has been considered evidence of Ford's romance with the military, as it seems "to articulate all his war-time emotions, his fascination with the American military tradition, and the special nobility he felt was born of combat,"[17] but when considering *Fort Apache*, Ford himself bluntly tells Peter Bogdanovich, "We've had a lot of people who were supposed to be great heroes, and you know damn well they weren't. But it's good for the country to have heroes to look up to." Returning to the subject of history, he then remarks, "Like

Custer—a great man. Well, he wasn't. Not that he was a stupid man, but he did a stupid job that day."[18]

If Little Bighorn was "a stupid job," as Ford says, then Lt. Colonel Owen Thursday's performance of his duties in *Fort Apache* must be regarded as Ford's own study of a stupidity so complete that it is, at times, stunning. Upon taking over his command, Thursday almost immediately manages to insult the entire post—officers, enlisted men, and their wives. Thursday (Henry Fonda) demotes a respected and well-liked officer, Captain Sam Collingwood (George O'Brien), without reason or explanation, and then offers the man who is an alcoholic a drink before breakfast. He can never remember his officers' names, insulting a Congressional Medal of Honor winner, Sergeant Major Michael O'Rourke (Ward Bond), and his son, Second Lieutenant Michael Shannon O'Rourke (John Agar). He puts a stop to the most important social function of the year, the annual noncommissioned officers' dance. He even invades the privacy of his men off duty and orders Lieutenant O'Rourke to "get out" of his mother's home, prompting the young man's father to remind his superior officer that "this is my home, Colonel Owen Thursday. And in my home I will say who is to get out and who is to stay. And I will remind the Colonel that his presence here—uninvited—is contrary to Army regulations . . . not to mention the code of a well-mannered man!"

It is extremely difficult to imagine how any cavalry officer (even George Custer) could have behaved in a more asinine way than Owen Thursday. Thursday's irrational decision to ride into a death trap cannot be considered a display of heroism but an act so ludicrous that it is a monumental piece of idiocy. Captain York (John Wayne) warns the lieutenant colonel that such a decision would be "suicide," but Thursday insults all reason by deciding to charge down a blind box canyon with his men—after being assured by the seasoned York that the Apaches will be waiting for him. Refusing York the privilege of accompanying the regiment because he will not have cowards in it, Thursday also punishes York by sending him (accompanied by Lieutenant O'Rourke) to the safety of the supply wagons that are waiting on a ridge well away from the action. Every man in the regiment knows that Thursday is making a terrible mistake. Learning of Thursday's plan, Sergeant Major O'Rourke is flabbergasted and exclaims, "Why, the madman!" Although Thursday's soldiers all know they will be riding to their deaths, they all follow him as he leads the charge. Revealed as a dead end (Ford's visual pun), the canyon into which the regiment charges is, as York predicts, a killing ground: the Apaches, hidden behind the rocks along the tops of the canyon walls, use their carbines to leisurely pick off the horsemen at will. They know that the men will have to ride back the way that they came in order to escape. As expected, Thursday's men are easily shot off their horses. He and a handful of survivors make a last stand in the canyon, replicating Custer's at Little Bighorn, but theirs is not a heroic melee or glorious conclusion. A wave of mounted Apaches simply overwhelms them in seconds.

With this in mind, it is not surprising that *Fort Apache*'s ending is the most controversial of all Westerns. Because Thursday's last charge and subsequent last stand, like Custer's, poorly planned and badly executed, is a disaster, one must ask, how can this be? How can men "willingly . . . charge into a canyon of slaughter led by a man particularly dedicated to ritual glory"?[19] More to the point, how could anyone follow a madman who has continually demonstrated his psychosis? And how could Lieutenant O'Rourke, who witnessed Thursday sacrificing his father to meet his own personal ends, have named his son after that man at the movie's end? Gallagher attempts to explain O'Rourke's (and York's) contradictory behavior at the conclusion of the movie by concluding that "the people of Fort Apache serve a system in which group, duty, and order are more important than individual, morality or life itself." In the end, Gallagher says, they are "destroyed by the system, by duty gone astray."[20] Duty in *Fort Apache*, however, not only goes astray, it is also savagely deconstructed—for its contradictions are never reconciled.

In the West, crude force is necessary to lead men. The conclusion of *Fort Apache* therefore is not an open acknowledgment of the complexities of command, but rather, the finale of a scalding critique of West Point and its graduates that underpins the action of this movie. Before the Second World War, Ford's optimistic and supportive portrayals of naval cadets in *Salute* and sailors in *Men without Women*, *Seas Beneath*, and *Submarine Patrol* depicted the military as a meritocracy in which the individual's attention to honor, duty, tradition, expressed by his self-sacrifice, was ultimately justified. In *Fort Apache*, however, behaving like an officer and a gentleman on the frontier is misplaced. It does not guarantee the individual social or moral superiority and thereby the individual's ability to command others. Fresh from West Point, Lieutenant Michael O'Rourke, for example, delivers his calling card to his commanding officer's residence on time, but he is not judged fit by Thursday to visit Philadelphia. On the parade ground, he is shown to be too well mannered. Apologizing to his recruits, he is unable to teach them how to march. When his father asks First Sergeant Festus Mulcahy (Victor McLaglen) how his son is faring, the sergeant's response is: "Aw, he's doin' fine, Michael; but, nevertheless, he's an officer . . . and that's no job for a gentleman." When Sergeants Mulcahy, Shattuck (Jack Pennick), and Quincannon (Dick Foran) take over from O'Rourke, they break the new recruits in with cudgels fashioned from planks. The sergeants' recruits are marching correctly in formation the same day.

Another West Point "gentleman," Owen Thursday fares no better on the frontier than his second lieutenant. Unable to adapt to relaxed standards of frontier living and the egalitarian behavior of his subordinates, he inexplicably wants to improve his troops by ensuring that they are dressed properly. "I intend to make this regiment the finest on the frontier," he says. "Prolonged duty in a small outpost can lead to carelessness . . . and inefficiency and laxity in dress and deportment. I call it to your attention that only one of you has reported here this morning properly dressed. . . . We're not cowboys at this post . . . or freighters with a load of alfalfa." Worrying about his men's galluses (suspenders) being exposed, Thursday is functioning like a senior West Point "kaydet," not a battle-seasoned lieutenant colonel. Failing to distinguish the field from the parade ground, Thursday may be excused in being overly concerned with his men's appearance, but he also proves to have difficulties differentiating the practical from the tactical. Attempting to emulate the exploits of Genghis Khan and Alexander the Great in Arizona, Thursday ignores the fact that, unlike Roman and Persian soldiers, the Apache are guerrilla fighters. He is therefore fortunate when his first feint against a band of Mescaleros succeeds. Unlike Khan's riders, who flanked their adversary by riding around a mountain to overcome highly unfavorable terrain, Thursday's cavalrymen do not have to execute a complicated maneuver: they outnumber and meet their opponents head-on in an open plain, thereby interrupting the Indians' pursuit of the detail sent out to repair the downed telegraph and retrieve the dead.

Unfortunately for the men under his command, Thursday's luck does not hold. Being a product of West Point, Thursday's arrogance and sense of entitlement make it impossible for him to accept his frontier posting ("Blast an ungrateful war department that sends a man to a post out here"). Like Custer, Thursday is an ambitious, career-oriented officer to whom posting in the West implies demotion. In order to be promoted, enjoy preferment, and return to Washington, he must attract the attention of the Eastern newspapers and therefore attempts to become "the man who brought Cochise back." Trained in Clausewitz's theories, Thursday is a Western military thinker, regarding war as an instrument used in a struggle between opposing wills. Ford heightens his viewer's awareness of Thursday's Eurocentricity by composing the landscapes through which Thursday and his regiment ride to meet with Cochise (Miguel Inclán) very differently from those that contain Cochise and his warriors. Landscapes associated with Thursday are shot according to the principles of the picturesque in which the viewer's eye is directed inward toward a distant horizon. When Cochise arrives with his band on horseback, Ford further emphasizes the difference between these two men's points of view. Shots composed behind Thursday continue to contain the picturesque, but those that foreground Cochise are composed from his point of view and express another aesthetic.[21]

The following morning, as Thursday and his cavalrymen line up against Archie Stout's startlingly brilliant clouds (created by Ford and Stout's unusual choice of infrared film stock for the outdoor shots in Monument Valley), there is no evidence of the picturesque, only horizontal planes that allow for motion through the frame. As Thursday charges, the frame remains unrestricted by flanking objects that direct the eye toward the picture's horizon. These shots encourage instead the movement of the running horses in and out of the picture's unrestricted, lateral edges, suggesting freedom of movement and a wide expanse of space, which contrasts sharply with the imposing frames created by the canyon into which they soon ride. Like the cavalrymen, the viewer's eye is constricted and directed down the canyon and into the killing field that is its floor.

Before the charge begins, Ford uses the dramatic effects of infrared film to their full advantage. Foregrounded and shot from low angles against bold streaks of sweeping clouds, Thursday and his waiting columns of men are positioned in a series of horizontal lines as the watching Apache would see them. As the bugle sounds "Forward," the men and horses move at a walk from left to right off the screen toward Cochise and into history. Ford then cuts to an even more extreme low-angle shot of Cochise and his generals, which awards the powerful figures precedence over the mounted men approaching them. Framed against a gigantic dramatic swirl of clouds, the Apache leader bends down, gathers a handful of dirt, and throws it downward toward the camera, consigning the regiment to its grave. Like the final shots at the end of *Torpedo Squadron 8*, this sequence in *Fort Apache* is also composed of remarkably bright shots. Throughout *Fort Apache*, this startling light indicates the presence of the Sublime in Monument Valley. The powerful luminescence of the glowing back-lit clouds prepares the viewer for the battle to come, foreshadowing Thursday's approaching transcendence—seeking glory, he will become a secular saint, immortalized, as one of the newspapermen at the conclusion of the film notes, the hero of "every school boy in America." The unnatural stillness of the men and horses while awaiting the bugle is accentuated by the unmoving clouds framing their forms. In the harsh light, the petrified men do not appear to be human. In *Monument Valley: John Ford Country*, Ford's compositions in this sequence catch the attention of Scott Eyman, who points out that "the clouds in the sky really look like explosions," and Joseph McBride, who remarks that Ford's use of sculptural lighting "almost turns the men into statues."[22]

However, what Thursday does, when the column does begin to move, is rash to the point of being almost incomprehensible. Pressing the attack, he disregards his subordinates' cautions about Cochise and ignores the fact that his regiment does not have the superior numbers needed to win this engagement. He and the viewer know that his force is outnumbered four to one, yet he gives the order to charge. Thursday's mental instability is also demonstrated in his attitude toward Native Americans. As a blatant racist, he neither understands nor respects the Apache; to him they are "cowardly Digger Indians." He cannot distinguish between Sioux and Apache warriors even though the difference between them could not have been made clearer to him. Prior to taking Thursday to meet Cochise, York had stressed the superiority of the Apache to his commanding officer, saying, "You could follow the Sioux's line of retreat from the Apaches by the bones of their dead."

MISPLACED DUTY AND HONOR

Because Ford was able to shape *Fort Apache* "as he saw fit,"[23] *Fort Apache*'s greatest strengths lie not in its action scenes, but in its powerful character studies. As a madman, Thursday is simply running true to form. Earlier, he had also proved himself unable to differentiate between the U.S. government and individuals who represent that institution. He supports Silas Meacham (Grant Withers), a corrupt Indian agent, even when presented with incontrovertible evidence that Meacham is a criminal, selling whiskey out of crates marked as containing Bibles and hawking carbine rifles to the Apache. Thursday knows that Meacham is "a blackguard, a liar, a hypocrite, and a stench in the nostrils of honest men," but unwilling to adapt to the situation at hand, he remains inflexible. Bound by his duty as an instrument of government to support the Indian agent, he pledges Meacham "the protection and cooperation of [his] command." Thursday further insults common sense when he ends his negotiations with Cochise. Power-crazed and conflating the personal with the professional, he snaps at his translator, Sergeant Beaufort (Pedro Armendáriz), "Tell them they're not talking to me, but to the United States government. Tell them *that the government* orders them to return" (italics mine).

Ford's critique of Thursday's misplaced emphasis on duty and honor is also articulated in his character study of Emily Collingwood (Anna Lee). Standing with Philadelphia and Mrs. O'Rourke, she is the epitome of a good "Army wife" as they watch the troops prepare to leave the fort. During the Civil War, Sam Collingwood, serving with Owen Thursday, made a mistake in battle that resulted in his posting to the West once hostilities ended. Like Thursday, however, Emily Collingwood is a careerist. Like her husband, whose posting to the West was the result of an error of judgment in battle during the Civil War, Emily deeply resents being stationed at Fort Apache and wants to return to the East. Thoughtful only of her husband's professional advancement, she, like Thursday, values her husband's honor above his life. She therefore does not allow Tom to inform him that his orders to transfer as an instructor to West Point have finally arrived even though Mrs. O'Rourke (Irene Rich) pleads with her not to be a fool. "Sam's no coward. He never was," she says, handing Collingwood's orders to Tom. "Keep this for the captain's return." Emily Collingwood is, as Mrs.

O'Rourke points out, "a fool." As Collingwood exits to meet Cochise, however, she experiences a chilling vision, similar to Libby Custer's premonition that her husband will not return. To Philadelphia (Shirley Temple) and Mrs. O'Rourke, who witnessed her sacrifice her husband in order to safeguard his honor and his reputation, she whispers, "I can't see him. All I see is the flags." Fittingly, Collingwood, like the others, dies ironically, a Victorian patriot.

PROFESSIONAL AND PERSONAL LIVES OVERLAP

As Slotkin points out, *Fort Apache* is both a Western and a platoon movie.[24] Capitalizing on genre conventions, Ford carefully uses small squads led by lieutenants and sergeants to create and further character studies that conflate and confuse the personal with the professional. The squads that Lieutenant O'Rourke commands consist of family members and close family friends. Sergeant Festus Mulcahy, for example, is O'Rourke's godfather. When Thursday selects O'Rourke to command an underarmed detail, his father, the top sergeant, ensures his son's safety, instructing his men to "go get Quincannon out of the guardhouse . . . and go to the stables and find Mulcahy, Shuttuck, and Johnny Reb. Tell them they're volunteering for an extra hazardous mission. Above and beyond the call of duty. Tell them their regiment is proud of them. Now get going." While emphasizing the teamwork of the sergeants who "volunteer" to accompany Lieutenant O'Rourke on his dangerous mission to repair the telegraph wire and band together to "destroy" contraband whiskey, Ford establishes the complexity of these sergeants' characters. Mulcahy, Shattuck, Quincannon, and Beaufort are all competent and compassionate noncommissioned officers. As York comments in the film's epilogue, they are "regular Army"—they may fight over cards or whiskey, but they will share the last drop of water in their canteens with each other. When Mulcahy finds his comrades' burnt corpses tied to wagon wheels, he is sickened by what he sees. He softly says, "Barry and Williams. Many a pint I had with both of them." Then, shaking his fist at the sky, he cries, "Why you . . ." Holding Meacham personally responsible for Barry's and Williams's deaths, he snarls at the sutler[25] during the noncommissioned officers' dance, "Get out of my way, Meacham, or I'll break both your legs."

Then, remembering his manners as an officer, he then turns to Mrs. O'Rourke on his arm and charmingly adds, "Of course, with your permission." Being "regular Army," Mulcahy understands how closely intertwined personal and professional relationships are in the military. When he sends O'Rourke back to the supply wagons with York, he does not give his lieutenant the opportunity to refuse York's orders or argue with his baptismal sponsor: "Get outta here, ya skirt!" Mulcahy, the affectionate godfather, shouts as he saves the young man's life. "Or I'll put ya across me knee and belt the pants off ya! Get out now!"

The overlap of personal and professional relationships in *Fort Apache* means that there are platoons marching everywhere—even at the dances that are the highlights of the fort's social season. It is no coincidence that the Thursdays' arrival at *Fort Apache* at the beginning of the film upsets the enactment of an annual series of dances—rituals that Slotkin argues symbolize and create the communal bond of those living and working at the fort.[26] The personal and professional bonds that exist between the members of the regiment and their wives are evident when the Thursdays momentarily suspend the George Washington Birthday Dance. Philadelphia and Captain York step onto the floor after their introductions, and the dance continues—as does the business of the regiment the next day—but Thursday, who will upset the highly regimented patterns of social and professional relationships at the fort, refuses to dance with the others. Immediately after taking command the next morning, he relieves his executive officers, Captain York and Captain Collingwood, of their duties. Thursday sends both men back to their troops before inexplicably and insultingly appointing a junior officer, Lieutenant Gates (Ray Hyke), as his adjutant. When Collingwood stays behind while the others leave for breakfast, Thursday declares "there is nothing personal" about his decision to demote him, but their shared combat history indicates otherwise. As Collingwood points out, no explanations from his senior officer are needed: during the Civil War, "You did what you did and rode on to glory. I did what I did and wound up here." Then, pointing out the irony attending Thursday's heroism, he says, "You wound up here too."

Ford's careful repetition of the elements of the next dance, the Grand March at the noncommissioned officers' ball, throughout *Fort Apache* further demonstrates how duty and decorum affect and determine the private and public lives of the cavalrymen. On their best behavior and setting a good example for the men, the officers and noncommissioned officers of the fort are, as Mulcahy promises to be, "the morals of decorum." As is customary at Fort Apache, the commanding officer, Thursday, leads out the wife of the sergeant major. Having personally and professionally insulted the O'Rourkes in their home the night before, Thursday hesitates before crossing the floor to ask for O'Rourke's permission to dance with his wife, but custom requires him to do so. Maintaining social custom, Thursday is the epitome of an officer and a gentleman as he says, "Mrs. O'Rourke, may I have the honor?" Standing and curtseying, Mrs. O'Rourke is the epitome of a lady when she replies, "It will be a pleasure, Colonel Thursday." Then, as custom demands, Sergeant Major O'Rourke leads out the colonel's lady, "in this case, his lovely daughter, Miss Philadelphia Thursday," knitting the social and professional fabrics of the fort together again.

Ford's careful overlapping of personal and professional relationships at the noncommissioned officers' ball illustrating the importance of military decorum in all aspects of Army life is repeated the next morning on the parade ground while the regiment prepares to leave the fort. Falling into columns, the cavalrymen enact the Grand March of the night before, reflecting on horseback their promenade through the dance hall that began the celebrations of the night before. Marching away to battle, the platoons of cavalrymen swing their horses into orderly columns of twos and fours, and, as on the dance floor, the cavalrymen adhere to a strict hierarchy of seniority, the senior officers leading the columns, the noncommissioned officers following their superiors, and the enlisted men following their superiors. Just as he did at the dance the night before, Thursday begins the military promenade and is followed by the members of his regiment in descending order according to their ranks.

Ford's re-creation of and attention to detail in the Grand March in *Fort Apache* is painstaking. As he tells Peter Bogdanovich in *John Ford*, "The Grand March in *Fort Apache* is typical of the period—it's a ritual, part of their tradition. I try to make it true to life."[27] In order to understand the significance of the scenes from the noncommissioned officers' ball, one must consider the finer points of the Grand March itself. The opening of a formal ball, the Grand March was a staple ritual enacted by the nineteenth-century American social and military elite. In *The Amateur's Vademecum* (1870), E. B. Reilley notes that "the Grand

March is properly executed as follows: The First Gentleman and lady will promenade around the room, the others will all follow: then the whole will form a single column of two lines, gentlemen on the left and ladies on the right, when they all execute the Grand March around the room, as directed by the Master of Ceremonies."[28] The Column of Twos is made when "the lead couple, having reached the center point at the foot of the hall, starts up the center of the hall, all the other couples following in turn. This Column is cast off . . . [and] a Column of Fours is then formed."[29] Blurring the distinction between civilian and military, Reilley notes that the set of two couples, four abreast, is called a *platoon*. "When Casting Off Fours," he says, "the first platoon wheels left, the first gentleman marching in place while the second lady curves around. The second platoon wheels right, third left, and so forth. Columns of Eight and Sixteen are possible if the hall and the number of dancers are both large. The whole series of figures above is often referred to as the March by Platoons."[30] The martial nature of the Grand March was recognized in 1863 by Mark Twain, who humorously describes the dance as a military engagement. In his article on the "Grand Ball at La Plata" published in *Territorial Enterprise*, Twain notes that "the dancers were formed in two long ranks, facing each other, and the battle opens with some light skirmishing between the pickets, which is gradually resolved into a general engagement along the whole line."[31]

It is no coincidence, then, that the horsemen who promenade from the fort mirror the activity occurring on the dance floor the night before. Following Thursday from the fort, the cavalry first exits in Columns of Twos. Platoons or Columns of Fours then leave to the strains of the "Garryowen." The cavalrymen not only promenade in columns from the fort but also prepare for battle in the same fashion. In the field, an abbreviated version of the March of Platoons takes place. Instructing his men to attack Cochise, Thursday could be announcing the first dance of the evening: "Gentlemen," he says, "*march* your troops. We'll charge in *a column of fours*" (italics mine). The tragedy created by Thursday's charge is intensified by the audience's intimate knowledge of its participants' personal lives. The men who die serving under Thursday were dancing with their friends and families only the night before.

COMEDY AND TRAGEDY

Commenting on the relationship of comedy and tragedy toward the end of his life, Ford says to his grandson, "I've always felt in every dramatic scene, any tragic scene, there's always the chance to slip in a little comedy. The two play against each other. Tragedy is very close to comedy. Every comedian wants to be a tragedian; every tragedian wants to be a comic. That's the nature of our business. And the two are akin. No matter what the situation there's always a chance to slip in a little comedy."[32] In *Fort Apache*, Ford's use of comedy critiques military culture. However competent and caring the sergeants who care for Lieutenant O'Rourke are, there is no question that they are, for the most part, working-class clowns. As American cavalrymen, these shanty Irishmen are incongruous—offered the opportunity to serve in what would be considered an aristocratic elite in a European theater of war. Aptly, Mulcahy points out to Philadelphia that Fort Apache is really an egalitarian society: in the West, the social classes are conflated (as Philadelphia and Michael's forbidden courtship and later marriage illustrate) and distinctions are observed more in their breach than in practice. "Ma'am, this is my godson, 'Leftenant' O'Rourke," Mulcahy says, after spanking Michael at the way station. "Many's the time he's come to me with a wet nose."

In *Fort Apache*, Ford's sergeants mix business and pleasure at every possible opportunity for comic effect. Beaufort, for example, finds a recruit, played by Hank Worden, who had "the honor of serving with the Southern arms during the late War Between The States." At Fort Apache, mixing business with pleasure is the reason one advances through the ranks. Preferment and patronage, not honor and merit, ensure that the low becomes the high: when the Southern recruit accepts the "honor" of buying Beaufort a drink, he is immediately preferred and promoted to the rank of acting corporal, and when he loses "his Yankee cap," Worden is congratulated. Beaufort shakes his hand. While the two Southerners take charge of the situation and care of one another, the Yankee recruits around them are thrown to the ground by their rearing horses. In the midst of the Army that defeated them, the Southerners are the only true cavaliers in this scene—they rise again, being the only horsemen left standing.

The sergeants quickly also erase distinctions between business and pleasure in the line of duty. Charged by their commanding officer with the task of destroying Meacham's "scripture," what Thursday terms the sutler's hidden store of illegal whiskey, they fill their tin cups full of what can only be said to be a highly flammable and dangerous liquid that "is better than no whiskey at all" and destroy the rotgut by drinking it on duty. Looking at the kegs of liquor to be consumed, Mulcahy comments incredulously to his partners on their good luck: "'Destroy it,' . . . Well, boys, we've a man's work ahead of us this day." Not surprisingly, "the boys" are found in the cooler the next day with huge hangovers, busted to privates, guarded by the recruits they have trained, and sentenced to shoveling manure in the hot sun. Ironically, Sergeant Beaufort, who escapes completing this punishment by leaving with York on what can only be considered a suicide mission, is considered by his fellows to be an "officer's pet."

In contrast to the sergeants, Ford's Apache are noble, tragic characters. As Gallagher notes, in *Fort Apache*, "Indians are outside the system; they are the Other."[33] Thursday's opposite, Cochise is the most rational, dignified, mature, flexible, and self-contained character in the movie. Interested in peace, he is also the most civilized: "It is not well for a nation to be always at war," he says. "The young men die . . . the women sing sad songs . . . and the old ones are hungry in the winter." Insultingly querulous when speaking with Cochise, Thursday does not respond to the Apache leader's appeal to his compassion while outlining the plight of the women, children, and old people who are suffering because of the war that Meacham has caused. Thursday also does not acknowledge Cochise's compelling and dignified petition to logic and personal honor. Instead, he petulantly snaps to Beaufort, "No preliminary nonsense with him. No ceremonial phrasing. Straight from the shoulders as I tell you. Do you hear me? They're recalcitrant swine. They must feel it. . . . Is there anyone in this regiment who understands an order when it's given?"

THE SUBTLE ART OF LYING

After Thursday and his men have been massacred, *Fort Apache* concludes with an epilogue in which York, now the regiment's commander, is preparing to lead his men against the Apache again. At the fort, a group of journalists from the East who are to ride with the cavalrymen ask York about Thursday's legendary charge. There is a picture of it in Washington. Even though York knows the picture to be inaccurate, he tells the reporters that it is "correct in every detail." Thursday's last campaign was not a glorious expedition. Ignoring the advice of his seasoned officers, he acted like a madman, galloping his troops into a blind canyon where they were shot off their horses. The survivors who made the last stand were simply overwhelmed in seconds by the hundreds of horsemen who rode over them. When one considers Thursday's self-interested behavior as a commanding officer, York's highly hypocritical speech to the newspapermen in front of Thursday's portrait at the end of *Fort Apache* should not be surprising or shocking. Nevertheless, when York lies by omission, it is. Prior to taking command of the regiment, York's assertion as a man and an officer to keep his word to Cochise had identified him as an honorable individual. When Thursday accused York of cowardice and ordered him back to the safety of the supply wagons, York had even thrown down his gauntlet and challenged his commanding officer to a duel to protect his personal and professional reputation.

Even more shocking is the newspapermen's eagerness to believe Thursday's lies. Both York and the viewer know that the sabre that hangs under Thursday's portrait is actually York's. Both York and the viewer know that Thursday's last stand, as Ford himself would say, was "a very stupid job." The press do not question how wildly inaccurate the official representation of Thursday's Charge and Last Stand is because they believe the stories that they have been told about it: "There were these massed columns of Apaches in their war paint and feather bonnets . . . and here was Thursday leading his men in that heroic charge!" Both York and the viewer know that Cochise and his Apaches did not mass in columns as Thursday's cavalrymen did or wear feather bonnets while doing so, but York allows the newspapermen to hang on his every word. He even substantiates the legend by telling reporters that their memories of those stories are "correct in every detail" and encourages them to continue printing the legend while they accompany him and the regiment on their patrol. York's reticence and self-control may be, as Ford says elsewhere, "good" for the country, but to his viewer, who knows the true story, the regiment's new commander has obviously learned the subtle art of lying to support the emphasis that military culture places on duty and tradition.

Again, *Fort Apache*'s self-critique is supported by visual nuance. Before leaving with the reporters, it becomes evident that York has exchanged his cavalry Stetson for Thursday's kepi as he picks up his headgear on the way out the door. Adopting Thursday's hat, York is following Thursday's last order. Having taken Thursday's place, he becomes like Thursday. Given the unnatural eeriness of the sequence preceding Thursday's charge, one must wonder if the spirit of the dead has returned to possess the living. Thursday, York says, made the regiment something to be proud of: "They're better men than they used to be." Again, unlike the newspapermen to whom York speaks, the viewer knows that York's eulogy is what Colonel Wesley Merritt—a member of the court of inquiry convened to consider the behavior of Major Markus Albert Reno at the Battle of the Little Bighorn—would have called a "whitewash." Moreover, York himself does not believe that the individuals in his command are better men than Collingwood and the others who died with Thursday. If one listens carefully to York, he changes horses in midstream during his speech, ending his eulogy by stating that the men of his regiment have not changed at all. They will still "fight over cards or rotgut whiskey, but share the last drop in their canteens." As York concludes, "The faces may change . . . the names . . . but they're there: they're the regiment . . . the regular Army . . . now and fifty years from now."

Whether one views *Fort Apache* as a combat film that deconstructs the Western, as Richard Slotkin suggests, or as a Western that deconstructs the combat film, watching *Fort Apache* today places the viewer in the position of the serviceman—someone who knows what has really happened during combat. In 1948, watching *Fort Apache*, what could men, recently returned from the Second World War, do but recognize the irrationality of the behavior of men serving their country and acknowledge their complicity in that state of affairs by their silence? Ford's final shot of the movie, presenting a blatant hypocrite, in his kepi, leading his regiment to destroy the Apache, could not be more cynical.

At the conclusion of *Fort Apache*, there is no one to look up to, and thus, at the beginning of the McCarthy era and the second Red Scare in the United States, Ford forces his viewers to consider who or what they have been worshipping. Or, as Cochise, whom Slotkin would recognize as an original and quintessential American, would have wondered, why are heroes necessary at all?[34] Ford returns to answer these questions two years later in *She Wore a Yellow Ribbon*, the next film of the Cavalry Trilogy, in which he further explores what Russell Campbell describes in his essay on *Fort Apache* as an ideal, organic community "at odds with the main current both of the American dream and the American experience."[35]

8

KEEPING THE FAITH

She Wore a Yellow Ribbon

Ford had a great sense of how the lines should go—how to get the last ounce of character out of a character. He had a slogan, "Never mind if it's corn if it makes them cry."[1]—James Warner Bellah

As Dan Ford points out, *Fort Apache* not only put Argosy Pictures back into the black, it also convinced his grandfather "that the public shared his visions of military glory and was ready for more pictures based on the stories of James Warner Bellah."[2] Ford's next cavalry movie was also a hit with its audiences: *She Wore a Yellow Ribbon*, released in October 1948, grossed $5.2 million at the box office. Depicting the military on screen in the Western, Ford touched a responsive chord with the American public. Recently returned from the Second World War, audiences in the United States responded enthusiastically to Ford's treatment of the dog-faced soldiers of the U.S. Cavalry in "dirty shirt blue." Like many other Americans, Ford, a returned veteran, was deeply committed to the memories of the men with whom he had served. As Dan Ford points out, before the Second World War, the military had been an avocation for his grandfather: it had been something that "John had played at for his amusement and used as a way of gaining social status"—after the Second World War, the military "became the centerpiece of [Ford's] life."[3]

Many commentators have remarked on Ford's obsession with all things military after his return from serving in the OSS. According to

Dan Ford, after returning home in September 1945, Ford appeared to reintegrate back into civilian life: he picked up the pieces of his "old life and slipped back into his old routine . . . [b]ut the war had profoundly changed him."[4] In part, this change was manifested in his attempts to "get more medals, decorations, and awards."[5] Ford "went to great lengths to enhance his own military record[;] he was also willing to go to great lengths to help others who had been in the service. He couldn't do enough for Francis' son, Billy Ford, who had served for three and a half years as an infantryman in the South Pacific, and was also materially helpful to Larry and Cecile Deprita, who spent three and a half years in a Japanese prisoner-of-war camp."[6] Seeking recognition for his wartime achievements and the achievements of others, however, was only part of the aftermath of Ford's service in the military. Carrying his experiences in the military into his civilian life, Ford joined the American Legion, the Motion Picture Chapter of the Military Order of the Purple Heart, the Veterans of the O.S.S., and the Veterans of the 101 Detachment. He also began wearing fatigues and his Navy baseball cap with his captain's eagle when directing. By 1946, he was putting the finishing touches on a multipurpose facility designed to be a home away from home for the veterans of the Field Photographic Unit and their families, into which he "poured the remaining $75,000.00 from his *They Were Expendable* salary" and his "love for military tradition and service."[7]

More than anything else, Dan Ford says, the care and attention that Ford devoted to building and maintaining Field Photo Home, affectionately termed the Farm, reflected the change that he had undergone: his grandfather immersed himself in dealings with carpenters, contractors, and landscapers. Off from the main house, he built a chapel of wood frame construction, white with a green roof and miniature porticoes. Inside, the setting was nondenominational: on the altar was a Protestant cross, a Catholic crucifix, and a Star of David.[8] Inscribed above it were the words of A. E. Housman: "Here dead lie we because we did not choose to live and shame the land from which we sprung."[9] For Ford, the Farm was "both a living memorial to the men of the Field Photographic and a recreational facility where the veterans would want to come."[10]

Ford's continued loyalty to the men with whom he had served and his careful maintenance of their wartime experiences were not part of his romance with an idealized life of the military, but the natural response to war of a combat veteran who has returned home. As Jonathan Shay points out in *Odysseus in America: Combat Trauma and the Trials of Homecoming*, "soldiers, sailors, marines, airmen, no matter how humble and undistinguished, abhor being *forgotten*."[11] Typically, Ford, the veteran, was keeping what Shay terms "the vow of the combat soldier to his dead comrades to keep faith with them."[12] His faithfulness to them (and to the living) served to alleviate what Yael Danieli has called the four "existential functions of guilt": by denying helplessness; by keeping the dead alive by making them ever present in thought; by sustaining loyalty to the dead; and by affirming that "the world is still a just place where someone (even if only the guilt-ridden survivor alone) feels guilt at what was done."[13] Ford, like many other veterans, remembered his fallen comrades because "to keep their memory alive resuscitates the dead."[14] Not surprisingly, Dan Ford himself remembers that the Farm "had a feeling of family about it that was very special. In 1946 there were 176 active members and their families. In a very real way my grandfather recreated the world of his pictures at the Farm; the gatherings had the same sense of community that his films had."[15]

Without a doubt, John Ford felt deeply and personally responsible for the deaths of the men who had served under him during the Second World War. As Shay states, "Veterans carry the weight of friends' deaths in war and after war, and the weight of all those irretrievable losses among the living that, like the dead, can never be brought back."[16] In 1944, "Butch" Meehan, a well-liked and highly respected member of Field Photographic, one of Ford's favorites, was killed while filming Kachin guerrillas behind enemy lines in Burma. After Meehan's death, his photo hung over the fireplace of the Field Photo unit operating in Burma. Clearly, to the men with whom he served and who were still fighting, Meehan was gone but not forgotten. Ford's letter to Meehan's father expresses the depth of his sorrow and his continuing sense of responsibility for Meehan and for the welfare of his parents:

> Dear George:
>   It is with the deepest sorrow that I write to you and Mrs. Meehan about Arthur. By now I understand you have been informed officially of his heroic death. George, it is hard for me to put it in words—he was such a wonderful lad, one of the finest I've ever known. I am heartbroken to think he has gone. He had volunteered to take the

place of one of his buddies who was down with fever; it was a dangerous mission and Butch went down with his machine gun blazing.

We are stunned with grief back here, but of course our sorrow is
nothing compared to yours. He was such a swell kid—brave, consid-
erate, hard working, always thinking of the other guy, never of himself—it is so ironic that fate should cause him to go that way doing
the other guy's job.

I am trying to get several days leave so I might come to the Coast
and see you and your wife, if you wish. Perhaps I could tell you
better in words what I'm trying to say on paper, but I know that our
country, our Navy and our home town Hollywood has lost the brav-
est, cleanest, most lovable boy that ever made the supreme sacrifice
for the thing he loved and for which he fought.[17]

In all, thirteen members of the Field Photographic Unit died while
serving under Ford. The importance that Ford awarded to the honoring
of each of the dead is evident in his memorial to them at the Farm. He
also honored the sacrifices of those not under his command. As Mark
Harris points out in *Five Came Back*, the loss of Torpedo Squadron 8
also haunted Ford after Midway: "In the weeks after [the battle,] he
assembled all of the film that been taken of the men of the squadron—
about eight minutes in total—into a reel memorializing them . . . had
the movie reduced to 8-millimeter film—a size that would allow it to
run on inexpensive home-movie projectors—and had copies of *Torpedo
Squadron 8* hand-delivered across the country to each of the dead
men's families."[18]

Ford's faithfulness also extended to the sons of his relatives, colleagues, and friends. In 1945, just before the shooting of *They Were
Expendable*, "Junior" Stout, the son of Ford's old colleague Archie
Stout, was shot while jumping out of an unarmed DC-3 transport plane
on the German-occupied island of Jersey because he was carrying his
Cunningham combat camera, which looked somewhat like a machine
gun. Around the same time, Ford received the news that Kim and
Rosina Wai's oldest son, Francis, had been killed at Leyte in the Philippines. Dan Ford notes that his grandfather began production of *They
Were Expendable* with a heightened awareness of the cost of war, by
citing John Wayne's memory of working on the movie: "Jack was awfully
intense on that picture and working with more concentration than I had
ever seen. I think he was really out to achieve something." To Dan

Ford, *They Were Expendable* was the culmination of four years of the most intense personal experience for his grandfather.[19]

When one considers *They Were Expendable*, its preproduction, production, and postproduction, the overlapping of Ford's military experiences and civilian life is particularly evident. He used MGM's salary of $300,000 (which he received to produce and direct the movie) to create a "living memorial" to the men of his unit.[20] Dan Ford notes that his grandfather "wanted a place that would help preserve the communal feeling of the unit . . . where they could gather on Memorial Day to pay tribute to their fallen comrades."[21] Keeping his faith with the dead and the living, the Farm (aka Field Photographic Homes, Inc.) was a nonprofit corporation that not only served as a clubhouse, a rehabilitation center for the paraplegic veterans in the hospital next door, and a community service venue—the Farm was also an expression of Ford's survivor guilt: "I'm getting a big chunk of dough for the picture," Ford said, "which I am turning into a trust fund for Pennick and the boys. That at least clears my conscience a bit. It will give Pennick a place to store his loot."[22]

SURVIVOR GUILT

As Shay points out, survivor guilt, expressed via "the resuscitative function of memory—that of bringing the dead back to life—takes many often unrecognized forms."[23] Ford's postwar Westerns often concern themselves with this phenomenon. Reflecting Ford's wartime experiences, the heightened sense of community among fighting men in the Cavalry Trilogy expresses, in part, the veteran's understanding of combat trauma that Ford himself was experiencing and unable to leave behind. Scott Allen Nollen points out that *She Wore a Yellow Ribbon* begins where *Fort Apache* leaves off, fading in on the flag of the U.S. 7th Cavalry and starting with narration that includes the fact that "Custer is dead."[24] *She Wore a Yellow Ribbon* is the psychological and social study of a professional soldier who survives his tour of duty and is about to end his military service. The movie's opening therefore is heavily ironic. Valorizing the Last Stand at the Little Bighorn—which, in *Fort Apache,* had been presented as a vainglorious, self-serving gesture on the part of the troop's commanding officer—a pompous narrative voice-over announces that George Armstrong Custer and the 212 dead men and officers of the 7th Cavalry at the Little Bighorn have become "immortal," and now, at war in the Southwest, the U.S. Cavalry is finding itself threatened by the "Kiowa, Comanche, Arapaho, Sioux and Apache under Sitting Bull, Crazy Horse, Gall, and Crow King." The narrator then introduces Captain Nathan Brittles (John Wayne) as the "one man [in this situation] fated to wield the sword of destiny." However, when Brittles appears in his union suit and galluses, it becomes apparent that the narrative voice-over is just government whitewash. Tag Gallagher points out that Brittles "is indistinguishable from the jargon and protocol of military duty . . . the mentality of a professional soldier has become his second nature,"[25] but the captain is also a man who has suffered from survivor guilt in his overlapping professional *and* personal lives throughout most of his career. Introduced to the viewer a mere six days before he retires from his commission, Brittles keeps the dead alive by making them ever present in thought. His quarters are graced by photographs of his deceased wife, Mary, and daughters, Jane and Elizabeth. Every evening, he visits their graves, sits down on a camp chair beside their tombstones, waters the flowers that are planted there, and discusses his plans for his retirement and the events of his work as if Mary were present. Sustaining loyalty to the dead, he has not remarried and started another family and even refuses to participate in a "Welcome Home" dance in honor of his promotion to lieutenant-colonel as the Army's chief of scouts until he has first "made his report" to his wife.

Brittles affirms that "the world is still a just place where someone feels guilt at what was done."[26] Enlisting the help of his old friend when attempting to stop another Indian War, he tells Pony That Walks (Chief John Big Tree) that his "heart is sad" at what he sees: "Your young men painted for war. Their scalp knives red. The medicine drums talking. It is a bad thing!" "We must stop this war," he says to Pony That Walks. When Pony That Walks agrees with Brittles but remarks that it is too late for him to convince his young men to lay down their weapons, Brittles reminds him, "Old men should stop wars." And Brittles does: commandeering his own regiment, he scatters the warriors' horses, leaving them with no choice but to return peaceably to the reservation on foot.

Warmly nostalgic, *She Wore a Yellow Ribbon* mythologizes the U.S. Cavalry. At the beginning of the film, "the bloody guidon of the immortal 7th Cavalry" is presented as a national icon. And as Tag Gallagher notes, "Gone already are the documentary reenactments of nineteenth-century life. . . . The palpable feel of grit and guts is transposed into the purely iconic, icons stunningly recreating the colors and movement of Remington."[27] Throughout the movie, Ford's treatment of the U.S. Cavalry references Remington's highly romanticized display of military culture that both the initiated and the uninitiated consider compelling. Shot from low angles calculated to create heroic, dashing figures, the cavalrymen re-create Remington's dramatic compositions on the silver screen. Throughout the film, prancing, running, and rearing horses are shot from low angles that reinforce and emphasize the extreme poses and positions that Remington favored. As in Remington's depictions of the U.S. Cavalry, the brims of Ford's cavalrymen's Stetsons are pinned to the crowns of their hats to allow their wearers to sight and shoot more accurately. Ford's studied moments of cinematic tableaus, featuring histrionic horses and their determined riders, that punctuate the action at hand have prompted Bill Levy to note that "one can't help notice that every time John Wayne's Captain Brittles rides ahead of the column, McGrath's bugler is right behind him, his horse dramatically rearing and McGrath theatrically raising his bugle, attempting to steal the scene from John Wayne."[28] McGrath, of course, is not attempting to steal the scene from Wayne, but is being used to create yet another "Remington" moment for the viewer. Even Ford's use of Technicolor in this movie is Remingtonesque. Winton C. Hoch, who won an Oscar for his color cinematography in this film, remarks that Ford said before production started, "I want Remington color."[29]

Ford's use of Remington color in *She Wore a Yellow Ribbon* is carefully contrasted against the reality of campaigning in the American Southwest. Life for Ford's cavalrymen may look romantic, but its reality is not. As Robert E. Lee commented to James Longstreet after witnessing a federal charge repulsed at the Battle of Fredericksburg:[30] "It is well that war is so terrible otherwise we should grow too fond of it."[31] Aware of the dashing display of the cavalry, Flint Cohill (John Agar) sarcastically remarks to Olivia Dandridge (Joanne Dru) that life in the cavalry is only attractive to those who do not actually live it: "Romantic, isn't it? Guidons gaily fluttering. Bronzed men lustily singing. Horses prancing," he says, and then undercuts his romantic description of the situation, which aptly describes many of Remington's works, with what Miss Dandridge considers to be a very "vulgar" expression of his personal experience that sums up being a cavalryman—"Bunions aching."

BROTHERLY LOVE

Because it is a record of men who became Great Men, History is personalized in *She Wore a Yellow Ribbon*. As Brittles, shaking his head, reads the list of the dead at Little Bighorn, he pauses, his silence giving life and meaning to the names of the dead. At Mary's grave that evening, he relates the sad news that her waltzing partner, Miles Keough, "that happy go lucky Irishman," was massacred at Little Bighorn with George Custer. "I guess I was a little jealous [of Keough]," Brittles admits. "Never could waltz myself." Throughout *She Wore a Yellow Ribbon*, Brittles's strong and lasting attachments to his wife, his men, and his fellow officers convey Ford's experience of military camaraderie, what the Greeks called *philia*. The experience of manly or brotherly love belonging to a "centuries-old tradition of strong non-sexual male friendship,"[32] *philia* is what McKubin T. Owens would recognize as "the glue of the military ethos . . . friendship, comradeship, or brotherly love."[33]

At first, the idea of brotherly love being the cohesive force that forges the U.S. Cavalry into being a crack fighting unit seems incongruous. However, as Shay points out, "modern American English makes soldiers' love for special comrades into a problem, because the word 'love' evokes sexual and romantic associations. But 'friendship' seems too bland for the passion of care that arises between soldiers in combat."[34] Throughout *She Wore a Yellow Ribbon*, one does not expect hard-bitten, grizzled veterans like Captain Brittles, Sergeant Quincannon (Victor McLaglen), and the troopers at Fort Sill to love one another or to express that love, but they do.

Generally considered the moment when John Wayne "blossomed into maturity as a professional actor,"[35] Captain Brittles's handing over of his command to Second Lieutenant Ross Pennell (Harry Carey Jr.) reveals the depth of his emotional commitment to the men who serve under him. Choking back his feelings, Brittles tells his men that he has always been proud of them and surreptitiously wipes away tears when his troop presents him with a solid silver watch with their sentiment, "Lest We Forget," engraved on its back. Brittles cares for the men whom he commands as if they were his children. He is old enough to "tan" Lieutenant Cohill's bottom. A paternal figure, he promises to return to the men whom he has left behind to guard the fort, assuring Cohill, "I'll get you out of this pocket, son"—his faithfulness to his men even supersedes his duty to his commanding officer. Brittles keeps his word to Cohill, risking a court-martial to save his men, and then further protects them by averting an Indian War. Throughout the movie, he ensures that his men are cared for: Corporal Mike Quayne (Tom Tyler) volunteers for duty after surgery to be told by Brittles, "Get back in that wagon, Quayne"; after accepting his silver watch, Brittles ensures that Top Sergeant Quincannon will spend the remaining two weeks of his service before his retirement in the cooler so he can retire "a top soldier."

The inhabitants at Fort Sill (with the exception of the sutler and his gun-runners) are all comrades. Gender makes no difference in this film—men and women are either "Army" or they are not. On one hand, Olivia Dandridge is not considered to be "Army enough to stay the winter." On the other, affectionately known as "Old Iron Pants," Abby Allshard (Mildred Natwick) *is*. She is an experienced campaigner who "planted 24 gardens in the first ten years of [her] marriage [and] never stayed long enough to see a single bloom." Brittles (whom Abby has affectionately dubbed "Marching from Georgia") pats her on the shoulder after Quayne's surgery and says, "Thanks, soldier." When Brittles does retire, he leaves "Old Iron Pants" one of his saddles so she will be more comfortable.

This attachment to beloved comrades inspires altruism and readiness to take risks against outsiders both defensively and offensively. Because of this, Cohill, Pennell, and the troopers follow Brittles's orders without hesitation. Even when they know that Brittles is acting without orders, they do not hesitate to help him stampede the Indians' ponies and follow the warriors who are on foot back to their reservation.

The charismatic impact of a leader rests on his passionate spirit—what Aristotle called *thumos*—the source "of any power of commanding and any feeling for freedom."[36] Trust goes to those leaders whose spirit leads them to follow a higher order morality, rather than blind obedience to hierarchy and protocol.[37] In *She Wore a Yellow Ribbon*, because power is used in accordance with "what's right," trust in one's comrades is evident up and down the chain of command. Brittles's men respect him because his obedience to his commanding officer is not blind but critical and questioning. Major Mac Allshard (George O'Brien) stays up half the night wrestling whether or not to send "the Dandridge girl" home. When he decides to do so, Brittles does not hesitate to respectfully protest in writing the decision of his commanding officer, Major Mac Allshard (George O'Brien), to "saddle his troop with his female relations at this critical hour." For his part, Allshard does not hesitate to reprimand Brittles when he requests permission to "rest the troop for three hours and start back" to relieve Cohill and his two squads who were left behind in the Paradise. As Allshard points out, "Every time he gave an order, the men would look at you. They'd wonder if he were doing the right thing. Do you want to ruin the boy?"

Loyalties between the men and their officers are not only predicated by the troop itself but also by the men's allegiances to one another during the Civil War. The camaraderie that existed between the Confederate War veterans while fighting for the Confederacy continues to bind Captain Tyree (Ben Johnson) and Trooper John Smith (Rudy Bowman). This bonding, however, does not interfere with the brotherhood of the troop as a whole. Old Iron Pants is "proud" to sew an approximation of the Stars and Bars for Tyree and his colleagues to spread over John Smith's coffin. When Brittles receives his letter announcing his appointment as "Chief of Scouts with a rank of lieutenant colonel" from "the Yankee War Department," Tyree wishes that Brittles had been holding a full hand—that the endorsements in the letter had been from Phil Sheridan, William Tecumseh Sherman, Ulysses S. Grant, *and* Robert E. Lee.

As Shay points out, the bond of camaraderie among the troops means that when one among them "does something magnificent, [his comrades] feel pride; when he does something vicious, [they] feel shame."[38] At Sudro's Wells, for example, Trooper John Smith, in the act of dying, tells Brittles that he would "like to commend this boy for how he handled his action in the best tradition of the Cavalry." And conversely, when Brittles reprimands Cohill and Pennell for fighting over Olivia, he and his lieutenants express shame over their breach of conduct. Addressing Cohill (and Pennell), Brittles points out their dereliction of duty to their comrades: "Mr. Cohill," he says, "it is a bitter thing indeed to learn that an officer who's had nine years' experience, the officer to whom I'm yielding command of the troop in two days, should have so little grasp of leadership as to allow himself to be chivvied into a go at fisticuffs while taps still sounds over a brave man's grave. God help this troop when I'm gone." Mumbling "Sorry, Ross" and "I'm sorry, Flint" after Brittles leaves, Cohill and Pennell hang their heads and admit their weakness while shamefacedly apologizing to one another.

Sergeant Quincannon's barroom brawl is another example of brotherly love. Following Brittles's order to have a drink to celebrate his captain's retirement, Quincannon dresses up in Brittles's civilian suit and derby, becoming his commanding officer's double. Encountering Sergeant Hochbauer (Michael Dugan) on the way to the bar to buy a drink, Quincannon, under orders, further emphasizes his status as Brittles's loyal brother-in-arms: When Hochbauer exclaims that Quincannon is improperly dressed and out of uniform, the sergeant retorts that he is correctly dressed because he is "wearing the uniform of a *retired gentleman*" (italics mine). A celebration of Brittles's retirement, the fistfight that ensues expresses the affection and loyalty that the men feel toward their captain out of uniform. Quincannon is drinking because he is following orders and having "a couple of drinks while [he's] waiting"; likewise, Hochbauer and every man attacking Quincannon in the bar is following Brittles's command to throw him "in the guardhouse."

As in the field, the troopers' cohesion in the bar creates courage by reducing fear. Thus, in spite of the terrible damage that Quincannon inflicts on his associates, the troopers helping Hochbauer persist in attempting to arrest him—and just as faithful to his commanding officer, Quincannon continues to resist their attempts. The direct emotional impact of Brittles's spirit is visible in the trust that his men place in him. The brawl continues unabated until "Old Iron Pants," who is not acting under Brittles's orders, arrives and marches Quincannon off at double time to the stockade herself.

As Shay points out, camaraderie produces courage in combat because a leader's love for his troops reduces his own level of fear, which in turn instills confidence in his troops. Beyond an imitative or contagious effect of the leader's confidence, fear is directly alleviated when troops can feel the leader's love for them. [39] Brittles's affection for his men is reflected in C Troop's complete confidence in him as their commanding officer. When Brittles returns to the Paradise to help Co-hill, Pennell, and their men who have been trailing the Kiowas, Coman-ches, Arapahoes, and Cheyenne dog-soldiers, his arrival spontaneously elicits a cheer. "Glad to see you," Cohill exclaims. "And I you," Brittles replies. Cohill does not "need a written order" from Brittles to obey his directives. His word is sufficient not only for Cohill and Pennell but also for Tyree, who accompanies Brittles into the enemy's camp. While dismounting to visit Pony That Walks, Brittles asks the Southerner, who is carrying the troop's guidon, "Were you ever scared, Captain Tyree?" Tyree, who has been ordered "to volunteer again," replies, "Yes, sir, up to and including now."

HONOR AND MORALITY

Based on the kind of courage that can only be the result of camaraderie and trust, the military culture in *She Wore a Yellow Ribbon* is a moral system expressed in highly sentimental terms. Francis Lieber's 1863 *Instructions for the Government of Armies of the United States in the Field* continues to be the continuing consensus of the serious military professional, be he a member of the United States Cavalry or the Con-federate States Army, for "men who take up arms against one another in public war do not cease on this account to be moral beings, responsible to one another and to God."[40] Thus, when Brittles offers a graveside eulogy in the memory of John Smith, he commends "the soul of Rome Clay, late brigadier general, Confederate States Army . . . known to his comrades here . . . as John Smith, United States Cavalry, a gallant soldier and a Christian gentleman."

Whether the cavalrymen fought for the North or the South during the Civil War, they all exhibit the qualities expected of the warrior ethos of Christian virtue and courtly manners. In the scene preceding Brit-tles's eulogy, which discharges the cavalryman's duty to God, for exam-ple, Tyree and his companions carry out their duty to women by chival-rously thanking Old Iron Pants, who (being "Army" herself) has fulfilled her own duty to her countrymen and fellow Christians by honoring their fallen comrade with a Stars and Bars. An honor code, chivalry requires moral conduct outside the rules of combat. Military culture, therefore, is a way of life as well as war.

Ford's presentation of the military as a moral system in *She Wore a Yellow Ribbon* not only reflects his own wartime experiences but also arises from his experience of returning to civilian life. As Dan Ford points out, on his return his grandfather found Hollywood more of a sham than ever before: "after four years with the O.S.S., after having served with the likes of Bill Donovan, Al Wedemeyer, and Claire Chennault," Hollywood did seem to be "seedy, shoddy, and full of hucksters."[41] As Bellah says to Dan Ford, "Hollywood is phony as all get out. The rule is that you're dear, dear friends with anybody you're working with and you don't know him the next day."[42] The divide between military and civilian life noted by Ford and Bellah is also apparent in *She Wore a Yellow Ribbon*. Civilians in *She Wore a Yellow Ribbon* who are not "Army" or Indians are hucksters: Karl Rynders (Harry Woods) and his henchmen are gun-runners who stand to profit from the escalating hostilities by hawking their wares to Red Shirt (Noble Johnson) and his followers. Rynders's highly unethical "right smart tradin'" displays neither *philia* nor *thumos*. After insulting Red Shirt's honor, Rynders receives a well-deserved arrow in his chest. He is immediately abandoned by his fellow traders: one is shot in the back as he attempts to flee; the other screams as he is burned alive. Brittles, Pennell, and Tyree witness the melee but do not attempt to intervene. The camaraderie that governs their conduct does not extend to Rynders and his men.

The completeness of the fraternity that exists among the cavalrymen is evident as they share a plug of tobacco while watching natural justice take its course in the Indians' encampment. Brittles's offer of chewing tobacco to his men not only signals the cavalrymen's commonality, it also expresses solidarity. Brittles's comment that excuses Tyree's reluctance to chew tobacco—"Chawing tobacco is a nasty habit. It's been known to turn a man's stomach"—has two functions. His reference to the nasty habit that has been known to "to turn a man's stomach" alludes to the spectacle of the gun-runner being tortured and burned alive in front of them. It also functions as an invitation to Pennell, who has been planning to leave the regiment, to rejoin the group. Pennell accepts Brittles's invitation: "I'll take a chaw if you please, sir," he says and takes the tobacco from his commanding officer. When the men mount their horses and prepare to leave, their camaraderie has been reestablished. Brittles asks Pennell, "Still figuring on resigning, mister?" and Pennell replies, "No, sir."

BEING GOLDEN

Emphasizing the high ethical standards of the military and the moral nature of life in the cavalry, wardrobe in this film is used, like Brittles's tobacco, to signal the principled ethos of military life. Ford, who "was always careful in choosing wardrobe," "would go down to every actor [with Bill Clothier] to Western Costume and . . . pick out clothes for actors."[43] As Harry Carey Jr. remembers, Ford "loved wardrobe fittings. He loved the western clothes of the 1870s and actually helped you put them on, especially the bandannas and the hats."[44] "Supposed to be a stickler for authenticity [in costuming],"[45] Ford, atypically, ignored historical accuracy when dressing the officers and men in *She Wore a Yellow Ribbon* and instead costumed them as he saw fit, standardizing the cavalrymen's uniforms and thereby translating the experience of the cavalrymen in 1876 into an experience that his twentieth-century viewers recently returned from the Second World War would recognize and identify as being like their own.

As Vincent A. Transano points out in "The 7th US Cavalry Regiment Fought in the Battle of the Little Bighorn," in 1876

> the soldiers' appearance was much at odds with popular portrayals of the Indian-fighting army. Their uniforms, especially those of the officers, were wildly non-regulation. Many officers wore custom-tailored sailor-style shirts, buckskins, straw hats (or any kind of hat that caught their fancy); the men wore blue shirts of various shades, battered black campaign hats or privately purchased civilian hats; and occasionally individual troopers even wore white canvas trousers or had their light-blue regulation trousers reinforced with canvas.[46]

At first glance, Ford's troopers appear to be popular portrayals of mounted infantry during the Indian Wars. Ford himself, however, modified the look of the cavalrymen to introduce a subtle aesthetic argument supporting his treatment of military culture into the film.

In 1876 (the year that Custer and his command died at Little Bighorn), the cavalry surtout or greatcoat would have been standard issue sky blue. As Gregory J. W. Urwin points out in *The United States Cavalry: An Illustrated History, 1776–1944*, "the enlisted man's overcoat did not actually receive a yellow lining until the 1880s."[47] Dressing officers and enlisted men in a cavalry greatcoat made of a darker shade, approaching royal blue wool, and sporting detachable cape with a yellow wool lining that would not have appeared on the frontier until well into the 1880s, Ford aligns deep shades of yellow with the cavalrymen throughout this film to associate military values with all that is superior—gold, in particular, is associated with the cavalry officers, a color that signifies that which is most valued, a hidden or elusive treasure, supreme illumination, and the final stage of spiritual ascension.

Throughout *She Wore a Yellow Ribbon*, the golden lining of the officers' capes and the officers' golden yellow stripes and chevrons not only signal the integrity of an officer and a gentleman, they also identify individuals as a fraternity—a band of brothers. As the narrator's voice-over announces, "There may be one man, one captain fated to wield the sword of destiny," the camera rests on a sign outside Brittles's quarters—over a blue background, the words "Nathan Brittles, Capt. Cav. U. S. A." are inscribed in large gold letters.

Ford also uses variants of the color yellow to link sentiment with morality, thereby consistently reinforcing the narrative's depictions of Brittles, his lieutenants, and his sergeants as moral individuals who function within an ethical system. Thus, a close-up of the bugler, played by Frank McGrath, begins the movie with his cape thrown back over his shoulder; the gold lining, golden trumpet, and its golden braid in the foreground dominate the screen, announcing the ideal nature of military culture. As the film's narrative action progresses, it becomes evident that the more gold a character exhibits, the closer to the ideal his behavior becomes. There are few opportunities for heroic action while the company is at Fort Starke. Thus, Brittles's and his men's yellow stripes and golden linings are not much in evidence. As McLaglen lectures the troops on minding their language in the presence of ladies, for example, he is the only man wearing gold. His sergeant's chevrons and the stripes on his pants contrast with the costuming of his men. In this scene, the troopers' pants do not sport yellow stripes and their motley red, blue, and white neckerchiefs outnumber the yellow bandanas found around their necks. As the company leaves Fort Starke, however, the honor guard that escorts them out the gate not only sports flags but also displays yellow strips and insignia. And on the trail, more gold is evident, with more officers wearing yellow scarves, gold insignia, and stripes. In the medium shots of the individuals riding in the column, the officers' stripes are necessarily foregrounded on horseback, and the linings of their capes often appear because of the action involved when riding and the wind that is blowing. By the time Brittles's column meets up with Quayne's patrol, it seems that every cavalryman (dressed in capes whose yellow linings appear as the horses run) is golden. Insignia and stripes are prominently displayed in each shot, identifying the relationships of speakers to one another. Despite the long, dusty miles that the cavalrymen have ridden, even the gold braid on the men's hats glistens in the sun.

When one considers this treatment of the color yellow among the men, Brittles's conversation with Quayne is extremely instructive. Having escaped a marauding band of Arapahoe warriors, Quayne and his men are reunited with their comrades, but their reunion is not joyous. Quayne has been severely wounded because Brittles's column did not relieve them in time. Surrounded and physically supported by his men, Quayne's golden insignia supports his men's well-founded trust in their officer: Quayne's leadership and his courage under fire cannot be doubted and his concern for his men's well-being is evident as he makes his report to Brittles. Aptly, Brittles, who had failed to be at their rendezvous, is relieved of the gold insignia that distinguishes Quayne. Covering his uniform, Brittles's surcoat hides even the stripes on his trousers. Although a brisk breeze is blowing, Brittles's cape does not reveal its lining as Quayne, making his report, looks at him accusingly and says, "They had us ringed. At night . . . we got away . . . made it to the relief point. But you were not there, sir." Unlike the faithful who have followed Quayne, Brittles has no yellow braid around the crown of his hat. As Brittles, who is clearly distressed by his inability to have relieved Quayne, replies, "I wanted to be there, Corporal," a slight breeze gently opens the edge of his cape, revealing a thin line of gold. Man-made, this breeze blows against the wind that causes Brittles's bandana to stream in the opposite direction. It becomes evident that Brittles's conduct has not met his men's expectations, but as he acknowledges Quayne's "good clear report" and lets him know that the report will stand on his record and earn him "that extra stripe in a couple of years," his fidelity and the company's brotherhood are re-established. Movement replaces stasis and the yellow lining of Brittles's cape billows out. As Quayne is helped to the wagon, more yellow insignia appear on the men's uniforms. While Brittles calls for a doctor to attend Quayne and whiskey for the wounded man, the moving interplay of blue and gold on the screen is re-established.

Ford's sentimental treatment of Brittles's last review of his men at Fort Starke showcases the entire company on horseback awaiting their captain with their capes thrown open on their shoulders. The waves of gold created by the exposed yellow linings of these capes as they wait in line express the depth of their love for and loyalty to their commanding officer. Not surprisingly, the sentiment on the silver watch they have bought for him reads, "To Captain Brittles . . . From C Troop . . . lest we forget." This highly emotional moment, which Quincannon describes as "a black day for the Army," is one of the movie's most colorful. Every man is wearing gold for the occasion—even the doctor sports a gold braid around the crown of his hat. The strong diagonal golden line formed by the horsemen is indeed something that Brittles is "proud of" and is almost overpowering. In a later scene, Brittles and Tyree enter the ballroom to discover a column of applauding men and women decorated in gold. As the camera dollies rapidly backward, the features of the individuals turned away from the camera toward the door are blurred. On the men's uniforms, however, the gleaming yellow badges, crests, insignia, and stripes are clearly visible. The women, their backs to the camera, are remarkable because of the startling and individual nature of the yellow ribbons that they are wearing in their hair. Promoted to top sergeant, Sergeant Quincannon is particularly notable. Stepping forward to welcome Brittles back to the fort, Quincannon is resplendent in his shining sergeant's regalia. His shoulders bristle with gleaming yellow bars and stripes—more golden chevrons and insignia have been added to his uniform. As the company applauds Brittles's return, the recently promoted top sergeant steps forward and welcomes the newly appointed chief of scouts with the words that succinctly define the two as comrades: "Welcome home, col'nel darlin'" (italics mine). As *She Wore a Yellow Ribbon* ends, it is apparent that military matters are always matters of the heart. Flint Cohill and Olivia Dandridge announce their engagement to Brittles, who has "known it all the time." "Everyone on the post knew it above the rank of second lieutenant," he says.

Ford also uses the color yellow to inform the romantic subplot concerning Cohill, Pennell, and Dandridge in *She Wore a Yellow Ribbon*. When "Trooper" Dandridge appears "ready for duty" with a pale yellow ribbon in her hair and refuses to tell her suitors for whom it is worn, romantic love disrupts the company's fraternity. Brittles, who does not take the young woman's flirting seriously, remarks, "For me . . . I'll make these young bucks jealous." Thinking the yellow ribbon may be for one of them, Cohill and Pennell, however, vie for Olivia's attention and at one point in the movie almost come to blows over her. And when the young men prepare to fight over Olivia, they remove their capes and begin stripping their blouses, removing all the golden emblems of their camaraderie.

Ford's sophisticated use of color throughout his portrayal of Dandridge subtly supports the transformation of a teasing minx into a mature young woman who becomes "Army enough to stay the winter." In 1876, a yellow ribbon in a woman's hair did not indicate that she had a sweetheart in the cavalry. In fact, a yellow ribbon denoted quite the opposite state of affairs. Speaking to Dan Ford, James Bellah, who "didn't like the idea [or] the title" of the movie, notes that "in the old days, a Yellow Ribbon in a girl's hair was the sign of a whore." Ford's attention to Dandridge's costuming can be seen in the contrast between the golden yellow used to denote rank and relationship between the men and the brighter, lighter shades of yellow used in the women's dress. Dandridge's ribbon is particularly interesting as its color slowly deepens as the action of the movie progresses. When she first accompanies the company to Sudro's Wells, her ribbon is such a light shade of yellow that it appears almost white. By the time she has returned to Fort Starke, the shade has deepened into a bright yellow. At the dance, like the other women who are "Army," she sports a vibrant yellow ribbon in her hair. When her engagement to Cohill is announced, she is ready to stay for the winter at the fort, having made the necessary transition from individual passion to a much deeper fraternity. In short, she has become a member of the community at Fort Starke. Having been initiated into military culture, she acquires the moral knowledge that she lacked at the beginning of the movie. As Brittles leaves the room "to make his report" at the graveside, she hands him a darker nosegay of golden flowers to lay beside his wife's tombstone.

FUNCTIONS OF GUILT

Unlike his critique in *Fort Apache*, which concerns itself with the individual and his ego, Ford's appraisal focuses here on how individuals are prepared socially and psychologically for war. Ford blends humor and sentiment in Quincannon's famous barroom brawl to comment on the resuscitative function of survivor guilt. Quincannon and several troopers honor Brittles's retirement and their memory of their commanding officer. The fight begins when Quincannon refuses to accompany Hochbauer to the guardhouse until he has toasted Brittles's memory. Once his attackers have been reduced to a pile of bodies on the barroom's floor, Quincannon announces, "Men, now we want no unpleasantness. A toast first and the guardhouse after, if you're able. And it's all on me I'm paying." The troopers stagger to their feet and join Quincannon in a drink to "Captain Nathan Brittles," afterward breaking their glasses in his honor, to ensure that those glasses cannot be used to drink a lesser toast. Overcome with emotion, Quincannon announces, "I . . . I . . . I thank you, comrades. . . . This has been a very pleasant moment" before punching a comrade in the face. About to be taken to the guardhouse, he turns around, returns to the bar, and solicitously inquires, "Are you hurt, Hanz?" On being told, "He's all right, Sarge," Quincannon begins throwing men out the door, and the fighting begins again. Ironically, Brittles's men respect his memory in the same way they honor the dead—by fighting. Violence, not tenderness, is the means by which cavalrymen live. As Quincannon informs Hochbauer before the melee begins, "Laddie, I've never gone any place peaceably in me life."

Ford's critique of military culture may also be found in the preparations for war that take place at Pony That Walks's camp. As the narrator's voice-over remarks, all the young warriors are prepared socially and psychologically for war. These horsemen are "young leaders" who "are ready to hurl the finest light cavalry in the world against Fort Starke." As in Fort Starke, war is a phenomenon that affects the entire community in the Indians' encampment. The voice-over notes, "In the Kiowa village the beat of the drums echoes in the pulse beat of the young braves. All chant of war." As with the cavalrymen, spirit is accompanied by camaraderie: the Indian warriors are "fighters under a common banner, old quarrels forgotten, Comanche rides with Arapaho, Apache with Cheyenne."

In *She Wore a Yellow Ribbon*, war is the province of young men. And here, Ford's critique offers a solution to the problem of war that has underpinned the action of the film's narrative. Throughout, it has been evident that older, experienced soldiers regard matters of honor and brotherly love differently than their younger colleagues. Unlike Cohill and Pennell, Brittles pays little attention to Olivia's flirting. Indeed, he cannot not take her attentions seriously. After exclaiming, "I'll make those young bucks jealous," he forgets about the encounter. He is far more concerned with the well-being of the entire command under his care. Unlike Red Shirt, Pony That Walks, who has experienced war, is not convinced that Custer's death and the return of the buffalo are signs that the time has come to drive American immigrants from Indian lands.

This divide between the old and the young is also showcased when Brittles visits the Kiowa village. As the voice-over notes, in the Kiowa village, unlike Red Shirt and his followers, "the old men stand silent. Even Pony That Walks has been howled down at the council fires." Valuing the lives of his men over his personal honor and peace over war, Brittles visits Pony That Walks to enlist his help to stop the oncoming war. War, Brittles says, "is a bad thing," and Pony That Walks agrees with him: "A bad thing, Nathan. Many will die. My young men, your young men." The situation, he says is "no good. No good." Unlike Brittles, Pony That Walks knows that it is too late to halt the young men from going to war. Having become a Christian, he has lost his ability to lead. His young men respect only "big medicine."

At this point, Ford's critique of "war fever" could not be stronger. As Brittles points out, the function of old soldiers is not to wage war but to stop it from occurring. He tells Pony That Walks, "We are too old for war, but old men should stop wars." Having experienced war, neither man desires it. McBride notes that "the poignant fellowship between these two old-timers of different races is unusual for a Western from that time," but feels that the men's friendship is an "easy sentimental" gesture: Ford's attention is focused instead on "the development of Brittles's character and romantic visual beauty."[48] *She Wore a Yellow Ribbon* is, as McBride points out, "a lyric poem about mortality, the bittersweet story of an old cavalry officer coming to terms with the necessity of turning over his command to a younger generation,"[49] but when one considers the distinction made here in such an unusual way for the Western between the old and the young, the film also insists that its viewers come to terms with the complicated (and often conflicted) nature of military culture itself. Wielding the sword of destiny, Brittles elects not to wage war. Instead, he chooses to ensure peace by scattering the Kiowa's pony herd, thereby disabling the warriors. Without their horses, the Kiowas cannot be warriors. Thus there are "no casualties, no Indian War, no court-martial." Without their mounts, the Kiowa can no longer be the "finest light cavalry in the world." Ultimately, the viewer learns what the old captain has known all along: war itself is simply a matter of pride. "You will have your soldiers follow the hostiles all the way back to the reservation," he tells Cohill and Pennell. "You'll follow a mile behind 'em. Walking hurts their pride. Your watching'll hurt it worse."

Like *Fort Apache*, *She Wore a Yellow Ribbon* is, at its base, a movie made for veterans. Indeed, the two may be seen as companion pieces, for *She Wore a Yellow Ribbon*'s loving treatment of Brittles balances *Fort Apache*'s scalding criticism of Thursday. By 1949, Ford and other veterans of the Second World War had discovered their return from the battlefields was much like that experienced by the soldiers after the Civil War. As S. L. A. Marshall writes in *Crimsoned Prairie: The Indian Wars*: "The common soldier who had lately saved the nation had that quickly ceased to be a popular hero. In fact, he became nigh an object of scorn."[50] And as Shay notes, Civil War veterans often wandered for long periods after the war's end and had trouble finding employment.[51] Ford himself went to great lengths to help others when returning from military service find work. Involved in Cold War hostilities at home, his recently demobilized audiences would have recognized his positive foregrounding of the dynamics of military culture in *She Wore a Yellow Ribbon* and agreed with his critique of the young men's eagerness to fight. Ford's audiences would also have understood the significance of his homage to the professional soldier at the film's end. They would also have known, when the narrator's voice-over proclaims, "So here they are, the dog-faced soldiers, the regulars, the fifty cents a day professionals, riding the outposts of a nation, men in dirty shirt blue and only a cold page in the history books to mark their passing, but wherever they rode, and whatever they fought for, that place became the United States," that they were looking not only at their antecedents but also at themselves.

It seems reasonable therefore to conclude that the popularity of *She Wore a Yellow Ribbon* rests on what Shay identifies as the "existential functions of guilt"[52]—denying the helplessness of survivors, sustaining loyalty to the dead, and keeping the dead alive by making them ever present in thought. Even more important, at the movie's end, the peace that is won and Brittles's appointment to the rank of chief of scouts as a lieutenant colonel affirm that the world is still "a just place." As Gallagher points out, in *She Wore a Yellow Ribbon*, "gone already are the documentary reenactments of nineteenth-century life[;] the palpable feel of grit and guts is transposed into the purely iconic, icons stunningly recreating the colors and movement of Remington."[53] These icons, re-creations of the military culture that members of Ford's audiences, in the process of readjusting to civilian life, would immediately have recognized, having experienced combat only a few years before, make the action on the screen meaningful and remind the ordinary man, returned from war, that, like Trooper John Smith, he too was "a gallant soldier and a Christian gentleman."

9

THE WAR AT HOME

Rio Grande

The first day on location in Moab, Utah, with Old Man Ford was something akin to my first day in the army. [1]—Chuck Roberson

Filmed in 1950 as *Rio Bravo* and retitled *Rio Grande Command* before its release, the final film of Ford's Cavalry Trilogy, *Rio Grande*, was shot on location in Moab Valley, Utah, instead of Monument Valley, and on Stage 11 at the Republic lot. *Rio Grande* was a Ford throwaway, made quickly and cheaply to secure funding from Herbert Yates at Republic Pictures for a project that the director was really interested in—*The Quiet Man*. Shot at an astounding speed in thirty-two days,[2] *Rio Grande* cost only $1.2 million to make and had earned $2 million at the box office by June 1952.[3] Based on James Warner Bellah's "Mission with No Record," *Rio Grande*, like *Fort Apache*, has been noted for its attention to historical realism. Ford chose to use authentic Sibley tents with Primus stoves sitting outside for cavalry housing and other articles used on the frontier at the time the story takes place. He also ordered the stuntmen and actors in the fighting regiment to drill on horseback and on foot until they "could have put any genuine army cavalry unit to shame. (Of course he called it rehearsing.)" As stuntman Bad Chuck Roberson remembers, "Pennick drilled us in the hot sun until the sweat poured off us, and our uniforms stuck to our bodies. Ford loved every minute of it. We were his personal soldiers, as dirty and stinking as any army that ever chased an Indian across the desert in the middle of July; probably dirtier."[4]

An examination of America's romance with combat culture in general—and the partisan nature of the American Character in particular—*Rio Grande* charts the complexities of military life caused by Colonel Kirby Yorke, a Civil War veteran who, like Owen Thursday in *Fort Apache*, stays in combat mode, privileging his oath of office over his duty to his family. Critical response to this film has been sharply divided. On one hand, one finds the perception that Ford was creating heart-warming Americana resembling that found in *Drums along the Mohawk* when making *Rio Grande*. Tag Gallagher, for example, points out that *Rio Grande* is "a storybook movie, accessible and privileged, cozy and strong, almost a chapter of reveille in an old man's fireside reverie, a mixture of epic and corn."[5] On the other hand, critics argue that *Rio Grande*'s depiction of military life promotes government propaganda. Max Westbrook, for instance, accuses Ford of being part of "a tradition of lying about the American experience": Ford's Americana in *Fort Apache*, Westbrook claims, justifies "the cover up of the Kennedy assassination, Vietnam, Watergate, and Contragate."[6]

Within these camps, critical responses to *Rio Grande* also conflict. Like Gallagher, Frank Wetta and Martin Novelli consider *Rio Grande* to be martial Americana, but they take a very different tack when discussing the movie by arguing that in it Ford simply endorses the military. Commenting on *Rio Grande* and the other films of the Cavalry Trilogy as examples of the Cold War Western,[7] they argue that "by the 1970s, the heroic West of John Ford had become 'the killing grounds of American imperialism.'"[8] Many critics agree with Wetta and Novelli's assessment of Ford's work: David Thompson, for example, asserts that the Trilogy "amounts to prettification of a lie . . . the lines of cavalry . . . the lone figure in Monument Valley": these images carry with them "no artistic integrity," Thompson says, "no intellectual honesty, and certainly nothing of historical value"—Ford's cavalry films are mere "'endorsements' of the military."[9] Paul Buhle and Dave Wagner also pronounce *Fort Apache* and *She Wore a Yellow Ribbon* "reactionary" and "distinctly conservative-patriotic (and racist)."[10]

It seems that the virulence of *Rio Grande*'s critical reception can also be attributed, in part, to its sensitive historical backdrop, the cavalry action during the Red River Wars in the Southwest, and, in part, to being released the same year that Ford made *This is Korea!* for Republic Pictures. Wetta and Novelli themselves conclude that *Fort Apache*, *She Wore a Yellow Ribbon*, and *Rio Grande* continue to resonate as "the American Army seeks to pacify the old imperial frontiers of Afghanistan, Iraq and other remote regions of the world, much as the British regiments had done earlier."[11] Even Joseph McBride's assessment of the film is that "Ford let his anti-Communist feelings run away with his reason."[12] Jörn Glasenapp also agrees with Michael Coyne's assertion that this movie is a "scantily disguised frontier equivalent of the communist threat."[13] *Rio Grande*, Glasenapp says, is a Western promoting postwar ideologies: in it, Natches's Apaches embody the "red anger" or "red hand," and overprotective mothers support "red infiltration."[14]

It is not difficult to imagine that John Ford would have been puzzled and appalled by *Rio Grande*'s critical reception. In *Rio Grande*, the regeneration of the individual, the family, and the state is not achieved by violence. As Lindsay Anderson points out, "to make films which are so dedicated to a military tradition as [the Cavalry Trilogy] are, and yet not make them militaristic, is an extraordinary achievement. . . . None of these stories can be called aggressive. . . . In *Rio Grande*, it is the Indians who attack; the cavalry foray is made to rescue the women and children who have been carried off by the marauders."[15] Another of Ford's veterans' movies, *Rio Grande* examines the postwar family as a casualty of war—its rupture and its repair. Ford's emphasis throughout rests on the social and psychological damage of individuals who have experienced war, which destroys the veterans' relationships with their loved ones, in particular, their wives and their families, after their return home. As Scott Eyman states, "*Rio Grande* is the beginning of a remarkable maturity in dealing with women in which complex mature explorations of all phases of adult love from the strong sexual yearnings of courtship to the uneasy compromises of daily life, to the bitter reality of separation and estrangement."[16] McBride finds Ford's "'emotionally complex family drama' treated with 'great delicacy,' intermittently elevating *Rio Grande* above its plot."[17]

PARTISANS

Rio Grande's narrative action begins when Jeff Yorke (Claude Jarman Jr.) arrives at his father's command on the Texas frontier. Unlike his father, Kirby Yorke (John Wayne), Jeff has failed. Unable to pass his mathematics exam at West Point, he has lied about his age and enlisted as a private in the Regular Army. The appearance of his mother, Kathleen (Maureen O'Hara), to take her underage son home begins the process by which the Yorkes resolve their differences and rebuild their family. Although some critical attention has been paid to the Yorkes' domestic difficulties, none has been given to the significance of the event during the Civil War that devastated their marriage—the Burning of the Shenandoah Valley.

A shattering experience, the burning was the first act of total war in North America. Late in July of 1864, the Confederate Army of the Valley (under Lieutenant General Jubal A. Early) defeated the Union Army of West Virginia (under Brigadier General George Crook) and drove it from the Shenandoah back over the Potomac River and into Maryland. Early then launched the Confederacy's last major raid into northern territory, attacking the Baltimore and Ohio Railroad in Maryland and West Virginia and burning Chambersburg, Pennsylvania, in retaliation for the burning of civilian houses and farms earlier in the campaign. Abraham Lincoln (with an election in the offing) and General Ulysses S. Grant then decided to crush Early's army and destroy the Confederacy's supply lines by burning the crops in the fertile Shenandoah Valley. As John F. Wukovitz points out, fighting in the lush Shenandoah prior to 1864 had been comparatively civilized: Union generals, when operating there, forbade the wanton destruction of property, and Southern civilians could successfully demand payment in gold for damages done by Union soldiers to fence rails and farmland.[18] In 1864, however, Confederate soldier Henry Douglas compared what he saw in the Shenandoah to a holocaust and termed the Burning "an insult to civilization and to God to pretend that the Laws of War justify such warfare."[19] Not surprisingly, Grant's scorched earth policy, intended to bring the valley to its knees in short order, had exactly the opposite effect. Partisan resistance to the Union Army became so great that General Philip Sheridan complained to Grant that since he "came into the Valley from Harper's Ferry, every train, every small part, and every straggler [had] been bushwacked by people."[20]

In *Rio Grande*, Ford uses the experience of the Burning of the Shenandoah Valley to establish (and critique) the conflict that partisanship creates in families. He also furthers his examination of partisanship by introducing the Irish American experience to support his investigation. Here it should be noted that the predominance of the Irish among the enlisted men and noncommissioned officers in *Rio Grande* (and the other movies in the Cavalry Trilogy) is historically correct. Twenty-one percent, or 38,649 men, from the Civil War's "green flag" regiments were recruited by the Army between the end of the Civil War and the Battle of the Little Bighorn.[21] In addition, given the preponderance of Irish Americans living in the East at the time of this story, it is also no coincidence that Kathleen Yorke, an Irishwoman from Virginia, a state founded by "that great Irishman Sir Walter Raleigh," is married to a man's whose last name indicates that he is either an Englishman or, worse, the son of Ulster Protestants.[22] As a reflection of the Irish-English conflict, Kathleen and Kirby's relationship not only conflates past and present and confuses the boundaries of civilian and military life, it also showcases antipathetic political and national sympathies.

In part, references to Fenianism form the building blocks of Ford's examination of partisanism throughout *Rio Grande*.[23] Like the supporters of the American Revolution and the Southern secessionists, the Fenian Brotherhood in America also believed that their Irish State's natural right to independence could only be achieved by armed rebellion. Ford himself was a Fenian sympathizer who is said to have supported and channeled funds to the Irish Republican Army all his life.[24]

In the film, the Regimental Singers serenade Lt. General Sheridan (J. Carrol Naish), whose father and mother, like Ford's, came from County Cavan, with the Irish Resistance folk song "Down by the Glenside (The Bold Fenian Men)." Reputed to be a Fenian sympathizer himself, Sheridan is supposed to have entertained overtures from the Fenian Brotherhood regarding the position of secretary of war in connection with their plans for the ill-thought-out and ill-fated 1866 invasion of Canada.[25] In *Rio Grande*, however, it is Sheridan's character who draws our attention to the rigidity and single-mindedness of the partisan, the man who sacrifices everything—friends, family, and even himself—to the cause that he espouses: "I sacrificed the happiness of

your home once, Kirby, to the needs of war," he says. "Now I'll probably ruin your Army career . . . hit the Apache and *burn him out*. I'm
tired of hit and run. I'm sick of hide and seek. If you fail, I assure you
that the members of your court-martial will be the men who rode with
us down the Shenandoah. I'll hand-pick 'em myself" (italics mine).

During the Civil War, Yorke was very much the Union partisan,
while his wife's sympathies were firmly planted in the South. While
obeying Sheridan's orders and participating in the Burning of the Shenandoah Valley, Yorke turned his wife and their infant son out of her
family's plantation home and then burned it while she watched. Remarkably, Yorke's marriage did not end, but understandably his wife
and his son could no longer continue to live with him. At the beginning
of the film, the family conflict that this action began fifteen years earlier
continues to be internecine. As in *Fort Apache*, privileging duty over
one's personal relationships in *Rio Grande* proves to be problematic.
Like Owen Thursday, Yorke feels that a man must honor his oath "even
if it means his destruction." Thus, through most of the movie, Yorke
remains caught between his duty to Sheridan and his responsibilities to
his wife and son. As a Southerner, his wife is equally partisan and self-
destructive: she is torn between her responsibilities as a mother to her
son, her duty to her family, and her desire to resume her life with her
husband. Their son, Jeff, is trapped by his obligations to obey both
parents, his stubborn father and his equally stubborn mother.

ENGAGING EMPATHY

Ford always considered himself to be "a silent picture man." As he said
to George Mitchell in 1964, "Pictures, not words, should tell the story."[26] *Rio Grande* is no exception to this rule. The film is a "textbook in
the rendering and exploiting of empathy."[27] In part, the success of this
film is due to "knee-level camera angles that evoke Remington's treatments of the frontier that both distance and personalize Ford's subjects." As Gallagher points out, empathy with the Yorkes is created by
Ford's extensive and atypical use of point-of-view shots—Kathleen
"stands in close shot while soldiers ride off behind her; she pops into an
empty frame after her son rides out of it; the reverse-angle shows a

desert vista with a speck of a rider, before we cut back to Kathleen gazing."[28]

As in *She Wore a Yellow Ribbon*, mise-en-scène in *Rio Grande* is an important element of Ford's critique of military culture. Throughout *Rio Grande*, Ford's focus rests on the norms and forms of Army life. The movie begins with the return of the cavalrymen from duty, rather than celebrating the column riding out to battle in the wilderness. Like Captain Brittles in *She Wore a Yellow Ribbon*, Yorke is a professional soldier, and like Brittles, Yorke's family is not in evidence at the start of the film. Unlike Brittles's family, however, they are not dead. The Yorke family's dysfunction is immediately attributed by Sheridan to Kirby's devotion to duty. His success as a professional soldier has resulted in his failure as a husband and a father, isolating him from those whom he loves. Jeff, who has not seen his father since the Burning of the Shenandoah, asks his mother, "Who is my father?" Kathleen replies, "He is a very lonely man."

Ford's subtle use of shadows and low-level lighting contributes to the viewer's understanding of the Yorkes and their story. When *Rio Grande* begins, Sheridan and Yorke first meet in his tent. During this sequence, a large, elaborate shadow representing the leafy branches of a tree acts as a backdrop behind Yorke, linking him with the ideal pastoral world of the Shenandoah Valley where his wife was born and raised. Next, a shadow in the shape of a cross on the low ceiling of Yorke's office is found the next day as the regiment's new recruits arrive. Located directly above the commanding officer's desk, this shadow reinforces Yorke's warning to his son that the military offers those serving in it only a life marked by suffering, hardship, and sacrifice, which must be endured. This shadow and another like it appear again above the heads of Yorke and Sheridan when they are in this office discussing orders and indicate that both men carry psychological and social burdens from their past: in Yorke's case, the burning of his wife's family's plantation, Bridesdale; in Sheridan's, the burning of the valley itself.

When Kathleen and Jeff are introduced to the viewer, the connotations of the shadows that accompany them are very different. Framed by backdrops of shadows cast by tree branches on the walls of Yorke's tent, these characters cast no shadows of their own. No guilt relating to their actions during the Civil War follows them about. Instead, Yorke casts a dark shadow on these walls. Ford's treatment of blacks in these shots creates a visual dialect that explores Yorke's guilt about the burning and his culpability for the disintegration of his marriage: his martial shade (reinforced by his cavalry sabre and riding boots emphasized by the large mirror at the back of his tent) contrasts sharply with the shadowy unspoiled garden of the Shenandoah that frames Kathleen and Jeff.

Ford also uses low-level lighting to heighten the couple's tension when expressing the contradictory emotions and political loyalties of husband and wife. As the two attempt to communicate with one another, Ford's expressionistic lighting reveals how different their points of view are: Yorke's passion is signaled by the shadow that clouds his face; Kathleen, on the other hand, uninterested in resuming a physical relationship with her husband, turns her back on him to look into the light. After the Regimental Singers serenade the couple with the romantic melody "I'll Take You Home Again Kathleen," Kathleen attempts to reconcile with her husband, but this time, her profile is darkened and Yorke's face is lit. Predictably, Yorke does not accept her invitation and politely wishes her a "good night."

Lighting levels also express the conflicted natures of the individuals themselves. Darkened, Yorke's and Kathleen's faces transmit the emotions that Ford ascribes to the partisan: hurt, anger, passion, fear, and loss. Darkness and light sculpt Yorke's features throughout *Rio Grande*, sometimes vertically, sometimes horizontally, transmitting his divided emotions as he tries to balance his military duties with his familial responsibilities. Yorke reminds Jeff that, as a commanding officer, he cannot function like a father because his duty overshadows his parental responsibilities. Yet, as a father, Yorke also recognizes his underage son is too young to fight in a battle. Attempting to resolve this situation, Yorke sends Jeff off to chaperone women and children to Fort Bliss, only to find his son embroiled in the very conflict with the Apaches that he had hoped Jeff would avoid. Heightening Yorke's tension, Trooper Tyree (Ben Johnson) chooses Jeff to accompany him on a dangerous rescue mission. After Jeff departs with Tyree and Trooper Boone (Harry Carey Jr.), Yorke, whose facial expression has been one of worry, steps forward into deep shadow. As the shadow overwhelms him, his features are completely darkened, signaling the intensity of his emotions: the highlights in his eyes as well as his mouth and chin are visible, emphasizing his dread of losing his son.

Ford's lighting of Kathleen is much more extreme and expressive than Yorke's, creating the impression of a very unbalanced personality—her face is often portrayed at crucial moments in the action as being either very brightly lit or completely existing in heavy shadow. Ford's most frightening presentation of Kathleen occurs after Yorke leaves her in his tent to search for the Apaches who raided his camp. Frustrated, emotionally and sexually, she stands waiting for his return, her face entirely darkened. Here, "the Colonel's Lady's" lighting levels, like her fortunes, are extremely low. As she watches Yorke and his men leave, the only detail given Kathleen's back-lit profile is a carefully placed highlight in her left pupil. Her darkened, featureless face and glittering eye held in a ten-second shot resembles a shadow figure from Celtic mythology, the banshee.

In short, Kathleen is revealed to be a man-eating monster. Sergeant Quincannon (Victor McLaglen) recognizes her true nature and crosses himself when he sees Kathleen first arrive at the fort and then crosses himself again before he takes his washing to her. The *bean sith* (or banshee) often appears in Irish legends as a washerwoman, cleansing the clothing and armor of those who are about to die. Ford's low-angle shots and shadows in Jeff's tent further establish his mother's need to devour others. Ignoring her son's need to make his own decisions, Kathleen announces that she has come to take him home. Her unnatural, devouring nature, signaled when she kisses Jeff full on the mouth, is then amplified as her cast shadow on the tent wall engulfs her sitting son.

Ford's use of key lighting at the regimental dinner, however, presents Kathleen in a very different light. Invited by Sheridan to offer the group a sentiment, she is radiantly lit and graciously toasts her "only rival, the United States Cavalry." Her husband, equally well lit at the opposite end of the table (and the political spectrum), finally capitulates to his wife's wishes. In this scene, Yorke publicly renounces his single-minded devotion to the cavalry to Kathleen by emptying his glass and turning it over on the tablecloth—announcing that he is drinking to comrades who have gone before. Seeing her husband declare her rival dead, Kathleen drains her glass as well, acknowledging and honoring his decision to privilege her above his men and his commanding officer.

Thus, when Yorke crosses the Rio Grande to rescue the children later in the film, he does so in accordance with her wishes, not Sheridan's. "We'll get 'em back," he tells her.

KIDDING THE CAVALRY

As in *Fort Apache*, Ford also uses humor to demonstrate the complexities of military life. In *New World Irish: Notes on One Hundred Years of Lives and Letters in American Culture*, Jack Morgan identifies Ford's distinct vision of Irish Americans in the Trilogy as being "narrowback," that of "the quintessential 1950s conservative Irish Catholic, the maudlin militarist, a kind of west Coast Cardinal Spellman,"[29] and, in "The Irish in John Ford's Seventh Cavalry Trilogy—Victor McLaglen's Stooge-Irish Caricature," complains that Ford's image of the Irish in the Cavalry Trilogy portrays the popular nineteenth-century stereotype of the Irish as "a fickle, ignorant and violent race, prone to treachery and the most outrageous superstitions."[30] "Assimilation being the measure," Morgan says, "the run of the mill immigrant Irish in the trilogy are so many micks suggesting only low-comic possibilities to Ford."[31] Morgan particularly objects to McLaglen's "low comic antics."[32] Sergeant Quincannon, he says, is such a "crude . . . caricature that there is no rehabilitating it."[33] Here it is important to take D. H. Lawrence's advice and "never trust the artist. Trust the tale."[34] Quincannon's clowning in the Cavalry Trilogy, in general, and *Rio Grande*, in particular, is not a mawkish, demeaning sentimentality on Ford's part, as Morgan suggests, but an essential element of his critique. Throughout the Cavalry Trilogy, Ford uses his Irish sergeant to kid the stereotype of the cavalryman as a romantic figure in much the same way that Cheyenne Harry, portrayed by Harry Carey Sr., kidded silent film's spotless Western hero, Tom Mix. As Victor McLaglen's Quincannon clowns around the fort in *Rio Grande*, Ford's visual nuances sophisticate the burlesque. Ford's evocative, painterly treatment of the sergeant in the Remington style parodies the romantic stereotype of the cavalry officer that the viewer expects to see. Playing with his viewer's expectations, Ford's medium shots emphasize McLaglen's barrel chest, short legs, jutting lower lip, and double chin, undercutting the romantic (and historically inaccurate) costuming of his subject's hat, boots, breeches, and horse furniture.[35]

Serving as a comic foil to Yorke's narrow-minded partisanship, Quincannon is the "Reluctant Arsonist" because he obeyed Yorke's orders to burn Bridesdale. "It was me cursed luck to be ordered to burn the crops and the barns at Bridesdale," he tells Wilkins, "with herself lookin' daggers at me and sabres at the colonel. He were a captain then. Silent as death she was, with a babe in her arms . . . little Jeff. Little Jeff!" Filled with remorse, Quincannon extends his right hand and spits on it in disgust: "And there's the black hand that did the dirty deed!" he shouts. "I wish you'd knock it off with that stick!"

The apolitical Quincannon is also a trickster. A symbol of resistance and power in Celtic society, the trickster is usually a male character with extreme appetites who fools the master or the king, breaks the law, and beats the system. Maintaining his agency in a difficult situation is undoubtedly the trickster's most salient characteristic. In general, the lowly trickster's overturning of a system is meant to address and correct social imbalance. Being neither tragic nor romantic, he is often an ambiguous figure. Another colorful example of this conflicted figure, Trooper Tyree earns a medal for bravery because he has done precisely what he should not have—gone AWOL. Tyree indeed takes his horse backward over its jumps as Quincannon (at the beginning of the movie) promises him that he will: the trooper from Texas not only saves his sister's reputation but also the lives of his comrades, their wives, and their children from the Apaches because he has stolen Yorke's horse. Ironically, he is decorated at the end of the movie and becomes a "hero" for being a horse thief.

Like Tyree, Quincannon also excels at beating the system. Instances of their overturning of military process and policy abound: the abuse of authority and intimidation (Quincannon disciplines Trooper Heinze [Fred Kennedy] cruelly after learning that the trooper believes him to be "a chowder headed mick"); the misuse of military assets (an excellent judge of horseflesh, Tyree steals Yorke's and Sheridan's horses to escape the law); the failure to supervise and dereliction of duty (Quincannon drinks with Tyree instead of guarding his prisoner and fails to prevent Tyree from escaping); and conduct unbecoming to military personnel (Quincannon encourages fighting among the ranks even though he specifies Marquis of Queensbury rules).

As a trickster, Quincannon reminds the viewer of the importance of balance in life and culture, offsetting his oath of office with the needs of others. Various officers (representing martial law and therefore the State) tell Quincannon that he'll be busted for his behavior—but he never is. Unlike Yorke, the canny sergeant avoids court-martial by following the letter of the law but not embodying its spirit. Quincannon, for instance, corrects the problem of the U.S. marshal's "Yankee justice" when guarding Tyree. Seated where he cannot see the door, he does not witness Tyree leaving the room. Thus he cheerfully shouts, "Hello!" when it bangs shut behind his escaping captive. After giving Tyree ample time to find a horse and ride away, Quincannon stands at the window of the guardhouse, calling loudly for the guard, but does not pursue his fleeing prisoner. Satisfying only the letter of the law, his behavior is perfectly ethical, perfectly obedient, and perfectly ineffective. Throughout *Rio Grande*, the wily Quincannon's behavior marks him as a life-affirming character. As "Uncle Timmy," he is the good father that Yorke cannot be. It is Quincannon, the reluctant "Arsonist" who burned Bridesdale, not Kathleen's husband, who ensures that the worried mother sees her son. Significantly, the children from the fort scream for their "Uncle Timmy," not Colonel Yorke, when the Apaches capture them. And it is "Uncle Timmy" who remembers to rescue Margaret Mary (Karolyn Grimes) and takes the time to have her genuflect in front of the church's altar before he whisks her out the door and into the safety of the waiting wagon.

OVERTURNING NORMS AND FORMS

A lord of misrule, Quincannon is delightfully incorrigible. When he is in charge and giving orders, his is a West full of the unpredictability. *Rio Grande* begins in true carnival fashion by presenting an orderly world that is about to be disrupted. The viewer is first introduced to the officers of the fort. Yorke's attachment to his duty establishes the primacy of military discipline, its hierarchy, its norms, and its ideologies. Yorke's relationship with Sheridan, for example, is one of unquestioning obedience even though Sheridan admits, "I sacrificed the happiness of your home once for the needs of war; now I'll probably ruin your Army career." After personally ordering Yorke to cross the Rio Grande and pursue the Apache in Mexico, he adds, "If you fail, I assure you the members of your court-martial will be the men who rode with us down the Shenandoah. I'll hand pick 'em myself." When Sheridan and Yorke first share duty coffee, Sheridan points out that Yorke has "the dirtiest job in the Army." At this point in the film, Yorke believes that the Army knows best. He replies that he is "not complaining sir. I get paid for it."

As the film continues, it becomes evident that an unlikely and alternative cosmovision characterized by the undermining of military norms is offered the viewer. Yorke's son's arrival as a regular Army recruit at the fort turns the strict chain of command within the Army topsy-turvy, for Kathleen arrives soon afterward. Military discipline breaks down and the hierarchy of command is overturned, as Yorke is unable to interfere while Jeff becomes good friends with Trooper Heinze, who blackens both his eyes; Quincannon and Doctor Wilkins (Chill Wills) band together to save Tyree from hanging even though the trooper, whom the colonel's lady describes as "a nice gentle soul who'd walk ten miles out of his way before he'd step on an ant," killed a man in cold blood; and Yorke and Kathleen fall in love with each other again. The mixing of social classes in *Rio Grande* is evident, particularly in the sequence in which the blue-blooded Kathleen rolls up her shirtsleeves and becomes a washerwoman, taking on the "trade" of scrubbing Quincannon's disreputable longjohns. Dirt, in all its manifestations, is leitmotif of the working class in this movie. The enlisted men are covered in dust and grime, while the officers' uniforms shine with spit and polish. In charge of the fort, Yorke is a particularly privileged individual, sporting elegant dress whites while courting Kathleen. By the movie's end, however, he is just as filthy as his men.

As Robert Stam points out, carnival is more than simple revelry because it raises questions about the nature of power and justice when a lord of misrule is put into the place of authority.[36] At the fort, the question of who is really in charge is raised when the U.S. marshal prepares to take Tyree prisoner. Acting on Kathleen's orders, Quincannon allows Tyree to escape on Yorke's horse. It is obvious to the viewer, if not Yorke, as his horse gallops away, that the nature of the authority conferred upon him by the U.S. Army is open to question and reinvention.

More nonsense ensues while the cavalrymen rescue the children who have been imprisoned by the Apaches in a church. Throughout this sequence, Jeff, Boone, and Tyree are hardly heroic figures. They are much more worried about what Margaret Mary, a pig-tailed ten-year-old girl, will do to them than they are about the Apaches. After braining Boone with the school bell when he steals into the sanctuary to rescue her, she exclaims, "Oh, Sandy, I'm sorry. I thought you were an Indian." Irrepressibly noisy, Margaret Mary is unable to be quiet even when hushed by Tyree. She can hardly wait for the shooting to begin. As Sandy says to Jeff, "I can't figure out what side that kid's on. Them or ours." Even Quincannon, the Lord of Misrule, falls under Margaret Mary's sway. Clearly she is a force of nature not to be resisted. When she scolds her "Uncle Timmy!" after he angrily hurls a bucket into the river by the fort after Tyree has been arrested, Quincannon immediately sits down on the dock and controls his temper.

Ford's treatment of the children's rescue carefully (and hilariously) overturns the romantic stereotype of the dashing cavalryman arriving at the very last moment to save the day. Yorke's troop crosses the Rio Grande but finds the Apaches to be a reluctant group of marauding murderers. Instead of torturing their victims, they spend the evening drinking, drumming, and dancing. The impending horror of a massacre of innocents that Yorke expects will occur is then also comically inverted. At dawn, outside the church, the Apaches are hardly menacing. Drunk and hungover from their evening's festivities, they can barely walk and have trouble making their way up the street toward their victims.

Inside the church, Trooper Boone is more concerned about having his bottom shot off by Jeff reloading a rifle than he is about repelling the oncoming enemy. When the Apache do attack, they do so illogically—continuing to try to open the front door after the shooting begins. During the battle for the children, the tropes of a last stand like the one at the Alamo are introduced: the church bell rings incessantly, and the defenders load their guns feverishly and shoot through a slit in the door that is fashioned in the shape of a cross, but as the cavalrymen charge up and down the main street of the town to save them, no blood is spilled. No Apaches fall dramatically from the tops of the buildings on which they were standing, and the bodies of cavalrymen also do not gallantly litter the street.[37] Even the bodies of the three Apaches who collapsed earlier on the steps of the church have mysteriously vanished.

When Yorke heroically rides into the building, he finds the children and Jeff are unharmed and hiding behind an overturned pew. No one dies while the children are hurried to their waiting wagon despite the bullets that continue to whizz about. Only one man is wounded after the children leave—Yorke, who (inexplicably) is able to still sit on his horse after Jeff pulls an arrow from his chest. After the battle, no land exchanges hands; no one is dispossessed; no one seizes power. Instead, everyone just goes home: the Apaches, presumably, to their camp—the troopers to their outpost.

Rio Grande concludes by returning to and re-establishing the social order and its accompanying hierarchies, which were inverted at the beginning of the movie. When Yorke returns to the fort on a *travois*, Kathleen takes his hand. She and Jeff walk together, accompanying Yorke to his tent. The family unit is reconstructed as wife and son return to husband and father, and the social, political, economic, and religious barriers that have been removed during Ford's carnival are put back in place.

Then, at the movie's end, regeneration in the West occurs, but in a most unusual fashion. At the review, the carnival begins again. After Trooper Boone, Trooper Yorke, and Trooper Tyree receive awards "for gallantry in action above and beyond the call of duty on 8th of July," Yorke and Sheridan join forces with Quincannon and his tricksters: when the U.S. marshal arrives again for Tyree, Yorke immediately grants the trooper a week's furlough so he can steal another horse and escape once more from the law. Everyone in uniform approves as Tyree steals Sheridan's mount and gallops away, noting that he is "an excellent judge of horseflesh."

"Dixie" plays as Sheridan takes the Regimental Salute—honoring Kathleen and suggesting that the South has finally risen again. The closing scene in *Rio Grande* reveals that not only have the Yorkes been reunited and the Army's coherence restored but the North has finally honored and reintegrated the South. Like a Shakespearean comedy, Ford's focus has been that of regeneration (individual, familial, and national) all along, as *Rio Grande* celebrates and affirms the blessings of civilization that have come to the West in the forms of marriage, family, and community.

10

VETERANS' AFFAIRS[1]

The Searchers

You didn't have to call me "an old bastard," you know. You should have had the courtesy to say "old gentleman."[2]—John Ford

Every studio in Hollywood was interested in producing *The Searchers*, a Ford-Wayne Western. As Dan Ford points out, *The Searchers* was a solid commercial venture not only because it was a John Wayne–John Ford vehicle but also because the film was partially financed by Cornelius Vanderbilt Whitney, the heir to the Minnesota Mining and Manufacturing fortune and one of the founders of Pan American World Airways.[3] After considering contracts from Columbia and MGM, Ford and Merian Cooper accepted Warner Bros.' offer, which entailed a 65/35 split and waived the studio overhead charges; Ford received $125,000 plus 10 percent of the net for directing the movie.[4]

Once Cooper signed the contract, preproduction for *The Searchers* began. In January 1956, Ford worked with Frank Nugent on the script. In February 1956, Ford's second unit began work in Aspen, Colorado, and Elk Island National Park, near Edmonton, Alberta, Canada. As he told Michael Killanin in March, "It's a rough and arduous job as I want it to be good. I've been longing to do a Western for quite some time. It's good for my health, spirit, and morale."[5] According to Jean Nugent, Ford needed to have "the same people around him all the time," so he told her husband that he had "to write a part for Dobe Carey, and he had to write a part for Ken Curtis."[6] Having gathered his Stock Company together, Ford began production in Monument Valley in mid-June of 1955. According to Pat Ford, Whitney, intent on supervising his investment, brought his wife and her poodle with him and "had to be in the middle of everything."[7] *The Searchers* was the first film to be produced by C. V. Whitney Pictures.

Ford deftly solved the problem of the presence of his high-maintenance partner by encouraging the stuntmen, who were wearing costumes that had been unwashed for weeks, to "pay strict attention to the young Mrs. Whitney on location." "Make her feel right at home," he told Bad Chuck Roberson and the stuntmen. "I don't want to see a man of you pass her without stopping to say a word to her."[8] Chuck Roberson "knew what he was up to. Although we were used to the smell of our own sweat after six weeks, Mrs. C. V. Bostonian Whitney had probably never smelled sweat in her entire delicate life. Every time one of us would pass and tip our hats, her lips said 'hello,' but her nose said 'oh no.'"[9] Ford then encouraged Fred Kennedy and Roberson to put on a stunt fight over supper one night. By the time Fred Kennedy and Roberson were pulled apart, "Miss Boston was boo-hooing and hollering that she wanted to go home."[10] Roberson further ensured she would leave after Ford assured the Whitneys that the gag had been put on for their benefit. After dipping his fingers into a glass of water, he faked a sneeze and flicked water onto the back of her neck—"her spine stiffened, and she pretended not to notice," Roberson says, "but the next morning, C. V. Whitney, wife, and poodle, and fourteen trunks loaded into their limousine and drove away."[11] Location work on *The Searchers* finished on July 10 and resumed at the studio on July 18. Ford finished shooting the picture on August 13.

Released on March 13, 1956, *The Searchers* easily recovered its cost of $2.5 million, grossing $5.9 million worldwide by April of 1958. Ranked among the greatest films ever made, John Ford's 115th film has lingered in America's memory.[12] As Arthur M. Eckstein notes, *The Searchers*, which critics consider socially and psychologically profound, is Ford's most influential work.[13] References to this movie have appeared in the works of other filmmakers again and again: from *South Pacific* (1958) and *Lawrence of Arabia* (1962) to *Star Wars: Episode II—Attack of the Clones* (2002) and *Dog Soldiers* (2002).[14] Even *Kill Bill: Vol 2* (2004) offers its audience what has become a standard compositional riff in Hollywood filmmaking: Uma Thurman is framed in the door of the chapel, in the same way as Ethan Edwards is in the final shot of the door of the Jorgensons' ranch house in *The Searchers*.

It is this closing shot of Ethan that also makes *The Searchers* one of Ford's most troubling films: John Wayne grasping his arm in tribute to Harry Carey Sr. before his character, Ethan Edwards, turns and walks away into the scorching wind and drifting sands of Monument Valley—the door swinging silently shut—the blackness falling. Lyrically closing Ford's narrative by returning the movie to its beginning, while reversing and unraveling its opening action, this sequence is unsatisfying. Although a new family is formed at the end of *The Searchers*—the Jorgensons walk into their ranch house with a new daughter and a new son—what should be renewal elicits instead pity and fear from the audience. Unwilling or unable to enter the ranch house, Ethan remains without. A good bad man, he must live out his days wandering. As Ford told Peter Bogdanovich, *The Searchers* is "the tragedy of a loner, of a man who could never be really part of a family."[15]

Ethan's inability to re-enter society has made him "one of the most famous characters in all of American motion picture history."[16] Much of his notoriety results from Ford's final depiction of the "loner," which prompts viewers like Tag Gallagher to ask *why* Ethan chooses to turn away from his kith and kin whom he had just recovered to wander in the desert.[17] After bringing Debbie (Natalie Wood) home, Ethan could have decided to walk into the Jorgensons' home, re-enter society, and reinvent himself. He could have started a new life with a new family. He had taken his revenge and recovered his kidnapped niece, thereby burying the past. What motivates him to turn away and continue to wander after the successful conclusion of his quest? Many commentators have attempted to answer this question by pointing out that Ethan has no other choice but to leave because he cannot give up his incestuous love for his brother's wife and his extreme horror of miscegenation.[18] Nonetheless, Ethan's return to the desert as the door swings shut is a highly disturbing moment at the movie's end.

It has been suggested that the troubling nature of Ethan's rejection of human society is due, in part, to our expectations of John Ford himself. A very puzzled Lindsay Anderson asks, "What is Ford, of all directors, to do with a hero like this?"[19] However, as Eckstein so capably demonstrates, Ford went to infinite trouble to develop Alan Le May's Ethan Edwards as a mentally unbalanced and highly antisocial character. Ford made significant changes to the script on location in Monument Valley and on the soundstage in Hollywood to create the dark and disturbing protagonist who turned his back on hearth and home at the movie's end.[20] Ford's choice of such a hero, however, is not so puzzling when one considers the historic moment during which *The Searchers* was made.

As Curtis Hanson points out in *A Turning of the Earth: John Ford, John Wayne and The Searchers* (1998), *The Searchers* is not about violence; it is about the effects of violence on individuals.[21] Released ten years after American troops who fought in the Second World War returned to the United States, *The Searchers* showcases the effects of the violence of war on the individual, in general, and the returning hero, in particular. Thus the subject of Ford's inquiry explored via the character of Ethan Edwards—that of blood pollution—is not limited to the unpleasant subjects of incest and racism even though those topics are crucial in recognizing and understanding Ford's view of Ethan as a negative, psychologically shattered, and tragic figure.[22] A thief, a predator, a murderer, a racist, *and* a sociopath, Ethan is, as Eckstein notes, "semi-psychotic,"[23] but Ford was not solely concerned with the plight of an extremely damaged *individual* when darkening the character of Ethan Edwards. Ford told Peter Bogdanovich that he meant *The Searchers* to be a "psychological *epic*" (italics mine).[24] Shared by every character in this movie, Ethan's dysfunctions are always related to a much broader, general dysfunction at work in *The Searchers* and, arguably, in American culture in 1956.

DAMAGED INDIVIDUALS

Every character in *The Searchers* is psychologically scarred by his or her involvement in some sort of war—the Civil War, the Texicans' war with the Comanche, or even the war waged between the Edwards brothers over Martha (Dorothy Jordan) within Nathan's home. At the beginning of the film, Ford's attention to mise-en-scène painstakingly identifies Ethan as a war veteran who has just returned home. Wearing a long Confederate overcoat, Ethan jogs into the yard on a horse sporting a Mexican saddle. Strapped to his saddle roll is a sabre with its scabbard wrapped in the gray silk of the Confederate Army. To further the impression of a Civil War veteran returning from the Mexican War, Ethan carries a folded serape in place of a Texas poncho. Later, he gives Debbie a beribboned medal that appears to have been won in Mexico.

Perceptions of (and attitudes toward) returning war veterans have varied widely—from culture to culture and from one historical period to another. Jonathan Shay observes that acts of war generate "a profound gulf between the combatant and the community he left behind" due to the fact that the returning veteran carries with him "the taint of a killer."[25] The widespread effects of this lingering blood pollution created by the Civil War and carried by Ethan are highly significant when one remembers that the Civil War divided families and was a war of homicides waged, literally and metaphorically, between fathers and brothers.

In the past, many cultures have responded to the veteran's blood pollution with ritual acts of cleansing: most warrior societies, as well as many not dominated by warfare, have historically had communal rites of purification of the returning fighter after battle. As Shay points out, during the Middle Ages, every returning warrior was required by the Church to do penance for spilling blood before he could rejoin his community. In fact, each warrior's penance for spilling blood was regulated according to the nature of the act he committed: "In the medieval Christian church, if you committed atrocities you had to do more penance, but even if you wore a white hat and were a perfect model of proper conduct you had to do penance . . . [but today] . . . our culture denies the need for purification and provides none."[26]

In contemporary American society, rites that cleanse the returning warrior of his blood pollution have been deleted from the rites of re-entry into polite society: as W. P. Mahedy observes, "Americans view war much differently than did our ancient ancestors. In America . . . the notion of cleansing has been . . . supplanted by the idea that the justice of our national cause renders all acts of war moral."[27]

As a veteran of the Civil War, Ethan, too, did not experience purification rites after the cessation of hostilities because they were not deemed necessary. Like other Civil War veterans who roamed as hobos on the fringes of society because they were unable to adjust to civilian life, Ethan wanders—for three years—spending some of that time in Mexico, before returning to the Edwards homestead.[28] At the beginning of *The Searchers*, the gap between the returning killer and his community could not appear to be greater. Still carrying his cavalry sabre—years after Lee's surrender at Appomattox—Ethan is living and thinking like a combatant. Unlike Reverend Captain Samuel Johnston Clayton (Ward Bond), an ex-soldier whose sword has become a ploughshare, Ethan, uncleansed, continues to identify himself as a member of the Confederate Army. He tells Clayton, "I don't believe in surrenders. I still got my sword." The importance of the Civil War as a backdrop against which *The Searchers* takes place should not be underestimated. Ethan is not just a returning veteran; he is a veteran on the losing side of a war that he has not yet conceded. He cannot be purified because, for him, the war has not ended.

Heroes of Ethan's day were men who were both needed by their people and considered to be dangerous to them. Society demanded the veterans' purification because, until they were cleansed, these men continued to function as combatants. Ironically, the living for which war best prepares a war hero upon return to civilian life is a criminal career.[29] In 1516, Sir Thomas More pointed out in *Utopia*, "Some thieves are not bad soldiers, some soldiers turn out to be pretty good robbers, so nearly are these two ways of life related."[30] In *The Searchers*, there is little doubt that Ethan has put his military training to use and embarked on such a career after the hostilities of the Civil War had officially ceased. When he offers to pay his way on Aaron's ranch with "fresh minted double eagles, Yankee dollars," he is continuing to carry on what appears to be a personal war with the North by robbing its banks. It is not surprising then that he arrives in Texas three years after the cessation of fighting between the North and South via Mexico.

In short, Ethan is still "at war" in a country nominally at peace. When searching for his niece, who has been kidnapped by a band of Comanche, Ethan's behavior continues to be homicidal: he murders Jerem Futterman (Peter Mamakos) by shooting the trader in the back and then callously rifles through the dead man's pockets looking for the money that he used to pay for his information about Debbie's whereabouts. Ethan's combat skills, which enable him to be a highly effective murderer and a thief, are accompanied by a type of psychological damage typical of war combatants: the complete absence of moral pain, guilt, self-reproach, and self-criticism.[31] He shows no regret at all for murdering Futterman and his henchmen. When Martin Pawley (Jeffrey Hunter) asks in astonishment, "What are you doing?" Ethan, pocketing a double eagle, replies, "I'm getting' my money back, ya idiot. Whadda ya suppose? We did all right." Of course, one could argue that Ethan cannot be considered a murderer because he was acting in self-defense, but when Martin complains to his uncle about endangering his life, by pointing out, "You just staked me out there like a piece of bait. I could have had my brains blown out," there is no apology for such antisocial behavior. Ethan merely grunts, "Never occurred to me," and goes to bed.

Throughout *The Searchers*, racism encourages and enables similar homicidal behavior. Notably, for Ethan, Martin's status as friend or foe is often unclear because he is part Cherokee. Ethan's comments about Martin's Native American heritage can be understood as manifestations of blood pollution instigated and informed by combat culture. The beginning of the Edwards blood feud is documented on the tombstone of Ethan's mother: Martha Edwards was "killed by Comanches." Early in the film, Ethan mistakes Martin for "a half-breed." Thereafter, according to Ethan, Martin is an "idiot." After desecrating a Comanche grave and shooting out the eyes of a dead warrior, Ethan turns to Martin and snaps, "Well, come on blanket-head." Ford extends his investigation of the racism fostered by combat culture when chronicling Ethan's shocking reaction to the women who have been recovered from their Comanche captors at a cavalry fort. There is no way of knowing how these women who rock back and forth and gibber to themselves have become insane. Nonetheless, Ethan, who regards them as tainted because of their sexual liaisons with the Comanche, is disgusted by their presence. "They're not white anymore; they're Comanch . . ." he says. Clearly, he considers them to be the enemy, less than human, although he himself, soiled with thoughts of incest, is also a "polluted" creature.

Grounded in the subject of blood pollution, Ford's interrogation of racism also extends from the psychology of the individual to that of the community or group. Like Ethan, most Texicans in *The Searchers* are psychologically damaged. Their racist attitudes are manifested in group hysteria akin to that of McCarthyism during the Cold War. In *The Searchers'* Texicana, as in America during the fifties, it is considered to be "better dead than Red." According to Laurie (Vera Miles), Martha would have wanted Ethan to put a bullet into Debbie's brain had she known that her daughter was living as a Comanche and had married into Scar's family.

THE POWER OF GRIEF

As Shay notes, bereavement is only one of the traumas of combat—grief is another. The powerful bond that arises between men in combat may be so intense as to blot out the distinction between self and comrade, leaving survivors to be condemned by their very survival.[32] As in *She Wore a Yellow Ribbon*, Ford's treatment of survivor guilt in *The Searchers* is also extensive and graphic. There is little doubt that Ethan feels responsible for his brother's death. Had he stayed at the ranch with Martha, his brother would have lived. Had he been defending the family, Martha, Aaron (Walter Coy), and Ben (Robert Lyden) might have survived. Had he been present, Debbie and Lucy might not have been kidnapped. In addition, it was his decision to break the news about Lucy's murder to Martin and Brad Jorgenson (Harry Carey Jr.), which precipitates Brad's suicidal charge into the Comanche camp. Again and again, bereavement is the catalyst that precipitates the berserk state. Ethan leaves Martha's funeral while it is in progress to seek revenge. His deep-seated guilt about surviving the massacre of his family and his mother's death also triggers other highly irrational and seemingly inexplicable acts, such as shooting the eyeballs out of a dead Comanche warrior or slaughtering a herd of buffalo. After both instances of killing rage, Ethan explains that he was getting even: without their eyes, the Comanche dead are doomed to wander forever between the winds, and without the buffalo, the Comanche will starve. Extreme manifestations of survivor guilt, these examples of berserk behavior, and others like them, are fueled by the desire for revenge—the means by which a combat soldier is faithful to his dead comrades and keeps their memory alive. Literally unable to bury Aaron, Martha, and Ben, Ethan leaves their funeral before it is finished, telling Clayton, who is delivering a graveside eulogy, to "put an amen on it." When Mrs. Jorgenson (Olive Carey) begs Ethan to do what Martha would have wanted—not to let the boys waste their lives in vengeance—he becomes enraged.

Oddly, this rage is also the means by which Ethan keeps Martha, Aaron, Ben, and Lucy present—if only in memory. As Shay points out, the existential function of rage keeps the dead alive by making them ever present in thought. "I won't forget a thing," is the vow of a combat soldier to his dead comrades to keep faith with them, to keep their

memory alive; asking the veteran to forget, the family asks him to dishonor himself.[33]

Sustaining loyalty to the dead can result in a combat veteran being
truly "haunted."[34] In *The Searchers*, Ford uses "Lorena," an authentic
Civil War ballad about thwarted love, as Martha's theme, to recall her
presence during Ethan's search and years after she has been murdered.
As Kathryn Kalinak notes, *The Searchers'* is a classical film score—
"identifiable, not only by its leitmotifs, but, on a structural level, by its
intricate interconnectedness between music and narrative action."[35]
"Lorena" returns in major and minor keys to to flesh out the unspoken
motivation and emotional content of several sequences": when Ethan
discovers Martha's body, "Lorena" can be heard in a minor key; during
the disbanding of the posse and the continued search by Ethan, Martin,
and Brad, "Lorena" returns; with the first glimpse of a grown-up Debbie as she descends a cliff toward Martin, "Lorena" is heard again;
Martin's embrace of Debbie when he rescues her in Scar's tepee is
underpinned by "Lorena"; and "Lorena" is used to score Debbie's return to the Jorgenson ranch at the end of the film.[36] Also reminding
viewers of the romantic tension between Ethan and his brother's wife,
Martha's haunting music recurs like a refrain when Ethan turns to ride
up a side canyon alone only to find Lucy's body. It repeats when Martin
evokes the happiness of Debbie's childhood: "Don't you remember
me?" he asks. "I used to let you ride my horse."

Perhaps the most disturbing scene of the film occurs when Ethan
finds Scar (Henry Brandon) dead and then proceeds to mutilate him.
Raising Martha yet again from the dead, Ethan takes Scar's scalp, thereby satisfying his need to avenge the death of a loved one. Re-enacting
Martha's murder, he balances the score by doing what had been done
before. Martin, who did not see the condition of his aunt's body earlier,
discounted the possibility of his aunt being mutilated after her death.
Nonetheless, when Ethan leaves Scar's tepee with a handful of long
black hair that could have been Martha's, it is impossible not to recall a
similar-looking scalp on Scar's spear and wonder uneasily whether Martha's daughter had been displaying her own mother's hair as a trophy
and whether the long, blonde, wavy lock beside it had been her sister's.

Of course, it is also possible to read Ethan's scalping of Scar less
literally: mutilating the war chief's dead body could be seen as a figura-
tive gesture by which Ford's hero expels his own demons. When viewed

as Ethan's double, Scar's head injury physically manifests the veteran's psychological damage. Scarred physically and psychologically, Ford's combatants are fated to be outcasts. Driven from his land, Scar is on the warpath and thus doomed to wander. Always at war, Ethan too must always be traveling.

Ford reinforces and advances his critique of post-traumatic stress disorder (PTSD) further by carefully paralleling Ethan's and Scar's behaviors. As critics have noted, Ford carefully presents Scar to the audience as Ethan's alter ego.[37] After kidnapping Debbie, Scar is never seen without Ethan's Civil War decoration around his neck. Like Ethan, he too is bereaved by the loss of his family and psychologically damaged by the deaths of his sons. Like Ethan, he too has gone berserk and is waging his own private war. His murderous raid on the Edwards homestead was an act of vengeance—of evening the score for his dead children. As Visser notes, vengeance must automatically follow the smirching of the family's honor; it requires "equality of damage done, and 'blood must have blood.'"[38] Thus, when Ethan and Scar finally do meet face to face, they speak and understand each other's language: one speaks "good English for a Comanche," the other "good Comanch."

THE VETERAN'S EXPERIENCE

Here, *The Searchers'* historic and cinematic moment offers its viewers much insight into Ethan's decision to walk away into the desert. First, it is necessary to revisit the situation of the returning American veteran just after World War II and its influence on both Ford and American society at the time of the film's making. In "Heroes and Misfits," David A. Gerber points out that it is now popularly assumed that the men who fought in World War II were greeted universally as heroes when they left the armed forces, because the "Good War" was considered a morally good cause. Few remember today that the prospect of World War II veterans' demobilization and reintegration was a cause for widespread concern, even alarm, that began long before V-J Day, evidenced by psychologists, psychiatrists, sociologists, physicians, clergymen, and military officials predicting "a major demobilization crisis" and considering every veteran a potential "mental case," even if he showed no symptoms.[39] These fears were popularly aired so often "in 1945 and 1946 that veterans, themselves, began to speak out against the stereotypes of criminality, violence, and psychopathology that established them as misfits unlikely to attain normal existences."[40]

As Gerber points out, Willard Waller, a Columbia University social work professor who was "a thoughtful analyst of veterans stated confidently that 'the political history of the next 25 years' in the United States would be determined when recent demobilized men concluded precisely whom to 'hate' among such potential targets as racial and ethnic minorities, capitalists, and those with draft exemptions."[41] Ironically, Waller's predictions about the social dangers of demobilization, wildly off target about the nature of the individuals returning from World War II, anticipated America's moral collapse into hatred on the national scale. For the next twenty-five years, the political history of the United States was determined by fervent anti-Communists and McCarthyites.

By 1956, Americans, John Ford among them, had not had much of an opportunity to socially and psychologically reintegrate to life in peacetime. Having returned from the European and Pacific theaters of war in 1946 and 1947, they found themselves involved from 1950 to 1953 in the Korean War and embroiled in Cold War hostilities at home. Given the circumstances, it is not surprising that Hollywood's response to World War II veterans' reintegration was extremely limited. Nonetheless, Gerber observes that "much of what is now popularly understood about World War II, the return of servicemen from the war . . . has been learned by watching Hollywood movies."[42] Notably, Ford did not make movies about the problems that Second World War veterans encountered when they returned home—*When Willie Comes Marching Home*, *What Price Glory*, and *Mr. Roberts* are all combat movies; *This is Korea!* is a documentary film made for the U.S. Navy; *The Long Gray Line* charts the training naval cadets receive at Annapolis.

Dore Schary's *I'll Be Seeing You* (1944), *The Enchanted Cottage* (1945), *They Dream of Home* (1945), and *Till the End of Time* (1946), made for RKO and United Artists, are prime examples of Second World War veteran narratives. During the mid- to late 1940s and into the early 1950s, other movies that also examine the readjustment problems of returning veterans include *Pride of the Marines* (Warner Bros., 1945), *The Blue Dahlia* (Paramount Pictures, 1946), *Crossfire* (RKO, 1947), *Key Largo* (Warner Bros., 1948), *The Clay Pigeon* (RKO, 1949),

Stanley Kramer's *The Men* (A Stanley Production, 1950), and *It's Al-ways Fair Weather* (MGM, 1955). The best known and most celebrated of those, William Wilder's *The Best Years of Our Lives* (Samuel Gold-wyn, 1946), garnered eight Oscars—one for its subject matter, which deals directly with the problems of social readjustment experienced by three World War II veterans.

During the Cold War, the returned veteran also became part of the cinematic coding that was a response to the blacklisting of the McCarthy period. American filmmakers and screenwriters created a prominent subgenre of film noir to express the postwar stigmatization and disillusionment that veterans experienced on their return. Direc-tors also used the nineteenth-century frontier for allegories on social and political issues that they could not treat elsewhere. Released while Hollywood blacklisting was still being enforced, *The Searchers* played to audiences composed of veterans and their families when all Americans were living and coping with the effects of social readjust-ment, PTSD, and Cold War hysteria. Placed in its cinematic moment, *The Searchers*, like *Fort Apache*, *She Wore a Yellow Ribbon*, and *Rio Grande*, recontextualizes the returning World War II veteran's experi-ence and haunts Americans with the proposition that it is impossible for the American war veteran to ever be able to return home. Simply put, Ethan's inability to return home did not puzzle his audiences—given their combat experience, highly ambivalent social status, and the chilly Cold War climate in which they lived. Ford's viewers would have recog-nized Ethan's dilemma as their own.

Given the similar situation of veterans who have returned home from more recent conflicts like the Vietnam War, the Persian Gulf War, the Iraq War, and the Afghanistan conflict, it is not surprising that *The Searchers* continues to be as relevant a film today as it was when it was first released. Post-9/11 viewers rate this movie as one of the greatest films ever made, and *The Searchers* is considered by the National Film Preservation Board and National Film Registry of the U.S. Library of Congress as culturally important.[43] Audience and industry responses to Ford's 115th movie indicate that America's attitude to its returning veterans has not changed since the end of World War II; however, the cultural transformation that such a change heralds is not yet complete.

In part, *The Searchers'* relevance today is attributable to John Ford, himself a veteran of World War II, creating the cinematic equivalent of classical Athenian theatre for the American audience when he made this movie. As usual, Ford, a trendsetter, was ahead of his time. Presently, the Office of Naval Research, funding the Honolulu Veterans Administration Medical Center (VAMC) virtual reality project for the treatment of PTSD, and Hunter Hoffman, a cognitive psychologist at the University of Washington, are in the process of discovering that a virtual reality can act as a trigger for bringing back those memories in a safe environment, enabling catharsis to take place.[44] Like the Honolulu VAMC virtual reality project for the treatment of PTSD, *The Searchers* triggers memories in its audiences in the safe environment of the movie theater. In doing so, the film functions as theater created by veterans for veterans—offering returning soldiers a distinctive therapy of purification, healing, and reintegration. Because the closing shots of *The Searchers* explicate Ethan Edwards's tragedy, Ford's audience members are invited to purge themselves of the experience that they share.

Thus, before John Wayne crosses his arm in tribute to Harry Carey Sr., before Ethan turns and walks away into the scorching wind and drifting sands of Monument Valley, before the door swings silently shut and the falling blackness becomes *The Searchers'* final moment, Lars, Debbie, and Mrs. Jorgenson have entered the house, Laurie and Martin have walked inside, and Ethan, left outside on the porch, steps back onto the land. Like the war combatant's, the viewer's social sphere is shrunk—from that of a tableau of the family composed of three individuals to that of a couple, Laurie and Martin, to that of one lonely and solitary individual. Reversing and unraveling *The Searchers'* opening, Ford's careful composition at the movie's end resists any possibility of closure for the viewer, returning its audience to the veteran, the man whose duty it is to protect and re-establish his community and who is doomed to never re-enter society. Ford's psychological epic concludes that the good bad man must live alone: uncleansed of his blood pollution, he is never able to return to hearth and home. It is not surprising that Ford insisted the scale of this movie be epic. What member of his audience who had fought in or experienced the trauma of World War II (or any war since) could have witnessed the ending of *The Searchers* and not have experienced the cleansing emotion of pity and fear for the returning veteran when Ethan says, "Let's go home, Debbie"?

11

A HOUSE DIVIDED

The Horse Soldiers

The Old Man had seen war, and of course, there is nothing pleasant about war. [1]—William Clothier

During the decline of the Hollywood studio system in the late 1950s and the early 1960s, Ford made five Westerns: *The Horse Soldiers* (1958), *Sergeant Rutledge* (1960), *Two Rode Together* (1961), *The Man Who Shot Liberty Valance* (1962), and *Cheyenne Autumn* (1964). As the movie industry changed, making pictures became "complex joint ventures between corporations," and independent producers had to assume responsibility for all the detail work that the studios had traditionally undertaken—everything from "the hiring of electricians, prop men, and makeup artists to the designing of sets and making up of payrolls." [2] In 1958, Marty Rackin and John Lee Mahin approached John Ford to direct *The Horse Soldiers*. Rackin, an independent producer/writer who later became the head of production at Paramount Pictures from 1960 to 1964, pitched *The Horse Soldiers* as a project to Ford for $200,000 plus 10 percent of the net. Rackin needed to convince the Mirisch brothers [3] to contribute $3.5 million, and Ford's willingness to direct the movie did just that—wanting to work with Ford, both John Wayne and William Holden agreed to star in the movie, and with Ford as director and two superstars as incentive, the Mirisch brothers invested in the project. A joint corporate venture, the complex deal for making *The Horse Soldiers* involved the Mirisch Company, United Artists, Mahin-

Rackin Productions, John Ford Productions, John Wayne's Batjac Productions, and William Holden Productions. Ford told John Lee Mahin, who was coproducing the picture, that *The Horse Soldiers* ought to be made in Lourdes, because "it's going to be a miracle to pull it off."[4]

Ford was an authority on the Civil War. Longtime cameraman and cinematographer William Clothier says of Ford that he could "tell you the name of every general who was in the Union Army and the Southern Army. He is absolutely familiar with every piece of wardrobe that was worn by troops in the Civil War."[5] Because of his interest in the subject, Ford should have been a perfect fit for *The Horse Soldiers*, a story based on Union Colonel Ben Grierson's mission to cut the railroad between Newton Station and Vicksburg. Mahin remembers that Ford fell for the script "like a ton of bricks,"[6] but the resulting movie was not what anyone, except perhaps its director, expected it to be. *The Horse Soldiers*, Mahin says, was "an unfortunate . . . a bad film."[7] Reviewers agreed: James Hawco dismissed it as "middle rung Ford," while Jeffrey M. Anderson considered it "lesser Ford." Complaining of narrative clichés and a "poorly-staged fist fight," Emanuel Levy pronounced it "not one of John Ford-John Wayne's best collaborations," and because if its "willingness to take liberties with history," Peter Canavese found it "flawed."[8]

In 1997, Dan Ford remarked that if he were writing *Pappy: The Life of John Ford* today, he "would give 'The Horse Soldiers' a better mention."[9] As he points out, *The Horse Soldiers* does merit "a better mention." Like Ford's other cavalry films, *The Horse Soldiers* is at once haunting and implausible, evocative and improbable. In spite of the problems experienced during its production, *The Horse Soldiers* still manages to convey an incisive critique of the American sociopolitical character, and what have been deemed to be the film's flaws (its anachronisms, problems with continuity, historical inaccuracies, and, at times, labored rhetoric) prove to be important components of Ford's deconstruction of popular notions of duty, honor, and patriotism found in his postwar Westerns. Advancing Ford's examination of partisanism in *The Horse Soldiers*, one finds a highly sophisticated treatment of perspective that is supported and furthered by Ford's and Clothier's close attention to the work of Mathew Brady, Alexander Gardner, and Timothy H. Sullivan during the Civil War.

PATRIOTISM IN POINTS OF VIEW

Based on the successful, daring, and surprisingly bloodless story of Union Colonel Ben Grierson and 1,700 men who set out from northern Mississippi and rode several hundred miles to cut the railroad between Newton Station and Vicksburg, *The Horse Soldiers* charts the (mis)adventures of a Union cavalry brigade that is sent behind Confederate lines. En route, Captain John Marlowe (John Wayne) and his officers' plans are overheard by a Southern belle, Miss Hannah Hunter (Constance Towers), and her slave, Lukey (Althea Gibson). At Greenbriar Plantation, Marlowe is forced to kidnap the women to protect the secrecy of their mission. Evading the Confederate forces in pursuit (with his captives in tow), he and his cavalrymen capture Newton Station and continue on to Baton Rouge, despite a skirmish with Southerners in which Lukey is killed and an encounter with cadets from a local military school (based on the Battle of New Market). Throughout, Marlowe's decisions are challenged by Hunter and Colonel Phil Secord (Willis Bouchey) and the troop's surgeon, Major Henry Kendall (William Holden).

When one considers the care given to point of view in *The Horse Soldiers*, it quickly becomes apparent that matters of perspective lie at the heart of this film. Ideologically driven, the viewpoints of the North and the South in *The Horse Soldiers* allow no middle ground to either its characters or its viewer. Romance, of course, is one method by which Ford quickly establishes the opposing viewpoints of North and South. Union Colonel John Marlowe's relationship with Hannah Hunter is confrontational throughout the narrative, often taking the form of a battle between the sexes. The skirmishes that occur between Marlowe and Hannah Hunter not only demonstrate their differing political and social philosophies but also showcase their competing ideologies of gender. In this theater of war, Marlowe, representing a rational, masculine North, finally capitulates to Hunter, who embodies an emotional, impulsive, feminine South. Ironically, as Kendall points out, the Southern belle, whom he implies to be a "ding dong," is the better general of the two, having no difficulty making fools of and captivating both men. Unable to anticipate Hunter's actions, Marlowe is unable to prevent her from learning his plans and cannot control her. She is able to escape at a gallop from the column, and when a cavalry brigade from the South appears on the opposite bank of a river, she breaks away from her captors and calls for help. Marlowe knocks her unconscious to subdue her as she attempts to bite the hand he has clasped over her mouth. As he relieves her guards of their stripes, his exasperated question, "How many men does it take to keep one lone female quiet?" makes it evident that no number of Northerners is equal to such a task. No one in the brigade, including Marlowe, is able to answer his question.

Carrying out their patriotic duty makes it impossible for Marlowe and his men to behave in accordance with "the social amenities" expected of gentlemen. Unquestionably in the wrong, they invade and loot Hunter's home before kidnapping her. Her discovery that Marlowe has instructed her guards to invade her privacy while using the privy earns him a well-deserved slap across the face. Declaring the belle the victor in this confrontation, Kendall wisely quits the field with what becomes a running gag, commenting to Marlowe, "You should see a doctor. Ding dong. Ding dong."

In this clash between the masculine and the feminine, the conflict between the North and the South is also represented as a disagreement between the traditions of pragmatism and chivalry. When Marlowe, for example, delivers the Confederate deserters Jackie Jo (Denver Pyle) and Virgil (Strother Martin) into the hands of the law with the compliments of "Miss Hannah Hunter of Greenbriar," Hunter believes that he has acted honorably. Marlowe, however, points out that his action is purely pragmatic—he does not trust them any more than her. Because Hunter is also partisan in her thinking, as Kendall remarks, Marlowe is "a hard man to understand."

Marlowe, however, is not really a complex character. Dubbed "Old Ironhead" by the doctor, the unemotional, duty-bound, conservative ex-railroad engineer embodies an epic type: he is the warrior who does "all the thinking" during the mission. Kendall, on the other hand, refuses to wear a gun and doctors the injured of both the North and the South. He too is a familiar figure, the liberal humanitarian pacifist. Also a liberal, Hunter is the epitome of the gentlewoman. Not a character study, the film's narrative is driven by the conflict generated by protagonists who do not (and cannot) change. At base, *The Horse Soldiers* is a Civil War romance in which characters' interactions illustrate *and* critique America's sociopolitical tensions. In order to do so, these characters' stories and rhetorical stances illustrate the flatness and rigidity of their roles.

DISRUPTED DUTY

The entanglement of the war hero and his rigid adherence to duty in the film's subplot not only drives the action of the film forward but is also a prime example of rhetorical absurdity. Indeed, it is difficult to decide which of Marlowe's pronouncements at Greenbriar is the silliest: his complaint that he will be put to "great inconvenience" by taking Hunter and Lukey with him on the raid after severely inconveniencing the women by stripping the plantation of its livestock and foodstuffs, or his offer to let Hunter and Lukey go if they promise on their "honor" to keep their mouths shut about the Union cavalry's presence in the South. As Kendall points out, both women are spies (and therefore without honor) and should be shot immediately. But however pragmatic (and sensible) such an act would be, Marlowe is unable to do so—the personal and professional dishonor of murdering civilians, women whose hospitality he has accepted, makes their execution unthinkable.

In short, Marlowe's decision to include women in the male-dominated world of the Union cavalry creates absurdity during the Civil War. Unlike *Rio Grande*, in which Ford's use of the carnivalesque is comic, in *The Horse Soldiers* it is a tragicomedy, fashioned out of what is already an impossible situation—soldiers in a war avoiding battle. A disorderly woman, Hunter inverts the military chain of command around her, making the high low and the low high. However much her male jailers may drag her about and however many times she may promise to behave, she does not obey orders. Rather, she acquiesces to requests that she deems reasonable because her captors are bound by social convention to protect and serve her. During the banquet scene at Greenbriar, for example, she has Marlowe and his staff chivalrously leaping to attention when she stands and sitting down again on her orders like a pack of trained seals. Even Kendall, who resists her charms and discovers her spying on Marlowe and his officers after supper, eventually retrieves her handkerchief for her. On the road, her delighted and solicitous jailers dry her underwear. When she refuses help mounting her horse, they accede to her wishes. She even disciplines Marlowe when he does not respect her privacy, slapping him across the mouth. At Newton Station, the situation becomes absurd: her captors ensure a hot bath is drawn for her so she may bathe while they kill Confederate troops and loot and burn Confederate contraband.

Finally, when attacked by "some kids from a military school," Marlowe has had enough of incongruities of the circumstances that he has created. He literally throws up his hands in disgust. Unaccompanied, Hunter has once more rushed to the front to witness the spectacle that is taking place. Viewing the young boys marching toward them, she asks, "Yes, Mister Colonel Marlowe, what are you going to do now?" His authority overturned by his social inferiors whom he may not harm, Marlowe gathers what remains of his dignity and replies, "With all due respect to your presence, ma'am, I'm going to get the hell out of here." Ordering recall as his troops are routed by children, he is reduced to shouting at Hunter's "constant companions," who have finally found her: "I told you to take care of this woman!"

Counterbalancing the comic disruption that her mistress creates, Lukey becomes a tragic figure. Throughout the raid, Lukey, a reasonable, rational individual, is a model prisoner. Her Union captors all become fond of her. After the battle at Newton Station, the brigade continues on toward Baton Rouge and is bushwhacked by Southern partisans. Inexplicably, Lukey, who is not a soldier, is the only casualty in this exchange. She dies in Hunter's arms, surrounded by their ineffectual captors. Aptly, when Sgt. Brown (Hoot Gibson) provides Hunter with a piece of looking glass that evening, she controls the situation, pragmatically comforting the men who are grieving with her over Lukey's death.

NO CHANCE OF RECONCILIATION

Ford's close-up of Hunter's reflection, looking back at her from the piece of mirror, reveals her face crowned by Brown's cavalry cap. This image, however, only suggests that her point of view has changed, that Hunter has changed sides and has become a "blue belly." Although Marlowe expresses his deep sorrow and regret about Lukey's death, Hunter refuses to change. She will not collaborate with him so she can be free: "It's too late. It's too late for all of that," she says. "No more promises. No more anything now."

At Williamsburg Bridge, Ford reminds the viewer that North and South cannot be united even though it appears that the antagonistic relationship between Marlowe and Hunter may be resolved by love. As

Marlowe informs Hunter that he is leaving her behind for the oncoming Union cavalry, his shadow dramatically envelopes her seated figure. At the end, they remain each other's shadows—separated by war, any relationship that they may have in the future is sure to fail.

At Newton Station, the antagonism between North and South is further developed as the conflict ceases to be personal and becomes professional. Before the battle at Newton Station begins, Marlowe asks his Confederate counterpart what contraband lies in the warehouses at Newton Station. Highly insulted, Colonel Jonathan Miles (Carleton Young) replies, "The property of the Confederate States of America is not contraband, sir." Marlowe's response—"Oh? Well, let's look at it from my side, Colonel"—emphasizes how different his perspective is from his Confederate counterpart's.

In the Union Army itself, another battle of opposing views is being fought. As Peter Cowie notes, *The Horse Soldiers* "encompasses two fundamental elements in Ford: the military man, for whom duty to the army precedes all else, and the ingrained humanism of the civilian doctor."[10] Throughout their journey into the South, Marlowe's patriotic duty as an officer and Major Henry Kendall's (William Holden) allegiance to the Hippocratic oath clash with one another. When Kendall, the brigade's reluctant doctor, leaves his wounded to deliver a baby, Marlowe places him under house arrest. When Kendall tends to the Union and Confederate wounded after the Battle of Newton's Station, Marlowe frets about the delay that this entails. When Kendall uses an "old Cheyenne Indian cure" on a scout's wound, Marlowe scoffs at the efficacy of green mold. And when the scout, Dunker (Bing Russell), contracts blood poisoning because he has discarded the tree moss and then dies of shock after the operation, the escalating hostility between the two men erupts into a brawl that is interrupted and reabsorbed by the larger conflict at hand, as Confederate forces, consisting of under-age cadets from a nearby military academy, launch an assault against the invading Union cavalry.

Ford based the tragicomic sequence, the Charge of the Cadets, on an incident that took place during the 1864 Shenandoah Valley Battle of New Market, during which Union troops were routed by cadets from the Virginia Military Institute. Filming of the Charge of the Cadets took place near the end of the location shoot, with 150 cadets between the ages of nine and sixteen from Jefferson Military College in Washington,

Mississippi, the alma mater of Confederate president Jefferson Davis. Ford's attention to historical detail for this sequence was painstaking: the cadets' uniforms were copied from an actual 1850s vintage college uniform preserved by a Natchez woman as a family heirloom.[11]

NOT A HEROIC ACTIVITY

Ronald L. Davis has suggested that Ford, after returning to Hollywood in October 1945, looked for answers to the changes in America during the Cold War in his country's military traditions.[12] The answer that Ford found while re-creating history becomes an important part of *The Horse Soldiers'* critique. Before the Charge takes place, it is made abundantly clear that fighting is not a heroic activity. A frantic Mrs. Buford (Anna Lee) begs the Reverend (Basil Ruysdael) of the Jefferson Military Academy not to take her son away to war: "Reverend, my boy Johnny he's all I've got left. First his Pa, then his Uncle, then his brothers, now him. He's all I have left, Reverend. I'm not going to let him go. I'm not going to let him go." Released of his duty, Cadet Drummer Buford is dragged kicking and screaming home by his determined mother and locked in his bedroom. No boy, however, can resist war. War seems to be, as Ford demonstrates, an activity for boys. In no time at all, Buford climbs out of his window, shimmies down the drainpipe, picks up his drum, and runs off to join his fellows.

Ford's treatment of the cadets' performance on the field of battle overturns the tragedy of children, as young as nine, marching off to be butchered. As the cadets begin their volleys, Marlowe orders his men not to return fire but to retreat. The only Confederate casualty is the unlucky Johnny (and his drum) caught by Corporal Wilkie (Ken Curtis). "Hey, Colonel, I've got me a prisoner here," Wilkie shouts. "What do you want me to do with him?" "Spank him," Marlowe replies. "On the bottom?" Wilkie asks. "Where do you think?" Marlowe snaps. Dishonored and squealing, "You dirty Yankee," the young Confederate hero is soundly spanked as the Union retreats from Jefferson. As the last Union cavalryman to scamper away, Marlowe gallantly doffs his hat as he leaves the playing field to the children chasing him.

Of course, war is not fun and games, and Ford is careful to point this out. The comedy created by the Charge of the Cadets is balanced by the tragedy found in Kendall's makeshift hospital at Newton Station. Wounded and dying in spite of Kendall's efforts to save him, the youthful Trooper Hoskins (Jan Stine) remains an idealistic boy who is unable to disappoint the expectations of others. Although he is afraid, Hoskins dies a "good death," dutifully claiming that he is "all right" because that is what Marlowe expects him to say. Brightly side-lit, his golden hair shines like a halo throughout this scene, suggesting his belief in the transcendent nature of self-sacrifice and helping to engage the viewer's sentiments in Marlowe's heartbreak as he attempts to comfort the young man. At base, Hoskins, who badly wants to be thought a hero, is really a child. At Hoskins's bedside, Marlowe's final bitter words to Hunter are: "Yes. I'm very proud of that *boy*" (italics mine).

Other soldier "boys" who play at war in this movie include the glory-seeker Colonel Phil Secord and the irresponsible armchair general Ulysses S. Grant (Stan Jones). Obsessed with himself and his political career, Secord, thinking only of furthering his public image, is not worried about the welfare of his men. Concerned with ends rather than means, Grant, who is also self-absorbed, is undisturbed by the problem of how Marlowe and his men will reach safety after they raid Newton Station. Answerable for the lives of his men, Marlowe, an adult father figure, views the matter of war very differently. As the Battle of Newton Station begins, Marlowe orders his men to fire and immediately regrets the slaughter that ensues on both sides. He shouts at Kendall, "I didn't want this. I tried to avoid a fight." With this in mind, Ford's comic critique of war in the Charge of the Cadets is scalding and apropos. Those involved in such reprehensible behavior should be spanked.

PRESENTATIONS OF THE CONFLICT

Ford's critique of war and its heroes is supported by the composition and framing of shots in *The Horse Soldiers*. Throughout this film, Ford's evocative, painterly treatments of war echo the work of Civil War photographers Mathew Brady, Alexander Gardner, and Timothy O'Sullivan. Broadly distributed during and after the Civil War, these photographs taught Americans to regard the violence of the battlefield as part of the Sublime nature of war in the terms of the pastoral ideal presented in American nineteenth-century landscape painting.

Because of the great demand for battlefield views and portraits, Gardner and O'Sullivan traveled to the battlefields and, competing with one another, produced a significant body of photographs.[13] Among the best known of these are Gardner's *Confederate Dead Gathered for Burial* (1862) and O'Sullivan's *A Harvest of Death, Gettysburg, Pennsylvania* (1863). Both images showcase picturesque arrangements of corpses that guide the viewer's eye through the landscape of the battlefield to a final release upward into the distant sky. Re-creating compositional elements used by these photographs, *The Horse Soldiers* features some of William Clothier's "most beautifully atmospheric cinematography" and includes "a sequence humorously re-creating the taking of a Matthew [*sic*] Brady photograph."[14] Throughout, Ford's treatment of perspective and leading lines indicate that his preproduction work with Brady's collection of Civil War images was a matter of concern for composition as well as an exercise ensuring verisimilitude—an exercise that led Clothier to declare that Ford "knew more about photography than any other man who ever worked in the movies. He was a genius. He'd force me into situations where I'd have to sit up and take notice."[15]

As in all photography, the meaning and reality of a subject in a Civil War photograph depend upon the perspective from which it is viewed and considered. To the untrained eye, Civil War landscape photography is believed to be a collection of accurate and truthful representations of the aftermath of battles and camp life. Arguably, the most famous of Brady's photographs is the iconic Civil War image *A Harvest of Death*, taken after the Battle of Gettysburg by O'Sullivan. In *A Harvest of Death*, the foreground, midground, background, and distant sky are all rendered in sharp delineation, de-emphasizing the picture maker's function as narrator who subtly directs the viewer, while meditating on the nature of war, to particular aspects of the scene. *A Harvest of Death* looks like an accurate representation of the aftermath of Gettysburg, but as in his other Civil War photographs, O'Sullivan rearranged his subjects (the corpses) and used perspective and composition to maximize meaning through symbolic associations, thereby legitimizing the photograph's apparent objectivity and truth.

A Harvest of Death is created by the repetition of the soldiers' bodies forming dynamic diagonals that guide the eye through the landscape of the battlefield from the foreground of the frame, back to a rider seated on a horse, and then farther back to the sloping hills at the picture's horizon and its empty sky. Gardner's approach to his subject in *Confederate Dead Gathered for Burial* is the same as O'Sullivan's but not nearly so subtle. Gardner's dynamic diagonal in this photograph is much bolder than O'Sullivan's. As Gardner's title indicates, these corpses have fallen in battle. They have been arranged tidily in a line that runs midframe in the foreground from right to left, before reversing direction and running from left to right. The first corpse encountered in this picture is posed for the shot, lying perpendicular to his fellows and thus drawing the line of sight to run from his feet over his bare stomach to his curved right arm and onto his hand, the fingers of which gesture toward the line of bodies immediately behind him.

Ford's compositions throughout *The Horse Soldiers* are mediated by visual strategies similar to those in the landscapes of the Civil War battlefields. Ford uses these to create a historically accurate look for the picture. Ford's first landscape is a wide shot in which cavalrymen, leading columns of horses from the horizon toward the front of the frame, canter by the camera and turn. The camera follows as it pans toward the horizon. Likewise, when Kendall is introduced, he walks from behind the camera to the conference table under a tree where Marlowe and his staff are discussing their battle plans. Later, when Marlowe's short brigade embarks on the raid, its column also trots away from the camera positioned in the camp toward the frame's horizon.

One of the most beautifully evocative landscape shots in *The Horse Soldiers*, which faithfully reconstructs the enormous depth of field found in photographs of Civil War battlefields, occurs when Marlowe, attempting to convince Southern scouts that he and his men are returning home, sends Blaney and his 2nd Iowa north. A tall tree trunk directs the eye from the lower left-hand corner of the screen along the natural diagonal created by the bank of the reservoir to Marlowe, who stands waving at the line of cavalrymen moving across the horizon from right to left. The viewer's eye continues along the water's edge to the right side of the screen, where it is met by the ridge on which the horsemen ride. After Marlowe has waved goodbye to the men with his hat, Ford reverses the motion to emphasize the opposite direction in which Marlowe and his men will ride. Marlowe turns and walks to the right of the screen. Following him, Ford's camera atypically pans to the right to reveal his waiting troops who will be taking the viewer south with them.

Ford's use of movement on screen becomes more complex once Marlowe and his men enter the gates of Greenbriar. As the South's opposing perspective of the war is introduced into the narrative, opposing points of view are also introduced by the camera itself. For example, after Lukey and Hunter look out a bedroom window at them, Marlowe and his men move up the front walk to the house against the natural movement of the viewer's perspective, which leads the eye toward the front gate. When Marlowe kicks open the front door of the house and enters it, the camera's straight-on point-of-view shot, extending over Marlowe's shoulder, carries the viewer's eye through the entrance hallway and up the stairs and then along the landing to Hunter's bedroom door. When Lukey enters the frame from Hunter's room and descends the staircase, her opposing movement reminds the viewer of the frame's stability. Visually, conceptually, and ideologically, the forward momentum that the viewer has been experiencing with the Union cavalry stops. Encountering Lukey, Marlowe (and the camera's gaze) can advance no farther into the house. His advance (and the viewer's) is stalemated.

Ford's decision to introduce movement within the frame that aggressively contradicts and halts the natural progress of the eye through a landscape creates a battle of perspectives. This is particularly evident during the Battle of Williamsburg Bridge. As Marlowe and his men, on the bridge, charge toward the cannons, their point of view is intercut with the opposing point of view of the Confederate artillerymen defending their position on the other side of the river. Aptly, movement away from the camera after Marlowe leaves Greenbriar complements the inclination of the eye to look toward the horizon, and what is recorded are moments of escape or retreat: Hunter on horseback attempting to flee from the column; Hunter attempting to run to the river to call for help; Marlowe's column following the diagonals of the battlefield landscapes of the Civil War to escape their Confederate pursuers in the swamp.

Thus it is a great visual relief when Ford dissolves this tension created by contrasting points of view when the ideological and emotional conflicts between the characters appear to be resolved at the movie's end. As Marlowe leaves Hunter behind "to her own kind" and rides off to fight his way to Baton Rouge, the camera (positioned at a respectable distance behind Hunter) records his exit toward the horizon. Hunter runs toward the bridge but stops at the wagon. Ford then cuts to reveal Hunter's face and Kendall appears behind her, entering via the side door of the cabin. He walks to join Hunter. As Kendall turns Hunter and guides her back to the cabin to tend the wounded, Ford varies his shots, but the camera angle remains the same and the camera itself continues to be stationary, recording the couple's progress to the log cabin in the background, directing the viewer's eye toward the small wooden structure.

Visually, the ending of *The Horse Soldiers* is a satisfying affair. Mahin was unhappy that Ford decided to drop the script's ending sequence of the troopers marching wearily but triumphantly into Baton Rouge, but as McBride points out, "Ford's decision to drop it arguably was aesthetically valid."[16] Stability in the South has been reintroduced with Marlowe's departure and by the arrival of Jeb Stuart's horsemen. As the Confederate cavalry pours by behind the cabin in pursuit of Marlowe and his men, the solid little building is not engulfed by the action going on around it. A home for the wounded, this cabin promises security and permanence for those within.

Ford's final shot of the small building is perhaps the movie's most telling, for at this point, all rhetoric has ended and Kendall and Hunter have returned to repair the human damage caused by the earlier conflict. An iconic image of America, which returns the audience to the frontier ideal found in *Drums along the Mohawk*, the cabin reminds its viewer of the resilience of the American Character. Throughout *The Horse Soldiers*, Ford's America has been a house divided, and it seems it will continue to be so. In spite of "The End" appearing, superimposed on the cabin, the war itself is far from being over—Marlowe has ridden on to join the Union forces in Baton Rouge, Hunter is staying behind in the South, and Kendall will soon be facing two long, terrible years in Andersonville Prison. Each character's "end" is motivated by his or her devotion to duty, self-sacrifice, and obedience to a higher cause. Ford's ending conceptually, ideologically, and visually renders the complexity of America's partisan sociopolitical character.

Neil York suggests that Ford's film demonstrates how historical "truths" are often omitted, fragmented, and altered before being assimilated into popular culture and how the events are often molded to fit the constraints of the present. But when one considers Ford's decision to end in "an elliptical and downbeat manner,"[17] the historical inaccuracies of *The Horse Soldiers* invite the viewer instead to identify with the characters on the screen and suggest that there really is little difference between America's past and its present. Ford's cavalry officers' lack of facial hair, for example, subtly modernizes the horse soldier—clean shaven, Marlowe and Kendall are men who belong to the twentieth, not the nineteenth, century. Kendall's white coats and jackets, which immediately identify him to Cold War audiences as a man of medicine, were never seen in the surgeons' tents during the Civil War. Even the unhistorical standardization of the cavalrymen's uniforms (especially the yellow stripe on their trousers) updates the martial look of the cavalryman to twentieth-century standards of military dress.

The Horse Soldiers presents a powerful irony created by Ford's treatment of multiple perspectives, landscapes, and anachronisms. In this film, America (earlier regarded as a pastoral ideal) is a battlefield. As *Stagecoach* pointed out in 1939, any man who lives in a state of nature must do so in a state of constant war with every other man. In 1959, to those who had not only lived through the Second World War and the Korean Conflict but were also heavily involved in the Cold War, this surely must have seemed to be the case. *The Horse Soldiers'* historical inaccuracies challenge Ford's viewers to recognize themselves, the nature of their own competing perspectives, and the nature of America on the screen. An important part of Ford's Western canon, *The Horse Soldiers* not only participates in and further develops its director's pessimistic postwar critique of the American Character, but also showcases and rationalizes what McBride deems to be Ford's tendency after the Second World War: to be "more nakedly individualistic, more deeply emotional, in many ways more pessimistic, fascinatingly and sometimes maddeningly self-contradictory."[18]

DEATH ON THE SET

After twenty-eight days on location, Ford stopped shooting *The Horse Soldiers* when veteran stuntman Fred Kennedy was killed while doubling William Holden in a saddle fall. Kennedy, who had worked with Ford for years, rolled off his horse on the mark but broke his neck when he hit the ground. He died almost immediately. As Chuck Roberson recalls, John Wayne, present at the accident, insisted that Kennedy, who had decided to retire after *The Horse Soldiers*, had been loping his horse at the time, but there hadn't been enough speed to make the stunt "*deadly.*"[19] It was a freak accident, but Ford, who had been a stuntman for his brother in his youth and was Kennedy's friend, felt responsible for the tragedy. Against his better judgment, he had allowed Kennedy to attempt the stunt. Hank Worden remembered "Ford walking away, blaming himself for Kennedy's death."[20] Kennedy's death "really knocked [Ford] out," Wayne said. "He just went back to the hotel, and he couldn't think or work for days."[21]

Katharine Hepburn's insight into Ford's character at the end of his life is particularly instructive here. Life for Ford, she remarks, "in actuality had been an extremely tough experience" because he was "sensitive to a great many things that people would never suspect [him] to be sensitive about." She asserts that he was "torn apart by a great number of things [that he] . . . could never admit to being torn by."[22] When one considers Ford's behavior after Kennedy's accident, it is evident that the stuntman's death had been one of the "great number of things" to which Hepburn alluded.

Ford could not just stop shooting the movie when Fred Kennedy died and still stay on time and in budget. *The Horse Soldiers* had to be finished. As Mahin remembers, Ford took to self-medicating after Kennedy's death and refused to shoot the last scene because "he didn't care about the picture anymore."[23] Tellingly, the scene Ford refused to shoot was a gory battle scene that would have involved more saddle falls. He instead improvised the visually satisfying ending that we see today. Mahin, however, was not happy with the results. "It was awful," he said. "They charged across that damned bridge and not one guy fell off the saddle. I didn't know what was the matter."[24] Ford's atypical behavior during the final days of production also disturbed John Wayne. "Pappy just doesn't seem to care anymore," he told Pilar. "He looks and acts like a beaten man."[25] Deeply affected, Ford was not just depressed and demoralized—his apathy toward the project and his inability to continue shooting the script as planned indicate he was also suffering from severe shock while attempting to complete shooting. As soon as *The Horse Soldiers* had been scored and dubbed, Ford flew to Honolulu in February 1959 to recover, swimming in the Ali Wai Yacht Harbor during the mornings and sitting in the deckhouse of the *Araner* during the afternoons.[26] Later in his life, he would not discuss *The Horse*

Soldiers with his interviewers. Speaking to Peter Bogdanovich, he even repressed his memory of the movie, saying, "I don't think I ever saw it. But a lot of the things in it actually happened—such as the children from the Military Academy marching out against the Union soldiers—that happened several times."[27]

12

THE NATURE OF ONE'S SERVICE

Sergeant Rutledge

I don't want to make great sprawling pictures. I want to make films in a kitchen. [1]—John Ford

Sympathetic to the fight for civil rights in the United States that took place after the Second World War, John Ford "liked the new liberalism—particularly the struggle for black civil rights, which in his mind was not unlike the struggle for Irish freedom." [2] In 1954, Ford approved of Chief Justice Warren's decision for Brown in *Brown v. Board of Education of Topeka*, which reversed the 1898 *Plessy* standard of "separate but equal" throughout the United States and overturned segregationist practice and thought. Acting as the touchstone of the social justice movement that followed, the *Brown* decision implemented the spirit of the Fourteenth Amendment, which guaranteed all Americans "equality of treatment and opportunity for all persons in the armed services without regard to race, color, religion, or national origin" in 1948 and paved the way for the Montgomery Bus Boycott in 1955, Martin Luther King's election as the president of the Southern Christian Leadership Conference, and federal intervention for the Little Rock Nine in 1957.

In 1958, a month after Ford arrived in Honolulu to recuperate from making *The Horse Soldiers*, Jim Bellah and Willis Goldbeck visited him with a script for *Captain Buffalo*, about the 9th Cavalry Regiment, the Negro unit that had fought some of the hardest fights of the Indian

Wars. In April, Ford returned to Hollywood to make a deal on the project. His decision to direct what was to become *Sergeant Rutledge* proved to be very timely. Mack Charles Parker's lynching on April 24 triggered national outrage,[3] and every studio, responding to public opinion, bid on *Sergeant Rutledge*. Warner Bros. settled with Ford for the film by offering him a "whopping $400,000; $100,000 for the property and $300,000 for [Ford] as the director."[4]

Although Ford began the project enthusiastically, it soon became evident that he had not recovered from the traumatic experience of making *The Horse Soldiers*. Bellah noted that the level of intensity that Ford displayed while working on the Cavalry Trilogy was not in evidence. "It was pretty obvious from the start that some of the old fire was missing in Jack," he says. "He had always been a real tyrant in story sessions, needling and picking away at you. It was his way of making you reach in and give your best. But on *Rutledge* he was really mild. Whenever an important subject came up he just said, 'Whatever you think is fine' or 'Just write it as you see fit, and I'll get it on film.' This wasn't the Jack Ford I knew."[5] Ford's shooting schedule for this film was also atypical: forty of the fifty working days it took to make *Sergeant Rutledge* were shot on the lot at Warner Bros.[6] Ford, as he told Colin Young, was making this movie "in a kitchen."[7] Ford was aware that the story of Captain Buffalo was the best one that had come his way for many years; he also knew that the subject was "a tricky one to be tackling" in 1959.[8] He told Young, "We have shaped the story to be told through a series of retrospects, as cutouts from the court-martial. As we develop it, he really looks guilty as hell."[9] A film with a black action hero well ahead of its time, *Sergeant Rutledge* uses highly sophisticated expressionistic techniques to raise questions for the viewer about the unreliability of memory and the prejudices underpinning social aberrance.

Sergeant Rutledge was released on May 18, 1960. Although Warner Bros. screened the picture for a number of civil rights leaders at various stages of its completion and received positive reactions to it, when the picture was released, "it was poorly received by critics both black and white."[10] At the box office, the film did not draw large audiences, grossing only $748,000 in the United States. Overseas, the film fared better, grossing $1.7 million. Ford blamed Warner Bros. for the film's financial failure, complaining, "Warners sent a couple of boys on bicycles out to sell it," he said.[11] Intent on breaking the color barrier in Hollywood,

Ford assumed his own stance on the subject of racism in *Sergeant Rutledge* to be apparent because its title character was "nobler than anybody else in the picture."[12] In 1966, however, Samuel Lachize, a critic for *L'Humanité*, the French Communist Party's official newspaper, pointed out that some people thought Ford's work had racist aspects. Ford, of course, was at once furious and flabbergasted—he had made *Sergeant Rutledge* in spite of movie executives who had told him that the project would lose money because it was about a "nigger" and therefore could not be shown in the South.[13] Ford made a point of informing Lachize that he had become angry and told the executives that they "could at least have the decency to say 'Negro' or 'colored man,' because most of those 'niggers' were worth better than they."[14] Incensed, he stated, "People who say such things are crazy. I am a Northerner. I hate segregation, and I gave jobs to hundreds of Negroes at the same salary the whites were paid. . . . Me a racist?" According to Ford, it was impossible not to consider African Americans "full-fledged American citizens" because when he "landed at Omaha Beach there were scores of black bodies lying in the sand."[15]

To date, *Sergeant Rutledge*'s critical reception has also been focused on issues of race. Joseph McBride, for example, notes that Ford painstakingly posed the ideal soldier, Rutledge (Woody Strode), in heroic low-angle shots while his fellow troopers serenade him with "Captain Buffalo," but argues that the director's racial perspective in *Sergeant Rutledge* is that of "an enlightened nineteenth century liberal" who is "honest enough to recognize and deal with his own complicity in racism," and thus "deserves credit for addressing such issues head on."[16] More recently, however, Jeffrey M. Anderson, in "Buffalo Stance," notes that "*Sergeant Rutledge* is an astonishing film not only for its sheer visual and narrative excellence but also for its early acknowledgement of race relations in America. It's strikingly similar to *To Kill a Mockingbird*, but two years earlier and a great deal angrier."[17] *Sergeant Rutledge*, Anderson says, should be given "enormous credit for its straightforward approach [to the problem of American racism], its bravery long before Hollywood was ready for it, and its noble beauties."[18] In part, questions about Ford's stance on race in *Sergeant Rutledge* may be attributed to a lack of understanding about the medium that he selected for his critique—the U.S. Army of the 1800s. As Frank Manchel points out in "Losing and Finding John Ford's 'Sergeant Rutledge'"

(1960)," Ford, like many men of his generation, believed "that the military, with all of its weaknesses, offered a better life than that found in civilian society. He felt that was particularly true for oppressed African-Americans."[19] The history of black regulars in the U.S. Army of the 1800s supports such beliefs. Historian William A. Dobak notes that the U.S. Army was one of the most impartial institutions of its day, and as such it attracted men whose ability and endurance ensured their regiments' survival and provided a place for black Americans in the nation's public life.[20]

CAPTAIN BUFFALO

Given Ford's love affair with Remington's images of the West, it is appropriate that *Sergeant Rutledge* was inspired by Remington's picture of black cavalrymen on the western frontier. The Tenth Cavalry was first sketched by Remington on an 1888 visit to Arizona. At this time, Remington noted, "The physique of the black soldiers must be admired—great chests, broad-shouldered, upstanding fellows."[21] In keeping with this model, Strode was a perfect fit for the part of Captain Buffalo, later known as Sergeant Rutledge. Strode was physically well suited to play the part of a superman. In fact, he had played the part before. As Manchel points out, Strode was "so impressive [that] . . . the controversial German film-maker Leni Riefenstahl, during a goodwill tour in California, used him as a model for a painting commissioned by Hitler for the 1936 Olympics in Berlin."[22] Thus Ford's extreme low-angle shots of Strode while he is serenaded by his unit with the song "Captain Buffalo" offer a military icon to the viewer—his presentation transcends the ordinary. Backlit, Rutledge emits light. He appears hardly human: physically, mentally, and emotionally perfect.

During the 1940s, Strode's powerful physical screen presence was a marketable commodity in Hollywood. Strode was cast in several films during the 1940s, including *Sundown* (1941), *Star Spangled Rhythm* (1942), and *No Time for Love* (1943).[23] Charlene Regester views the character of Rutledge as stereotypical, arguing that in the courtroom, he is put in the position of a "weak black male,"[24] but Strode's experience of the character differs vastly from Regester's perceptions of it. Strode not only regarded his role of hero as "an accolade for his service in the John Ford Stock company,"[25] but also insisted that the role elevated the status of African Americans: "I've never gotten over *Sergeant Rutledge*. It had dignity. John Ford put classic words in my mouth," Strode said late in his career.[26] "You never seen a Negro come off a mountain like John Wayne before. I had the greatest Glory Hallelujah ride across the Pecos River that any black man ever had on the screen. And I did it myself. I carried the whole black race across that river."[27] Yet in spite of Strode's own affirmation of his role and the movie, the question of Ford's racial perspective in *Sergeant Rutledge* remains so hotly debated that Tag Gallagher comments, "It is a pitiable reflection on American criticism that Ford, virtually the *only* filmmaker to concern himself with racism before it became commercially fashionable to do so, is virtually the only filmmaker whom critics attack as racist."[28] Perhaps it is a result of Ford's treatment of miscegenation or, as Rutledge terms the matter, "white woman business," another central issue in *Sergeant Rutledge* that has elicited curious critical responses. McBride finds *Sergeant Rutledge* "bluntly provocative" in its treatment of miscegenation, but believes Ford himself was conflicted about the subject of sex shown on screen.[29] Claiming that he did not want any part of the "market for sex and horror" that Hollywood had become, in *Sergeant Rutledge*, he nevertheless took advantage of "the climate of sexual frankness through the prism of race relations, the most controversial political issue in the country at the time."[30]

In part, the critical debate remains without resolution because of its attention to race relations in this film. Published on May 26, 1960, the *New York Times* review of *Sergeant Rutledge* begins by stating that "the theme of racial tension—as a Negro soldier is tried for a double-murder and the rape of a white girl—has been firmly imprinted by director John Ford on his favored post–Civil War canvas of the Southwest in 'Sergeant Rutledge,'" but does not go on to discuss the issues of race and miscegenation in the film at all. Instead, *Sergeant Rutledge* is simply assessed as a film about "a little-known chapter in Army history; the solid, brave service of a group of Negro recruits, including former slaves, under white officers during the Indian Wars," and summed up as "a good picture—thoughtful, well-acted, biting, interesting and stimulating—with the steady hand of an old pro like Mr. Ford every step of the way." "The picture succin[c]tly etches the court-martial testimonies and atmosphere, beset with bias, sympathy and ugly evidence," the unnamed reviewer says, noting that "it is impossible to believe that such a proud, professional Army man would yield to heinous crimes."[31]

As the *Times* reviewer points out, *Sergeant Rutledge* is the character study of a professional soldier whose actions are circumscribed by duty, honor, and military codes of conduct. In this film, no member of the U.S. Army is exempted from its rules of conduct. Duty-bound, Lieutenant Tom Cantrell (Jeffrey Hunter) and Sgt. Matthew Luke Skidmore (Juano Hernandez) capture Rutledge and return him to the fort for his court-martial, even though they cannot believe him to have committed the crimes of which he was accused. Mary Beecher (Constance Towers) finds Cantrell's devotion to duty excessive and calls him a "cheap contemptible tin-plated book-soldier," but Rutledge would not agree with her. His powerful courtroom speech demonstrates that he gave up his liberty to save the patrol and return to face the court-martial, not because of his own values, but because of his devotion to duty. He returns to be tried because "the Ninth Cavalry was [his] home." In court, Rutledge says that the regiment is "my real freedom. And my self-respect. And the way I was desertin' it [the Ninth Cavalry], I wasn't nothin' but a swamp-runnin' nigger. And I ain't that! Do you hear me? I'm a *man!*"[32]

ON TRIAL

Listening to Rutledge, it is impossible not to respect his sincerity and his self-control. In the courtroom, Ford is at great pains to establish Rutledge's moral goodness to convince the viewer that he could not have committed the crimes of murder and rape of which he is accused. However, truth is indeed an elusive item in *Sergeant Rutledge*. As Cantrell points out, the prosecuting attorney Capt. Shattuck (Carleton Young), a Southern anti-abolitionist, plays "cheap legal tricks" with his witnesses' testimonies to bias the judges. As in *Young Mr. Lincoln*, Ford's court of law in *Sergeant Rutledge* is presented as theater, with the five judges along the rear, contained within a proscenium frame in which the lights are theatrically dimmed as the witnesses testify. When Mary Beecher, for example, first takes the stand and answers the prosecutor's questions, she is in the spotlight as the lights dim. As she continues her testimony for the defense, her figure is also darkened and reduced to that of a speaking silhouette.

As she speaks, her testimony takes on a life of its own. Ford cuts from the courtroom to the interior of the train that she describes to the court. While Mary's story and those of the other witnesses called to the stand unfold, Ford's representations draw heavily on expressionist techniques found in film noir to reveal character and convey discrepancies in the witnesses' stories. Conveying moral, ethical, and political comments, shadows indicate the characters' psychological realities. Their inferences of psychological and social aberration are inescapable. The guards at the courtroom door cast heavy shadows of watchful minutemen. Unreliable witnesses who have something to conceal are accompanied by shadowy doppelgangers on the wall behind them. Chandler Hubble (Fred Libby), the guilty party, is represented as having two selves on the stand: seated in the witness's chair, he is at once the grieving father testifying his son's guilt and the oversized shadowy figure standing behind him. Psychologically "clean" witnesses without pasts to hide, like Mary Beecher and Lt. Cantrell, cast no shadows when testifying. Others, like Doctor Eckner (Charles Seel), are under-lit, the unnatural lighting erasing shadows and suggesting severe psychic imbalances.

As Gallagher notes, in *Sergeant Rutledge*, "high-angle shots, numerous close-ups, foreground figures glaring wrathfully down screen toward background figures, all add portentous tones quickly undercut by their own exaggeration, as well as by the court's idiotic dickerings, by prosecutor Shattuck's racist demagogy and caricatured mannerisms, and by Cordelia Fosgate (Billie Burke) befuddling his name—Shattuck, haddock—and calling him Captain Fish."[33] High- and low-angle shots of those involved in the proceedings but not on the stand are also significant because Ford's camera also comments on the status of these individuals as the trial proceeds. When Rutledge enters the courtroom, for example, he is shot at eye level. As damning evidence is introduced, his reaction is shot at an unnaturally high angle. When witnesses recognize his good character, Rutledge's reaction is captured by a low angle. The lowest angle shot in the courtroom, elevating Rutledge heroically, occurs when he testifies that he rejoined his unit voluntarily because he is not "a swamp-runnin' nigger"—it is at this point that Rutledge proclaims his humanity: he is "a man."

UNRELIABLE WITNESSES

Even a cursory glance of the film reveals that Ford's treatment of the witnesses' narratives differs radically from the expressionist style he uses in the courtroom scenes. Gallagher complains that "the twelve flashbacks do not reflect their six narrators' personal knowledge."[34] Ford, however, did not exploit the discrepancies between the stories because his purpose was to outline and highlight the discrepancies within each witness's rendition of the events. Thus, the action of the courtroom is sustained throughout the entire film, which moves outside the courtroom only during the arrival and departure of Lt. Cantrell. The action of every flashback, with the exception of Chandler Hubble's, is presented as testimony. Presented as evidentiary film, these flashbacks are the force at the heart of the trial's arguments, in the crisscrossing of views and the confrontation of points of view in the courtroom. Ford includes the viewer as a member of the court, not only as a witness to the action but also as a judge of each story's probative value. Only when the honesty and authenticity of the memories have been verified can the witnesses' accounts be considered "real evidence."

As McBride notes, at this stage in his career, Ford had achieved "an elegant simplicity and precision of style that some have mistaken for a perfunctory attitude toward his craft."[35] At first, the witnesses' flashbacks appear to be representational. Their use of hyperreal color, however, reminds the viewer that he or she is not witnessing reality but memories, reconstructions, and interpretations of the past. Throughout these memories, Ford's use of shadows is extremely sparse. Rather than working expressionistically with shadows and harsh lighting as he does in the courtroom to comment on the credibility of the witnesses, Ford uses visual, verbal, and acoustic discrepancies between the image on the screen and the spoken word in the courtroom to deconstruct the stories of the witnesses, revealing how memory and bias can render testimony unreliable.

Mary's reconstruction of the train on which she first meets Cantrell is an excellent case in point. Brightly lit and highly artificial, the caboose in which she rides does not sway as it travels. Despite the jacket swinging on the wall behind Mr. Owens (Shug Fisher) and the smoke flowing beside the window, the tables, bunks, walls, floors, and occupants of the carriage are noticeably static. In *Pappy*, Dan Ford points out that his grandfather "didn't bother to place the set on jacks and hire extra men to rock it—the usual method for producing a sense of motion" and attributes this lapse of realism to his grandfather's "crisis in enthusiasm," which had been evident earlier in meetings with Willis and Goldbeck about the script.[36]

Another continuity problem early in the movie occurs when Mary Beecher remembers entering the telegraph office late at night with Rutledge. Incongruously, a daylight scene of the desert is shown outside the window. Later, when she sits in the office as Rutledge sleeps in the adjacent bedroom, the desert scene shown outside the same window is considerably darker, lit by the lamp outside the railway station. Such discrepancies encourage the viewer to recognize the unreliability of memory. Mrs. Cordelia Fosgate, for example, claims on the witness stand that she heard two shots before running to the window and seeing Rutledge leave the Dabney house, but when the camera cuts to her opening the window as a single shot is fired, the viewer must question her testimony. Did the camera document the third shot fired by Rutledge in self-defense or is Mrs. Fosgate reacting to the second of the two shots that she claimed to have heard? When she states that Rutledge rode past her window at exactly eight o'clock, her exasperated husband, Colonel Otis Fosgate (Willis Bouchey), further undermines his wife's credibility as a witness by exclaiming, "Cordelia, you haven't known what time it is since the day we were married."

Similarly, although Dr. Walter Eckner testifies that it was obvious upon examination that Lucy Dabney was beaten and violated, no bruising is evident on her arms, back, or face when he and Lt. Cantrell examine her body. Only bloody cuts from a whip or fingernails that score her back are evident. Another disturbing discrepancy in Eckner's testimony arises when Lt. Cantrell leaves the Dabney's home and asks Skidmore to call Rutledge in on the case. During this sequence, Eckner remains inside with the body. He was not privy to Cantrell and Skidmore's conversation and could not have reported their exchange—yet Ford includes this scene as part of Eckner's testimony on the stand. Later, Rutledge's touching conversation with Moffat (Naaman Brown) as the corporal dies in his arms could not have been witnessed by Skidmore. Skidmore, however, includes this exchange as he answers questions on the stand.

Throughout, the unreliability of the witnesses' accounts is carefully balanced against the reliability of physical evidence. In the field, Chris Hubble's red shirt allows Skidmore to identify his charred remains, but in the courtroom, items like Lucy's "little golden cross" and Chandler Hubble's hunting jacket, introduced as pieces of tangible, direct evidence, may not be what they seem. Shattuck points out that Cantrell's introduction of Lucy's cross is a "cheap theatrical device" on the part of the defense attorney because it cannot be distinguished (immediately) from a boxful of other crosses with broken golden chains. Likewise, the initials CH burned into Hubble's jacket could also identify that garment as belonging to Charlie Haight or Clay Hagathorne.

Gallagher suggests that the inconclusive nature of the evidence presented by Cantrell, Shattuck's vicious, racist innuendos, and the sodden judges reveal the court-martial to be a farce. Ford's intention, he says, is to "exalt character,"[37] but Fosgate dispels the possibility that the trial is farcical when Cantrell attacks the court's integrity for its continuing to allow Shattuck's racist innuendos. Reminding the viewer that the system at work is above reproach, the judge forcefully declares that "the one over-riding rule of this court martial, or of any court martial, is to seek out truth and to administer justice." He then proceeds to do exactly that. In Fosgate's opinion, direct evidence is the crux on which the judges must base their decision. The entire case, he says, "hangs upon [Lucy's] little cross." As it turns out, he is absolutely correct: Lucy's cross being in the pocket of Chandler Hubble's hunting jacket proves the sutler to be her murderer.

In *Sergeant Rutledge*, Lucy's cross speaks for itself. As direct evidence, it is testimony that Hubble cannot refute. On the stand, he is unable to offer a plausible explanation to Cantrell's question, "Why did you tell me at Fort Lincoln that you could not identify Lucy's cross?" Having just identified the cross as Lucy's in an effort to shift the blame for the rape and murder onto his dead son, Hubble cannot answer Cantrell's question. To do so would be to admit his guilt. Instead, he directs attention away from himself, saying, "It was too soon. Chris [Ed Shaw] was my son. My only son. It's hard for a man to admit." Significantly, while Hubble is lying to the court, Ford does not cut to the action that is described. Simply, it is impossible to do so, for no memory of this act exists for the camera to document and make substantial.

THE IMPORTANCE OF EVIDENCE

As historian Christian Delage points out, jurisprudence built around the assumed truth of the still image's objective neutrality was established by the mid-nineteenth century. Fritz Lang, however, demonstrated in *Fury* (1936) that a film of an event cannot constitute "objective" proof because it always "proceeds from a point of view that puts it in the same category as testimony."[38] The latter is a reality with which John Ford was well acquainted. Ford spent his final weeks of active service duty in Washington, D.C., in communication with George Stevens. Still in Europe, Stevens was traveling between London and Berlin and working hard to compile footage for *Nazi Concentration and Prison Camps* (1945) and *The Nazi Plan* (1945), two documentaries that were to be entered into evidence at the Nuremberg Trials. Ford assigned the few remaining staffers in Field Photo to help him from Washington in any way they could; his division had over the years come into possession of a wealth of filmed Nazi propaganda and newsreels, and he had Robert Parrish search the Navy's archives for images that could be used to demonstrate a long-standing pattern of intentional abuse in the camps over the previous decade. He had fourteen hours of footage flown to Europe, where Stevens quickly culled it to one hour.[39]

On November 29, 1945, Stevens's *Nazi Concentration and Prison Camps* was shown. The movie began with two sworn affidavits of authenticity, the first signed by Stevens and the second signed by Field Photo's acting head, Ray Kellogg, and witnessed by Ford. The audience was presented with the "actual," for Stevens had omitted nothing—from the vermin-infested bunkhouses, to the thumbscrews, to the gas chambers and ovens, to the harvesting of gold from the teeth of the murdered, to the lampshades made of human skin for the amusement of an officer's wife. Two weeks later, Stevens's second evidentiary film, *The Nazi Plan*, charting Hitler and the Nazi party's rise to power, was shown at the trial with narration that Budd Schulberg had written. Stevens's films had done what weeks of testimony had not: they had made the defendants' crimes irrefutable and their fates inevitable.[40]

In part, the success of Stevens's films rests on the popular perception of the documentary film's authenticity. When introduced as evidence, Stevens's documentaries, much like still photographs, were accepted as being objective accounts of the camps devoid of personal and political bias. The materials that they contained were so shocking, it was felt that the pictures of the camps were artifacts that spoke for themselves.

As the director of *Midway*, *Torpedo Squadron 8*, and *December 7th*, Ford knew how carefully documentaries must be constructed to advance a critique and to evoke desired reactions from its viewers. In *Sergeant Rutledge*, Ford emphasizes the importance of point of view and the subjective nature of the evidence presented, reminding his viewers that only the image should be considered authentic. Intimately acquainted with the fictions produced by the big Hollywood studios to celebrate national pride and American mythology, Ford warns the viewer of mistaking testimony for real evidence. In the courtroom, the movement from word to image to artifact insists that the truth lies not in the subjectivity of the witness's story but in the objective neutrality of Lucy's little cross.

ANOTHER CRITIQUE OF RACE RELATIONS

Two Rode Together, the movie that Ford made immediately following *Sergeant Rutledge*, continues to express Ford's concerns with social and political issues. In June of 1960, Ford was offered the opportunity to film a novel called *Comanche Captives* by Will Cook. At first, he was not interested in the story of two men, a cynical sheriff and an idealistic Army lieutenant, searching for a group of white children who had been captured by Indians years before. A violent and disturbing story, *Comanche Captives* is a realistic captivity narrative. When they are found, the children have become more Indian than white and must be imprisoned by their rescuers. In an escape attempt, one of them kills his own mother. Ford undertook the directing of *Two Rode Together* as a favor to Columbia's Harry Cohn. As with *Sergeant Rutledge*, Ford directed *Two Rode Together* for the money ($225,000 plus 25 percent net profits) and, as with *Sergeant Rutledge*, lost enthusiasm for the film early in preproduction, while working on the script with Frank Nugent. A joint venture between John Ford Productions and Sam Sheptner Productions, *Two Rode Together* was released by Columbia first in Japan on May 24, 1961, and then in the United States on July 26, 1961.[41] Both the box office and critical responses were lukewarm.[42]

Tag Gallagher considers this throwaway film to be a prime example of Ford's postwar bitterness and revisionism. In *Two Rode Together*, he says, one finds the disjunction and experimentation of Ford's "transitional period."[43] Harry Carey Jr.'s assessment of *Two Rode Together*, however, provides the viewer with valuable insider's insight into Ford's filming. "*Two Rode Together* seems to me to be a hodgepodge of incidents and pieces of business from every western Jack ever made. It was good old Irish stew. He threw everything in," Carey says. "If ever Ford was on vacation, doing exactly what he damned-well pleased, and having one hell of a good time doing it, it was on *Two Rode Together*." *Two Rode Together* was the first time that Ford and Richard Widmark worked together. "As it turned out, Jack and Dick got on marvellously; it was a mutual admiration society," Carey continues. "Dick kept telling me how amazed he was at Ford's genius at simplifying a sequence, at the way he could get across so much drama with a minimum of camera moves. It knocked Dick out."[44] Widmark "loved Uncle Jack." As far as he was concerned, "even a gone-screwy Ford is a hundred times better than all these other idiots."[45]

While Richard Robertson suggests that Ford handles his material in *Two Rode Together* "gingerly and a little awkwardly,"[46] Ford's contemporaries found the depictions of murder, miscegenation, and rape in *Two Rode Together* convincing. On July 27, 1961, *New York Times* reviewer Eugene Archer applauded Ford for his "realistic approach to frontier existence" and his "no nonsense direction." As "an extension of the Indian prejudice theme of his earlier *The Searchers*, *Two Rode Together* has rough edges," Archer says, "but it also has a point. . . . Mr. Ford has told an ugly story in direct, uncompromising fashion."[47] Donald Dewer considers *Two Rode Together* to be one of the bleakest films Ford ever made: "The Comanches are brutal opportunists, the army officers are crude, hypocritical racists, the civilians are a naïve conglomerate waiting only to become a rabid mob."[48] Ford himself has been said to be unsatisfied with the movie from beginning to end. As Dan Ford remarks, the more Ford worked on *Two Rode Together*, the less he liked it. Before the script was finished, he was calling it "the worst piece of crap I've done in twenty years."[49]

Two Rode Together is a social and psychological film, but its tone, unlike *Sergeant Rutledge*'s, is tragic. *Two Rode Together* is a captivity narrative in which a crooked marshal, Guthrie McCabe (James Stewart), and an honest cavalryman, First Lieutenant Jim Gary (Richard Widmark), join forces to rescue white prisoners many years after they have been abducted by Comanche raiders. Gary and McCabe ride into Quanah Parker's camp looking for individuals on their list of captives, which includes Marty Purcell's brother and Harry Wringle's stepson, now known as Running Wolf (David Kent), Hanna Clegg (Mae Marsh), and Frieda Knudsen aka Wakanana (Regina Carrol). They are able to negotiate the release of only two captives: Running Wolf and Elena de la Madriaga (Linda Cristal). Neither hostage can be reintegrated into white society. Running Wolf and Elena have become Comanche—foreign to their own people, they are treated like prisoners when they return to the fort. Reflecting the somber tone of its material, *Two Rode Together* is "a grim, claustrophobic movie set mostly at night against solid black, occasionally in overcast daytime."[50]

REPRESENTATIONAL AND HISTORICALLY ACCURATE

Ford's treatment of Western iconography here is highly representational, and his treatment of the settlers' responses to the abduction and recovery of their children is historically accurate. As Glenn Frankel notes, abductions became the "the abiding fault line" in "the vicious struggle between Texans and Comanches": "There was no chance for peaceful coexistence so long as Comanches held white captives, and they grasped the deep cultural, religious, sexual, and racial hatred that kidnapping Texan women and children aroused. Texans quickly came to see Indians as subhuman in part because of the seemingly casual cruelty with which they treated the captives."[51] In *Two Rode Together*, before McCabe leaves for Quanah Parker's camp, he regards Marty's brother as subhuman. He tells her that her brother will have "forgot his English. He just grunts Comanche now. Grunts Comanche." Displaying the sexual and racial hatred that Texans held for the Comanche, McCabe assures Marty that she would suffer a Fate Worse than Death because of her brother's bestiality: "Given the chance, sister, he'd rape you. And when he's finished, he'd trade you off to one of the other bucks for a good knife or a bad rifle."

Frankel points out that, in Texas, "what had started as a tit-for-tat struggle over horse thievery and hunting rights quickly evolved into a forty-year blood feud between two alien civilizations": "Neither side believed the other was fully human. Comanches saw the Texans as invaders without conscience who occupied their lands, destroyed their hunting grounds, and broke every promise. Texans saw Comanches as human vermin, brutal, merciless, and sadistic."[52] Aptly, on the one hand, the Comanche leader, Quanah Parker, does not trust McCabe to honor his agreement to trade six rifles for Elena. Wringle, on the other, refuses to claim Running Wolf for the Army, saying, "You couldn't pay me to take in a mad dog like that."

Throughout, Ford's depiction of the Comanche is not sentimental. Instead of "the modern image of Indians—nurtured by the Native American rights movement, revisionist historians, and the film *Dances with Wolves* (1990)—[which] has been one of profoundly spiritual and environmentally friendly genocide victims seeking harmony with the land and humankind," the viewer finds Ford's Comanches are "nobody's victims and no one's friends. They [are] magnificent, brutal, and relentless."[53] Ford's Comanches resemble historical accounts, in both action and demeanor. Jean-Louis Berlandier, a French-born naturalist who traveled through Comancheria in the late 1820s, wrote, "The Comanche constitute the largest and most terrible nomadic nation anywhere in the territory of the Mexican republic."[54] Historically, most of the captives taken by the Comanche were Mexican. As Frankel points out, one rough estimate suggests there were at least two thousand captives by the early 1800s abducted because of the Comanche's need for labor and exchangeable commodities.[55]

While Ford's *The Searchers* investigates one family's search for their abducted children, *Two Rode Together* explores what *The Searchers* did not—what happens after the individual who has been abducted returns home. In *Two Rode Together*, the settlers' expectations that their children will be returned to them seem at first to be reasonable. They expect their loved ones to come back with their memories of their families intact, eager to reintegrate into white society. The settlers also expect themselves to be able to accept their children no matter how they have changed, and to be able to welcome them back into their families, but, unable to resolve their memories of the children abducted with those who return, they are unable to distinguish the past from the present.

DENIAL

The most heart-wrenching example occurs when Ole Knudson (John Qualen), who has waited seven years for the opportunity to reclaim his daughter abducted at the age of nine, begs McCabe and Gary to bring her back. When McCabe, a pragmatist, advises him to forget that he ever had a daughter, because she would have "a couple of half-breed kids," Knudson snaps back that he will not leave without her. "Dat makes no matter to me, no, by golly she's still my little girl Freda," he says. Offering McCabe $285 to find Freda, Knudson, in deep denial, begins to sob as he describes her: "Eyes was blue. Hair was yellow . . . yellow like corn silk, yellow like gold." For Knudson (and his fellow settlers), their children will always be as they are remembered. Unable to listen to Knudson, Gary has to leave the tent. He knows that the Freda Knudson loves is lost forever. As Gallagher points out, "No other Ford picture is played so constantly at the level of gut response."[56] Like Knudson, Marty Purcell (Shirley Jones) also hopes to reclaim her brother, who has been missing for nine years. Holding herself responsible for his capture, she tells Gary, "It was my fault, you know; I was supposed to look after him. When the Indians came, I ran and hid. He was only eight years old. I was still hiding when father came home . . . too frightened to come out even when I knew the Comanches had ridden away." Unable even to listen to Guthrie's description of what her brother would be like if he were to be found, Marty, like Knudson, breaks down, admitting to Gary that she is "a fool for cryin' over someone who died nine years ago." *Two Rode Together* is an unrelenting examination of anger, desperation, and despair. In it, Ford's depiction of the people inhabiting the West is deeply tragic, and his treatment of the American Character far from romantic.

The film's lack of closure, created by the abductions of the settlers' loved ones, intensifies the desperation of their families to reclaim them. Ironically, even when the captives are returned, they remain lost to their families. Like their historic counterparts, they have grown older and been assimilated, no longer resembling the children they once were. When Running Wolf is brought back to Fort Grant, no one, not even Harry J. Wringle (Willis Bouchey), will claim him as one of their own. With his face painted and his long hair braided, Running Wolf looks like one of those "dirty devils." Completely assimilated by the

Comanche, the boy's English name *and* his English have disappeared—even his father and sister do not mention his Christian name when speaking of him. Like thirteen-year-old John Parker, who spoke only Comanche after being returned from living with the Comanche for six years, Running Wolf resists the Army's attempt to repatriate him. Thoroughly indigenized, he attempts to escape the moment he dismounts from his horse at the fort and has to be restrained. In order to keep him at the fort, the Army holds Running Wolf in a jail cell until he is claimed by Mary McCandless (Jeanette Nolan), who has lost her mind since her own son's disappearance.

Soon after being taken into the McCandless family in order to give Mary "comfort in a lie," Running Wolf kills his foster mother. While he is being dragged away to be lynched, the music box he loved as a child falls to the ground and begins to play. Revealing himself to be Marty's brother, and clutching his music box and screaming, "Mine, mine!" he reverts back to being the child he was before he was abducted. Marty recognizes her brother immediately, but once again when she should, she cannot bring herself to intercede on his behalf. Horrifyingly, she remains silent. Not calling out his name—the act that would have reintegrated him back into his family—she again condemns him. No one else speaks up for the boy who is clutching the music box.

Tragically, the settlers who witness the boy's memories return prove to be as remorseless as the Comanches they hate. Gary, the cavalryman, being the most ethical character in the movie, attempts to reason with the crowd but without the force of law is unable to stop the lynching. Only Running Wolf's dangling legs are visible after the horses and their wagon have been whipped away from the tree. Intensifying the emotional impact of the lynching, Ford leaves the image of the dead boy's face to the imagination of the viewer, who knows his true identity.

UNPLEASANT SOCIAL AND PSYCHOLOGICAL TRUTHS

Like *Sergeant Rutledge*, *Two Rode Together* sets memory against reality. Ford heightens the movie's social and psychological horror by contrasting it with the natural gentleness found in characters when interacting outside social constraints. His use of improvisation during "long single takes . . . such as the three-minute fifty-one-second riverbank chat between McCabe and Gary, improvised by the actors when they thought they were rehearsing,"[57] is a studied, stylistic experiment. As Martin Scorsese attests, John Ford

> could go in some surprising directions. There's a scene in *Two Rode Together*, which was made in the early 1960s that I'm particularly fond of. James Stewart and Richard Widmark are sitting by a river and they're talking and the camera stays on them for a long period of time. The dialogue is very funny, and the rapport between the two men is also quite endearing and sweet—it reminds me of a Renoir film. It doesn't feel staged, it feels like life at the moment it's happening, between two actual people of that period in the west. You feel that you're looking directly into the world these men inhabit. In other words, the documentary impulse at the heart of a dramatic film made in Hollywood. If you look at Hollywood cinema very closely, you see many more examples like this—natural behavior unfolding in real time. This is where fiction and documentary cross over.[58]

As in Gary and McCabe's conversation, there is also sweetness in the romance that blossoms between Gary and Marty. At times, they also seem to be like "innocent teenagers."[59] Their spontaneous love for one another is juxtaposed against McCabe and Elena's much more studied relationship, just as the settlers' delusions of being loving parents are contrasted with their savage and brutal behavior toward those who have been returned to them. Unlike Gary and Marty's, McCabe and Elena's relationship is not sanctioned by the community. Ford's critique of the fort's social rejection of Elena as a "polluted" woman is direct and forceful. As she tells McCabe, the people who should be her saviors are actually her jailers: "These people, they smile at me and show their teeth, but it is the eyes that bite," she says. "I have not seen the back of anyone's head since I came here." Elena understands that she is feared and reviled: "The eyes are all over my body like dirty fingers," she tells McCabe. "As if they turned their backs I would leap upon them and my touch would have to be washed off like filth." The thought of miscegenation is so socially repugnant that Elena, who was Stone Calf's wife, is considered a freak by saloonkeeper Belle Aragon (Annelle Hayes), herself a social outcast. On meeting Elena, who is modestly dressed in bonnet, gloves, and a high collar, Belle sneeringly offers her work in her saloon: "You can drop the phony airs," she sniffs. "I know all about you,

Mrs. Stone Calf. New travels fast in this country. How'dja like a job, honey? I can put your hair in Indian braids . . . a short skirt . . . some squaw boots . . . a little bear grease . . . you'd be quite an attraction." Like Dallas (Claire Trevor), the prostitute run out of Tonto by the "Law and Order" League at the beginning of *Stagecoach*, Elena in *Two Rode Together* discovers that "civilized" people "are worse things than Apaches." During the five years that she lived with the Comanche, she recalls that her eyes "never saw a tear."

Although romance appears to win out over reality, and comedy attempts to overturn tragedy, in *Two Rode Together*, neither the pastoral nor the picturesque support the ending of this movie. McCabe and Elena take a stagecoach to escape their social debasement and reinvent themselves, but it is doubtful that they will be able to leave Elena's scandal behind—they are leaving to start a new life, not in Mexico (like Ringo and Dallas in *Stagecoach*), but in San Francisco, where the West, once a pristine wilderness, has become an urban jungle. Made and released as the Hollywood blacklist was breaking down, *Two Rode Together* is a timely critique, transmitting social and psychological truths about racism, mass hysteria, and individual hypocrisy—while inviting parallels with the behavior of studio owners and movie stars who ruined the careers and lives of many of their colleagues during the House Un-American Activities Committee's investigation of the film industry.

As Scott Eyman notes, what continued to appear to be indifference on Ford's part while shooting *Two Rode Together*, turned into something considerably darker when Ward Bond died suddenly of a heart attack on November 13 in Dallas, Texas.[60] Chuck Roberson, who was present when Ken Curtis and Harry Carey Jr. broke the news of Bond's death to Ford, remembers that "the Old Man hung his head for a minute, and when he looked up again, I could see tears trickling down from beneath his dark glasses. He had lost a friend of nearly thirty years, and it was a hard thing to accept."[61] Ford temporarily shut down production on *Two Rode Together* as he did when Fred Kennedy died during the shooting of *The Horse Soldiers*. He chartered a plane and flew with Curtis and Carey to Dallas to collect Bond's body before continuing on to Los Angeles to make the arrangements for the funeral that took place at the Field Photo Home. Ford ensured that Bond was accorded full military honors: his body was placed in a flag-draped casket in the chapel with a uniformed honor guard while flags flew at half-mast. Ford completed *Two Rode Together* on December 16 and then left for Honolulu, where he started drinking heavily—where, after several weeks of self-medication, he had to be checked into Queen's Hospital for alcoholic dehydration.

In 1961, Andrew Sarris, who considered *Two Rode Together* to be a "dark, savage movie," observes that in it "the classical Ford images of Indian war parties, frontier dances and cavalry formations are subtly debased and dusted over in the dim twilight of the Western epic."[62] As he considers Ford's canon, Sarris does not side with critics of Ford who consider him to be "a grizzled old prospector who lost his way out in Monument Valley," but he does believe that Ford, whom he considered to be conservative, "preferred to accept history and even legend as it was written rather than revise it in a radical or derisive spirit."[63] "In accepting the inevitability of the present while mourning the past," Tellingly, Sarris says, what Ford "wishes to conserve are the memories of old values even if they have to be magnified into legends." Sarris could not have been more mistaken. In his next Western, *The Man Who Shot Liberty Valance*, Ford savagely deconstructed the legend of the American West while criticizing those who made and printed it.

13

DECONSTRUCTING THE LEGEND[1]

The Man Who Shot Liberty Valance

Generally, I hate music in pictures—a little bit now and then, at the end or the start—but something like the Ann Rutledge theme belongs. I don't like to see a man alone in the desert, dying of thirst, with the Philadelphia Orchestra behind him.[2]—John Ford

As Dan Ford remarks, *The Man Who Shot Liberty Valance* was "an auteur project all the way": Ford discovered Dorothy M. Johnson's story, developed it into a script with Willis Goldbeck and James Warner Bellah, and recruited the all-star cast.[3] Joseph McBride points out that Ford not only paid $7,500 for the film rights to the story, published in *Cosmopolitan* magazine in 1949, he also raised half of the $3.2 million needed to cover the production costs of the movie through John Ford Productions, awarding himself a salary of $150,000 and 25 percent of the net profits.[4] In doing so, Ford largely freed himself from the tyranny of a studio and its producers overseeing his work—the investment of his own money procured the artistic freedom he desired. Intriguingly, *The Man Who Shot Liberty Valance* lacks the qualities in his Westerns that have come to be considered distinctively Fordian. As Dan Ford remarks, the movie "doesn't really look like [his grandfather] made it. There is none of the special quality that was uniquely his."[5]

Ford chose to shoot the project in black and white and, in July 1961, wrote to John Wayne, who also starred in the film, that "for a change, no locations. All to be shot on the lot."[6] Production began on September 5, and shooting ended on November 7, 1961. Dan Ford remarks that everyone that he talked to about this movie noted his grandfather's lack of energy, complete disregard for background effects for extras, and disinterest in smoke and commotion.[7] While shooting, Ford worked quickly with "an attitude that bordered on indifference, trimming corners whenever possible."[8] Newcomers Lee Marvin and Edmond O'Brien enjoyed working with Ford immensely, but John Wayne's and Ken Murray's experiences proved to be extremely difficult. On set, Ford exploded at Wayne, whom he was convinced had been avoiding his telephone calls, and stuntman Ken Murray remembers that "Ford was a monster." "He was an ogre," Murray said. "I was scared of him."[9] Ford's lack of personal hygiene appalled Hal Nesbit, a stagehand at Paramount, who remembers Ford's assistant carried a bucket filled with sand: "[Ford would] go behind a set and use it to go to the bathroom. He wouldn't leave the stage."[10]

Ronald L. Davis concludes that toward the end of production, Ford was tired, had grown bored, and had begun to slough off.[11] But even without the sublime landscapes of Monument Valley, *The Man Who Shot Liberty Valance* suggests otherwise. Ford's radically different approach to the genre he knew so well has enjoyed, as Dan Ford remarks, "a very rich critical history and has attracted an enormous amount of attention from writers, critics and film buffs."[12] Critical commentators agree that *The Man Who Shot Liberty Valance* is a Cold War Western concerned with the misrepresentation of the past, in general, and the self, in particular.[13] Highly complex, the film has been considered a staple Western, as the work of an auteur director, and as a valuable Cold War artifact. Douglas Pye notes that the film presents a complex structure of bitter ironies that rest upon the Western's traditional opposition of East and West, civilization and savagery, order and disorder, law and outlaw, and legend and history. "The film," Pye says, "denies the possibility of transcendence—it demonstrates that in fact, no-one can unite the opposites."[14] Like Pye, Mark W. Roche and Vittorio Hösle argue that Ford's movie, at a fundamental level, is "a film about transition—the movement of history from heroes to men."[15] Film historian Andrew Sarris notes that "a Ford film, particularly a late Ford film is more than its story and characterizations; it is also the director's attitude toward his milieu and its codes of conduct."[16] Sarris regards *The Man Who Shot Liberty Valance* as a political Western *and* a psychological murder mystery *and* a confrontation with John Ford's personal, professional, and historical past.[17] Following Sarris's reasoning, Alan Nadel proposes that Ford's preoccupation with the problem of misrepresentation in the film mirrors the state of American propaganda during the chilliest days of the Cold War.[18]

Like *Fort Apache, Rio Grande, Sergeant Rutledge*, and *Two Rode Together, The Man Who Shot Liberty Valance* displays Ford's concern with "the disparity between historical fact and tradition."[19] Like these movies, *The Man Who Shot Liberty Valance* examines the fallibility of limited points of view while relying heavily on the average American's understanding that truthfulness is the basis of a successful social contract. Throughout *The Man Who Shot Liberty Valance*, Ford uses subtle shifts in narrative technique to create disturbing complexities that encourage the viewer to critique Ransom Stoddard's Hollywood version of the Wild West.

DECONSTRUCTING THE LEGEND

The Man Who Shot Liberty Valance is an aging politician's life story. Stoddard (Jimmy Stewart) and his wife, Hallie (Vera Miles), arrive in the town of Shinbone to attend the funeral of the man to whom Stoddard owed his career and his marriage. Recognized by a reporter when he steps off the train, Stoddard agrees to talk with the editor of the *Shinbone Star*. He begins the story of his rise to fame and fortune in a flashback, recounting his adventures as a young lawyer in search of employment, traveling West in a stagecoach that is robbed. Stoddard is beaten by one of the outlaws, Liberty Valance (Lee Marvin), because he champions Law and Order. Left for dead, he is saved by the "toughest" rancher in the territory, Tom Doniphon (John Wayne), who takes him to the town of Shinbone where he is nursed back to health by his future wife, a waitress working at Peter's Place. Stoddard decides to stay in Shinbone. He not only washes dishes at Peter's Place while recovering from his injuries, but he also works as a reporter for the local newspaper *and* teaches Hallie and other townspeople and their children how to read and write.

Because he is an earnest and educated humanist intent on improving his community, Stoddard quickly becomes a respected citizen. He runs against Valance (who has been terrorizing the town) and becomes a state representative. Enraged by his loss, Valance retaliates by beating Dutton Peabody (Edmond O'Brien), the editor of the *Shinbone Star*. In response, Stoddard calls the outlaw out, even though he is a poor marksman. Surprisingly, it is Valance, not Stoddard, who is shot during their showdown. On the strength of appearing to have shot and killed Liberty Valance, Stoddard goes on to defeat his political competition, Major Cassius Starbuckle (John Carradine), and becomes governor. He ends the movie a successful politician, married to Hallie, and living in Washington—a man who, with a "snap of his fingers," could become the vice president of the United States of America.

At first, Stoddard's rendition of his life appears to be convincing, even though it is an Easterner's version of the Old West, replete with clichés and stereotypes gleaned from dime novels and newspaper serials. Embedded in what is essentially a twelve-year-old boy's dream of individual glory are the concepts of rugged individualism, Manifest Destiny, moral simplicity, and idyllic perfection. It is a tale no one should accept, yet it has been accepted by many audience members— perhaps because, like Frederic S. Remington's more than half a century earlier, Ford's vision of the American frontier had begun to be regarded as a reality as well as an interpretation of American history. [20]

According to historian Peter Flynn, the characteristic moments of dime novels, later transmitted in film, "are not real—yet they have come to represent the real" and are to be found in later Westerns: Shane riding toward the fragile frontier town with the Teton Range mountains rising behind him; the Ringo Kid's shootout with the Plummer Boys on the streets of Lordsburg; Butch and Sundance held frozen forever in a single image of outmoded heroics. All are epic moments found only in "a Neverland whose landscape was mapped by turn-of-the-century popular media and then held timeless, frozen for posterity on the silver screen." [21] Ford, who grew up on Western dime novels and made some fifty Westerns, was himself keenly aware of the discrepancy that existed between the reality of settling the American frontier and the distortion of the American West in Hollywood. His own early Westerns "weren't shoot-em ups" [22]—they were character stories. Making Harry Carey into "sort of a bum . . . instead of a great bold gun-fighting hero," [23] he decided to mock the studios' Western leading men a little— but not the Western. "We tried to do it the real way it had been in the

West," Ford said to Peter Bogdanovich. "None of this so-called quick-draw stuff, nobody wore flashy clothes and we didn't have dance hall scenes with girls in short dresses. As Pardner [Jones, one of Ford's script consultants who knew Wyatt Earp and Bat Masterson] said, 'In Tombstone, we never saw anything like that.'"[24]

Aptly, Stoddard's version of his gunfight with Liberty Valance is a showdown, albeit a pathetic, implausible one. Stoddard's memories of the event have all the elements of a dime novel gunfight: the dance hall band playing in the saloon down the street, the villain winning his last game of poker with the Death Hand, the decent law-abiding man doing the right thing, the Colt .45s, the deserted streets, and the emptied sidewalks. At work in Stoddard's tale is what Richard Slotkin identifies as a system of clichés whose resonance is so strong that their truth is unquestioned. In part, the success of these clichés may be attributed to their power to generate the audience's collective memory of the American male's character and bourgeois values.[25] As Gary Johnson notes, the iconography of the Western with "its settings, lassos, Colt .45s . . . hanging trees, stagecoaches, Stetsons, outlaws, lawmen, gamblers, and gunfighters, is the largest, and richest of all film genres, and Hollywood has burned it into the minds of movie goers from Dodge City to Timbuktu."[26] Thus, a dishwasher who patterns his career on those of Horatio Alger's characters and Horace Greeley's advice can succeed in the West if its icons are aligned in his favor.

IF THE HAT FITS . . .

Tom Doniphon's version of Stoddard's gunfight with Liberty Valance, which appears well after Stoddard's account of the event, is more believable, despite the fact that in Doniphon's anecdote Valance's body faces toward Peter's Place instead of the saloon, as in Stoddard's story. For the majority of the audience, who knows little or nothing about firearms, the plausibility of Doniphon's story rests on his hat—the high-crowned Stetson of the Jazz Age cowboy—and not the fact that he uses a rifle instead of a revolver. Known as the "Boss of the Plains," the Stetson, with its high crown and wide brim, is an American hero's icon, calling forth the qualities of integrity, honor, pride, and distinction. Because he wears a white Stetson at the gunfight, Doniphon's character and motives must be considered indisputably pure, despite the fact that he murders Valance in cold blood. The outlaw's hat, of course, signifies a worldview antithetical to that of the hero in any dime novel set in the Wild West.[27] Liberty Valance's black *vaquero*, with its low crown and narrow rim, immediately identifies him as the villain of the story because it resonates with "the danger and violence associated with lawlessness."[28]

Suitably, Ransom Stoddard has no hat for much of his screen time. Given the importance of this mise-en-scène element, it is not surprising that his identity remains uncertain until the end of his tale. As a young man, he travels to Shinbone hatless and works bare-headed as a dishwasher, educator, lawyer, and reporter. Always the odd man out, he carries, but does not wear, a businessman's Homburg to Capital City. In spite of his efforts to adapt to Western culture and society, Stoddard never dons a cowboy hat. Instead, he plays the disconcerting part of the Southern gentleman. His white, low-crowned, small-brimmed town hat was the favorite civilian hat of that most powerful and civilized of America's men, Confederate general Robert E. Lee.

Because hats signify character type in a Western, the enigma of an empty hat box when Stoddard and his wife, Hallie, arrive in Shinbone is tantalizing. Whose hat box is it? It isn't a gentleman's box although it appears large enough for Stoddard's hat. Hallie's hat is far too small. Used as a cactus rose container, this box is carried to Tom Doniphon's funeral, where a simple pine box emphasizes that one's identity is erased by time and, finally, death. Stoddard is incensed that Doniphon's body is about to be buried without the hieroglyphs of a Western hero: his boots, his spurs, and his gun. The vital importance of Doniphon's boots and spurs to Stoddard (and no one else at the funeral) draws attention to his subsequent attempts to appropriate the power of these symbols when reconstructing his version of the Wild West.

At the outset of his interview with the *Shinbone Star*, Stoddard prefaces his memories with the highly theatrical act of brushing dust off an old stagecoach. Claiming to recognize the coach, he invokes the spirit of Horace Greeley, a showman and newspaperman whose specialty, Dutton Peabody, the editor of the *Shinbone Star* notes, was tearing his readers' hearts out. Unfortunately for the credibility of Stoddard's story, one stagecoach looks just like any other of the same make and model. Stoddard's rendition of his adventures is fanciful rather than factual. While the stagecoach is being robbed, for example, there are two glaring inconsistencies in Stoddard's presentation of the Wild West. First, Valance's line "Stand and deliver" belongs to an English highwayman, not an American desperado. Second, Valance is wearing the black hat of Deadwood Dick, the first Western dime villain, and a bandana over his nose, but the color-coding of his slicker is jarring. In the dime novel, the villain simply does not wear white. Additionally, when Doniphon escorts a bruised and bloodied Stoddard into town, no Jazz Age Cowboy, however extreme his costume for publicity stills, had such ridiculously long leather covers adorning his stirrups. More obvious and jarring is the lack of aging or weathering of the set—Shinbone looks like it has just been constructed—and so it has . . . in Stoddard's imagination.

As Stoddard's story continues, Shinbone and its characters exhibit so many oddities that they cannot be excused as problems with continuity during shooting or John Ford's drinking or as the result of the head injury that Stoddard the storyteller received when Valance beat him. True to the imagination of the typical dime novel reader (a twelve-year-old boy), dinners are bigger and better out West. At Peter's Place, Peter Ericson (John Qualen) helps his wife cook grotesquely oversized steaks with frying pans that would cover the entire cooking surface of an ordinary stovetop. Reduced to being a dishwasher, Stoddard scrubs dinner plate after dinner plate. As the men in the dining room eat off serving platters to accommodate their gargantuan servings of meat and potatoes, the viewer is prompted to ask, "Where are those dirty dinner plates coming from?" The nightlife in Shinbone is also unrealistic. The honkytonk band in the saloon plays music, but there are no dance hall girls tempting the men to dance. And strangely, the stamped-tin ceiling that belongs above the band is pasted to the wall behind them.

Surely the most outrageous moment of mise-en-scène in the movie occurs when Stoddard gallops a buckboard past a line of large Saguaro cacti. Situated in a West that has resonated in baby boomers' imaginations since early childhood, Doniphon's ranch sits on the original Ponderosa—the Janss Conejo Ranch, located well north of the native habitat of Saguaros. In 1959 there was not a Saguaro cactus to be seen on the Ponderosa. If one looks closely, it is possible to see the mounds of soil supporting the bases of the Saguaros, which are standardized in terms of size and shape and planted like a line of telephone poles.

Arguably, the Saguaros' blatant artificiality and the other discrepancies noted here are not merely the results of sloppy set dressing but important and necessary parts of Stoddard's story. As well, only three days were spent doing the location work in the Conejo Valley. Ford wanted the hold-up of the stagecoach to have, as Lindsay Anderson notes, "the cramped artificiality of a scene in a 'B' Picture."[29] When Wingate Smith, Ford's assistant director, complained about the set, saying that it didn't look "lived in," Ford replied curtly, "If they notice it, then we'll give 'em their nickel back."[30]

Quite simply, Ford showed no interest in creating the verisimilitude on which the Hollywood Western rested when making *The Man Who Shot Liberty Valance* because his primary interests lay in conveying the psychological elements of the story. Like *Sergeant Rutledge* and *Two Rode Together*, *The Man Who Shot Liberty Valance* is concerned with the dark side of human nature—the mind's proclivities toward aberrance, madness, insanity, and betrayal. *The Man Who Shot Liberty Valance* returns the viewer to mise-en-scène and lighting found in *Stagecoach*. At night, Shinbone's honkytonk saloon and darkened streets resemble the shadowy, red-light district of Lordsburg.

Ford's sophisticated use of overdrawn stirrup covers, ridiculous frying pans, elephantine steaks, and artificial cacti point toward a very unpleasant mind—the mind of a politician that attempts to portray itself as balanced and fair but presents the world around it in terms of clichés. How sincere is Stoddard's story? It is impossible to tell. The audience never does find out why Dutton Peabody fired him—Stoddard omits this scene while actually telling his tale. When one considers the details of Stoddard's account, it seems probable that, like Major Cassius Starbuckle's bombast, ostensibly written from the heart but actually a blank piece of crumpled paper, Stoddard's story, too, is simply made up as it goes along.

Whether Stoddard is telling his tale to set the record straight and unburden his conscience, or to further rearrange the facts in his favor, we will never know. In either event, Stoddard's confession must be considered a case of very special pleading for a public that he knows will judge him. Kent Anderson is absolutely correct when he notes that this is one of the bleakest endings in film history. If Stoddard did not shoot Liberty Valance, he is guilty of lying by omission and thereby duping the American public that he was elected to represent. If he did shoot

Liberty Valance, then the American public is guilty of supporting and promoting the career of a vigilante and a murderer. Whatever the case may be, the West that Stoddard has created is not the pastoral utopia it seems to be when seen as the train goes back to Washington. Ford's evocative shot of a cactus rose appearing to grow out of the lid of Doniphon's coffin suggests that Stoddard's West should be considered little more than a grave—a gruesome garden fashioned out of a prickly pear sitting on a pine box.

CHAMBER FILM

Like chamber music, a chamber film's internal organization is structured on the principles of repetition and variation. In chamber music, a musical passage repeats and varies to create and amplify the work's emotional impact. In chamber film, a similar effect is created. In *The Man Who Shot Liberty Valance*, musical and visual motifs are repeated and varied to heighten audience response. As Lindsay Anderson notes, this movie functions like "a poem" that "develops with the simplicity and concreteness of a ballad."[31] Ford's uncharacteristic and highly ironic use of Ann Rutledge's sweetly tender theme from *Young Mr. Lincoln* accompanies Hallie and repeats itself at key moments, building the elegiac impact of her lost relationship with Tom Doniphon. Visual motifs are also repeated and varied—often book-ending the action to balance and enhance emotional impact: the cactus rose, for example, dug up at the beginning of Hallie's visit to Shinbone, is planted on Doniphon's coffin when she leaves; buckboards bring Stoddard into Shinbone and take the body of Liberty Valance out of the town; the delegates' meeting in Capital City repeats and amplifies Stoddard's election in Shinbone; an empty hat box accompanies the Stoddards' arrival in Shinbone and Doniphon's simple pine box is the final image presented before they step back on the train.

As in a musical score, point and counterpoint impart a sophisticated and elegant balance that compensates, in part, for Ford's irreverent revision of the Western's conventions. Ford's treatment of movement is an important part of this balancing. *The Man Who Shot Liberty Valance* begins with the image of a train, that American icon of progress, traveling from East to West, from Washington to Shinbone. At the movie's end, this scene's mirror image is presented when the same train returns to Washington, with the Stoddards traveling from the West back to the East. When traveling to Shinbone, the Stoddards are returning to their past lives; when traveling to Washington, they are moving into their future. This movement supports the ambiguities in Stoddard's story, for caught between the past and the future, the present itself is easily overlooked. Because the story is fashioned from flashbacks, little is revealed about who the elderly characters have become. Rather, we are only told what Stoddard wants us to believe.

Stoddard wants us to believe his story, but Ford's presentation is that of a dark melodrama that raises questions rather than providing answers, often through the use of light and shadow. Conveying moral, ethical, and political comments, shadows from the window panes cast on the walls by the mourners indicate that every character who sits looking at Doniphon's coffin has either something to hide or, like Kirby Yorke and Phil Sheridan in *Rio Grande*, a metaphorical cross to bear. Ford's inferences of political corruption, psychological dislocation, and social aberration are inescapable: Stoddard and his wife cannot meet each other's eyes during the movie's conclusion. Clearly, the senator has not given Hallie something to read and write about in Washington. More overtly expressionist than the cross created by light pouring into the room containing Doniphon's coffin is Doniphon's ominous shadow cast in a back alley just before Stoddard's shoot-out with Valance. The shadow of Valance's *vaquero* that hangs between Doniphon and Stoddard in Peter's kitchen also confirms the vicious nature of lawlessness in the American West. At the end of this scene, Stoddard, engulfed in Doniphon's shadow, is awarded the identity of the man who murdered Liberty Valance long before the gunfight actually happens.

Ford's most poignant use of shadows occurs during Stoddard's attempt to teach his pupils what it means to be an American. Standing beside a picture of Thomas Jefferson, a slave owner and lawyer, Pompey (Woody Strode) forgets to include equality in his recitation of the Declaration of Independence. Reciting with his hands behind his back, Strode creates the shadowy image of a bound man beside and behind him on the wall. His character is indeed held in bondage, as Doniphon summarily interrupts his schooling and orders him back to work as if he were a slave. To emphasize the emptiness of Lincoln's gesture of political freedom to African Americans in 1864, Stoddard gives Pompey a handful of "pork chop" money just before leaving Shinbone.

"GERMANIZING" AMERICANA

Thus, despite its elegantly balanced and sophisticated presentation, Stoddard's account of his life rings false. And it is meant to. His story fails to convince because John Ford "Germanizes" one of America's foundational myths. His use of expressionist detail undermines the notion that Western iconography is representational—and makes it apparent that the senator's juxtaposition of dime novel opposites is a matter of "smoke and mirrors" designed to divert his listener's attention away from the facts of his story. In short, despite (or arguably because of) its epic elements, Stoddard's story fails. There are no heroes in this film because a dishwasher gets the girl in the end. Ironically, the black-hatted villain who steps out in the street pulls his gun "in self-defense" and is murdered in cold blood. Lindsay Anderson says that it is tempting to think of *The Man Who Shot Liberty Valance* as an elegy for the heroic simplicities of the pioneering West,[32] but Ford makes it necessary to think of *The Man Who Shot Liberty Valance* as an elegy for the simple, unvarnished truth. We will never know what really happened in Shinbone. In 1968, talking to the student Documentary Film Group at the University of Chicago, Ford muddied the waters further by saying, "Ah, Liberty Valance! Yes. The man didn't kiss his horse and ride off into the sunset."[33]

You have to hand it to him—John Ford had guts. As Peter Cowie points out in *John Ford and the American West*, 1962 was a juncture in American history that did not relish either satire or the lampooning of history.[34] President John F. Kennedy was "stirring the youth of the world with grandiloquent rhetoric," and his vision of a New Frontier moved the American public to accept military debacles like the Bay of Pigs.[35] When one considers the chilly climate of American politics then, what form of critique could have been more dangerous for its director in 1962 than a challenging of the popular Western tradition, with its patriotic promotion of Manifest Destiny? Although Dalton Trumbo had been the first to break the Hollywood blacklist in 1960, it would still be years before many of Ford's colleagues who had been blacklisted worked again.

Ford's final caution to his viewer concerning the manipulation and misrepresentation of history occurs shortly after the *Star*'s editor, Maxwell Scott (Carleton Young), insists on printing a version of the past that is not Stoddard's. It is the movie's most shattering moment, when Stoddard, who has asked us to put our trust in him, travels back to Washington and does not correct the conductor when he is mistaken for the man for whom nothing is too good. However jaded we may have become about the inevitability of history's manipulation of information, Stoddard's gross display of personal misrepresentation is still very shocking. Here, Ford's critique of politicians and politics could be hardly more damning. Personal values, it seems, have no place in a politician's life, even though John F. Kennedy's Inaugural Address in January of 1961 envisaged the very same values that Stoddard also promoted for the West: "a new world of law, where the strong are just and the weak secure and the peace preserved."[36] Only four months after this statement, Kennedy, much like Stoddard addressing the staff of the *Shinbone Star*, assured his audience, the American Association of Newspaper Editors, that he and the editors of newspapers owed "a common obligation to the people: an obligation to present the facts, to present them with candor, and to present them in perspective"[37]—before he immediately misrepresents his government's involvement in the Bay of Pigs to the American public in his next paragraph.[38] As Ford points out, any version of history, whatever it may be, could be hardly less factual than the political and personal nonsense to which the editor of the *Shinbone Star* and we (the public) have been witnesses. We will never know what really happened in Shinbone, just as the American public will never know what really happened in the White House during the Cold War.

As a Cold War critique, *The Man Who Shot Liberty Valance* offers its audience parallels between Ransom Stoddard and John F. Kennedy that are deeply disturbing when one considers the canonizations of Stoddard's character at the movie's end and Kennedy's after his assassination. Newspapers, it seems (and by extension, Hollywood), create legends, and as Ford points out, that person—be he hero or villain—rarely gets what he really deserves.

Generally, however, this film is regarded by its commentators as an elegy for the past. Andrew Sarris says, "Everything that Ford has ever thought or felt is compressed into one shot of a cactus rose on a coffin."[39] However, Ford, as a veteran, was not only committed to honoring the dead, he was also obligated to tell their story. To further address the presence of ellipses in the legend, he turned to a story about the collective trauma of the American frontier in his next Western, *Cheyenne Autumn*.

14

QUESTIONS OF JUST CONDUCT

Cheyenne Autumn

Do I contradict myself? Very well, then I contradict myself, I am large, I contain multitudes. [1]—Walt Whitman

John Ford began work on his final Western in 1963. [2] In 1964, he reported to Michael Killanin, "Right now I am working on a very big picture. This, I think, will be a welcome [change from] the movies and TV's of the past. It will be a costly picture and entail much physical labor." [3] To launch *Cheyenne Autumn*, Ford teamed up with Bernard Smith, with whom he had worked while shooting the Civil War segment of *How The West Was Won*. When Ford initially asked Smith, "What kind of uniform should Grant be wearing?" Smith did not take the bait. He wisely replied, "Mr. Ford, don't ask me a question like that. You can answer that question better than I ever could." [4] The pair quickly forged a friendly working relationship and convinced Warner Bros. to finance *Cheyenne Autumn* for $4.2 million; the director would receive $200,000 for his work and the Ford-Smith partnership, which shared in the financing, would keep 65 percent of the net profits. [5]

Dramatizing the Native Americans' side of Manifest Destiny, *Cheyenne Autumn* promised to be a timely addition to the Western canon, but it was "an exceptionally difficult picture" for its director. In September, the weather did not cooperate in Monument Valley, and C. V. Whitney would not release second unit footage from *The Searchers* for the project. As in the planning stages of *The Horse Soldiers*, *Two Rode*

Together, and *Liberty Valance*, Ford again appeared to lose his enthusiasm during preproduction. He did not participate in the story writing
sessions, giving Jim Webb carte blanche with the script. On location, his
problems seemed to be compounded. At sixty-nine, he was physically
incapable of working eighteen-hour days on location. He became exhausted after thirty days of shooting and fell ill. In addition to fatigue,
he had also been attempting to cope with uncooperative actors Sal
Mineo and Ricardo Montalban, who did not respond positively to his
abrasive directing style. Finally, depressed and despondent, "morbid
and morose," he went to bed and refused to leave it for five days—
"word was passed among the company that he had the flu, but most of
the people who were close to him knew that his problems were largely
psychological."[6] Dan Ford notes that George O'Brien, who was cast in
the movie, attempted but was unable to boost Ford's morale: whenever
O'Brien mentioned *Cheyenne Autumn*, Ford would grow "sullen and
withdrawn and simply [say,] 'It's just no fun anymore.'"[7]

It has been generally assumed that Ford's problems on set grew as
he aged and lost touch with the film industry—Dan Ford remembers
that February 1959 was a particularly difficult time for his grandfather.
The elder Ford realized that there was "change in the air; there were
new currents of thought blowing in over Hollywood, and John wasn't
sure he understood the scent they carried. The mood of the country was
changing, and Hollywood was changing with it. There was a new, more
liberal, more permissive spirit in the air."[8] Ford's difficult postwar behavior while working with actors and being interviewed by the press
had increased over the years. By 1968, he deeply resented being labeled
"a bit eccentric," telling Philip Jenkinson: "Everybody has a little eccen-
tricity in their character, I believe, but if you ask me to define it in what
way I don't know I'm eccentric . . . probably because I'm very courteous
to my equals, more than courteous to my inferiors (I'm speaking in
terms of pictures), and I'm horribly rude to my superiors, so that's
probably what they mean by eccentric."[9]

In 1964 while making *Cheyenne Autumn*, Ford remarked to Bill
Libby that he expected people to say, "There goes senile old John Ford
out West again, but I don't give a damn."[10] Yet, when one considers the
sophistication and speed with which Ford's last movies were shot, it is
evident that he had not lost his ability to script, direct, edit, and score
motion pictures. Dan Ford observes that when his grandfather did get

out of bed and return to the set of *Cheyenne Autumn*, the picture was shot quickly and efficiently, but something was missing. Ford worked "mechanically and without feeling, glossing over whole sections and shooting them with a single camera set-up. Instead of going after the best possible locations, he set up whenever possible right in front of Goulding's."[11] George O'Brien observed to his son after *Cheyenne Autumn* had been shot that Ford no longer had any real interest in making movies.[12]

Prior to Fred Kennedy's death, the John Ford Stock Company had been, as Harry Carey Jr. notes, an extension of Ford's family and served as a source of camaraderie, providing him with comrades-in-arms like Jack Pennick. As individuals within the Stock Company died, retired, or began working in television, its esprit de corps lessened, and Ford's social (and moral) world started to fall apart. The deaths of Fred Kennedy and Ward Bond ruptured the social cohesion upon which Ford had built his own character. Some actors, like Richard Widmark, Karl Malden, and Lee Marvin, were added to the company. The time that Malden spent as a noncommissioned officer in the 8th Air Force stood him in good stead when working with Ford on *Cheyenne Autumn*. Malden recognized Ford's style of command and the martial culture of Ford's fraternity—"Does it matter?" asked Ford when the actor objected to the same pose in two scenes: *"No sir*, not at all," was Malden's reply (italics mine).[13] "I'd never want to get in a fight with John Ford," Malden says. "It was his picture. He brought the bat and ball and you played the game his way. He was directing every day I was there."[14] With this in mind, it is not surprising that Malden was admitted to the cast's inner circle and invited to the director's daily afternoon tea. Ford and Lee Marvin also formed a close working relationship almost immediately. As Eyman points out, "The two men had a great deal in common: periodic alcoholism, a passion for the sea, brave showing in World War II—Marvin had been a Marine and was badly wounded on Saipan—and surprisingly liberal politics."[15] But even Marvin, a veteran whose postwar character and behavior was very much like Ford's, could not fill the gap that Ward Bond's irretrievable loss had created. In 1964, Ford still missed "old Ward Bond very much."[16]

Notably, other newcomers were not added to the Stock Company. Unlike Malden and Marvin, Ricardo Montalban and Sal Mineo did not understand military codes of order and discipline. A Mexican, Montalban did not fight for America during the Second World War, and Mineo, born in 1939, had no memories of the war at all. Ford, who insisted on total command on the set, found working with Mineo particularly difficult. The young method actor did not catch on to what Ford wanted from him until one night after supper when the director took out his knife, opened it, and laid it on the table beside Mineo's phonograph: "Can it you play it a little softer?" he asked. It was only then that actor finally understood what his relationship with Ford should be and replied, "*Yes sir,* I can play it very soft" (italics mine).[17] William Clothier remembers that Ford's good working relationship with his crew and technicians was also that of total command—at one point during the shooting of the movie, Ford, for instance, refused to begin work until "the little electrician who called [him] a son of a bitch" and had been fired by Wingate Smith (without Ford's permission) was rehired and brought back to the set via a limousine.[18]

Loosely based on the story of the Northern Cheyenne Exodus, *Cheyenne Autumn* is an account of combat, combat trauma, and self-healing, and oddly, is the John Ford film that everyone in 1964 seemed to love to hate—everyone that is except John Ford, who thought it "a hell of a good story";[19] Mark Haggard, who argued that "at 70 [Ford was] . . . still exploring and experimenting, moving in a new direction as an artist";[20] and Bosley Crowther, who considered *Cheyenne Autumn* to be "a stark and eye-opening symbolization of a shameless tendency that has prevailed in our national life—the tendency to be unjust and heartless to weaker peoples who get in the way of manifest destiny."[21]

Cheyenne Autumn was released on October 3, 1964, in the United States, and then again, later in October, in Spain and in France. The film, received enthusiastically in Europe, was a critical failure and a box office flop in the United States. Richard Oulahan of *Life* magazine labeled *Cheyenne Autumn* "a turkey";[22] Stanley Kauffman of the *New Republic* described it as a "pallid" version of the best Ford, its cast "beyond disbelief";[23] *Newsweek* declared "Ford has apparently forgotten everything he ever knew, about actors, about cameras, about Indians, and about the West";[24] and *Mad Magazine* dubbed the movie "*Cheyenne Awful*" in September 1965.

BROKEN EXPECTATIONS

As director Toshi Fujiwara points out, *Cheyenne Autumn* has been disparaged, respectfully ignored, or defended by most of its critics for not being what it was expected to be—either a historically accurate representation or a sentimental account of Dull Knife's and Little Wolf's attempts to return home with their people.[25] Joseph McBride finds *Cheyenne Autumn* conceptually flawed. His objection to the movie lies in Ford's decision to tell both sides of the story. *Cheyenne Autumn* would have been more successful in its treatment of the Exodus, McBride says, had Ford been less even-handed and used more of Howard Fast's *The Last Frontier* as source material for the film.[26] Unlike Mari Sandoz's *Cheyenne Autumn*, which romantically idealizes the exodus of the Northern Cheyenne, *The Last Frontier* is told from the white pursuers' point of view, principally that of Captain Murray, a hard-nosed cavalryman trying to do what he considers his duty while troubled by the irrationality of government policies.[27]

Katherine Cliffton, Ford's principal researcher on *Cheyenne Autumn*, however, disagrees with McBride. Assigned to verify the historical data from *The Last Frontier* in original sources like the Dodge City and New York newspapers, Cliffton believes "where *Cheyenne Autumn* went wrong was in trying to put into it what [Ford] admired in Fast's book."[28] Because of Ford's appreciation for *The Last Frontier*, she says, "[*Cheyenne Autumn* was a] poor imitation of his better films."[29] Perhaps Mari Sandoz's objection to the film adaptation of her book best sums up why audiences in 1964 had been disappointed by *Cheyenne Autumn*. John Ford, known for his exciting chase sequences, had not delivered an action film: "I don't see how you can make a slow story about one of the greatest chases of history," Sandoz said. "They made it dull."[30]

Ford, of course, was well aware that the Exodus, which began on September 9, 1878, had been anything but dull. Katherine Cliffton, Dudley Nichols, Pat Ford, and Richard Widmark had meticulously researched the historical background of the Exodus and its major figures for him. He knew that the 89 Northern Cheyenne warriors and 246 Northern Cheyenne women and children who traveled across Kansas and Nebraska to return home near the Great Lakes in present-day Minnesota had been harried by close to ten thousand soldiers and three thousand settlers,[31] but the dramatic value of their pursuit was not his primary concern. A movie made for the thinking man, *Cheyenne Autumn* offers its viewer opportunities to analyze the action on screen. Appropriately, it begins like a documentary. A voice-over narrates the traumatic history of the Northern Cheyenne as they prepare themselves to meet with officials from the U.S. Department of the Interior's Agency of Indian Affairs to discuss their deplorable living conditions, but almost immediately, the narrative announces its fictionality to those familiar with the Exodus—attributing the Cheyenne's decision to leave the reservation and return home to Tall Tree (Victor Jory), a chief who never existed. Throughout, only the most general outlines of the Exodus are discernible as Captain Thomas Archer (Richard Widmark) and his cavalry pursue men, women, and children for seven hundred improbable miles in a huge circle that begins and ends in Monument Valley.

Ford's treatment of the indigene during this journey has also raised many eyebrows. Critical commentators, among them Brian Spittles, have suggested that Ford's treatment of the Exodus is an apology for presentations of Native Americans in his earlier Westerns. However, Harry Carey Jr. disagrees with assessments like Spittles's: "Uncle Jack never apologized for anything in his life," he says. "The fact that the Indians were not the enemy in this picture might have given him some comfort but no more than a fleeting thought."[32] Actually, the Northern Cheyenne's Exodus had interested Ford for "a long time" because there "are two sides to every story."[33] Accordingly, Ford offers his viewer an even-handed examination of the Exodus via the Northern Cheyenne's "point of view" *and* the U.S. Army's. His treatments of the characters in this movie are also carefully balanced, not privileging one above another. As Pat Ford's memoranda and preproduction treatment of *Cheyenne Autumn* reveal, John Ford intended to make the movie *without* Western heroes or villains: he specified that the Army was to be "an underpaid, undermanned force trying to maintain a virtually impossible peace" and the Cheyenne were not to be "heavies."[34]

HELLENIZING THE WEST

Making this Western without heroes or villains presented an enormous artistic challenge because Ford, nonetheless, considered the Exodus "a tragic story."[35] Adapting the conventions of classical tragedy to the actuality of the American West, Ford's modification of the tragic form is at once startlingly simple and profoundly radical in its scope and complexity: his Cheyenne are not individual onlookers who comment on the action at hand. The band is represented as a composite character. As Pat Ford's preproduction notes demonstrate, his father decided instead to have the Cheyenne "serve" as a "Greek Chorus."[36]

The U.S. Cavalry, led by Captain Archer, and the members of Fort Robinson's garrison, led by Captain Wessels (Karl Malden), also function as choral ensembles. Because there are no heroes (and no villains) in *Cheyenne Autumn*, its narrative action is also modified. Conflict and dramatic tension in this movie are produced by the clash of cultures, not individuals.

Ford's use of the Greek choruses as composite characters generates *Cheyenne Autumn*'s "tragic and epic grandeur,"[37] transforming what is described by the film's narrator as "a footnote in history" into a significant exercise in ethics that encourages the viewer to reconsider the nature of justice and viability of the Absolute Good. In part, his presentation of the Cheyenne invites the audience to participate in this exercise. Because the Cheyenne function as an ensemble, Ford typically uses wide shots that distance the viewer from and encourage his or her contemplation of the action. When Little Wolf and Dull Knife are shown in a two-shot or a medium shot, for example, they invariably speak for their group. Dull Knife reminds the audience of the closeness of the relationship that Ford's Cheyenne have with one another, stating in one scene that he and Little Wolf have "always thought as one. Never has the thickness of a straw come" between them. In a bold experimental gesture, Ford also carefully forges a strong sense of identification between the viewer and the Cheyenne. A Greek chorus not only represents the general population on the stage and comments on the action of individual protagonists, but it also speaks for the members of its audience. Using perspectives that include the viewer in shots containing the Cheyenne, Ford, at times, blurs traditional boundaries and barriers that separate the audience from the actor on stage by including the viewer in the action taking place on the screen, as at the beginning of the film when the Cheyenne march (toward the camera) to arrive at the U.S. Department of the Interior's Agency of Indian Affairs.

Before the Cheyenne's arrival, Ford's camera establishes the place of the viewer in the action on screen via the road leading into the valley. In this shot, the vanishing point is located near mid-center, on the butte occupying the horizon. The telegraph poles and rows of cannons and men create horizontal lines that intersect the road and direct the eye toward the butte. Extending backward, through the screen and into the audience, these sightlines also embrace the viewer, who becomes a choral member. This inclusion of the viewer is further reinforced as the camera functions like an onlooker, panning to peruse the Cheyenne as they walk by. Later, when the disgusted Cheyenne leave the agency to return home, Ford again reinforces the viewer's relationship with them, enabling the viewer to not only witness but also to join the Exodus, as the ensemble following Tall Tree draws the eye down the road.

Dignified and stately, the Cheyenne's departure from Indian Territory is also orchestrated as a procession, during which the chorus expresses itself in terms of its movement rather than its dialogue. In doing so they express the warlike nature of the Cheyenne culture, in which a baby is a soldier when he takes his first breath.[38] Harry Carey Jr. remembers that during the shooting of this movie, Victor Jory, Dolores del Rio, Gilbert Roland, and Ricardo Montalban marched and marched "across the red sand of Monument Valley. Every so often, one of them would say something as though it were a world-shattering statement, and then they would continue to march, stop, make another announcement, and march, march."[39]

INVESTIGATING VIRTUE

Ford's treatment of Little Wolf (Ricardo Montalban) is also an integral element of the film's investigation of virtue and the conflicted nature of duty, honor, and morality. Historically, Little Wolf was one of the four "Old Man" chiefs among the Council of Forty-four and the Northern Cheyenne's Sweet Medicine Chief. A master strategist, Little Wolf was a far-sighted leader whose command skills elevated him to leadership within the prestigious Elk Society. Aptly, in *Cheyenne Autumn*, it is

Little Wolf who is chosen to be his people's leader and to whom Tall Tree entrusts the Sacred Bundle. As the Cheyenne's representative, spokesman, and war chief, he exemplifies their martial culture.

According to Aristotle, virtue is a character trait that is the ethical midpoint between two vices, one of excess and one of deficiency.[40] Positioned between Red Shirt's aggressive behavior and Dull Knife's cautious conduct, Little Wolf must be considered a virtuous individual. Ford, however, complicates Little Wolf's character. Pledged to lead his people home, Little Wolf steers his starving followers into a Catch-22 situation. If they continue their Exodus with him, the children will surely die. If they leave him and go to Fort Robinson with Dull Knife (Gilbert Roland), the Cheyenne will never attain their homeland. Ford expects his audience to think the decision to follow Little Wolf is immoral, and even reinforces such a reaction for the viewer by having Little Wolf's youngest wife, Little Bird (Nancy Hsueh), abandon her morals (and her virtue) to travel north with her lover, Red Shirt (Sal Mineo), and Dull Knife's group. As half of the Cheyenne start to split away to follow Little Wolf and the other half begin to turn one by one to follow Dull Knife, Ford cuts to a closer straight-on view of the division, in which men on horseback and walking women and children stream to the left and right, thereby carefully positioning the viewer between the two groups. Just before what is left of the group splits apart, Little Bird breaks out of line and runs across the screen to join her lover. The camera pans to follow her flight, but its gaze (and the viewer's) abandons the search for home and does "the right thing" to save the children. The camera (and the viewer) follow Dull Knife to Fort Robinson. Terribly, at Fort Robinson, "doing the right thing" results in a massacre.

Ford's ethical exercise appears to be highly unorthodox until one also considers the police action undertaken by Archer's ensemble in pursuit of the Cheyenne. As historian Jeff McMahan points out, the traditional theory of a just war is predicated on two sets of principles, one governing the resort to war and the other governing the conduct of war. These principles are, as Michael Walzer says, "logically independent"—because it is possible for a just war to be fought unjustly and for an unjust war to be fought in strict accordance with the rules.[41] Thus, in war, the moral position of unjust combatants is indistinguishable from that of just combatants: unjust combatants do not do wrong merely by participating in an unjust war; they do wrong if they violate the principles of just conduct in war.[42]

Ford emphasizes the nature and the severity of the violation that the Cheyenne have experienced not only as prisoners of the state but also as prisoners of war. At the beginning of the movie, their reservation is presented as a prison, with Archer's voice-over noting that the Cheyenne are "as out of place in this desert as eagles in a cage." More than merely a prison, it is a death camp. After pledging to provide the inhabitants of reservations with adequate clothing and rations, the Indian Bureau has ignored the Cheyenne and left them to starve, until only 335 of the more than 1,000 men, women, and children who arrived a year earlier remain. Decimated by disease and hunger, the survivors wait for hours under the hot sun for the moment when "the white chiefs from Washington would see for themselves how the Cheyenne had been forgotten." Supporting the Cheyenne, Deborah Wright (Carroll Baker) asks Major Braden (George O'Brien) to "plead [with the Congressional Committee at Fort Reno] for justice." A professional soldier, Braden interprets his duty to be that of perpetuating injustice. He replies, "Miss Wright, my responsibility to the Indians is only to guard them. When you have reached my age, you will have realized that it pays to stick to your knitting. That's exactly what I intend to do."

In the military, professional standards of ethical behavior are organized into general rules and principles to guide the Officer Corps. In *Cheyenne Autumn*, these are standards with which most of Ford's contemporaries, having served in the Second World War, would have been familiar. These principles are transmitted to the viewer via Captain Archer's relationship with Lieutenant Scott (Patrick Wayne). At the beginning of the cavalry's pursuit, Archer's ensemble immediately begins its mission by investigating the nature of virtue. A seasoned soldier, Archer's moderate and reasonable behavior exemplifies the middle ground between the vices of excess and deficiency. Archer is a consummate professional. Scott, on the other hand, to whom the pursuit and capture of the Cheyenne is a "personal matter" of revenge, behaves excessively. On learning that the Cheyenne have "skipped," Scott's response is "Thank God." Impatient, he can hardly wait to begin chasing them. Not heeding Archer's comment that he is a "damned idiot," Scott oversteps his authority and acts unethically, bringing E Troop up too quickly.

While Archer and Scott pursue the Cheyenne, the older officer attempts to mentor the younger, inexperienced man. Reminding his lieutenant that "the trick to being brave is not to be too brave," Archer emphasizes the need for ethical behavior while soldiering. Scott, however, does not take Archer's advice to heart—disobeying his orders and rashly leading a cavalry charge into an ambush, he is responsible for his men's casualties and the loss of his company's wagons. Scott's excessive behavior is so appalling that the veteran artillerymen, bewildered when the charge begins, ask, "What in the *hell* is that kid doing? What the *hell* is he doing?"

Unlike Scott, Sr. Sergeant Wichowsky (Mike Mazurki), a veteran of thirty years and ten days in the Army, understands and values the Army's professional standards, which ensure virtuous behavior among enlisted men and their officers. "Proud to be an American soldier," Wichowsky, a Pole, however, refuses to re-enlist and continue pursuing the Cheyenne because to do so would mean he has become a Cossack. As a professional, Wichowsky knows that the activities of war are not those of genocide. He says to Archer, "Do you know what a Cossack is? He is a man on a horse with a fur hat on his head and a sabre in his hand. Now he kills Poles just because they're Poles. Like we're killing Indians just because they're Indians."

Ford's treatment of the cavalrymen in *Cheyenne Autumn* differs from that of his more action-oriented Cavalry Trilogy. McBride, for example, points out that Captain Thomas Archer in *Cheyenne Autumn* and Captain Kirby York in *Fort Apache* are both "obedient rebels," that is, like York, Archer is a conflicted character, sympathetic to the Indians but forced to execute unjust orders. Also like York, Archer acquires stature because of his principled opposition to his commanding officer.[43] When closely examined, however, Archer cannot be considered "obedient." Unlike York, who supports and perpetuates the story of Thursday's glorious Last Stand to protect the reputation of his regiment (and his father-in-law), Archer challenges the authority of Fort Robinson's commanding officer and his divisional commander in Omaha, traveling to Washington to discuss the plight of the Indians imprisoned at Fort Robinson with Secretary of the Interior Carl Schurz (Edward G. Robinson).

NECESSITY OF DISCRIMINATION

When making decisions, officers are expected to discriminate between the demands of situations in the field and those thought out before. With this in mind, Captain Oskar Wessels's actions showcase and emphasize the ethical nature of Archer's actions. Ford's depiction of Wessels, whom McBride terms "grotesquely caricatured," is an important element in *Cheyenne Autumn*'s critique.[44] Unlike Archer and his ensemble, who execute unethical orders in an ethical manner, Wessels and his troupe carry out unethical orders in the most unethical way imaginable.

In historical reality, Oskar Wessels never existed. Captain Henry W. Wessells Jr., born in Sacketts Harbor, New York, and educated in Connecticut, was in command when the Fort Robinson tragedy occurred. He had served in the West since 1870. A fictional character, Ford's Wessels is, as McBride points out, a German stereotype—speaking with a heavy German accent and following a Prussian code of military discipline. In his fur hat, Wessels looks like, and indeed is, the Cossack that Wichowsky refuses to become.

At first, Wessels appears to conform to the high standards of honor, integrity, loyalty, and justice that combat demands of officers. When the Cheyenne arrive at Fort Robinson, he welcomes them and provides them with food, shelter, and warmth. He seems to be a European who is fascinated by the indigene. "Good. Good," he says. "Feed them. Give them good fire. Make them comfortable." His character, however, soon proves to be much more complex than it first appears. Tapping his shoulder, he tells another officer, "This will make me a major."

When orders arrive from Omaha to restrain the Cheyenne and march them back to their reservation, Wessels's self-serving actions become much more extreme. Archer argues with Wessels's off-hand observation that returning the Cheyenne to their reservation is "just military routine." "Murder is not routine," he snaps at Wessels. "They could never survive that march in the dead of winter." Following his superiors' directive, Wessels's actions become excessive. He imprisons women and children in an unheated warehouse at 10 below zero. For Wessels, orders are to be obeyed blindly. "It is an order," he tells Archer, excusing his behavior. "An order."

After Wessels leaves the table to talk to the Cheyenne, Ford heightens the dramatic tension in this scene via Archer's exchange to Dr. O'Carberry (Sean McClory). Appealing to the doctor's professional ethics, Archer challenges him, saying, "You claim to be a doctor. You gonna let him put those women and children in a warehouse at 10 below zero? What are you gonna do about it?" The doctor replies, "What are you gonna do about it?" When both men act according to their ethics, they dissolve the tension: Archer goes to Washington and convinces Schurz to intercede; O'Carberry, after much deliberation, declares Wessels unfit for duty and places him under house arrest. Tragically, he acts too late—the Cheyenne escape from the warehouse just after Wessels is imprisoned, and although Lieutenant Scott intervenes and stops the shooting, noncombatants, women, and children have been cut down by soldiers as they try to flee from Fort Robinson. Surveying the massacre, Scott finally recognizes that the members of the ensemble at Fort Robinson have been behaving like "idiots."

THE DEATH CAMP

Ford's critique of the actions that take place at Fort Robinson could not be more scalding: Wessels cannot be mistaken for anything other than a war criminal and the Cheyenne, his victims. At the fort, Ford's treatment of the Cheyenne carefully aligns them with images of prisoners in Nazi death camps during the Second World War. When the Cheyenne are herded into the warehouse, Ford's exterior close-up of Spanish Woman (Dolores del Rio), draped in a gray Army blanket, her face pressed against a pane of a warehouse window, evokes memories of documentary images of blanketed prisoners marching to or being incarcerated in prison camps. Then, as the Cheyenne prepare to escape, Ford further emphasizes the presence of noncombatants in the group. Knives and guns are recovered from their hiding places while women and infants watch. One baby whose cradleboard serves as a hiding place for knives appears in three shots. In the last of these, the child's eyes follow the passage of weapons passed above him from one man to another.

Ford presents the viewer with an unlit interior that reads as a barracks found in a prisoner of war camp or concentration camp after lights out as the Cheyenne prepare to break out of the warehouse. The darkened interior appears to be discernible because the bright light from the lantern of the soldiers patrolling the outside of the building shines into the windows of the warehouse. Against these frosted windows, the silhouette of a backlit guard with his fur hat and rifle appears to be a gigantic shadow. Supported by powerful backlighting, the effect of the moving lantern is that of a prison camp's searchlight.

When Wessels finally breaks out of his room, the massacre is over. His point of view reveals the bodies of his troopers and those of the Cheyenne warriors. Arguably, this sequence is Ford's most effective in the film. Even though the viewer has seen women and babies drop to the ground during the shooting, the angle of this shot excludes the viewer seeing their corpses. Instead of a massacre, the viewer is presented with what appears to be the aftermath of a battle. Ford then cuts to a shot that reverses the point of view 180 degrees, allowing Scott's and Wessels's faces to be apparent when the lieutenant shouts bitterly to Wessels, "Has authority been sufficiently obeyed, sir?" Wessels, approaching the camera, does not answer this question, but Ford's camera does, maximizing the viewer's shock by revealing the bodies of noncombatants. A baby off screen begins to wail after Scott speaks, and as the camera tracks backward, Wessels walks toward the audience and then out of the shot toward the fort's gate. Left behind is Ford's final wide shot of the massacre.

This tableau of corpses lying on the snow before the surviving soldiers standing behind them does not evoke memories of photographs taken of Native Americans massacred during the 1880s. Documentation of Washita and Wounded Knee, generally considered to be among the best-known images of such atrocities, reconstructs the landscape of the battlefield via the picturesque paradigm used by Civil War photographers. In these images, the viewer is allowed to transcend the tragedy of war by ascending (in graduated stages) to heaven in the distant sky. In the grisly situation at Fort Robinson, however, there is no route by which the viewer's eye may ascend the horror that Ford's camera documents in the compound.

Ford uses the camera's perspective to align the viewer with the dead and convey the enormity of the Fort Robinson massacre in *Cheyenne Autumn*. The viewer's eye is directed through the bodies, to Scott and Wessel's soldiers, who stand in the midground and background surveying the atrocity. Behind them, the wall of a cabin prevents the eye's natural inclination to rise upward. There is no question as to who is responsible for the slaughter of the innocents lying in the foreground. Ford's use of visual irony here could not be more biting: in the foreground, the blanketed bodies of two women are discernible. Flanking one of the corpses are two very young children, one kneeling, the other standing. Both are in shock. As the camera fades to black, the child who is kneeling presses her forehead to her mother's body. Foregrounded, the motherless children are awarded precedence over the soldiers who stand well behind them, emphasizing the vileness of their act. As Walzer points out, in war "the moral equality of soldiers" awards combatants "an equal right to kill"—but they do not have a right to kill just anyone.[45] The central requirement is that of discrimination. All combatants, just and unjust alike, must discriminate between combatants and noncombatants, intentionally attacking the former and not the latter.

THE POLITICAL DIMENSIONS OF GENOCIDE

The murder of these women, children, and elders was intentional and must be considered a means by which political objectives (those of the U.S. government) as well as aims of personal gain (those of Wessels) would be achieved.[46] Thus, the genocide experienced by Native Americans in the West is not confined to the actions of a self-serving captain and his band of "idiots" at Fort Robinson. Ultimately, Washington is responsible for the massacre that occurs. Because the state that they serve is corrupt, the cavalrymen are unable to serve the greater good. Archer, Scott, Mazurski, and Wessels, servants of the state, ultimately support the interests of corporate America. In Washington, politicians, responding to the needs of businessmen characterized by Schurz as "the leeches and vultures upstairs," therefore support and further the annihilation of those impeding the progress of profit.

Ford's critique of the U.S. government in *Cheyenne Autumn* is counterbalanced by his assertion that, in America, the moral worth of the individual can enable individuals to effect political and social change. Schurz demonstrates that the individualism of the American Character is a "progressive force" that can reconcile "liberty and social justice"[47] and supports "the idea of perfect and free individuals" in

Cheyenne Autumn.[48] After learning the plight of the Cheyenne, he addresses the portrait of Abraham Lincoln, another "leader of leaders," in his office: "Old friend . . . old friend," he asks, "what would you do?" Schurz's question directs the viewer to consider the moral and political dimensions of the situation. Alone with his conscience, Schurz finds his face, reflected in the glass protecting the portrait, doubling Lincoln's. "The Battle Hymn of the Republic" playing in the background indicates that Schurz, a moral individual, will do what Lincoln, who freed the black slaves and united a divided nation, did. Little Wolf and his group finally find their way home, much to the relief of the viewer, who has witnessed the injustice that has taken place.

Thus, in spite of the horrors and injustices of war, Ford's West remains an ideal place—the America that attracted its settlers and Ford's own family. The presence of the Sublime, which disappeared during Ford's social and psychological studies of the darker side of the American Character in *Two Rode Together* and *The Man Who Shot Liberty Valance*, reappears at the end of *Cheyenne Autumn*, presented in pastoral and picturesque terms—the tepees in the sunny foreground of the North Cheyenne village, like the high ridges that flank it, direct the eye through the community to the gleaming lake, ridges, and mountains of the background before ascending into the distant cloudless sky. In this shot, Man and Nature, reflections of one another, become integrated.

At the closing of the Exodus, Carl Schurz assures the Cheyenne that "a new tradition" of trust and reconciliation between them and the U.S. government has begun, but Ford does not provide *Cheyenne Autumn* with the happy ending that Schurz promises. The America conceived by Alexis de Tocqueville, that self-conscious and actively political society in which self-interested individuals bond for the purpose of mutual benefit, proves to be short-lived. In what Fujiwara terms *Cheyenne Autumn*'s "most ambiguous scene,"[49] Ford again problematizes the character of Little Wolf, the war chief who kills Red Shirt immediately upon his arrival at the Cheyenne village in their homeland. By doing so, Little Wolf regains his personal honor but is unable to continue as the Cheyenne's leader. He passes the Sacred Bundle to Dull Knife since "no one could carry it who had shed the blood of another Cheyenne."

Little Wolf's actions send him into exile because "a war chief of the Cheyenne can only raise his hand against the enemy." No longer a member of his community and unable to return home, Little Wolf cannot attain the Absolute Good that is expressed in this peaceful, pastoral ideal of the Cheyenne's homeland. In the closing shot of *Cheyenne Autumn*, Little Wolf is doomed to wander. Ford's final vision of the Cheyenne warrior evokes pity and fear for Little Wolf from his viewer. Last seen moving along on the horizon, Little Wolf is presented as a mere silhouette, at once alienated and tragic.

Wandering without community, Little Wolf is visually, literally, and metaphorically a "Vanishing American," and as such invites comparison with George B. Seitz's *The Vanishing American* (1925), which was shot in Monument Valley. An early (and also compromised) attempt to address the mistreatment of Native Americans by the U.S. government, *The Vanishing American* was one of Paramount/Famous Players-Lasky's most ambitious projects of the 1920s, was well received at the box office, and later was remade, adapted, and directed by Joe Kane for Republic in 1955.

Seitz's Vanishing American, Nophaie, dies at the end of the movie, but in Kane's 1955 version, he survives his gunshot wound and stays with the white missionary teacher with whom he has been romantically involved at the Indian School. In 1964, Ford's Little Wolf is a much more problematic character. He does not die or assimilate. Unlike Seitz and Kane, Ford simply leaves the war chief suspended on the screen, riding not into the sunset but along it. As in Greek tragedy, Little Wolf's exit serves as a curtain closing on the story, and when the film goes black, the viewer, unable to join Little Wolf, is equally unable to return to the Edenic homeland envisioned by early Americans, presented in the Americana of *Drums along the Mohawk* and recovered in *Cheyenne Autumn* by the Cheyenne Nation. Highly sophisticated, *Cheyenne Autumn* reminds the viewer that there are always veterans on both sides after a war is over. The conflicted nature of duty, honor, and morality at the conclusion of this movie leaves Little Wolf, the First American, unable to return home, like Ethan Edwards in *The Searchers*.

John Ford achieved in his final Western what he had envisioned during its preproduction: *Cheyenne Autumn* is an American tragedy that tells the story of a West without tragic heroes. Complex and conflicted, *Cheyenne Autumn*'s presentations of Native Americans and cavalrymen call for the recognition of Native American history, the realization of the viewer's own place in the story of the West, and the response of pity and fear to that realization. When speaking of *Cheyenne Autumn* to Peter Bogdanovich, Ford says, "Let's face it, we've treated them very badly—it's a blot on our shield; we've cheated and robbed, killed, murdered, massacred and everything else, but they kill one white man and, God, out come the Troops."[50] Progressive and far-sighted, Ford not only revealed the tragedy created by the martial nature of the American Character, but he also used the historical and cinematic resources of the Western to shine a spotlight on the irrationality of government policies. Despite Warner's interference with *Cheyenne Autumn* during its editing—at the age of sixty-nine—Ford continued to be a filmmaker on the cutting edge. In 1964, *Cheyenne Autumn* questioned the ethical behavior of the American Army in war and, in doing so, predicted the American public's protest of Vietnam a few short years later.

AFTERMATH

They won't let me make one. They won't let me do another movie.[1]—
John Ford

In 1970, John Ford told Joseph McBride that he would "still enjoy doing a Western." "If a story came along, I'd go out and do it now, but hell, they're not coming," he said. "I get two or three scripts a week, but they're remakes or rewrites of pictures I've already done. Or they're all filthy or sexy, and that would be against my nature, my religion, and my natural inclinations to do those things."[2] Ford had been waiting to direct a movie for four years. His career as a director had ended quietly in 1966 when Samuel Goldwyn Jr. offered him the opportunity to direct *April Morning*, but MGM had been unwilling to work with the Old Man again—*Young Cassidy* (1965) and *7 Women* (1966) had been producers' nightmares and box office disappointments. And, as Goldwyn noted, Ford "was too far gone physically. I don't think he would have made it through the picture."[3] As early as 1964, Ford, who continued to drink heavily, suffered from hardening of the arteries and began to take sleeping pills without prescriptions. He had also begun to display alarming signs of weakness and fatigue. As Wingate Smith pointed out, Ford "wasn't feeling good in *Cheyenne Autumn*. He started sloughing [while setting up and shooting scenes]. . . . I noticed that his circulation wasn't too good. . . . He'd be walking along and he'd stop . . . and he would look all around . . . and you knew he was not going to shoot any scenes there." Ford, however, would not see a doctor about his failing health. "He wouldn't go to a doctor for a complete examination, for the simple reason I think your grandfather was afraid," Smith said to Dan Ford.[4] When Ford finally did see a doctor in October 1971, he was diagnosed as having stage 4 stomach cancer.

As Scott Eyman comments, during his retirement years, Ford "entered that twilight world of the director who is too old to work; a world of tributes, interviews, and making the rounds of film festivals to collect awards."[5] While doing so, Ford continued to protect his public image. When interviewed, he was, at times, direct, but generally he could be counted on to pretend not to understand questions and to conveniently forget which movies he had made and his motives while making them. Ford also continued to evade talking about his work even when no longer making movies. His elusive behavior has come to be considered evidence of Irish perversity by his interviewers, but it should not be considered unusual or eccentric. Ford and his family were professionals who maintained a strict policy of not talking about films with industry outsiders: even as children, "Pat and Barbara were always sure to tell their friends, 'Now, listen, when you walk in the front door, don't mention anything about movies.'"[6]

Ford's evasiveness about his work is perhaps best understood via a scene in *The Searchers*. Midway in that movie, Ethan Edwards and Martin Pauley visit forts and trading posts while looking for Debbie. After talking with Jerem Futterman, Martin wonders why he hadn't heard "mention of any Nawyecky Commanche" when they passed through these places the previous winter. Ethan reminds Martin that the absence of the Nawyecky Commanche is not odd at all. Masters of indirection, the Nawyecky never tell anyone where they are going or what they are doing: the word *Nawyeka* means "sorta like 'roundabout,'" Ethan says. "Like a man says he's goin' one place when he means to go just the reverse." When one considers John Ford's career and life, it seems that his survival (and maintenance of being a "money" director) in Hollywood should be attributed (in part) to *his* mastery of the art of indirection. When Ford told interviewer Eric Leguèbe in 1965 that he wanted to be remembered as the "author" of Westerns, war stories, and comedies, he again upset his interviewers' expectations: his Oscar-winning dramas and wartime documentaries were to be his legacy and not just "the rest."[7]

Late in 1968, Ford was overseeing the production of *Vietnam! Vietnam!* Recruited by Bruce Herschensohn, the head of the United States

Information Agency (USIA), Ford met with director Sherman Beck to discuss the documentary and flew to Vietnam to view locations. According to Beck, Ford said, "As far as I'm concerned, Sherm, you're the director. This is your film. I'm here to do whatever I can to help make it a good one."[8] Like his mentor, Darryl Zanuck, John Ford did not interfere with the director's work. At base, Ford was a studio man. Like Zanuck, he knew he was part of a large system of production. Appropriately, he influenced the film later, during its postproduction. Herschensohn, editing in Washington, D.C., brought his assemblies to Hollywood, where he and Ford screened and discussed them.

Vietnam! Vietnam! was the last film that John Ford produced. But by the time it was completed in 1971, Ford, Herschensohn, and Beck were unable to shape American culture. Their government's policy toward the Vietnam War had changed, making its message passé. Considered an "irretrievably hawkish" USIA film even at the end of the twentieth century, *Vietnam! Vietnam!* was officially "retired" in 1975.[9] As Eric Spiegelman points out, federal law at that time prohibited the domestic exhibition of any motion picture financed by the USIA, so *Vietnam! Vietnam!* was locked in a vault, where it remained for twenty-seven years until the National Archives were allowed to make it public.[10]

Scott Eyman believes that John Ford, at the age of seventy-four, agreed to work with the United States Information Agency on *Vietnam! Vietnam!* because he could not adjust to being sidelined during his retirement,[11] but Ford's working relationship with the military continued unabated after his discharge and throughout his retirement: as a naval reservist, he would "periodically train Navy film crews at sea or make a documentary, not so much in support of a war, as of the men fighting it."[12] Ford's lasting commitment to the U.S. military was further strengthened by his deeply personal interest in the Vietnam War— both his grandsons were serving.[13] "Of course, their grandmother is proud," he wrote Michael Killanin. "But I shiver in my boots."[14]

Particularly concerned about Dan, Ford made sure that his grandson, who had begun his tour of duty during the Tet Offensive, was all right. "It was November of 1968, I'd been there since June," Dan Ford told Eyman. "I was a forward observer in the 25th Division, a first lieutenant. I had just come out of the jungle, on a five-day sweep, and was dressed in muddy clothes, when I got word that Admiral Ford wanted to see me. I got a helicopter back to Cu Chi, where all the tunnels were, about thirty miles north and west of Saigon."[15]

After spending half a day with his grandson, Ford toured parts of Vietnam before returning to the United States. Ford's personal stance on the war was conflicted. He knew (after touring "pacified" villages) that the war was a fiasco. "All that bullshit," Dan Ford said to Scott Eyman. "He didn't buy it."[16] Ford himself privately commented, "What's the war all about? Damned if I know. I haven't the slightest idea what we're doing there."[17] Tellingly, *Vietnam! Vietnam!* offers two clips featuring President Lyndon B. Johnson, whom Ford personally considered "a despicable man" and "a go-getter."[18] In these, Johnson frames the United States' obligations to its allies in the moral code that every honor-bound military man recognizes and respects, proclaiming that "this nation will keep its commitments from South Vietnam to West Berlin" and that "we cannot just now dishonor our word or abandon our commitment and leave those who believed us and who trusted us to the terror and repression and murder that would follow."

But to his grandson, Ford appeared to be unaware of the reality of fighting in Vietnam. "He would make a big thing about me being in the Army, but my military wasn't his military, my war wasn't his war," Dan Ford observed. "He wasn't in the real Navy, he was in John Ford's Navy. His war was Washington and Wild Bill Donovan and flying the Hump to China. My war was tedium and boredom and mud. He loved the service; I hated it. I don't think he understood the real service."[19]

Ford, however, had not lost contact with the times as much as commentators might believe. In 1965 Bob Stephens, a young Navy man who lived over Ford's garage for eight months while recuperating from wounds he had suffered in Vietnam, found working for the Old Man the turning point of his life. Stephens believed that he gained "a better understanding of what [his] military life was going to be like" from Ford even though he had been in service for fifteen years. "I had 2,500 men working for me when I was finished, and Ford taught me how to make sure that the job got done," he said. "Ford gave me the ins and outs of leadership, how to display it. Mostly, he could be hard-ass, but if he was hard with you, he knew that you were able to do it, but were lazy. Ford taught me how to handle people, how to motivate them, how to keep them from getting killed."[20]

When John Ford was discharged from the OSS, his final Officer Fitness report praised the "superb accomplishments" of Field Photo and cited Ford's "outstanding ability, his devotion to duty, and"—somewhat unusually—"his loyalty to and love for his subordinates."[21] Pat Grissom, a paralyzed Second World War veteran who shared his rehabilitation with Herb Wolf, one of the Field Photo men, told Eyman,

> I've always said that John Ford saved my life. Not literally, but by inviting us out to the Farm, paying attention to us. I met people like John Wayne and Gregory Peck and Maureen O'Hara and Ollie Carey and Cliff Lyons. Being there did more for our rehabilitation and getting us ready to go back to life than anything else. It gave us a drive, an impetus, it made a significant impact on our lives. Because of John Ford, we realized that we weren't just old soldiers waiting to die.[22]

Military life had always been a medium sympathetic to the concepts and principles that anchored Ford's New England upbringing and sense of community. Very much the head of his household at home, on the soundstage, and in the service, John Ford functioned as a New England father figure, serving as a motivator, an educator, and a disciplinarian. Directing the lives of his wife and children, the careers of the actors of his Stock Company, and the fortunes of his men in the field, Ford encouraged his subordinates to call him Pappy and tolerated other monikers as long as they identified him as being in control. Chuck Roberson observes that

> Ford had several different names among the guys who were regulars in his company. I called him Mr. Ford, or Skipper, to his face, and of course, "The Old Man," behind his back (sometimes, a few other choice things when he beat me at cards), but to Duke and some of the other guys that had been around a lot longer than the rest of us, he was "Pappy." The name fit him. He watched over us with his one good eye like a stern father ready to yank us up by our hair and boot us out to his wood shed, just to show us who was boss.[23]

The OSS training films that Ford produced, directed, and occasionally acted in during the Second World War are particularly illuminating when one considers Ford's role as a father figure to his men, because they reveal the Skipper in the act of preparing his "boys" to keep themselves from being killed.[24] *Undercover: How to Operate Behind Enemy Lines in World War 2* (1943) is a rare opportunity to see the director at work on film. Acting as J. P. Baldwin, Attorney at Law, Ford is unmistakable, playing the part of an OSS operative with his own trademark pipe and large handkerchief stuffed in the breast pocket of his jacket. Rocking in a chair that barely accommodates his long, lanky frame, he grills a recruit named Charlie, with his left hand stuffed in his pants pocket while his right hand, holding his pipe, emphasizes points and questions in front of the young man's face.

During Charlie's second interview, Baldwin sends him off to sea to rehearse his role of a fisherman by living the part. "You talk a good fisherman, now you've got to learn to be a good fisherman," he tells his student. "You've got to know the ropes literally." A "couple of weeks of salt water and hard work" on a boat off the Grand Banks toughen Charlie physically and mentally and make him appear to be what he claims to be. While watching the film, it is very difficult to determine where Ford the director and Ford the OSS man begin and end. Baldwin also stresses the importance of teamwork (critical to casts and crews as well as commandos): "Once you join our team, it isn't a question of your own neck anymore," he says to Charlie. "Those brains of yours are a vital connection point in our system of intelligence. When one fuse is blown, the lights go out all over the house, so we're just as interested in safeguarding that neck of yours as you are."

After the Second World War, this overlapping of Ford's professional lives continued, extending into his personal life and even his relationships with his grandchildren. Encouraging Dan Ford's desire to work in the movie business, Ford trained his grandson to see the world as an OSS deskman and a film director by sharpening his powers of observation. While driving along Waikiki Beach with his grandson, Ford pointed out a man walking through a crosswalk and asked what he did for a living. When Dan guessed that the man might be in the Navy, Ford replied, "No, he's too old." "Look at him," Ford instructed his grandson. "He's got Navy shoes on, but he's in civilian clothes. He's probably a steward on the [cruise ship] *Lurleen*. He doesn't work on the deck crew because he looks like he's got soft hands."[25]

Examining Americans was more than just a pastime for Hollywood's Old Master. His Westerns and war stories are important cultural artifacts that reveal a progressive, self-reflexive process at work. A spokesman for America, John Ford obeyed Horace Greeley's injunction: as a young man, he went West and then to war. In the Western tradition, epic adventure has always been a man's rite of initiation, and Ford's Westerns and war stories trace the initiations of both individual *and* national character. Eyman, who believes that Ford's "greatest gift was his ability to combine the epic with the intimate—not just in the same film, but in the same moment, the personal moving side by side with the mythological,"[26] argues that "Ford's vision of America became America's vision of itself and the world's."[27] Always in touch with his own cultural conditioning, Ford repeats, reinvents, and regenerates the beliefs and concerns of his generation. His films transmit what D. H. Lawrence would recognize as being "a whole human experience" that arouses "the emotional self" and "the dynamic self" in Ford's viewers.[28] Ford remarked to Walter Wagner in 1973 that the Western is designed to do exactly this: "*Stagecoach* was a typical Western," he says. "Lots of emotion, lots of action."[29] As Gaylyn Studlar comments, Ford's Westerns are satisfying because they are challenge the emotions of the viewer by revealing the sensitivity of men and women.[30]

Often considered depictions of America's attempts to come to terms with itself, Ford's Westerns communicate "American myths."[31] Richard Slotkin explains that the frontier (and its attendant myths) became America's "structuring metaphor," explaining and justifying the establishment of the American colonies and charting America's progress as it became a powerful nation-state.[32] In Westerns, Slotkin says, viewers rediscover American history. In Ford's Westerns, they also discover American icons. As Scott Eyman says, Ford "shaped a vision of America for the twentieth century every bit as majestic and inclusive as the one Jefferson crafted in the eighteenth century. It's made up of soldiers and priests, of drunks and doctors and servants and whores and half-crazed men driven by their need to be alone, even as they journey toward home, toward reconciliation."[33]

Central to Ford's vision, the journey homeward in the American West frames the American experience as a veteran's experience. Ford's individuals in the West, war veterans all, are transitional figures who have left behind a moral order and experienced lawlessness before attempting to establish that order elsewhere. As Jonathan Shay points out, the homecoming experience for the veteran, conflicted and complex, always raises the question, "What is 'home' anyway?"[34] Deeply concerned with this question, Ford's Westerns ask whether it is possible to actually go H-O-M-E (to that perfect place where one may find the Absolute Good). Can that place be found, as it is depicted at the conclusion of *Cheyenne Autumn*, or is the individual's homecoming yet another expression of the American Dream, something to be pursued but never attained?

The darkening of Ford's vision in his postwar Westerns and war movies, often linked by his commentators to what they see as America's loss of innocence and coming of age during the Second World War, is part of the veteran's homecoming experience. Ford could not ignore Hollywood's sordid corporate greed or the effect of the Cold War on his fellow film industry workers when he returned home. Arguably, the onset of the Cold War in America kept Ford, like many veterans, in combat mode, and thereby sharpened the work of the man whom Andrew Sarris describes as "America's cinematic poet laureate."[35] In complete command of his medium after the Second World War, this master filmmaker's touch was so deft that only a few strokes were needed to create his vision of the American Character, present the nation as an ideal waiting to be realized, or forward his critique of corporate America.

A virtuoso, Ford never lost sight of the fact that the Americana he created was but a dream. At night, Ford commented on every factual and dramatic inaccuracy while watching *The Battle of the Bulge* (1965) on television with his grandson Tim, while printing his own legend with his grandson Dan during the day.[36] In 1971, at the Venice Film Festival, after receiving the Grand Lion of Venice award, Ford told reporters that he "worked out" every day in his swimming pool, that he "was never feeling better," and that he had "half a dozen projects in the works": as Dan Ford recalls, "None of it was true."[37]

John Martin Feeney died peacefully at 6:35 p.m. on August 31, 1973, but John Ford continues to live on in his work. His Westerns and war stories will always be an important part of our conversations about American film and culture because, like their picture-maker, they do not provide their viewers with easy answers—their images of America provoke praise and condemnation, admiration and attack, nostalgia and criticism. As long as America continues to be dreamed into being, Ford and his work will continue to be relevant to her audiences. As Eyman observes, "like Tom Joad " John Ford is "all around us in the dark."[38]

Fittingly, Ford wanted to be remembered for his work, not his personal peccadillos. Tellingly, at the end of his life, Katharine Hepburn observed that life for John Feeney "in actuality had been an extremely tough experience" because he was "sensitive to a great many things that people would never suspect [him] to being sensitive about." Sitting at his bedside in Palm Springs, she remarks that the dying man she is visiting had been "torn apart by a great number of things." It is only then that John Ford, director, patriot, and critic, after a very long and carefully considered pause, replies to her with total conviction and complete honesty—it is only then, speaking also for John Feeney, that he says, "I think that's true. Yeah."[39]

NOTES

INTRODUCTION

1. John Wayne to Dan Ford, Tape 80, Ford, J. Mss., Lilly Library, Indiana University, Bloomington.

2. Carl Jung, "Concerning Rebirth," in *Collected Works of C.G. Jung*, volume 9, part I: The Archetypes and the Collective Unconscious (New York: Routledge, 1969), 221.

3. "Hollywood's Calmest Man Gets Action," *Picture Show*, The Associated Press Feature Service, 21 January 1939.

4. Bertrand Tavernier, "Notes of a Press Attaché: John Ford in Paris," in *John Ford: Interviews*, ed. Gerald Peary (Jackson: University of Mississippi Press, 2001), 109.

5. Scott Eyman, *Print the Legend: The Life and Times of John Ford* (New York: Simon & Schuster, 1999), 565.

6. Ibid.

7. Ibid.

8. Ibid.

9. Ibid.

10. Joseph McBride, *Searching for John Ford: A Life* (New York: Faber and Faber, 2003), 5.

11. Olive Carey, the wife of Harry Carey Sr. and mother of Harry Carey Jr., made her acting debut in Edwin S. Porter's *Tess of the Storm* (1914). In 1916, she married Harry Carey Sr., the popular Western actor who gave John Ford his start as a director, and retired from films to become a homemaker. The Careys and John Ford remained close friends after their professional careers parted. After Harry Carey Sr. died in 1947, Olive returned to the screen, acting

in many of Ford's movies. Her son, Harry Carey Jr., who also appeared in many of John Ford's postwar movies, was also a member of Ford's Stock Company.

12. McBride, *Searching for John Ford*, 5–6.

13. Ibid., 6.

14. John Ford to Dan Ford, Tape 21, Ford, J. Mss., Lilly Library, Indiana University, Bloomington.

15. McBride, *Searching For John Ford*, 31–32.

16. John Ford to Dan Ford, Tape 21, Ford, J. Mss., Lilly Library, Indiana University, Bloomington.

17. Katharine Hepburn to John Ford, Tape 50, Ford, J. Mss., Lilly Library, Indiana University, Bloomington.

18. Tavernier, "Notes of a Press Attaché," 107.

19. McBride, *Searching For John Ford*, 649.

20. Tavernier, "Notes of a Press Attaché," 108.

21. Eyman, *Print the Legend*, 567.

22. Ibid., 17.

23. Ibid., 18.

24. Jean Narboni and Andre S. LaBarthe, "Filmmakers of Our Time: The Twilight of John Ford," in *John Ford: Interviews*, ed. Gerald Peary (Jackson: University of Mississippi Press, 2001), 76.

25. Kay Gardella, "A Very Special Tribute to a Very Special Guy," in *John Ford: Interviews*, ed. Gerald Peary (Jackson: University of Mississippi Press, 2001), 144. At the time of Gardella's interview with John Ford, he was also watching his own movies and fascinated by Spaghetti Westerns on late night television.

26. Desiderius Erasmus, "Praise of Folly," in *Praise of Folly and Letter for Maarten Van Dorp, 1515* (London: Penguin Books, 1971), 104.

27. McBride, *Searching For John Ford*, 5.

28. Steven Spielberg, Brian Grazer, and Ron Howard, "John Ford," https://www.youtube.com/watch?v=tfiCdpmuFUE.

29. Ibid.

30. Spielberg discussing John Ford in a clip from the AFI Archive, https://www.youtube.com/watch?v=DfUw4SN1Nig.

31. Dan Ford, *Pappy: The Life of John Ford* (New York: Da Capo Press, 1979), 7.

32. Ibid., 7.

33. John Wayne to Dan Ford, Tape 75, Ford, J. Mss., Lilly Library, Indiana University, Bloomington.

34. Gaylyn Studlar, "Sacred Duties, Poetic Passions," in *John Ford Made Westerns: Filming the Legend in the Sound Era*, ed. Gaylyn Studlar and Matthew Bernstein (Bloomington: Indiana University Press, 2001), 47.

35. Ibid.

36. Cynthia J. Miller and A. Bowdoin Van Riper, "Introduction," in *Undead in the West II: They Just Keep Coming* (Lanham, Md.: Scarecrow Press, 2013), xviii–xix.

37. Ibid., 3. Further, Slotkin comments on page 5 of *Regeneration through Violence* that American settlers viewed the Western frontier as an opportunity to "regenerate their fortunes, their spirits, and the power of their church and nation; but the means to that regeneration ultimately became the means of violence, and the myth of regeneration through violence became the structuring metaphor of the American experience."

38. Jonathan Shay, *Odysseus in America: Combat Trauma and the Trials of Homecoming* (New York: Scribner, 2002), 76.

39. Dan Ford to Katharine Hepburn, Tape 51, Ford, J. Mss., Lilly Library, Indiana University, Bloomington.

40. Katharine Hepburn to Dan Ford, Tape 51, Ford, J. Mss., Lilly Library, Indiana University, Bloomington.

I. A CAREER MAN

1. Katharine Hepburn to Dan Ford, Tape 50, Ford, J. Mss., Lilly Library, Indiana University, Bloomington.

2. Excellent considerations of Ford's work, among them Tag Gallagher's *John Ford: The Man and His Films*, Joseph McBride's *Searching for John Ford: A Life*, Scott Eyman's *The Life and Times of John Ford*, Ronald L. Davis's *John Ford: Hollywood's Old Master*, and Andrew Sinclair's *John Ford*, have traced the events of his life and concentrated on his Irish American origins while examining and commenting on his silent films, his successful transition to sound in the film industry, his Second World War documentaries and movies, and his films released during the 1950s and 1960s.

3. Andrew Sarris, *The John Ford Movie Mystery* (Bloomington: Indiana University Press), 18.

4. *Becoming John Ford*, DVD, directed by Nick Redman (Denver, Colo.: Boston Road Productions, 2007).

5. *Becoming John Ford.*

6. Katharine Hepburn to John Ford, Tape 49, Ford, J. Mss., Lilly Library, Indiana University, Bloomington.

7. John Ford to Katharine Hepburn, Tape 49, Ford, J. Mss., Lilly Library, Indiana University, Bloomington.

8. John Ford to Dan Ford, Tape 51, Ford, J. Mss., Lilly Library, Indiana University, Bloomington.

9. John Ford to Dan Ford, Tape 21, Ford, J. Mss., Lilly Library, Indiana University, Bloomington.

10. Katharine Hepburn to John Ford, Tape 50, Ford, J. Mss., Lilly Library, Indiana University, Bloomington.

11. Dan Ford, *Pappy: The Life of John Ford* (New York: Da Capo Press, 1979), 158.

12. Katharine Hepburn to John Ford, Tape 49, Ford, J. Mss., Lilly Library, Indiana University, Bloomington.

13. Katharine Hepburn to John Ford, Tape 49, Ford, J. Mss., Lilly Library, Indiana University, Bloomington.

14. Katharine Hepburn to John Ford, Tape 51, Ford, J. Mss., Lilly Library, Indiana University, Bloomington.

15. John Ford to Dan Ford, Tape 51, Ford, J. Mss., Lilly Library, Indiana University, Bloomington.

16. Ford, *Pappy*, 106.

17. Ibid.

18. Ford bought the *Araner*, a 110-foot ketch, in 1934 as a way of escaping from the pressures involved in filmmaking.

19. C. G. Jung, *Two Essays on Analytical Psychology* (New York: Pantheon 1953), 190.

20. John Wayne to Dan Ford, Tape 75, Ford, J. Mss., Lilly Library, Indiana University, Bloomington.

21. *Becoming John Ford.*

22. Harry Carey Jr., *The Company of Heroes: My Life as an Actor in the John Ford Stock Company* (New York: Taylor Trade, 2013), 178.

23. John Wayne to Dan Ford, Tape 75, Ford, J. Mss., Lilly Library, Indiana University, Bloomington.

24. Peter Bogdanovich, *John Ford* (Berkeley: University of California Press, 1978), 108.

25. Walter Wagner, "One More Hurrah," in *John Ford: Interviews*, ed. Gerald Peary (Jackson: University of Mississippi Press, 2001), 152–53.

26. Ibid., 158.

27. Ibid.

28. Ibid.

29. *Becoming John Ford.*

30. Mary Ford to Dan Ford, Tape 41, Ford, J. Mss., Lilly Library, Indiana University, Bloomington.

31. William Clothier to Dan Ford, Tape 13, Ford, J. Mss., Lilly Library, Indiana University, Bloomington.

32. John Wayne to Dan Ford, Tape 39, Ford, J. Mss., Lilly Library, Indiana University, Bloomington.

33. Bogdanovich, *John Ford*, 19.

34. Charles J. Maland, "From Aesthete to Pappy: The Evolution of John Ford's Public Reputation," in *John Ford Made Westerns*, ed. Gaylyn Studlar and Matthew Bernstein (Bloomington: Indiana University Press, 2001), 223.

35. Ford, *Pappy*, 218.

36. Frank S. Nugent. "Hollywood's Favorite Rebel," in *John Ford Made Westerns*, ed. Gaylyn Studlar and Matthew Bernstein (Bloomington: Indiana University Press, 2001), 235.

37. Ibid.

38. See Joseph McBride's *Searching for John Ford: A Life*, Tag Gallagher's *John Ford: The Man and His Films*, Ron L. Davis's *John Ford: Hollywood's Old Master*, Peter Bogdanovich's *John Ford*, and Andrew Sinclair's *John Ford*.

39. "Hollywood's Calmest Man Gets Action," *Picture Show*, January 21, 1939, Weekly Picture Page.

40. Ibid.

41. Ibid.

42. Ibid.

43. Ibid.

44. Ford, *Pappy*, 87.

45. Ibid., 101.

46. Ibid., 102.

47. Ibid.

48. Ibid., 86.

49. Joseph McBride, *Searching for John Ford: A Life* (New York: Faber and Faber, 2003), 603.

50. John Ford to Dan Ford, Tape 21, Ford, J. Mss., Lilly Library, Indiana University, Bloomington.

51. John Wayne to Dan Ford, Tape 39, Ford, J. Mss., Lilly Library, Indiana University, Bloomington.

52. Katharine Hepburn to Dan Ford, Tape 49, Ford, J. Mss., Lilly Library, Indiana University, Bloomington.

53. Carey, *Company of Heroes*, 100.

54. Ibid., 125.

55. John Wayne to Dan Ford, folder 15, box 12, Ford, J. Mss., Lilly Library, Indiana University, Bloomington.

56. Carey, *Company of Heroes*, 56.

57. Ibid., 59.

58. Ibid., 185.

59. Ibid., 181.

60. Ibid., 180.

61. Ibid., 78.

62. Ibid., 47.

63. Ibid., 181, 180.

64. Ibid., 22.

65. Ibid., 21.

66. Ibid.

67. John Ford to Dan Ford, Tape 31, Ford, J. Mss., Lilly Library, Indiana University, Bloomington.

68. Carey, *Company of Heroes*, 193.

69. Ibid., 5.

70. "Twinkle Twinkle Little Star," *Variety*, October 25, 1948, 24.

71. Ibid.

72. Ben Johnson to Dan Ford, Tape 60, Ford, J. Mss., Lilly Library, Indiana University, Bloomington.

73. John Ford to Dan Ford, Tape 31, Ford, J. Mss., Lilly Library, Indiana University, Bloomington.

74. Andrew Sarris, *The John Ford Mystery Movie* (Bloomington: Indiana University Press, 1983), 12.

75. George F. Custen, *Twentieth Century's Fox: Darryl F. Zanuck and the Culture of Hollywood* (New York: Basic Books, 1997), 228.

76. Ibid., 228–29.

77. Ibid.

78. Kay Gardella, "A Very Special Tribute to a Very Special Guy," in *John Ford: Interviews*, ed. Gerald Peary (Jackson: University of Mississippi Press, 2001), 144.

79. Eric Leguèbe, "John Ford," in *John Ford: Interviews*, ed. Gerald Peary (Jackson: University of Mississippi Press, 2001), 74.

80. Mel Gussow, *Don't Say Yes Until I Finish Talking* (London: W.H. Allen, 1971), 94.

81. Custen, *Twentieth Century's Fox*, 371.

82. Gussow, *Don't Say Yes Until I Finish Talking*, 97.

83. Ibid., 74–75.

84. Custen, *Twentieth Century's Fox*, 374.

85. Emanuel Eisenberg, "John Ford: Fighting Irish," in *John Ford: Interviews*, ed. Gerald Peary (Jackson: University of Mississippi Press, 2001), 12.

86. Michel Mok, "The Rebels, If They Stay Up This Time, Won't Be Sorry for Hollywood's Trouble," in *John Ford: Interviews*, ed. Gerald Peary (Jackson: University of Mississippi Press, 2001), 23.

87. Rudy Behlmer, *Memo from Darryl F. Zanuck: The Golden Years at Twentieth Century-Fox* (New York: Grove Press, 1993), 105.

88. Custen, *Twentieth Century's Fox*, 235.

89. Gussow, *Don't Say Yes Until I Finish Talking*, 92.

90. Custen, *Twentieth Century's Fox*, 239.

91. Ibid., 374.

92. Ibid., 260.

93. Ibid., 4.

94. Wagner, "One More Hurrah," 158.

95. Ford, *Pappy*, 136.

96. Ibid., 193.

97. Scott Eyman, *Print the Legend: The Life and Times of John Ford* (New York: Simon and Schuster, 1999), 556.

98. Custen, *Twentieth Century's Fox*, 67.

99. Ford, *Pappy*, 112.

100. Custen, *Twentieth Century's Fox*, 171.

101. Ford, *Pappy*, 103.

102. Mary Ford to Dan Ford, Tape 41, Ford, J. Mss., Lilly Library, Indiana University, Bloomington.

103. Ford, *Pappy*, 103.

104. Ibid.

105. Custen, *Twentieth Century's Fox*, 200.

106. Ibid.

107. Ibid., 223.

108. Ibid.

109. Ford, *Pappy*, 212.

110. Eyman, *Print the Legend*, 315.

111. Ibid.

112. Ford, *Pappy*, 206.

113. Ibid., 207.

114. Custen, *Twentieth Century's Fox*, 264.

115. Ford, *Pappy*, 206.

116. Ibid., 211.

117. Custen, *Twentieth Century's Fox*, 265.

118. Ibid.

119. Dan Ford to John Wayne, Tape 39, Ford, J. Mss., Lilly Library, Indiana University, Bloomington.

120. Ford's letter to Thomas A. Dawson in Ronald L. Davis, *John Ford: Hollywood's Old Master* (Norman: University of Oklahoma Press, 1995), 236.

121. McBride, *Searching for John Ford*, 413.

122. In 1946, Ford used the money that he received for directing *They Were Expendable* to create Field Photo Home near Encino in the San Fernando Valley. A recreation center for the 180 men who had served with the Field Photographic Unit of the OSS during the Second World War, Field Photo Home was also a memorial to the memories of the thirteen men in the Field Photographic Unit who had been killed during the war. For more information see Davis, *John Ford*, 177–78.

123. McBride, *Searching for John Ford*, 421.

124. Ibid., 417.

125. For more information regarding Custen's discussion of how Zanuck's creation of Twentieth Century-Fox's studio house image was transmitted to its products, see page 81 in *Twentieth Century's Fox*.

126. McBride, *Searching for John Ford*, 421.

127. As Roland Barthes in *Camera Lucida* would agree, details of the visual dialectic within Ford's presentations of an idealized West that appear after the Second World War disturb its surface unity and stability, opening his subjects to critical analysis.

128. John Ford to Dan Ford, Tape 49, Ford, J. Mss., Lilly Library, Indiana University, Bloomington.

129. Katharine Hepburn to Dan Ford, Tape 49, Ford, J. Mss., Lilly Library, Indiana University, Bloomington.

130. Leguèbe, "John Ford," 72.

2. EARLY DAYS IN THE HOLLYWOOD WEST

1. Custen, *Twentieth Century's Fox*, 82.

2. Ford, *Pappy*, 14.

3. Olive Carey to Dan Ford, Tape 11, Ford, J. Mss., Lilly Library, Indiana University, Bloomington.

4. Ford, *Pappy*, 19.

5. Sarris, *The John Ford Movie Mystery*, 20–21.

6. Eyman, *Print the Legend*, 55.

7. Ibid.

8. Tom Paulus, "'If You Can Call It An Art,'" in *Ford in Focus: Essays on the Filmmaker's Life and Work*, ed. Kevin L. Stoehr and Michael C. Connolly (Jefferson, N.C.: McFarland, 2008), 136.

9. Eyman, *Print the Legend*, 498.

10. Ibid., 18.

11. Ibid., 61.

12. Ibid., 60.

13. Mark Haggard, "Ford in Person," in *John Ford: Interviews*, ed. Gerald Peary (Jackson: University Press of Mississippi, 2001), 134.

14. Bogdanovich, *John Ford*, 40.

15. Ibid.

16. Ford, *Pappy*, 21.

17. Ibid., 20.

18. Ibid., 27.

19. Richard Ashton, "The Silent Years: A Chronology," in *Ford at Fox* (Los Angeles: Twentieth Century Fox Home Entertainment LLC, 2007), 27.

20. George Mitchell, "Ford on Ford," in *John Ford: Interviews*, ed. Gerald Peary (Jackson: University Press of Mississippi, 2001), 66.

21. Ibid., 65.

22. Ibid.

23. Ford, *Pappy*, 30.

24. Ashton, "The Silent Years," 29.

25. Ford, *Pappy*, 32, 34.

26. Ibid., 32.

27. Ibid., 32–33.

28. Mitchell, "Ford on Ford," 66.

29. Ibid.

30. Barbara Novak, *Nature and Culture: American Landscape and Painting, 1825–1875* (New York: Oxford University Press, 1980), 38.

31. Ibid., 34.

32. Ibid., 35.

33. Ibid., 41.

34. Howard Sharpe, "The Star Creators of Hollywood," in *John Ford: Interviews*, ed. Gerald Peary (Jackson: University Press of Mississippi, 2001), 18.

35. Ford, *Pappy*, 34.

36. Eyman, *Print the Legend*, 91.

3. THE HEROIC WEST

1. George J. Mitchell, "Ford on Ford," in *John Ford: Interviews*, ed. Gerald Peary (Jackson: University Press of Mississippi, 2001), 66.

2. Ibid., 95.

3. Richard Ashton, "The Silent Years: A Chronology," in *Ford at Fox* (Los Angeles: Twentieth Century Fox Entertainment LLC, 2007), 32.

4. McBride, *Searching for John Ford*, 157.

5. Ibid.

6. Ibid.

7. Ford, *Pappy*, 39.

8. Tom Paulus, "'If You Can Call It An Art . . . ': Pictorial Style in John Ford's Universal Westerns (1917–18)," in *John Ford in Focus: Essays on the Filmmaker's Life and Work*, ed. Kevin L. Stoehr and Michael C. Connolly (Jefferson, N.C.: McFarland and Company, 2008), 135–36.

9. Barbara Novak, *Nature and Culture: American Landscape and Painting, 1825–1875* (New York: Oxford University Press, 1980), 184.

10. Graham Clarke, *The Photograph* (New York: Oxford University Press, 1997), 58.

11. Ibid., 60.

12. Ralph Waldo Emerson, "The Over-Soul," in *The Selected Writings of Ralph Waldo Emerson*, ed. Brooks Atkinson (New York: Modern Library, 1950), 263. Cited in Novak, *Nature and Culture*, 43.

13. Andrew Sinclair, *John Ford* (New York: Dial Press, 1979), 41.

14. Ford, *Pappy*, 38.

15. Eyman, *Print the Legend*, 106.

16. Mitchell, "Ford on Ford," 62–63.

17. Sinclair, *John Ford*, 40.

18. In McBride, *Searching for John Ford*, 247.

19. Ibid., 281.

20. Ibid., 282.

21. Ibid.

22. Ibid., 283.

23. Ibid., 283, 283–84.

24. Richard Slotkin, *Regeneration through Violence: The Mythology of the American Frontier, 1600–1860* (Norman: University of Oklahoma Press, 1973), 5.

25. Mary Ford to Dan Ford, Tape 41, Ford, J. Mss., Lilly Library, University of Indiana, Bloomington.

26. Richard Slotkin, *Gunfighter Nation: The Myth of the Frontier in Twentieth-Century America* (New York: Atheneum, 1992), 304.

27. Ibid., 159.

28. Tag Gallagher, *John Ford: The Man and His Films* (Berkeley: University of California Press, 1986), 147.

29. Bill Libby, "The Old Wrangler Rides Again," *Cosmopolitan*, March 1964, 56.

30. Michel Guillaume Jean de Crèvecoeur, *Letters from an American Farmer*, introduction and notes by Warren Barton Blake, http://www.gutenberg.org/cache/epub/4666/pg4666.html.

31. McBride, *Searching for John Ford*, 289.

32. Novak, *Nature and Culture*, 78.

33. As Edward Morris points out in *Constable's Clouds: Paintings and Cloud Studies by John Constable* (Edinburgh: National Galleries of Scotland, 2006), chiaroscuro depends primarily on the nature and position of the source of the light. Whatever the source of light and shadow giving the illusion of solidity and recession, in a landscape, "it is the clouds, as they partially or wholly obscure the sun that control the nature and fall of the light and thus also the chiaroscuro of the landscape" (10). John Constable remarks in his third lecture on the history of landscape painting (given at the Royal Institution in London on June 9, 1836) that "Chiaroscuro is by no means confined to dark pictures. . . . It may be defined as that power which creates space; we may find it everywhere and at all times in nature; opposition, union, light, shade, reflection and refraction, all contribute to it. By this power, the moment we come into a room, we see that the chairs are not standing on the tables, but a glance shows the relative distances of all the objects form the eye, although the darkest or the lightest may be the furthest off" (9).

34. Zanuck on Ford in Mel Gussow's *Darryl F. Zanuck: A Biography* (London: W. H. Allen, 1971), 163–64.

35. Courtney Fellion, "On Death's Horizon: Wandering Spirits and Otherworldly Landscapes in Western Art and Cinema," in *Undead in the West II*, ed. Cynthia J. Miller and A. Bowdoin Van Riper (Lanham, Md.: Scarecrow Press, 2013), 68, 69.

36. Ibid., 69.

37. McBride, *Searching for John Ford*, 285.

38. Ibid., 22.

39. Michel Mok, "The Rebels, If They Stand Up This Time, Won't Be Sorry for Hollywood's Trouble," in *John Ford: Interviews*, ed. Gerald Peary (Jackson: University of Mississippi Press, 2001), 22.

40. Ibid., 21.

41. Gallagher, *John Ford*, 152.

42. Christopher Flynn, *Americans in British Literature, 1770–1832: A Breed Apart* (Farnham, Surrey: Ashgate Publishing, 2008), 83.

43. Crèvecoeur, "Letter III," *Letters from an American Farmer*.

44. Robert C. Sickels, "Beyond the Blessings of Civilization: John Ford's *Stagecoach* and the Myth of the Western Frontier," in *John Ford in Focus: Essays on the Filmmaker's Life and Work*, ed. Kevin L. Stoehr and Michael C. Connolly (Jefferson, N.C.: McFarland and Company, 2008), 152.

45. Edward Buscombe, "Painting the Legend," in *John Ford Made Westerns*, ed. Gaylyn Studlar and Matthew Bernstein (Bloomington: Indiana University Press, 2001), 163.

46. Libby, "The Old Wrangler Rides Again," 56.

47. Buscombe, "Painting the Legend,"156.

48. Mitchell, "Ford on Ford," 56.

49. Buscombe, "Painting the Legend," 158.

50. Ibid.

51. McBride, *Searching for John Ford*, 449.

52. Libby, "The Old Wrangler Rides Again," 58.

53. Buscombe, "Painting the Legend," 166.

54. Libby, "The Old Wrangler Rides Again," 56.

55. Ronald L. Davis, *John Ford: Hollywood's Old Master* (Norman: University of Oklahoma Press, 1995), 103.

56. Ford, *Pappy*, 134.

57. McBride, *Searching for John Ford*, 285.

58. Gary L. Bloomfield and Arlen C. Davidson, *Duty, Honor, Applause: America's Entertainers in World War II* (Guilford, Conn.: The Lyons Press, 2004), 18. For details about European directors, writers, composers, and actors who fled to America during the 1930s, see Bloomfield and Davidson's excellent discussion on pages 14 to 18.

59. Mark Harris, *Five Came Back* (New York: Penguin Press, 2014), 88.

60. Ibid., 17.

61. Rudy Behlmer, *Memo from Darryl F. Zanuck: The Golden Years at Twentieth Century-Fox* (New York: Grove Press, 1993), 16.

62. Harris, *Five Came Back*, 16.

63. Alan Gevison, ed., *Within Our Gates: Ethnicity in American Feature Films, 1911–1960* (Oakland: University of California Press, 1997), 223.

64. Harris, *Five Came Back*, 58–59.

65. Bosley Crowther, review of *The Long Voyage Home* (Twentieth Century-Fox movie) *New York Times*, October 9, 1940, http://www.nytimes.com/movie/review?res=9F05EED9103EE432A2575AC0A9669D946193D6CF.

66. Harris, *Five Came Back*, 68.

67. Bosley Crowther, review of *A Yank in the R.A.F.* (Twentieth Century-Fox movie) *New York Times*, November 12, 1941, http://www.nytimes.com/movie/review?res=9900E7D7163DE333A25751C1A9679D946093D6CF.

68. *Variety*, July 7, 1941.

69. Harris, *Five Came Back*, 88.

70. Ibid.

71. Bogdanovich, *John Ford*, 80.

72. Darryl F. Zanuck to John Ford, Twentieth Century-Fox Inter-Office Correspondence, January 25, 1941, Ford, J. Mss, Lilly Library, Indiana University, Bloomington.

73. Ibid.

74. Darryl F. Zanuck to John Ford, Letter, War Department, January 27, 1941, Ford, J. Mss., Lilly Library, Indiana University, Bloomington.

75. Ford, *Pappy*, 162.
76. Mary Ford to Dan Ford, Tape 42, Ford, J. Mss., Lilly Library, Indiana University, Bloomington.
77. Ibid.

4. NOT FOR SELF BUT FOR COUNTRY

1. Bogdanovich, *John Ford*, 45.
2. *Becoming John Ford*, DVD, dir. by Nick Redman (Twentieth Century Fox Home Entertainment, 2007).
3. Ibid.
4. Ibid.
5. McBride, *Searching for John Ford*, 172.
6. Gallagher, *John Ford*, 64.
7. Ibid., 64–65.
8. Ibid., 66.
9. Ibid., 68.
10. Ibid., 67.
11. Ibid., 69.
12. McBride, *Searching for John Ford*, 173.
13. Ford, *Pappy*, 74.
14. John Ford (Lieutenant Commander USNR) to Capt. Elias Zacharias, USN, Report, undated, Ford, J. Mss., Lilly Library, Indiana University, Bloomington.
15. Ibid.
16. Ford, *Pappy*, 76.
17. Gallagher, *John Ford*, 98.
18. Ibid., 216.
19. Ibid., 98.
20. McBride, *Searching for John Ford*, 308.
21. Ibid., 306.
22. Gordon S. Wood, *Empire of Liberty: A History of the Early Republic,1789–1815* (New York: Oxford University Press, 2009), 45.
23. Ibid.
24. Ibid.
25. Ibid., 288.
26. Ibid., 10–11.
27. Ibid., 10.
28. Ibid., 13.
29. Ford, *Pappy*, 7.

30. McBride, *Searching for John Ford*, 308.

31. *Becoming John Ford*.

32. Ford, *Pappy*, 36.

33. Ibid., 164.

34. The first Allied airstrike over Japan, the Doolittle raid, occurred on April 19, 1942. For more information regarding the Doolittle Raid see Harris, *Five Came Back*, 109–10.

5. IN THE NAVY

1. John Ford, Letter, January 19, 1942, Ford, J. Mss., Lilly Library, Indiana University, Bloomington.

2. McBride, *Searching for John Ford*, 358.

3. Directed by John Ford and Gregg Toland, *December 7th* is a docudrama that charts the Japanese invasion of Pearl Harbor, showcasing the sinking of the *Arizona*, the bombing of Hickam Field, and the reconstruction of the American fleet.

4. McBride, *Searching for John Ford*, 358.

5. Ibid., 359.

6. Ibid., 360.

7. Eyman, *Print the Legend*, 258–59.

8. Ibid.

9. Louella O. Parsons, "Midway Raid Shrapnel Hits Film Director," *Los Angeles Examiner*, June 19, 1942, 1.

10. McBride, *Searching for John Ford*, 363.

11. Ibid., 364.

12. Gallagher, *John Ford*, 206–7.

13. McBride, *Searching for John Ford*, 364.

14. Ibid., 361.

15. Ibid.

16. Ibid.

17. John Ford, "Reflections on the Battle of Midway: An Interview with John Ford (August 17, 1943)," in *John Ford in Focus: Essays on the Filmmaker's Life and Work*, ed. Kevin L. Stoehr and Michael C. Connolly (Jefferson, N.C.: McFarland, 2008), 103. Also see *Recollections of Commander John Ford, USNR Adapted from Commander John Ford USNR interview in box 10 of World War II Interviews, Operational Archives Branch, Naval Historical Center*, http://www.history.navy.mil/research/histories/oral-histories/wwii/battle-of-midway/john-ford-remembers-filming-battle-of-midway.html.

18. Present at Midway Island was "the Marine Sixth Defense Battalion, commanded by Lt. Col. Harold D. Shannon, [and] reinforced by part of the Second Raider Battalion, which had equipment for meeting a mechanized landing." See *Combat Narratives: Battle of Midway, June 3–6, 1942. US Confidential—British Secret* (Washington, D.C.: Publication Section, Combat Intelligence Branch, Office of Naval Intelligence, United States Navy, 1943), https://archive.org/details/BattleOfMidwayJune1942.

19. Ibid., 7.

20. Ibid., 8.

21. Ibid.

22. Ibid., 6.

23. Ford, "Reflections on the Battle of Midway," 107.

24. *Combat Narratives: Battle of Midway*.

25. *ExO Marine Aircraft Group 22. Action Report, June 7, 1942*, 8. Available at http://www.midway1942.org/docs/usn_doc_15.shtml.

26. Ibid.

27. Ibid.

28. Ibid.

29. McBride, *Searching for John Ford*, 360.

30. Ibid., 361.

31. Vincent Casaregola, *Theatres of War: America's Perceptions of World War II* (New York: Palgrave Macmillan, 2009), 52.

32. Ford, *Pappy*, 171.

33. Ibid., 171.

34. McBride, *Searching for John Ford*, 362.

35. Robert J. Mrazek, *A Dawn Like Thunder: The True Story of Torpedo Squadron 8* (New York: Back Bay Books, 2008), 180.

36. Spruance to Nimitz, Report, 16 June 1942, Action Reports microfilm, reel 3. Also in Craig L. Symonds, "Mitscher and the Mystery of Midway," *Naval History Magazine* 12, no. 3 (June 2012), http://www.usni.org/magazines/navalhistory/2012-05/mitscher-and-mystery-midway.

37. McBride, *Searching for John Ford*, 362.

38. Ibid., 363.

39. Ibid., 383.

40. Ibid., 364.

41. Mrazek, *A Dawn Like Thunder*, 184.

42. Ibid.

43. Ibid.

44. McBride, *Searching for John Ford*, 364.

45. Ibid., 353–54.

46. Ibid., 355.

47. Ibid., 384.

48. Ibid., 361.

49. Gallagher, *John Ford*, 216.

50. Ford, *Pappy*, 178.

6. WAR STORIES

1. McBride, *Searching for John Ford*, 451.

2. Ford, *Pappy*, 192.

3. Ibid., 194.

4. Mark Armistead to Dan Ford, Tape 1, Ford, J. Mss., Lilly Library, Indiana University, Bloomington.

5. Ford, *Pappy*, 197.

6. Rear Admiral Aaron S. Merrill to Charles Cheston, acting director of the OSS, Letter, September 14, 1944, Ford, J. Mss., Lilly Library, Indiana University, Bloomington.

7. Ford, *Pappy*, 198.

8. Ibid., 199.

9. McBride, *Searching for John Ford*, 410.

10. Ibid., 199.

11. Ibid.

12. Ford, *Pappy*, 198.

13. Ibid., 199.

14. Anthony E. Rotundo, *American Manhood: Transformations in Masculinity from the Revolution to the Modern Era* (New York: Harper Collins, 1993), 7.

15. Ford, *Pappy*, 200.

16. Anthony E. Rotundo, "Learning about Manhood: Gender Ideals and the Middle-Class Family in Nineteenth-Century America," in *Manliness and Morality: Middle-Class Masculinity in Britain and America 1800–1940*, ed. J. A. Mangan and James Walvin (New York: Palgrave Macmillan, 1987), 38.

17. Rotundo, *American Manhood*, 38.

18. Mary Ford to Dan Ford, Tape 41, Ford, J. Mss., Lilly Library, Indiana University, Bloomington.

19. Ford, *Pappy*, 178.

20. Rotundo, *American Manhood*, 2.

21. McBride, *Searching for John Ford*, 411.

22. Rotundo, *American Manhood*, 13.

23. McBride, *Searching for John Ford*, 411.

24. Ibid.

25. Ford, *Pappy*, 201.

26. Ibid., 206.

27. Ford, *Pappy*.

28. Ibid.

29. Barbara Ford to Dan Ford, Tape 19, Ford, J. Mss., Lilly Library, Indiana University, Bloomington.

30. Ibid.

31. McBride, *Searching for John Ford*, 477.

32. In William T. Walker, *McCarthyism and the Red Scare: A Reference Guide* (Santa Barbara, Calif.: ABC-CLIO, 2011), 137. Also in William K. Klingaman's *Encyclopedia of the McCarthy Era* (New York: Facts on File, 1996), 431.

33. John Ford to John Wayne, Western Union Telegram, 1 June 1950, Ford, J. Mss., Lilly Library, Indiana University, Bloomington.

34. For more information about *Red Channels* and the Hollywood blacklist, see David Everitt's *A Shadow of Red: Communism and the Blacklist in Radio and Television* (Lanham, Md.: Ivan R. Dee, 2007); Paul Buhle and David Wagner's *Hide in Plain Sight: The Hollywood Blacklistees in Film and Television, 1950–2002* (New York: Palgrave Macmillan, 2003); and Paul Buhle and David Wagner's *Blacklisted: The Film Lover's Guide to the Hollywood Blacklist* (New York: Palgrave Macmillan, 2003).

35. Wingate Smith to Major General Lawton, deputy chief signal officer, Letter, August 2, 1950, Ford, J. Mss., Lilly Library, Indiana University, Bloomington.

36. Ibid.

37. Gallagher, *John Ford*, 277.

38. Frank Capra to John Ford, Letter, December 19, 1951, Ford, J. Mss., Lilly Library, Indiana University, Bloomington.

39. Victor W. Phelps, Colonel, MPC to Frank Capra, Army-Navy-Air Force Personnel Security Board, Letter, December 14, 1951, Ford, J. Mss., Lilly Library, Indiana University, Bloomington.

40. John Ford to Frank Capra, Letter, undated, Ford, J. Mss., Lilly Library, Indiana University, Bloomington.

41. Frank Capra to Ford, Letter, January 14, 1952, Ford, J. Mss., Lilly Library, Indiana University, Bloomington.

42. Dalton Trumbo, *The Time of the Toad: A Study of the Inquisition in America* (London: The Journeyman Press, 1982), 12.

43. John Wayne to Dan Ford, Tape 80, Ford, J. Mss., Lilly Library, Indiana University, Bloomington.

44. Ford, *Pappy*, 269.

45. Gallagher, *John Ford*, 287.

46. John Wayne to Dan Ford, Tape 80, Ford, J. Mss., Lilly Library, Indiana University, Bloomington.

47. *Dulce et decorum est pro patria mori.*

48. Gallagher, *John Ford*, 275.

49. Carey, *The Company of Heroes*, 129.

50. Ibid., 130.

51. Ibid.

52. McBride, *Searching for John Ford*, 538.

53. Ibid., 539.

54. Ibid., 230.

55. A favorite in the Crimean war, the "Garryowen" is an Irish tune that has a long history with the British, Canadian, and American military. The official regimental marching song of Second Regiment of Irish Volunteers, the "Garryowen" is more notably the marching tune of General George Armstrong Custer's 7th Cavalry Regiment.

56. Gallagher, *John Ford*, 1.

57. John Ford to Katharine Hepburn, Tape 51, Ford, J. Mss., Lilly Library, Indiana University, Bloomington.

7. CRITIQUING COMBAT CULTURE

1. Emanuel Eisenberg, "John Ford: Fighting Irish," in *John Ford: Interviews*, ed. Gerald Peary (Jackson: University of Mississippi Press, 2001), 13–14.

2. Ford, *Pappy*, 214.

3. Ibid., 215.

4. McBride, *Searching for John Ford*, 447.

5. Ibid., 447.

6. Bosley Crowther, "*Fort Apache* (1948)," June 25, 1948, *New York Times*, http://www.nytimes.com/movie/review?res= 9B0DE5DA123EE03BBC4D51DFB0668383659EDE.

7. Ford, *Pappy*, 213.

8. Crowther, "*Fort Apache* (1948)."

9. Ibid.

10. Max Westbrook, "The Night John Wayne Danced with Shirley Temple," in *Old West—New West: Centennial Essays*, ed. Barbara Howard Meldrum (Moscow: University of Idaho Press, 1993), 65.

11. Ibid., 69.

12. Ibid., 71–72.

13. Slotkin, *Gunfighter Nation*, 343, 342

14. Ibid., 335.

15. McBride, *Searching for John Ford*, 386–87.

16. Gallagher, *John Ford*, 253.

17. Ford, *Pappy*, 214.

18. Eyman, *Print the Legend,* 341.

19. Gallagher, *John Ford*, 249.

20. Ibid., 253.

21. The Claudian presentation of the picturesque associated with Thursday directs the viewer's eye toward the distant horizon via diagonals created by objects carefully placed in the foreground that flank the lateral sides of the frame and direct the eye inward toward objects placed in the midground and background planes. The Luminist aesthetic, on the other hand, is known for the open lateral sides of its frame. The Luminist school of landscape painting encourages the viewer's eye to move unimpeded from one side of the picture to the other.

22. *Monument Valley: John Ford Country*, DVD (Burbank, California: Warner Home Video, 2007).

23. Ford, *Pappy*, 218.

24. Slotkin, *Gunfighter Nation*, 336.

25. A civilian merchant, a sutler (or victualer) sold provisions and wares to armies in the field, in camp, or in quarters. In *Fort Apache*, Meacham is both an Indian agent and a sutler.

26. Slotkin, *Gunfighter Nation*, 338.

27. Bogdanovich, *John Ford*, 86.

28. E. B. Reilley, *The Amateur's Vademecum* (Philadelphia: J. Nicholas, 1870), 199.

29. Ibid., 199.

30. Ibid.

31. See Mark Twain's description of a Grand March in "Grand Ball at La Plata" from the *Territorial Enterprise* at http://www.territorial-enterprise.com/gr_ball.htm.

32. John Ford to Dan Ford, Tape 51, Ford, J. Mss., Lilly Library, Indiana University, Bloomington.

33. Gallagher, *John Ford*, 249.

34. Slotkin, *Gunfighter Nation*, 455.

35. Russell Campbell, "Fort Apache," *The Velvet Light Trap*, August 1971. Also in McBride, *Searching for John Ford*, 452.

8. KEEPING THE FAITH

1. James Warner Bellah to Dan Ford, Tape 3, Ford, J. Mss., Lilly Library, Indiana University, Bloomington.
2. Ford, *Pappy*, 218.
3. Ibid., 206.
4. Ford, *Pappy*, 206.
5. Ibid., 206–7.
6. Ibid., 207.
7. Ibid. Ford purchased a twenty-acre ranch, known as the Farm, at 18201 Calvert Street in Reseda, California, and created the Field Photo Homes, Inc., for the members of the Field Photographic Unit. The Farm served as a memorial for members of the Field Photo Unit who had died in the war and was also a place where the surviving members of Field Photo (and their families) could maintain their friendships.
8. Ibid.
9. Ibid., 206–8.
10. Ibid., 208.
11. Jonathan Shay, *Odysseus in America: Combat Trauma and the Trials of Homecoming* (New York: Scribner, 2002), 80.
12. Ibid.
13. Ibid.
14. Ibid.
15. Ford, *Pappy*, 208.
16. Shay, *Odysseus in America*, 76.
17. Ford, *Pappy*, 189–90.
18. Harris, *Five Came Back*, 159.
19. Ibid., 199.
20. Ibid., 198.
21. Ibid.
22. Ibid.
23. Shay, *Odysseus in America*, 80.
24. Scott Allen Nollen, *Three Bad Men: John Ford, John Wayne, Ward Bond* (Jefferson, N.C.: McFarland, 2013), 189.
25. Gallagher, *John Ford*, 255.
26. Shay, *Odysseus in America*, 80.
27. Gallagher, *John Ford*, 254.
28. Bill Levy, *Lest We Forget: The John Ford Stock Company* (Duncan, Okla.: BearManor Media, 2013), 93.
29. McBride, *Searching for John Ford*, 460.
30. The Battle of Fredericksburg was fought on December 13, 1862.

31. Available in *Robert E. Lee Quotes* at http://www.sonofthesouth.net/leef-oundation/Notable%20Lee%20Quotes.htm.

32. Jeffrey Richards, "'Passing the Love of Women': Manly Love and Victorian Society," in *Manliness and Morality: Middle-Class Masculinity in Britain and America, 1800–1940*, ed. J. A. Mangan and James Walvin (Manchester: Manchester University Press, 1987), 117.

33. McKubin T. Owens, "Military Ethos and the Politics of 'Don't Ask, Don't Tell,'" http://ashbrook.org/publications/onprin-v8n1-owens/.

34. Shay, *Odysseus in America*, 40–41.

35. Ford, *Pappy*, 229.

36. Shay, *Odysseus in America*, 227.

37. Ibid.

38. Ibid., 158.

39. Ibid., 211.

40. Francis Lieber, *Instructions for the Government of Armies of the United States in the Field* (Washington, D.C.: War Department, Adjutant General's Office, 1863), 4. Also in Shay, *Odysseus in America*, 224.

41. Ford, *Pappy*, 206.

42. James Warner Bellah to Dan Ford, Tape 3, Ford, J. Mss., Lilly Library, Indiana University, Bloomington.

43. William Clothier to Dan Ford, Tape 13, Ford, J. Mss., Lilly Library, Indiana University, Bloomington.

44. Carey, *A Company of Heroes*, 11.

45. Ibid., 13.

46. Vincent A. Transano points this out in "The 7th U.S. Cavalry Regiment Fought in the Battle of the Little Bighorn," http://www.historynet.com/battle-of-little-bighorn.

47. Gregory J. W. Urwin, *The United States Cavalry: An Illustrated History, 1776–1944* (Norman: University of Oklahoma Press, 2003), 114.

48. McBride, *Searching for John Ford*, 459.

49. Ibid., 458.

50. S. L. A. Marshall, *Crimsoned Prairie: The Indian Wars* (Boston: Da Capo Press, 1984), 453.

51. Shay, *Odysseus in America*, 155.

52. Ibid., 80.

53. Gallagher, *John Ford*, 254.

9. THE WAR AT HOME

1. Chuck Roberson, *The Fall Guy* (North Vancouver: Hancock, 1980), 63.

2. Eyman, *Print the Legend*, 390. Scott Eyman points out that Ford shot *Rio Grande* so efficiently that of the 646 individual camera setups involved in making *Rio Grande*, there were only 665 takes.

3. Ibid., 394.

4. Roberson. *The Fall Guy*, 66.

5. Gallagher, *John Ford*, 256.

6. Max Westbrook, "The Night John Wayne Danced with Shirley Temple," *Western American Literature* 25, no. 2 (Summer 1990): 159.

7. Richard Slotkin, *Gunfighter Nation: The Myth of the Frontier in Twentieth-Century America* (New York: Atheneum, 1992), 504. Richard Slotkin identifies the Cold War Western as part of that postwar development in the genre that rationalized, identified, and reconciled democratic values and practices with the imperatives of military power.

8. Frank Wetta and Martin Novelli, "'Romantic, Isn't It, Miss Daindridge?': Sources and Meanings of John Ford's Cavalry Trilogy," *American Nineteenth Century History* 7, no. 2 (June 2006): 300.

9. David Thompson, *The New Biographical Dictionary of Film* (New York: Knopf, 2002), 304–5.

10. Paul Buhle and David Wagner, *Radical Hollywood: The Untold Story Behind America's Favorite Movies* (New York: The New Press, 2002), 138.

11. Wetta and Novelli, "Romantic, Isn't It, Miss Daindridge?" 317.

12. McBride, *Searching for John Ford*, 274.

13. Jörn Glasenapp, "John Ford's Rio Grande: Momism, the Cold War, and the American Frontier," *Zeitschrift für Anglistik und Amerikanistik: A Quarterly of Language, Literature and Culture* 53, no. 3 (2005): 273.

14. Ibid., 274.

15. Lindsay Anderson, *About John Ford* (London: Plexus Publishing, 1981), 122. Also found in Ken Nolley's excellent discussion of Ford's Cavalry Trilogy in "Printing the Legend in the Age of MX: Reconsidering Ford's Military Trilogy," *Literature Film Quarterly* 14, no. 2 (1986): 87.

16. Eyman, *Print the Legend*, 394.

17. McBride, *Searching for John Ford*, 503.

18. John F. Wukovitz, "John Mosby and George Custer Clash in the Shenandoah Valley," *America's Civil War Magazine* (HISTORYNET.com), http://www.civilwar.org/battlefields/thirdwinchester/third-winchester-history-articles/john-mosby-and-george-custer.html.

19. Ibid.

20. Ibid.

21. Robert Doyle, "Part 1: The 'Greening' of the 7th Cavalry" in "Custer's Last Irishmen: The Irish Who Fought at the Battle of The Little Bighorn,"

http://thewildgeese.irish/profiles/blogs/custer-s-last-irishmen-the-irish-who-fought-at-the-battle-of-the.

22. The names York and Yorke in Ireland are usually of immigrant origin, having been brought into the Province of Ulster by settlers who arrived from England, especially during the seventeenth century.

23. Fervent supporters of Irish nationalism, Fenians belonged to the Fenian Brotherhood, an Irish republican organization founded in the United States in 1858 by John O'Mahony.

24. McBride, *Searching for John Ford*, 141. Joseph McBride also comments that it would not have been out of character for Ford to be an occasional contributor and collector of IRA funds during its continuing fight against British control, as Andrew Sinclair claims in *John Ford: A Biography*. Discrepancies in business travel expenses overseas claimed by Ford for income tax purposes in 1921 suggest that he may have been contributing to the flying column of his cousin Martin Feeney. On page 24, McBride notes that Feeney claimed to Dan Ford that "his cousin John had sought him out in the hills to give him food and money."

25. Jack Morgan, *New World Irish: Notes on One Hundred Years of Lives and Letters in American Culture* (New York: Palgrave Macmillan, 2011), 139.

26. Mitchell, "Ford on Ford," 64.

27. Gallagher, *John Ford*, 257.

28. Ibid., 259.

29. Morgan, *New World Irish*, 144.

30. Jack Morgan, "The Irish in John Ford's Seventh Cavalry Trilogy—Victor McLaglen's Stooge-Irish Caricature," *MELUS* 22, no. 2 (Summer 1997): 33–44.

31. Morgan, *New World Irish*, 139.

32. Morgan, "The Irish in John Ford's Seventh Cavalry Trilogy," 33, 35.

33. Ibid., 35.

34. Morgan, *New World Irish*, 139.

35. Ford's historically inaccurate costuming of Quincannon's hat, boots, and breeches makes the sergeant an easily recognizable figure and fulfills his audience's expectations of the appearance of a cavalry sergeant established in *Fort Apache* and *She Wore a Yellow Ribbon*. In the field, Quincannon continues to wear a kepi, not the broad campaign hat. His boots lack the flat heels, square toes, and square cut across the back that distinguished cavalrymen's boots in the 1870s. Insignia of rank was never worn on the men's shirts, but Quincannon's shirts display his top sergeant's stripes. His dark galluses are unusual. The width of the yellow stripe on his breeches that should indicate his rank is incorrect being the same width as the other officers'. Quincannon's horse furniture is also inaccurate, not being a Model 1859 curb bit. For more infor-

mation about the U.S. Cavalry's uniforms and equipment, garrison life, people, and events that inform Ford's Cavalry Trilogy, see Jeffrey C. Prater, Maj. USAF, *John Ford's Cavalry Trilogy: Myth or Reality?* (Fort Leavenworth, Kans.: U.S. Army Command and General Staff College, 1989).

36. Robert Stam, *Subversive Pleasures: Bakhtin, Cultural Criticism, and Film* (Baltimore: Johns Hopkins University Press, 1989), 173.

37. Roberson, *The Fall Guy*, 120.

10. VETERANS' AFFAIRS

1. Portions of this chapter appear in "'Let's Go Home, Debbie': The Matter of blood Pollution, Combat Culture, and Cold War Hysteria in *The Searchers* (1956)," published in *Journal of Popular Film & Television* 39, no.2, and in *Westerns: The Essential Journal of Popular Film and Television Collection*, ed. Gary R. Edgerton and Michael Marsden (New York: Routledge, 2012), and are included with permission.

2. Carey, *The Company of Heroes*, 171.

3. Ford, *Pappy*, 270.

4. Ibid.

5. Eyman, *Print the Legend*, 444.

6. Ibid.

7. Ibid., 446

8. Roberson, *The Fall Guy*, 163.

9. Ibid.

10. Ibid., 164.

11. Ibid., 165.

12. See Eckstein's discussion of the choices made in *Sight and Sound*'s worldwide poll of film critics on page 927 in Roger Ebert's *Ebert's Video Companion*. In 1972, *The Searchers* appeared in *Sight and Sound*'s list of the greatest films ever made. It has been on the list ever since and was named the Greatest American Western ever made by the American Film Institute in 2008.

13. Arthur M. Eckstein, "Darkening Ethan: John Ford's *The Searchers* (1956) from Novel to Screenplay to Screen," *Cinema Journal* 38, no. 1 (1998): 3.

14. References to *The Searchers* also appear in *Major Dundee* (1965), *The Longest Yard* (1974), *The Wind and Lion* (1975), *Jaws* (1975), *Taxi Driver* (1976), *Star Wars* (1977), *Close Encounters of the Third Kind* (1977), *Hardcore* (1979), *Paris, Texas* (1984), *Dances with Wolves* (1990), *Unforgiven* (1992), *Saving Private Ryan* (1998), and *O Brother Where Art Thou?* (2000).

15. Bogdanovich, *John Ford*, 92.

16. Eckstein, "Darkening Ethan," 4.

17. Gallagher, *John Ford*, 337; Phillip J. Skerry, "'What Makes a Man to Wander?' Ethan Edwards of John Ford's *The Searchers*," *New Orleans Review* 18, no. 4 (1991): 86.

18. See Douglas Pye's "Double Vision: Miscegenation and Point of View in *The Searchers*" in *The Book of Westerns*, ed. Douglas Pye and Ian Cameron (New York: Continuum, 1996), 229–35; Joan Dagle's "Linear Patterns and Ethnic Encounters in the Ford Western" in *John Ford Made Westerns: Filming the Legend in the Sound Era*, ed. Gaylyn Studlar and Matthew Bernstein (Bloomington: Indiana University Press, 2001), 102–31; *Carlton Smith's Coyote Kills John Wayne: Postmodernism and Contemporary Fictions of the Transcultural Frontier* (Hanover: University Press of New England, 2000); Marty Roth's "'Yes My Darling Daughter': Gender, Miscegenation, and Generation in John Ford's *The Searchers*," *New Orleans Review* 18, no. 4 (1991): 65–73; Pat Miller's "The Race to Settle America: Nice Guys Do Finish and Last," *Literature Film Quarterly* 29, no. 4 (2001): 315–20; Arthur M. Eckstein's "Darkening Ethan: Jon Ford's *The Searchers* (1956) from Novel to Screenplay to Screen," *Cinema Journal* 38, no. 1 (1998): 3–24; Christian L. Pyle's "'The Injun in Ya': Racial Ambiguity and Historical Ambivalence in *The Searchers*" in *The Image of the American West in Literature, the Media, and Society*, ed. Will Wright and Steven Kaplan (Pueblo: Society for the Interdisciplinary Study of Social Imagery, University of Southern Colorado, 1996), 100–105; Susan Courtney's "Looking for (Race and Gender) Trouble in Monument Valley," *Qui Parle: Literature, Philosophy, Visual Arts, History* 6, no. 2 (1993): 97–30 and "Picturizing Race: Hollywood's Censorship of Miscegenation and Production of Racial Visibility through Imitation of Life," *Genders* 27 (1993): 2–20; and Peter Lehman's "Texas 1868/America 1956: *The Searchers*" in *Close Viewings: An Anthology of New Film Criticism*, ed. Peter Lehman (Tallahassee: Florida State University Press, 1990), 387–415.

19. Marty Roth, "'Yes My Darling Daughter': Gender, Miscegenation, and Generation in John Ford's *The Searchers*," *New Orleans Review* 18, no. 4 (1991): 65.

20. Eckstein, "Darkening Ethan," 3–4.

21. *A Turning of the Earth: John Ford, John Wayne and The Searchers*, directed by Nick Redman (DVD, 1999; Warner Home Video, 2006).

22. Eckstein, "Darkening Ethan, 1.

23. Ibid., 16.

24. Ibid., 3.

25. Shay, *Odysseus in America*, 152.

26. Ibid., 152.

27. W. P. Mahedy, *Out of the Night: The Spiritual Journey of Vietnam Vets* (New York: Ballantine, 1986), 56–57.

28. Shay, *Odysseus in America*, 155. Civil War veterans often wandered for long periods after the war's end and had trouble finding employment.

29. Ibid., 19.

30. Ibid.

31. Ibid., 80.

32. Johnathan Shay, *Achilles in Vietnam: Combat Trauma and the Undoing of Character* (New York: Scribner), 69.

33. Shay, *Odysseus in America*, 80.

34. Ibid.

35. Kathryn Kalinak, "'What Makes a Man to Wander': *The Searchers*," in *How the West Was Sung: Music in the Westerns of John Ford* (Berkeley: University of California Press, 2007), 169.

36. Ibid., 168.

37. Joseph McBride and Michael Wilmington propose that Scar mirrors Ethan's desires in "Prisoner of the Desert," *Sight and Sound* 40, no. 4 (1971).

38. Margaret Visser, "Vengeance and Pollution in Classical Athens," *Journal of the History of Ideas* 45, no. 2 (1984): 194.

39. David A. Gerber, "Heroes and Misfits: The Troubled Social Reintegration of Disabled Veterans in *The Best Years of Our Lives*," *American Quarterly* 46, no. 4 (1994): 547, 549.

40. Ibid., 549–50.

41. Ibid., 548.

42. Ibid., 551.

43. *The Searchers'* listing in the National Film Registry of America is available at http://www.loc.gov/programs/national-film-preservation-board/film-registry/complete-national-film-registry-listing/.

44. Bob Brewin, "Combat Duty in Iraq and Afghanistan, Mental Health Problems of Care," *Government HealthIT*, http://www.govhealthit.com/news/combat-trauma-theater-0.

11. A HOUSE DIVIDED

1. William Clothier to Dan Ford, Tape 13, Ford, J. Mss., Lilly Library, Indiana University, Bloomington.

2. Ford, *Pappy*, 278.

3. Walter, Marvin, and Harold Mirisch founded the Mirisch Company in 1957. Walter Mirisch began producing with Allied Artists in 1947 and was in charge of production there until he founded his successful independent pro-

duction company with his brothers. The Mirisch Company produced sixty-eight motion pictures over seventeen years in an agreement with United Artists. Nominated for seventy-nine Academy Awards, Mirisch films won twenty-three Oscars.

4. Ford, *Pappy*, 280.

5. McBride, *Searching for John Ford*, 595.

6. Davis, *John Ford*, 595.

7. Ibid., 595.

8. See James Hawco's review, "John Ford's *The Horse Soldiers*," http://sensesofcinema.com/2005/feature-articles/horse_soldiers/; Jeffrey M. Anderson's review "Civil Western," http://www.combustiblecelluloid.com/classic/horseold.shtml; Emanuel Levy's review of *The Horse Soldiers* in *Cinema 24/7*, http://emanuellevy.com/review/horse-soldiers-the-1959-4/; and Peter Cavanese's review of *The Horse Soldiers*, http://www.grouchoreviews.com/reviews/4108.

9. Neil Longley York, *The Horse Soldiers and Popular Memory* (Kent, Ohio: Kent State University Press, 2001), 155.

10. Peter Cowie, *John Ford and the American West* (New York: Harry N. Abrahms, 2004), 112.

11. McBride, *Searching for John Ford*, 596.

12. Davis, *John Ford*, 178.

13. Timothy O'Sullivan's Civil War photographs were attributed to his employer, Mathew B. Brady, who insisted "that the photographs he distributed had to be labelled, 'Photo by Brady' no matter who had actually operated the camera. . . . [O'Sullivan] turned down Brady's offer of the job of managing the Washington studio after Appomattox." James D. Horan's *Timothy O'Sullivan: America's Forgotten Photographer* (New York: Bonanza Books, 1964), 2–3.

14. McBride, *Searching for John Ford*, 594.

15. Ibid., 291.

16. Ibid., 599.

17. Ibid.

18. Ibid., 421.

19. Roberson, *The Fall Guy*, 227.

20. Davis, *John Ford*, 293.

21. Ibid., 228.

22. Katharine Hepburn to Dan Ford, Tape 51, Ford, J. Mss., Lilly Library, Indiana University, Bloomington.

23. Ford, *Pappy*, 283.

24. Davis, *John Ford*, 293.

25. Ibid., 294.

26. Ford, *Pappy*, 283.

27. Bogdanovich, *John Ford*, 96.

12. THE NATURE OF ONE'S SERVICE

1. Colin Young, "The Old Dependables," *Film Quarterly* 13, no. 1 (Autumn 1959): 8.

2. Ford, *Pappy*, 284.

3. Howard Smead, *Blood Justice: The Lynching of Mack Charles Parker* (New York: Oxford University Press, 1999), 120.

4. Ford, *Pappy*, 284.

5. Ibid.

6. Ibid., 285.

7. Colin Young, "The Old Dependables," 8.

8. Ibid.

9. Ibid.

10. Ford, *Pappy*, 286.

11. Eyman, *Print the Legend*, 478.

12. McBride, *Searching for John Ford*, 607.

13. Tavernier, "Notes of a Press Attaché," 106.

14. McBride, *Searching for John Ford*, 607.

15. Ibid.

16. Ibid., 610.

17. Jeffrey M. Anderson, "Buffalo Stance," in *Combustible Celluloid*, July 8, 2014, http://www.combustiblecelluloid.com/classic/sgtrut.shtml.

18. Ibid.

19. Frank Manchel, "Losing and Finding John Ford's 'Sergeant Rutledge' (1960)," *Historical Journal of Film, Radio and Television* 17, no. 2 (June 1, 1997): 250–51.

20. William A. Dobak, " Black Regulars on the Frontier," *Wild West* 15, no. 6 (April 2003), http://eds.a.ebscohost.com/eds/results?sid=e6d3994b-8d6c-4b93-a0f6-a863d5991ba0%40sessionmgr4003&vid=0&hid=4213&bquery= black+regulars+on+the+frontier&bdata= JmNsaTA9RlQxJmNsdjA9WSZ0eXBlPTAmc2l0ZT1lZHMtbGl2ZQ%3d%3d.

21. William Loren Katz, *The Black West: A Documentary and Pictoral History of the African American Role in the Westward Expansion of the United States* (New York: Harlem Moon, 2005), 216.

22. Frank Manchel, "The Man Who Made the Stars Shine Brighter: An Interview with Woody Strode," *Black Scholar* 25, no. 2 (1995): 37–39.

23. Charlene Regester, "From the Gridiron and the Boxing Ring to the Cinema Screen: The African-American Athlete in pre-1950 Cinema," *Culture, Sport, Society* 6, nos. 2–3 (2003): 277.

24. Ibid., 279.

25. Sinclair, *John Ford*, 191.

26. Ibid.

27. Ibid.

28. Gallagher, *John Ford*, 341.

29. McBride, *Searching for John Ford*, 665.

30. Ibid.

31. *"Sergeant Rutledge,"* *New York Times*, May 26, 1960, http://www.nytimes.com/movie/review?res=9904E7D8153DE333A25755C2A9639C946191D6CF.

32. Sinclair, *John Ford*, 191.

33. Gallagher, *John Ford*, 373.

34. Ibid., 375.

35. McBride, *Searching for John Ford*, 604.

36. Ford, *Pappy*, 285.

37. Gallagher, *John Ford*, 374.

38. Christian Delage, *Caught on Camera: Film in the Courtroom from the Nuremberg Trials to the Trials of the Khmer Rouge*, ed. and trans. Ralph Schoolcraft and Mary Byrd Kelly (Philadelphia: University of Pennsylvania Press, 2014), 13.

39. Harris, *Five Came Back*, 400–401.

40. Ibid., 402.

41. Ford, *Pappy*, 290.

42. Davis, *John Ford*, 485.

43. Gallagher, *John Ford*, 376.

44. Carey, *A Company of Heroes*, 180.

45. Ibid., 185.

46. Richard Robertson, "New Directions in Westerns of the 1960's and 70's," *Journal of the West* 22, no. 4 (1983): 44.

47. Eugene Archer, "Two Rode Together," *New York Times*, July 27 1961, http://www.nytimes.com/movie/review?res=9E06E2DC1138E03BA15754C2A9619C946091D6CF.

48. Eyman, *Print the Legend*, 486.

49. Ford, *Pappy*, 290

50. Gallagher, *John Ford*, 376.

51. Glenn Frankel, *The Searchers: The Making of an American Legend* (New York: Bloomsbury, 2013), 53.

52. Ibid., 52.

53. Ibid., 32.

54. Ibid.

55. Ibid., 40.

56. Gallagher, *John Ford*, 377.

57. Ibid., 377.

58. Raffaele Donato and Martin Scorsese, "Docufictions: An Interview with Martin Scorsese on Documentary Film," *Film History* 19, no. 2 (2007): 204.

59. Gallagher, *John Ford*, 377.

60. Eyman, *Print the Legend*, 485.

61. Roberson, *The Fall Guy*, 246.

62. Sarris, *The John Ford Movie Mystery*, 151.

63. Ibid., 124, 128.

13. DECONSTRUCTING THE LEGEND

1. Portions of this chapter appear in "John Ford on the Cold War: Stetsons and Cast Shadows in *The Man Who Shot Liberty Valance* (1962)," published in *Journal of Popular Culture* 45, no. 2, and are included with permission.

2. Bogdanovich, *John Ford*, 99.

3. Ford, *Pappy*, 291.

4. McBride, *Searching for John Ford*, 623.

5. Ford, *Pappy*, 293.

6. Ibid.

7. Ibid., 292.

8. Davis, *John Ford*, 307.

9. Ibid., 308.

10. Eyman, *Print the Legend*, 489.

11. Davis, *John Ford*, 309.

12. Ford, *Pappy*, 293.

13. For discussions of misrepresentation in *The Man Who Shot Liberty Valance* (and Ford's other works), see Kent Anderson's "The Man Who Shot Liberty Valance," *Journal of Popular Culture* 39, no. 1 (February 2006): 10–28; Lindsay Anderson's *About John Ford* (New York: McGraw, 1981); John Baxter's *The Cinema of John Ford* (New York: A. S. Barnes, 1971); Peter Bogdanovich's *John Ford*; Stanleye Corkin's *Cowboys as Cold Warriors: The Western and U.S. History* (Philadelphia, PA: Temple University Press, 2004); Peter Cowie's *John Ford and the American West*; Robert Murray Davis's *Playing Cowboys: Low Culture and High Art in the Western* (Norman: University of Oklahoma Press, 1992); Ron Davis's "Paradise among the Monuments: John Ford's Vision of the American West," *Montana Magazine*, Summer 1995a and

John Ford: Hollywood's Old Master; Scott Eyman's *Print the Legend: The Life and Times of John Ford*; Tag Gallagher's *John Ford: The Man and His Films* and "Dialogue"; Gaylyn Studlar and Matthew Bernstein's *John Ford Made Westerns*; Peter Lehman's "An Absence Which Becomes a Legendary Presence: John Ford's Structured Use of Off-Screen Space," Wide Angle 2, no. 4 (1978): 36–42; Bill Libby's "The Old Wrangler Rides Again"; Richard A. Maynard's *The American West on Film: Myth and Reality* (Rochelle Park, NJ: Hayden Book Company, 1974); Joseph McBride and Michael Wilmington's *John Ford* (New York: Da Capo Press, 1975); Walter Metz's "Have You Written a Ford Lately? Gender, Genre, and the Film Adaptations of Dorothy Johnson's Western Literature," *Literature Film Quarterly* 31, no. 3 (2003): 209–20; Alan Nadel's *Containment Culture: American Narratives, Postmodernism, and the Atomic Age* (Durham, NC: Duke University Press, 1995); Douglas Pye's "Genre and History: *Fort Apache* and *The Man Who Shot Liberty Valance*" in *The Book of Westerns*, ed. Ian Cameron and Douglas Pye (New York: Continuum, 1996), 111–22; Mark W. Roche and Vittorio Hösle's "Vico's Age of Heroes and the Age of Men in John Ford's Film *The Man Who Shot Liberty Valance*," *CLIO: A Journal of Literature, History and the Philosophy of History* 23, no. 2 (1994): 131–47; Cheyney Ryan's "Print the Legend: Violence and Recognition in *The Man Who Shot Liberty Valance*" in *Legal Realism: Movies as Legal Text*, ed. John Denvir (Chicago: University of Illinois Press, 1996), 23–43; Andrew Sarris's *Interviews with Film Directors* (New York: Avon, 1967) and *The John Ford Movie Mystery*; Brian Spittles's *John Ford* (Harlow, England: Pearson Education Ltd., 2002); and Mike Yawn and Robert Beatty's "The Frontier of John Ford" in *The Image of the American West in Literature, the Media and Society: Selected Papers*, ed. Will Wright and Steven Kaplan (Pueblo: Society for the Interdisciplinary Study of Social Imagery: University of Southern Colorado, 1996), 113–22.

14. Douglas Pye, "Genre and History: *Fort Apache* and *The Man Who Shot Liberty Valance*," *The Book of Westerns*, ed. Ian Cameron (New York: Continuum; 1996), 122.

15. Mark W. Roche and Vittorio Hösle, "Vico's Age of Heroes and the Age of Men in John Ford's Film *The Man Who Shot Liberty Valance*," *CLIO: A Journal of Literature, History, and the Philosophy of History* 23, no. 2 (1994): 147.

16. Sarris, *The John Ford Movie Mystery*, 46–47.

17. Ibid., 174.

18. Alan Nadel, *Containment Culture: American Narratives, Postmodernism, and the Atomic Age* (Durham, N.C.: Duke University Press, 1995), 159, 166.

19. Gallagher, *John Ford*, 409.

20. Cowie, *John Ford and the American West*, 35.

21. Peter Flynn, "The Silent Western as Mythmaker," *images: a journal of film and popular culture* 6, http://www.imagesjournal.com/issue06/infocus/silentwesterns.htm.

22. Bogdanovich, *John Ford*, 39.

23. Ibid.

24. Ibid., 40.

25. Gary North, *In Defense of the Classic Western*, http://lewrockwell.com/north/north409html.

26. Gary Johnson, "The Western: An Overview," *images: a journal of film and popular culture* 6, http://www.imagesjournal.com/issue06/infocus/western.htm.

27. Daryl Jones, *The Dime Novel Western* (Bowling Green, Ohio: Popular Press, Bowling Green University, 1978), 180.

28. Ibid., 148.

29. Lindsay Anderson, *About John Ford* (New York: McGraw-Hill, 1981), 180.

30. Ibid.

31. Ibid., 181.

32. Ibid.

33. Documentary Film Group, *John Ford Interviews*, ed. Gerald Peary (Jackson: University of Mississippi, 2001), 126.

34. Cowie, *John Ford and the American West*, 191.

35. Ibid.

36. "John F. Kennedy: Inaugural Address," *Inaugural Addresses of the Presidents*, http://www.bartleby.com/124/pres56.html.

37. "The Bay of Pigs Invasion Speech by John F. Kennedy," *Speeches of John F. Kennedy*, John F. Kennedy Presidential Library and Museum, http://www.jfklibrary.org/Historical+Resources/Archives/Reference+Desk/Speeches/JFK/003POF03NewspaperEditors04201961.htm.

38. Kennedy states, "On that unhappy island, as in so many other arenas of the contest for freedom, the news has grown worse instead of better. I have emphasized before that this was a struggle of Cuban patriots against a Cuban dictator. While we could not be expected to hide our sympathies, we made it repeatedly clear that the armed forces of this country would not intervene in any way," although the American government had been recruiting, housing, and training anti-Castro Cuban exiles on military bases in South Florida and at American military bases in Panama since 1960.

39. Sarris, *The John Ford Movie Mystery*, 182.

14. QUESTIONS OF JUST CONDUCT

1. Walt Whitman, "Song of Myself," *Modern American Poetry*, http://www.english.illinois.edu/maps/poets/s_z/whitman/song.htm.

2. Ford had approached Columbia Pictures in the 1950s to direct a screenplay about the Exodus based on Howard Fast's *The Last Frontier*. Fast, however, was blacklisted, and the project fell through. Then, claiming the story belonged to the public domain, Ford and Bernard Smith sold Warner Bros. a different version of the screenplay loosely based on Mari Sandoz's *Cheyenne Autumn*. After a lengthy legal battle over plagiarism, which Columbia won, *Cheyenne Autumn* was released in 1964.

3. Davis, *John Ford*, 321.

4. Ibid., 497.

5. Ford, *Pappy*, 296–97.

6. Ibid., 300.

7. Ibid., 301.

8. Ibid., 283.

9. John Ford, interview by Philip Jenkinson, "The John Ford Interview," in *Stagecoach*, directed by John Ford (1939; Criterion Collection, 2010), DVD.

10. Libby, "The Old Wrangler Rides Again," 47.

11. Ford, *Pappy*, 301.

12. Eyman, *Print the Legend*, 503.

13. Ibid., 505.

14. Ibid.

15. Ibid., 489.

16. Libby, "The Old Wrangler Rides Again," 52.

17. Eyman, *Print the Legend*, 325.

18. Ibid., 490.

19. Carey, *Company of Heroes*, 169.

20. Mark Haggard, "A New Direction," *Newsweek*, February 1, 1965, 2.

21. McBride, *Searching for John Ford*, 659.

22. Richard Oulahan, "John Ford's Trojan Horse Opry," *Life*, November 27, 1964, 19.

23. Stanley Kauffman, *The New Republic*, January 23, 1965, 36.

24. Joseph McBride, *Searching for John Ford*, 659.

25. Toshi Fujiwara, "The People. Who Will Tell The People? Who Will Tell Them?" *FIPRESCI* 5 (2009), http://old.fipresci.org/undercurrent/issue_0509/cheyenne.htm.

26. McBride, *Searching for John Ford*, 647–48.

27. Ibid., 646.

28. Ibid.

29. Ibid, 646–47.

30. James N. Leiker and Ramon Powers, *The Northern Cheyenne Exodus in History and Memory* (Norman: University of Oklahoma Press, 2012), 167.

31. The soldiers pursing the Cheyenne were a mixed command from the 19th Infantry and 4th Cavalry under Lt. Colonel William H. Lewis and by men from Fort Wallace, Fort Hays, Fort Dodge, Fort Riley, and Fort Kearney.

32. Carey, *Company of Heroes*, 192.

33. Bogdanovich, *John Ford*, 104.

34. McBride, *Searching for John Ford*, 645.

35. Bogdanovich, *John Ford*, 106.

36. McBride, *Searching for John Ford*, 645.

37. Bosley Crowther, "Screen: John Ford Mounts Huge Frontier Western," *The New York Times*, December 24, 1964, http://www.nytimes.com/movie/review?res=9B0DE3DB1F3FE13ABC4C51DFB467838.

38. McBride, *Searching for John Ford*, 645.

39. Carey, *Company of Heroes*, 194.

40. Aristotle, *Nicomachean Ethics*, ed. W. E. Ross (Oxford: Clarendon Press, 1908), http://classics.mit.edu/Aristotle/nicomachaen.html. In Book Two of the *Nicomachean Ethics*, Aristotle points out that the virtuous character trait of courage lies between the extremes of rashness and cowardice.

41. Michael Walzer, *Just and Unjust Wars* (Harmondsworth: Penguin, 1977), 21. Also in Jeff McMahan, "The Ethics of Killing in War," *Ethics* 114 (July 2004): 693.

42. McMahan, "The Ethics of Killing in War," 694.

43. McBride, *Searching for John Ford*, 647.

44. Ibid., 647.

45. McMahan, "The Ethics of Killing in War," 694.

46. Ibid.

47. Steven Lukes, *Individualism* (Colchester: EPCR Press, 2006), 39.

48. Walt Whitman, *Leaves of Grass and Selected Poems and Prose*, ed. Peter M. Coviello (London: Penguin, 2014), 11.

49. Fujiwara, "The People. Who Will Tell The People? Who Will Tell Them?"

50. Bogdanovich, *John Ford*, 104.

AFTERMATH

1. Tavernier, "Notes of a Press Attaché," 109. As Joseph McBride points out on page 5 of his introduction to *Searching for John Ford*, in 1962, John Ford noted moviegoers' shifting tastes when talking to Hedda Hopper: "I have

no choice but to make westerns," he told her. "Talk about moral bankruptcy! In the past 18 months I've had three good stories okayed at the studios—warm, human stories. It's not the studio that turned them down, but the Madison Avenue and Wall Street people who do the financing. They sent them back, say there wasn't enough sex and violence!" Scott Eyman notes on page 523 of *Print the Legend* that as late as June of 1965, MGM announced that Ford's next project, *The Miracle of Merriford*, a rewrite of John Hersey's *A Bell for Adano*, in which American soldiers raise money to repair an English church damaged during World War II, would begin shooting that October, but the project was canceled. The public preview failure of *7 Women* (1966), deemed sexually perverse and violent by its reviewers, on July 16, 1965, at the Academy Theatre in Pasadena, California, however, and Ford's preference for war movies and Westerns made him, despite his strong international reputation, unemployable. Ford continued to pitch projects to the studios but was unable to find the financing and executive will to support them: among the films he proposed were a biographical treatment of Wild Bill Donovan; a movie codirected with the American Revolution; another Midway film, "about the way it was"; and *Tora! Tora! Tora!* with Akira Kurosawa.

2. Eyman, *Print the Legend*, 679.

3. Ibid., 531.

4. Wingate Smith to Dan Ford, folder 15, box 12, Ford, J. Mss., Lilly Library, University of Indiana, Bloomington.

5. Eyman, *Print the Legend*, 538.

6. Ibid., 299.

7. Leguèbe, "John Ford," 72.

8. McBride, *Searching for John Ford*, 694.

9. Ibid., 534, 538.

10. See Eric Spiegelman's comments about *Vietnam! Vietnam!* in *Bus Your Own Tray*, http://spiegelman.tumblr.com/post/29921323/the-last-film-ever-produced-by-the-legendary-john.

11. Eyman, *Print the Legend*, 533.

12. Gallagher, *John Ford*, 342.

13. Dan Ford served in the Army's 25th Division, and Tim Ford served in the Merchant Marine during the Vietnam War.

14. McBride, *Searching for John Ford*, 694.

15. Eyman, *Print the Legend*, 536.

16. Ibid., 534.

17. Ibid., 538.

18. Ibid., 432; Tavernier, "Notes of a Press Attaché," 107–8.

19. Ibid., 538.

20. Eyman, *Print the Legend*, 566.

21. Harris, *Five Came Back*, 400.

22. Eyman, *Print the Legend*, 287.

23. Roberson, *The Fall Guy*, 159.

24. With or without voice-overs, Ford's OSS documentaries, now in the public domain, like *Training Group* (1942) and *The Mole* (1943), are straightforward reports on the effectiveness of methods to be used by agents in the field: in the first instance, types of hand-to-hand combat are shown and discussed; in the second, ways by which trains may be blown up in tunnels are examined. *Caccolube* (1943) and *Disassemble and Reassemble of the M-1 Carbine* (1944) are useful and pertinent sets of instructions: the first about destroying the engines of medium-sized vehicles and the second about the ins and outs of the M-1 rifle. The Field Photographic Branch of the OSS also excelled in making docudramas. The first film ever produced by a secret intelligence service to train its own agents, Ford's *Undercover: How to Operate Behind Enemy Lines in World War 2* (1943) dramatizes the experiences of agents in the field in order to teach correct procedure and protocol to its recruits.

25. Eyman, *Print the Legend*, 451.

26. Ibid., 565.

27. Ibid., 561.

28. D. H. Lawrence, "Introduction to Frederick Carter's *The Dragon of the Apocalypse*," *Apocalypse and Writings on Revelation*, ed. Mara Kalnins (Cambridge: Cambridge University Press, 2002), 49.

29. Walter Wagner, "One More Hurrah," in *You Must Remember This* (New York: Putnam's, 1975), 155.

30. Gaylyn Studlar, "Sacred Duties, Poetic Passions," in *John Ford Made Westerns*, ed. Gaylyn Studlar and Matthew Bernstein (Bloomington: Indiana University Press, 2001), 69.

31. John G. Cawelti, *The Six-Gun Mystique Sequel* (Bowling Green, Ohio: Bowling Green University Popular Press, 1999), 2.

32. Slotkin, *Regeneration through Violence*, 5.

33. Ibid., 451.

34. Shay, *Odysseus in America*, 4.

35. Sarris, *The John Ford Movie Mystery*, 90. Also in McBride, *Searching for John Ford*, 11.

36. Eyman, *Print the Legend*, 551.

37. Ford, *Pappy*, 314.

38. Eyman, *Print the Legend*, 568.

39. Katharine Hepburn to Dan Ford, Tape 51, Ford, J. Mss., Lilly Library, University of Indiana, Bloomington.

INDEX

ABOUT THE AUTHOR

Sue Matheson is an associate professor of English literature at the University College of the North in Manitoba, Canada. She teaches in the areas of American film and popular culture, Canadian literature, children's literature, and detective film. Western film is one of her specializations. Her interests in film, culture, and literature may be found in more than forty essays published in a wide range of books and scholarly journals. She is the editor of *Love in Western Film and Television: Lonely Hearts and Happy Trails* (2013) and is also the founder and coeditor of *the quint: an interdisciplinary quarterly from the north*. Additionally, she serves as the book review editor of the *Journal of Popular Film and Television*.